GLOBAL LEADERSHIP
IN TRANSITION

GLOBAL LEADERSHIP IN TRANSITION

Making the G20 More Effective and Responsive

COLIN I. BRADFORD
WONHYUK LIM

editors

KOREA DEVELOPMENT INSTITUTE
Seoul

BROOKINGS INSTITUTION PRESS
Washington, D.C.

Library of Congress Cataloging-in-Publication data

Global leadership in transition : making the G20 more effective and responsive / Colin
I. Bradford and Wonhyuk Lim, editors.
    p.   cm.
Includes bibliographical references and index.
ISBN 978-0-8157-2145-1 (pbk. : alk. paper)
1. Group of Twenty. 2. International economic relations. 3. Economic development—
International cooperation. I. Bradford, Colin I. II. Lim, Wonhyuk.
HF1359.G575 2011
337—dc22   2011015741

9 8 7 6 5 4 3 2 1

Printed on acid-free paper

Typeset in Adobe Garamond

Composition by Cynthia Stock
Silver Spring, Maryland

Contents

Foreword

The G20 Seoul summit came at a crucial moment for both the global economy and global governance. The global economy, thanks to an international, concerted policy effort led by the G20, has avoided catastrophe. Consequently, there is a general view that the G20 has been successful as a global crisis committee. In the leaders' communiqué issued at the Pittsburgh summit, G20 leaders designated the G20 as "the premier forum for international economic cooperation."

Now that the sense of crisis has receded, the question for the G20 is how to keep the momentum intact and continue to be effective beyond the crisis as a bona fide steering committee for the global economy. Korea, as the chair of the G20 summit in Seoul in November 2010, made the utmost effort to dispel concerns about the G20's future effectiveness and to build confidence in the G20 as the premier forum for international economic cooperation. Toward that end, we must continue to make sure that the previous commitments and promises made by the G20 leaders are delivered within the given timeframe.

At the same time, we must pay due attention in the G20 process to the views and concerns of non-G20 countries. Although more than 85 percent of global GDP is produced by the G20 countries and two-thirds of the global population resides in these countries, more than 170 UN member countries do not belong to the G20, and the credibility and legitimacy of the G20 as a steering committee cannot be upheld without their support. Under the leadership of Korea, the first non-G7 country to chair the G20, the G20 added two new agenda items, development and the global financial safety net, to address the pressing needs of mostly non-G20 countries.

The G20 Seoul summit can be seen as a litmus test of the future of the G20 as a global steering committee. Korea hopes that the Seoul summit's success will pave the way for solidifying the G20's position as a steering committee. Obviously, to make it an effective and relevant steering committee, G20 leaders will have to consider the institutionalization of the G20. In that context, the Seoul international symposium "Towards the Consolidation of G20 Summits: From Crisis Committee to Global Steering Committee," September 27–29, 2010, could not have been more appropriate and timely. We commend the Korea Development Institute and the Brookings Institution for having co-organized this significant symposium, supported by the *Dong-A Ilbo,* Korea's leading daily newspaper. With the participation of the world's leading scholars and practitioners in the field, this symposium served as a landmark platform for the global discussion of the future of the G20. This book is a compilation of the proceedings of this symposium, which will stimulate further discussion on the G20 and global governance.

IL SAKONG
Chairman
Presidential Committee for the G20 Summit
Republic of Korea

Preface and Acknowledgments

The origin of this book goes back to a seminar that two Brookings Institution scholars, Colin Bradford and Johannes Linn, gave at the Korea Development Institute (KDI) in November 2009. A month and a half earlier, the leaders at the G20 Pittsburgh summit had agreed to make Korea the G20 chair for 2010, and Korean policymakers and scholars were trying to come up with ideas and proposals that would make the G20 the global leadership forum for international cooperation. At the KDI seminar, the two speakers and KDI scholars quickly agreed that Korea could make a significant contribution toward that goal by placing development on the G20's agenda and initiating discussion on the establishment of a secretariat. They felt that the introduction of a development agenda would allow the G20 to move beyond crisis-focused macroeconomic and financial issues and to address the concerns of many countries left out of the G20 process while pursuing its core objective of "strong, sustainable and balanced growth" through international economic cooperation. They believed that Korea's own remarkable development over the past half-century would add credibility.

The Brookings and KDI scholars also thought that the establishment of a small nonbureaucratic secretariat driven by the G20 leadership—in cooperation with the key international organizations, notably the International Monetary Fund—would help to facilitate summit preparations and consultations, ensure systematic monitoring and implementation, and preserve institutional memory and continuity. Together, they felt, the introduction of a development agenda and the establishment of a secretariat would enhance the G20's legitimacy with respect to both its representativeness and its effectiveness as the group makes its transition from a crisis management committee to a global steering committee.

Korea's Presidential Committee for the G20 Summit had been thinking along those lines as well. In fact, when the KDI seminar was held, the committee was developing preliminary ideas for the introduction of global financial safety nets and a growth-oriented development agenda as well as for institutional innovations such as a permanent secretariat and a systematic approach to consultations with non-G20 members. When Brookings and KDI—the oldest and best-known think tanks in the United States and Korea, respectively—began to explore ideas for a joint project on the G20, the committee was more than happy to provide its support.

Brookings had played a leading intellectual role in making the leaders' G20 (L20) a reality. In particular, Colin Bradford and Johannes Linn had advocated a new global governance structure based on the G20 at least since 2004, co-editing in 2007 a book entitled *Global Governance Reform: Breaking the Stalemate.* Complementing their work at the Global Economy and Development Program, Bruce Jones, Carlos Pascual, and Stephen John Stedman led multi-year efforts at the Brookings Foreign Policy Program and published in 2010 a book entitled *Power and Responsibility: Building International Order in an Era of Transnational Threats.*

KDI had a rather late start in global governance research but expended considerable time and energy on G20-related issues in support of Korea's efforts. Hyeon Wook Kim and his colleagues worked on a project commissioned by the G20 committee analyzing the policies of the G20 member countries as a part of the mutual assessment process (MAP) to ensure collective consistency. Wonhyuk Lim focused on the growth-oriented development agenda as well as institutional innovations such as systematic consultations with non-G20 members.

In January 2010, KDI leaders came to Brookings to define the contours of our joint project. We decided that it would focus on innovations to "institutionalize" the G20—to consolidate the G20 to become "the premier forum for international economic cooperation" beyond the global financial crisis that created it. We then designated Colin Bradford and Wonhyuk Lim to lead the project from Brookings and KDI, respectively.

In February 2010, Bradford and Lim met at Brookings to discuss the details of the joint project. They quickly saw eye-to-eye on two critical issues. First, to solidify the status of the G20 from a crisis management committee to a global steering committee, the project would have to cover not only institutional innovations but policy and political innovations as well. Having a permanent secretariat and regular meetings does not guarantee success for a leadership forum unless it deals effectively with problems that matter to the global community. Second, the two co-editors agreed that the breadth of the project required that it draw talent from as wide a pool as possible, from both policymakers and scholars, transcending national borders.

To generate institutional, policy, and political innovations for the G20, the Brookings Institution, the Korea Development Institute, and the Centre for International Governance Innovation (CIGI) joined together to organize a day-and-a-half-long conference held on April 21–22, 2010, in Washington. The purpose of the off-the-record conference was to identify and explore promising ideas and proposals to facilitate preparation for the Seoul G20 summit and beyond.

The G20 Seoul International Symposium, a large public symposium based on the Washington conference, was held September 27–29, 2010, in Seoul, organized by KDI, Brookings, and the renowned Korean newspaper *Dong-A Ilbo*. Several hundred people attended the symposium, which was held in the COEX Center, where the G20 Seoul summit also took place. The symposium program combined officials, experts, academics, and journalists in discussing a broad range of issues, and the proceedings were published by the Korea Development Institute in time for distribution at the November G20 summit in Seoul. This volume also is based on the Seoul Symposium.

Having completed this project, we would like to extend particular thanks to the Presidential Committee for the G20 Summit. Il SaKong, chair of the G20 committee, provided strategic guidance and valuable advice from the project's inception. Changyong Rhee, sherpa to the president of the Republic of Korea, shared his ideas with the co-editors on a number of occasions and engaged in intensive discussions with the participants at the Washington conference and the Seoul Symposium. We also would like to thank Thomas Bernes, vice-president of programs and acting executive director of the CIGI, for co-hosting the Washington conference and helping us to draw from the excellent international network of experts that the CIGI has developed over the years. Similarly, we would like to thank Jae Ho Kim, president of the *Dong-A Ilbo*, for co-hosting the Seoul Symposium and making it a signature international event for the newspaper's ninetieth anniversary.

No project of this magnitude can succeed without research and logistical support, and the co-editors would like to thank Yoon Jung Kim, research associate at KDI, for her meticulous work over the course of the project. They also would like to thank Kyunghye Lee and her colleagues at the COEX convention team for their splendid logistical support for the Seoul Symposium.

The Korea Development Institute and the Brookings Institution hope that this volume will provide useful ideas for officials, experts, and civil society for adopting innovations for the G20 and facilitate a larger public dialogue in Korea and around the world that will help generate momentum for the transformation of the G20 into a more inclusive, effective, and enduring form of summitry for the twenty-first century.

OH-SEOK HYUN
President
Korea Development Institute

KEMAL DERVIŞ
Vice President
Global Economy and Development
Brookings Institution

Toward the Consolidation of the G20: From Crisis Committee to Global Steering Committee

COLIN I. BRADFORD AND WONHYUK LIM

The Republic of Korea hosted the fifth G20 summit on November 11–12, 2010. As Paul Martin, the former prime minister of Canada, emphasizes in chapter 1 of this book, it was a historic moment in summitry, when a non-G8, recently developing country chaired an "apex summit" for the first time. G7/8 summits, consisting of four European nations (France, Germany, Italy, and the United Kingdom), two North American nations (Canada and the United States), Japan, and Russia, have met yearly from 1975 to the present. There has been increasing dissatisfaction with the G8 in recent years due to the fact that it represented less than 1 billion people of a world population of roughly 6 billion at the turn of the millennium and that the eight countries, except for Japan, were Western, industrial countries in a world in which dynamic non-Western emerging economies were becoming increasingly important.

The G8 responded to the new realities through "outreach" efforts, by inviting selected non-G8 countries to G8 summits to discuss specific topics or for specific segments, such as breakfast, lunch, or dinner. For a short period following the Heiligendamm G8 summit in Germany in June 2007, the G8 included five emerging market economies (Brazil, China, India, Mexico, and South Africa) in parts of the summit meetings. As a result, one issue that presented itself was whether to make the G8 Plus 5 the new apex summit grouping (see chapter 2 by John Kirton).

During those years, a substantial number of people in major countries were pushing for reform to make summits both more representative and more effective than G8 summits. One of the options proposed for future summits was that the G20 grouping of finance ministers and central bank presidents created at the time of the 1997–98 Asian financial crisis become an L20 or leaders-level summit that would replace the G8. Despite the growing dissatisfaction with both the substantive performance and the representativeness of the G8, it took the global financial crisis of 2008–09 to trigger the transition from the G8 to the G20 at the leaders' level, which began with the first G20 summit, in Washington on November 15, 2008 (see chapter 3 by Ngaire Woods).

Next, the London G20 summit (April 2, 2009) constituted an unprecedented effort by major economies to stimulate their economies together through expansionary fiscal and monetary policies; to put in motion domestic and international efforts to strengthen the oversight, supervision, and regulation of financial markets and institutions; and to fund and reform the International Monetary Fund to put it back in the center of the international monetary system.

The Pittsburgh G20 summit in September 2009 put in place its new and challenging Framework for Strong, Sustainable, and Balanced Growth in order to place the macroeconomic policies of major economies within a medium-term context and to achieve "collective consistency" among them. At Pittsburgh, G20 leaders declared G20 summits and ministerial meetings to be "the premier forum for international economic cooperation," upstaging the G8 if not replacing it. (See chapter 4 by Gordon Smith and chapter 5 by Lan Xue and Yanbing Zhang.)

Challenges for the Seoul G20 Summit

Since late 2009, when Korea's responsibilities for the 2010 G20 summit became clear, the Korean government began to encourage efforts to address multiple challenges to make the G20 a more enduring, inclusive, and credible form of summitry for the twenty-first century.

The first set of challenges is to make the G20 an enduring body for providing strategic direction for the world even after the global financial crisis abates. There is great concern, expressed by Il SaKong in his preface to this volume, that the G20 may fade away as a significant forum for global leadership as the global financial crisis subsides and the current focus on financial and macroeconomic issues increasingly shifts to technical matters unsuitable for discussion at the leadership level (see parts 2 and 3 of this volume, respectively); or that the G20 will become overwhelmed by expanding its agenda to include global poverty and development (see part 4), energy and climate change, and health and human security, for example, thereby reducing its focus and impact. Either scenario would be unfortunate because globalization is producing an increasing number of cross-border and cross-sectoral issues that must be addressed by the global community.

This force field defines the trade-off between focus and delivery on one hand and relevance and continuity on the other. The challenge is one of identifying policy innovations for the G20 that are intrinsically inclusive in their scope and specific in their reach and impact to address challenges of high consequence for the public interest.

The second set of challenges is to address the trade-off between achieving legitimacy as a representative body and achieving legitimacy as an effective body. The truth of it is that it is easier to reach agreement and forge conclusions in smaller rather than larger groups, especially if those groups are limited to like-minded countries. However, the evidence of recent G8 summits has been that a small like-minded group like the G8 does not have legitimacy in the rest of the world, which is not represented in it. Moreover, the increasing importance of dynamic emerging economies implies that the effectiveness of a small like-minded group in addressing global problems is likely to decline over time. That said, a large summit grouping that provides wide scope for inclusiveness, such as the United Nations climate change conference in Copenhagen, Denmark, in December 2009, demonstrates the perils in terms of effectiveness of taking representativeness to its logical extreme by including all nations.

It remains to be seen if the G20 is "the golden mean" between the G8 and G192. (See chapter 22 by Colin Bradford and chapter 23 by Stewart Patrick on the new dynamics of summitry.) Even though the G20 is significantly more representative than the G8, the question of inclusiveness remains alive for the many countries, regions, and peoples that feel left out of direct representation. The G20, even though more inclusive than the G8, still is a self-selected group based on size, wealth, and power. In the eyes of the rest of the world, it still has a representativeness deficit. At the same time, the increased diversity in the membership of the G20 calls for a more systematic and structured approach to summit preparation and implementation. So the challenge is to come up with institutional as well as policy innovations for the G20 that enhance its legitimacy in terms of both representativeness and effectiveness. (See part 5 as well as chapter 24 by Andrew Cooper and chapter 25 by Barry Carin in part 6.)

Finally, the third set of challenges for the G20 concern leadership and communication. They arise from the fact that the current crisis is essentially a triple crisis: a crisis of confidence in markets, a crisis of faith in the capacity of domestic and international institutions to avoid and manage financial instability, and a crisis in public trust in political leadership. What that means is that while it is absolutely essential for the G20 to generate institutional and policy reforms and innovations to address the current crisis, it must also restore public trust in national and global political leadership. Therefore, greater emphasis, consciousness, and intentionality with regard to political innovations for the G20 are a vital part of the agenda to transform summitry. (See part 7.)

More deliberate efforts need to be made by G20 leaders and officials to focus more clearly on connecting the actions and messages of G20 summits to the broad public concerns of their people. The forging and delivery of effective policy outcomes by summits are crucial. But, in addition, the articulation of the meaning of these policy results for their people and the linking of policy actions to public anxieties about jobs, secure incomes and pensions, and personal security are as vital for successful summits as the policies themselves. To make the G20 successful in managing the ongoing financial crisis, restoring trust in political leaders is as important as renewing confidence in markets.

G20 chairs need to use their leadership and membership in the G20 troika over three years to bring about changes in summitry that can make the G20 both more inclusive and more effective than the G8. Such innovations can enable the G20 to become the global steering committee for the world economy beyond the financial crisis.

Multiple Dimensions of Global Leadership

The G20's biggest challenge is to define itself as the global leadership forum to make globalization work in the twenty-first century. Hence, in the overview of the issues facing the G20 discussed in this book, the multiple dimensions of leadership are taken up to situate the G20 in the political context between leaders and their publics. Viewing the G20 from the perspective of leadership challenges embraces the institutional and policy challenges and makes vivid the complexity of the daunting task of leadership facing the heads of state and government who constitute the G20 summit grouping.

Strategic Leadership

The primary function of the G20 is to provide strategic guidance, vision, and a sense of direction for the global economy. The G20 is an informal mechanism, not a "decider." Nor is it an authority with legal powers to generate final decisions or instructions for action. Rather, it is a strategic guidance mechanism acting as a steering committee for the global economy to provide vision for the general direction for the world and policy frameworks and recommendations for national officials, especially officials of the G20 nations, and for international organizations that have their own decisionmaking bodies and procedures.

As a consequence, the G20 provides vital strategic leadership for the global economy, which is crucial to its functioning as a complex system of national and supranational economic interactions. At the same time, the G20 is limited by its informality, its lack of authority, its periodicity, and its essential nature as a steering or coordinating committee rather than as a formal institution per se.

The current financial crisis has made clear that the absence of strategic leadership creates unacceptable risks in the new global economy. The institutionalization of the G20 becomes critically important in providing a means to fill the void in strategic leadership left by the G8, which was inadequate to the task of global leadership of the global economy because of its lack of representativeness and effectiveness and hence its lack of legitimacy.

Political Leadership

As indicated, the current crisis is simultaneously an economic crisis, an institutional crisis, and a political crisis. What has been revealed for all to see is that there is a crisis of confidence in markets, a crisis of capacity of the international institutional system to cope with the global dimensions of the financial crisis, and a crisis of trust in political leadership. If the void revealed by the inadequacy of the G8 to cope with the financial crisis also manifests an inability to answer the fundamental strategic question—"Where are we going?"—the political crisis casts in high relief the question "Who is in charge?" The answer in the case of the financial crisis seems to be that no one "was minding the store," especially when it came to oversight, supervision, and regulation of financial institutions and markets.

The public perception of the failure of public responsibility for outcomes generated by markets makes it imperative to fill this void in the public square by consciously reasserting public responsibility over markets and restoring public trust in national leaders and governments. Summits, then, provide an opportunity not only to set strategic directions in the global economy but also to consciously and visibly assert political leadership on behalf of the public for economic outcomes.

Financial markets have failed to protect the public interest because political leaders failed to assert public responsibility for them. Part of the agenda of political innovations for the G20 becomes generating conscious attention by leaders and their senior advisers to the manifestation of both national and global leadership by heads of state and government in G20 summits in order to deliberately address the fundamental issue of public trust in political leaders and public institutions as a critical part of the economic crisis itself.

Integrative Leadership

The challenges presented in the twenty-first century are fundamentally different from the challenges of the twentieth century. Whereas the new realities are driven by spillover effects from one domain to another, in the twentieth century progress was made by considering challenges within domains through specialization, focused expertise, and depth. In economics, insights were based on the assumption of the autonomy of economic actors from one another, which permitted competitive markets to act as allocators and mediators. In international relations, autonomous national entities related to each other at arm's length through "foreign policy," diplomacy, and external relations. Now, globalization presents a new reality: the interpenetration of domestic forces, which means that we are all present in each other's worlds in terms of products, people, culture, and information.

Spillover effects reveal fundamentally new dynamics that require horizontality to balance verticality, coordination to supplement competition, and integration to enhance specialization. Instead of problems being managed by "specialized" agencies, institutions, and ministries, global challenges and the linkages among them require communications, concertation, cooperation, and coordination. Competitive markets, the adjudicators and allocators of the twentieth century, must be supplemented now by integrated approaches involving intersectoral, interministerial, and interinstitutional strategies rather than stove-piped management. Global challenges today are fundamentally characterized by their interconnectedness as well as their internal complexity. As Paul Martin points out in chapter 6, the very idea of sovereignty itself needs to be understood in new ways when actions in one country have drastic effects on domestic conditions in other countries.

Of all national officials, national leaders are unique in having overall responsibility for society as a whole, in all its interrelated dimensions. All other senior officials have partial responsibilities. Most governments and the international institutional system itself are organized around specific sectors and issues. In the global age, summit leaders face the additional challenge of providing integrative leadership across issues and domains that must explicitly address the spillover effects and linkages to be effective.

These are new challenges that manifest themselves both domestically and globally. The institutionalization of G20 summits, as a twenty-first-century forum, must squarely face and deal with this new dynamic of the twenty-first century in order to be effective in addressing the global challenges that are the summits' primary mandate.

Institutional Reform Leadership

Filling the void in strategic leadership at the global level, restoring trust in political leaders at the national level, and providing integrative leadership in addressing the interlinked issues of today are prerequisites for achieving institutional reforms to deal with current challenges. Domestically, there has been an institutional failure in relation to financial institutions and markets whereby the invisible hand of the market was assumed to relieve the public hand of the government of responsibility. In addition, most national governments are better organized vertically to deal with sectoral challenges than they are horizontally to deal with today's interconnected challenges. By extension, the system of international institutions also is organized to deal with problems by separating energy from agriculture, from health, from environment, and from security when in fact at all levels the determining forces of social outcomes now lie as much in the links between sectors as they lie within them.

G20 leaders, in their role of providing strategic guidance for the global economy, have already begun focusing on the need for institutional innovations at the domestic, national, and international levels to strengthen the capacity of public institutions to exercise guidance, oversight, supervision, and regulation of markets and societal challenges. G20 governments are each reviewing, strengthening, and reforming their financial regulatory institutions. They are establishing greater global supervision and surveillance by establishing the Financial Stability Board in Basel, with expanded membership, and by reforming and redefining the role of the International Monetary Fund in the global financial system. Finally, G20 summits have given significant attention to providing adequate financial resources to the IMF, the World Bank, and the regional multilateral development banks as instruments for the prevention of future financial crises.

Not only are the mandates, missions, and operations of international institutions outdated and outstripped by current global challenges, but their power structures also are better equipped to reflect the mid–twentieth century dominance of Western industrial countries than the world population's current geopolitical and economic weights and those in the anticipated future. Therefore, G20 leaders already have given impetus to governance reforms in international economic institutions—especially the Financial Stability Board, the IMF, and the World Bank—but significant shifts in voting shares and chairs in these institutions have yet to be realized.

Substantial international leadership on behalf of institutional reform remains to be taken to reduce the dominance of Europe and the United States in the IMF and the World Bank and thereby to transform them from essentially transatlantic institutions into truly global institutions. As reform occurs, there will be a delicate balance to strike between increasing the alignment of power in the World Bank and the IMF with G20 realities—without allowing the G20 leadership in both institutions to overexert itself against the universal membership—and creating more inclusive power arrangements in them. (See chapter 19 by Thomas A. Bernes and chapter 20 by Johannes F. Linn.)

Pragmatic Leadership

Much of the twentieth century was driven by ideological conflicts between democracy and authoritarianism, capitalism and communism, and the market versus the state. Twenty-first-century relationships are characterized by a more

complex set of forces and factors. Global challenges have imprinted themselves on the fabric of the twenty-first century in indelible ways, forcing new
behaviors, norms, and orientations. Ideological lenses are less dominant, and
more pragmatic leadership is required to reach agreements and to make progress collectively. Pragmatic leadership is more focused on substance, functionality, effectiveness, and public outcomes than on values, narrow constructs of
national interest, posturing, and use of the international arena for domestic partisan political gain. The urgency of the problems, challenges, and approaches is
becoming dominant over ideological articulations, value constructs, abstractions
of like-mindedness, and a priori alliances.

One of the great challenges for G20 leaders is to deal sequentially with global
challenges by pragmatically aligning substantive policy positions on different
issues in varying country groupings. This approach would be far better than
resorting to breaking countries down on all issues into blocs of East versus West,
North versus South, industrial countries versus emerging market economies, G8
versus the rest, or the West and "the Rest" or other rigid configurations (see
chapter 23 by Stewart Patrick). The great promise of the G20, because of its
ample and diverse membership, is that varying alignments could predominate
over a priori alliances and that shifting coalitions of consensus could develop as
the agenda evolves. If a G20 leadership culture could evolve in this pragmatic,
undogmatic, flexible, and substantive fashion, it would be an immense step forward for international understanding and cooperation that would demonstrate
to the larger world a form of institutionalized leadership that could hold promise
for other forums.

Part of what is at issue here is a new balance between individualism, autonomy,
and competition on one hand and social cohesion, solidarity, community, and
cooperation on the other. Excessive market fundamentalism based on individualism and competition is being harnessed by the current reform effort to ensure that
private interests do not again harm the larger public interest. Pragmatic rather
than ideologically driven leadership as the basis for a new culture of cooperation
in G20 summits could be a major institutional innovation in global relations.

The stakes are high. As Paul Martin states in chapter 6, on financial reform
and the G20: "More and more the issue is whether the markets are going to
dictate a country's economic and social policy or whether national governments
are going to recognize their duty to their own citizens to adhere to international
norms and to work with other countries so that the fear of contagion ceases to
be a sword of Damocles hanging over an increasingly integrated global system."

Inclusive Leadership

Global leadership needs to be exercised on behalf of the world, not just the G20.
The four G20 summits that took place before the Seoul summit had focused

on the global financial crisis and economic recovery, where the size, weight, and clout of the G20 countries had been crucial to the successful policy effort and reform agenda forged to that point. Questions arise now about whether and how to broaden the agenda of the G20 beyond the crisis to include other related issues, such as climate change and energy security, in which the rest of the world also has an enormous stake.

In this context, despite the significant leap forward in achieving representative legitimacy by moving from the G8 to the G20 as "the premier forum for international economic cooperation," potentially divisive issues remain regarding whether the G20 is fully representative of the rest of the world and whether it has the right to assert itself as the global steering committee for the global economy given the self-selected nature of its members. For the G20 to be successful, it must demonstrate that it is representing more than the interests of the nineteen countries composing it, both in its agenda and in its process of considering policy ideas and actions. For that to happen, G20 leaders will need to be open to representing more than their own interests at future G20 summits and to make specific efforts to include the perspectives and views of non-G20 countries in its deliberations (see chapter 24 by Andrew Cooper.)

The G20 will need to consider how issues central to the rest of the world can be brought into the framework of G20 strategic leadership without offending other countries by seeming to govern for them, without them. On the other hand, beginning now to discuss questions of membership, composition, and broader representation in G20 summits could threaten the ability of the G20 to deliver the better public outcomes and tangible improvements in economic conditions that are both expected and urgently needed.

Concluding Remarks

The emergence of the G20 as the steering committee for the global economy, possibly replacing the G8, poses an opportunity not only to have a larger and more representative summit grouping but to have a qualitatively better form of summitry. For that to occur, the confluence of the economic, political, and institutional aspects of the current crisis would have to compel a transformative approach to the institutionalization of the G20. Such an approach to the G20 is necessary to make it different from the G8, not only in size and representativeness but also in effectiveness and in the way that it functions. Viewing summitry as a multidimensional process based on new forms of strategic, political, integrative, institutional, pragmatic, and inclusive leadership defines the focal points for institutional innovations for the G20 discussed in this book.

The transformation of G20 summitry put forth here involves a fluid, flexible, evolving set of processes and institutional innovations meant to move forward continuously as additional G20 summits occur. The thirty-year history of the G8 is characterized by continuous change and adaptation to changes in circumstances. Such evolutionary transformation entails a search for new forms, modalities, processes, interactions, and procedures to strengthen the effectiveness of summits as complex events in which important consequences are at stake. The G8 summits not only became increasingly anomalous but also increasingly ineffective because the dynamics were stale and stultifying (see chapter 2 by John Kirton and chapter 3 by Ngaire Woods.)

The goal of innovations for G20 summits is *not* to be interpreted as an attempt to consolidate G20 summitry into a rigid set of rules and procedures so that G20 summits will endure and the twenty members that now compose it will prevail as permanent members for the next thirty years. Rather, the intent is to be conscious and intentional about the leadership, process, and institutional aspects in an attempt to avoid letting this transformative moment pass when innovations could be made that would enhance the productivity, meaning, and impact of summitry for the international community as a whole. (For a summary of innovations discussed in this volume, see the conclusion.)

The hope is that G20 summits will not be just annual events but opportunities through time for global guidance, policy innovation, and reform with enduring real consequences for people and nations everywhere. Then, the G20 will have made the transition from crisis committee to global steering committee and in the process transformed itself into a more representative, more effective, and hence more legitimate mechanism for global leadership than the G8 that preceded it.

PART I

History and Prospect

1

The G20: From Global Crisis Responder to Global Steering Committee

PAUL MARTIN

There have been three steps in the evolution of the G20 to date. The first, not surprisingly, was its founding during the turmoil of the Asian crisis over a decade ago, when the G20 finance ministers met for the first time. The second was the series of G20 leaders' summits that began in Washington in 2008, arising out of the current financial upheaval. The third step, which occurred in 2009, was the announcement that Korea would be the first non-European, non–North American country to host a G20 summit. This decision spoke in a way that no communiqué ever could to the fact that the G20 had come of age and that its perspective extends to a horizon far beyond that of the G8.

This became immediately evident when Korea championed the need for global financial safety nets, a need experienced by those economies sideswiped by the 2008 financial crisis. In this context the enhancements to the IMF's crisis prevention instruments and the discussions on a global stabilization mechanism are most welcome. Korea's initiative was evident again when the host, one of the few international aid recipients to become a donor, put development on the G20 agenda. What Korea has done within a generation is virtually unprecedented. This is not an idle statement. Its focus on education, infrastructure, and the synergy between government and the private sector—the three pillars of Korea's economic growth—carries with it a lesson that is irrefutable for both recipients and donors alike.

Furthermore, if, in parallel with Korea's economic model, the G20 confirms a renewed and enhanced commitment to the Millennium Development Goals, I believe the positive effect will be incalculable.

All of this is to say that as the G20's evolution continues apace, it is now critical that it complete the cycle from global crisis responder to global steering committee, for that is what is required if globalization is to work. This is the challenge
of the G20. Its success in this role depends on three things. First is the breadth
of issues that it addresses and the results that it achieves. Let me be clear. The
G20 must pick its spots, and they must be the ones that count. But there can be
no upfront restrictions placed on its scope. The reason that the G20 came into
being was that the G8, without the resurgent or emerging economies at the table,
was no longer able to function as the world's steering committee. Thus the only
restrictions on the issues that the G20 can accept should be those that arise from
the priorities that it sets for itself at any given point in time.

Nor is it mandatory that each meeting result in symbolic agreement. There
must be true commitment to whatever is agreed. The reason for creating the G20
was not simply to have more people in the leaders' photo-op. There are real differences between nations, and they must ultimately be bridged if globalization is
to work. But that will not happen if instead of being confronted those differences
are perpetually papered over by pretty words signifying nothing.

The second key to the success of the G20 will be its capacity to coordinate
the response to the crisis of the day, whatever that may be, while at the same
time organizing to mitigate if not prevent the crises on the horizon. The needed
economic recovery, with unequivocal bank regulation at its core, is a priority of
today's crisis; climate change and food security are the most immediate examples
of the next crises that must be dealt with.

The third key is the G20's preparedness to reach out to those who are not at
the G20 table. Here again Korea took the lead, and for that it is to be congratu-
lated. G20 multilateralism demands more than a camouflaged concern for what
is all too often little more than a country's narrow national interests. The world's
new steering committee came into being because the interdependence of nations
has changed the paradigm. The G20's members are members because they have
power and position, but they also have a responsibility to the rest of the world, a
responsibility that they must live up to, a responsibility that begins by listening
to what others have to say. For example, the failure of adequate financial regulation in the United States and Europe, the moral hazard that it represented, and
the devastating contagion that ensued was an infringement on the sovereignty of
every country on every continent in the world. Those populations have the right
to be heard.

In summary, what is the measure by which the new steering committee should
be judged? The answer, I believe, is the degree to which it improves the way that
globalization works in the here and now and in the way that it prepares for the
road ahead. This is not an academic yardstick. The goal is to relieve the gridlock

that is paralyzing the international system; how well the G20 achieves that, on issue after issue, is the litmus test it will be called upon to pass.

The future of globalization is the great issue of our time. The challenges that the G20 has before it now are all manifestations of the need to make the world work better. Even more to the point, how the summit deals with them will provide an indication of how the G20 will deal across the board with the interdependence of states in the future. Over the years to come the issues that the G20 will have to confront will be as varied as the pebbles on a beach. But whether they will be successfully dealt with is another question, one that will depend on a fundamental truth.

Bargaining at the G20 will inevitably begin as it does everywhere else, on the basis of the self-interest of nations. No one who witnessed the disarray at Copenhagen or the never-ending disagreements over bank regulation between and within the United States and Europe over the last two years should hold any other expectations. But in the end, success can and will be achieved if the member countries recognize that in today's highly interdependent world, the furtherance of a country's self-interest depends more than ever before on the degree to which it furthers the global interest. That, I would submit to you, is the message that the world looks for as the G-20 completes its evolution from crisis responder to steering committee.

2

The G8: Legacy, Limitations, and Lessons

JOHN KIRTON

On June 21, 1997, at their Denver summit, the Group of Seven (G7) leaders confidently proclaimed:

> We have been encouraged by the many positive indicators in our economies: inflation remains low, growth continues at a solid yet sustainable pace or is increasing, and fiscal actions are reducing budget deficits. We welcome the impressive gains of the emerging economies, which have contributed significantly to global growth.

Less than two weeks later the Thai baht collapsed, catalyzing what turned from an Asian to a global financial crisis that spread to consume Indonesia, Korea, Russia, and Brazil and even afflicted the United States over the subsequent year and a half. Over a decade later, on July 8, 2008, at their Hokkaido-Toyako summit, the Group of Eight (G8) leaders also confidently declared: "We remain positive about the long-term resilience of our economies and future global economic growth. Financial market conditions have improved somewhat in the past few months." Less than two months later, the U.S. government seized bankrupt mortgage lenders Fannie Mae and Freddie Mac and then let investment bank Lehman Brothers collapse, catalyzing the American-turned-global financial and economic crisis, which spread within months to generate the greatest global recession since the Great Depression eight decades before.

The chapter appendixes are available at www.g8.utoronto.ca.

The G8 was by no means alone in its failure to predict or prevent those expanding financial crises, bred by a globalizing world. Indeed, even when professionals within leading international organizations such as the Bank for International Settlements (BIS) saw the 2008 crisis coming, they were unable to get the members to act in any serious way. Perhaps the greatest failure came from the Group of Twenty (G20) finance ministers' forum, for it had been created in 1999 to preserve global financial stability in the wake of the inability of the multilateral economic institutions established in the 1940s and their subsequent plurilateral supplements to comprehend and cope with the new era of interconnected, complex, uncertain, private sector–driven finance. But the blame had to be shared by the G7/8, which, since its start as a forum of the G5 finance ministers of the United States, Britain, France, Japan, and Germany in 1973, had been governing global finance.

In its performance as a global financial forecaster and economic governor in the twenty-first century, the G7/8 was in part a victim of its striking success in accomplishing the historic mission that it had been created to achieve. As it declared at its first summit in Rambouillet, France, on November 17, 1975, that mission was to preserve within its members and promote on a global basis the values of "open democracy, individual liberty and social advance." The G7 accordingly led the peaceful destruction of the Soviet Union, bloc, empire, and ideology; its replacement by democratic alternatives in much of the world; and the inclusion of a reforming Russia as a full member of its democratic concert club. In 1999, the G7 politically initiated at the leaders' level the war that saved Kosovo from an erupting genocide, with the G7-led North Atlantic Treaty Organization (NATO) delivering the required military force. In 2009 the G8, now with Russia, condemned Iran's leader, Mahmoud Ahmadinejad, for his denial of the holocaust. In 1978 it initiated the campaign against global terrorism, with a new regime to stop skyjacking. In 1979, long before the UN became politically active, the G7 invented global climate change governance by producing the most ambitious and effective control regime that the world has seen to this day. It came to consensus that carbon concentrations in the atmosphere must immediately be stabilized at existing levels and acted to ensure that G7 members reduced their emissions into the atmosphere for the following five years.

In the twenty-first century, through its dialogue with the Group of Five (G5)—China, India, Brazil, Mexico, and South Africa—and then through the broader Major Economies Meeting (MEM) and Major Economies Forum (MEF), it moved all consequential carbon powers to agree to contribute to the cause of controlling emissions. In 2005 it eliminated the debt of the deserving poorest countries, pledged to double official development assistance (ODA) by 2010, and did much to meet that pledge, even during economically contracting times. In 2001 it launched the Global Fund against HIV/AIDS, Tuberculosis, and Malaria. In 2010 the G8 raised $7.3 billion at its Muskoka summit to help the UN save the lives of millions of poor children and mothers around the world. In its early years, the G7/8 also produced several successes in the finance and economics field. It oversaw the post–Bretton Woods regime of floating but managed exchange rates and launched and concluded successive rounds of multilateral trade negotiations.

Yet as the twenty-first century approached and the Asian-turned-global crisis struck, the G7/8 acknowledged its own shortcomings by creating the broader G20 of both established and emerging systemically significant countries to lead the required reform of global finance. When the American-turned-global crisis erupted a decade later, the G7, led by the leaders of the United States, France, and Britain, reluctantly went beyond its own elite club to elevate to the leaders' level the broader G20, which had worked well in most respects since its start. This leap of faith was fulfilled by the successful performance of the G20's first summits: Washington with its large-scale stimulus and stronger financial regulation; London with its mobilization of $1.1 trillion for stimulus with a pro-poor tilt; Pittsburgh with its Framework for Strong, Sustainable, and Balanced Growth and its agreement to eliminate inefficient fossil fuel subsidies; and Toronto with its credible message for containing the Euro-crisis—stimulus now, exit soon, and fiscal sustainability over the medium term.

How and why did the G8 succeed so well from 1975 to 1999, and why did it increasingly cede center stage to its G20 offspring as the global economic governor from 1999 to 2010? The G8, as a major democratic concert, combined globally predominant power with the shared social purpose of promoting democracy in a world in which the relative capability of self-contained sovereign states defined power and in which democracy had the decisive soft-power advantage in the ideological struggle that defined polarity in the world. The G7 completed its success in the quest that it was designed for by acting from 1989 to 2006, in accordance with the concert principle, to include a defeated, democratizing Russia as an equal in an expanded G8, even though Russia's declining power put its relative capability in a class below that of the rest of the members of this exclusive club of major powers.

But then a self-confident G8 stopped expanding, just as twenty-first-century globalization and democratization placed a premium on connectivity rather than relative capability and on systemic significance rather than major power status in a world in which many more politically open, well-connected, rising democracies were available to help supply the new needs for global governance. Only after their political victory in the cold war had turned into economic defeat from post–cold war globalization did all G8 leaders learn that they needed the newcomers in their club, at the hub of a network to govern an open, tightly wired world. The G8's legacy and limitations suggest that the

G20 will succeed if it becomes a club with a comprehensive agenda, with social and political as well as economic openness and progress as its defining principles, with leadership from its emerging members that are most advanced in that regard, with a dense network connecting it broadly with civil society, with stronger accountability, and with a willingness to hold longer and even intersessional summits at critical times.

The G8's Legacy, 1975–2010

The G8 was conceived and created to deal with the concentrated, comprehensive, interconnected cascade of global crises that assaulted the major democracies from 1971 to 1975. On August 15, 1971, U.S. president Richard Nixon unilaterally imposed a 10 percent import tax on America's closest friends and ended the currency convertibility that had made the U.S. dollar as good as gold. Post–World War II progress in opening trade ground to a halt after the launch of the Tokyo Round in 1973. In October 1973 the oil shock from a new war in the Middle East suddenly made Americans and many others pay much more for their sometimes suddenly unavailable oil and gas. Further south, it led India to claim that it needed alternative energy and therefore to explode its first nuclear device, in May 1974. As Euro-communism swept the southern tier of Europe from Greece to Spain, Christian Democratic Italy, facing bankruptcy, considered letting the Communist Party into a coalition government. The Soviet Union accumulated loans from Western banks, which it might bankrupt by refusing to repay. And New York City itself faced bankruptcy, with President Gerald Ford refusing to bail it out. With these compounding crises, America alone could not cope, especially as its Watergate-catalyzed constitutional crisis reached its climax and its last helicopters lifted off from its embassy in Saigon in April 1975, marking the final defeat of the United States in its then longest war.

This cadence of crises led the leaders of the Atlantic Alliance's "Berlin dinner four" to meet at the British embassy in Helsinki in July 1975, on the margins of the summit of the Conference on Security and Cooperation in Europe (CSCE), to discuss the economic dimensions of the democratic West's relationship with the communist East (Putnam and Bayne 1984). They met again, with their finance and foreign ministers at their side, at Rambouillet, France, in November, joined by Italy and Japan. The finance ministers, save for Italy's, had been meeting separately in the "Library Group" at the White House in Washington since 1973. When two of them, Valéry Giscard d'Estaing of France and Helmut Schmidt of Germany, became their country's leaders, they wished to continue their intimate dialogue at the leaders' level.

Yet the more important founding father of the G7 was U.S. secretary of state Henry Kissinger. He concluded, drawing on his doctoral dissertation on the

Concert of Europe, that America and the embattled democratic West needed
not just a cohesive Atlantic community but a modern democratic global concert to stave off its crisis-bred decline (Kissinger 1964, 1973). He therefore had
America's first post-Watergate president create it, with America's rising democratic allies of Canada, Italy across the Atlantic, and Japan on the far western
front as full members, so that all of and only the world's democratic major powers would be in the new concert club (Kissinger 1975, 1979, 1982). He also had
it created with foreign and finance ministers at their leaders' side.

The opening passage of the communiqué issued at the conclusion of the
Rambouillet summit accurately and transparently reflects the primacy of the
political in the central purpose and policy agenda of this democratic concert.
In a mission statement inserted at Japan's initiative, it declared (Dobson 2004):

> In these three days we held a searching and productive exchange of views
> on the world economic situation, on economic problems common to our
> countries, on their human, social and political implications, and on plans
> for resolving them. We came together because of shared beliefs and shared
> responsibilities. We are each responsible for the government of an open,
> democratic society, dedicated to individual liberty and social advance-
> ment. Our success will strengthen, indeed is essential to, democratic soci-
> eties everywhere. . . . To assure in a world of growing interdependence the
> success of the objectives set out in this declaration, we intend to play our
> own full part and strengthen our efforts for closer international coopera-
> tion and constructive dialogue among all countries, transcending differ-
> ences in stages of economic development, degrees of resource endowment
> and political and social systems.

As the communiqué revealed, the leaders' agenda covered the key issues
that they confronted in international finance, macroeconomics, employment,
trade, and development, in the face of a commodity-empowered South and its
demands for a new international economic order. But it also explicitly embraced
the central political-security issue in its statement: "We look to an orderly and
fruitful increase in our economic relations with socialist countries as an important element in progress in détente." Moreover, it extended to environmental
issues: "Our common interests require that we continue to cooperate in order to
reduce our dependence on imported energy through conservation and the development of alternative sources." Behind the scenes, the G7 intrusively induced
an America jealously guarding its sovereign prerogatives for domestic policy to
give its bankrupt financial capital a loan that President Ford had hitherto refused
to provide. And going on the offense, it discussed how it could help democracy
prevail in Spain, which was then being released from its long authoritarian grip
(Hajnal 2007).

As Kissinger had always conceived of the summit as a continuing concert club, he had the United States host the second summit soon after Rambouillet. Here, with the prerogatives of chair, he fulfilled his pre-Rambouillet promise to the commodity-empowered Canadians to invite them into the club. At Puerto Rico, the leaders discovered how their unilateral bank lending to the Soviet Union cumulatively made them all vulnerable should a hostile Soviet Union abandon détente and refuse to repay. They also kept communists out of a desperate Italian government by offering Italian leaders the loans that they needed, but only if the communists were refused a place. At London in 1977, the European Community was added. At Bonn in 1978, in an act of spontaneous combustion among leaders, they accepted, along with their big package deal on macroeconomic management, a German-Canadian initiative for a novel and effective regime to counter terrorism, in the form of "skyjacking" (Kirton 1993).

At Tokyo in 1979 the leaders confronted the second oil shock from the Middle East and the first Islamic revolutionary "terrorist" threat from Iran by assembling an energy-environment policy that soon defeated stagflation in the North and the commodity threat from the South. At the initiative of Helmut Kohl of Germany, supported by the United States and Canada, the G7 also invented global climate change governance. Through economic contraction and emissions control, its members complied as best they could for the following five years with its ambitious consensus that carbon concentrations in the atmosphere must immediately be stabilized at existing levels (Kirton 2008). In 1981, faced with the new cold war catalyzed by the Soviet invasion of Afghanistan, a new right-wing president in the United States, and a new left-wing one in France, Canadian prime minister Pierre Trudeau, as summit host, induced all his fellow leaders to engage in global negotiations to produce a new international economic order, which socialists wanted but Ronald Reagan did not. By the end of the first cycle of summitry, each country member of this expanding club had equally secured the rights and responsibilities of host.

During the subsequent seven-year and then eight-year hosting cycles, from 1982 to 1988, 1989 to 1995, 1996 to 2002, and (with Russia inserted) 2003 to 2010, the performance of the G7/8 expanded in most ways. At its annual summits and its two intersessional ones in 1985 and 1996, its standout achievement, flowing from its core mission, was peacefully winning the cold war and post–cold war peace, the latter by incrementally accepting a democratically committed Russia as a full member of an enlarged G8 concert club. To be sure, several international institutions, notably NATO and the CSCE, also played a vital role in winning the cold war. But it is striking that on July 16, 1989, Soviet leader Mikhail Gorbachev sent his "surrender letter" on behalf of the Soviet system to none of them or their ranking members. Rather, he sent it to the G7 leaders, including Japan, gathered in Paris for their G7 summit that year.

The G7 subsequently stopped a second holocaust in Europe, by politically initiating at the leaders' level what appeared legally to be an act of aggression against a sovereign state and fellow member of the United Nations. Over Kosovo on March 24, 1999, it used the North Atlantic Treaty Organization to implement the political decisions that the G7 leaders had made and to which a democratically committed Russia subsequently acquiesced. Starting in 1986 it conducted a successful campaign against apartheid in South Africa, supporting the democratic revolution that arrived there in the 1990s. Since the 1970s, it has had an ongoing concern with the wars in Afghanistan and the Middle East and with terrorism around the world.

The Dimensions of G8 Governance

A systematic assessment of the dimensions of governance undertaken by the G8, along with similar international institutions, confirms the G8's generally increasing success. G8 performance showed a notable spike in 1989 when the cold war was won and another in 2000 as globalization took hold (appendix A). During its first thirty-five years it held ninety-five days of leaders' discussions whose outcomes were recorded in 195 public documents. In addition to its annual gatherings it held two intersessional summits, in New York in 1985 and in Moscow in 1996, both designed to win the cold war and secure post–cold war peace. During the first thirty-five years, G8 leaders used the summit to manage their domestic politics, in part by securing individual compliments for their country in the communiqué (appendix B). The summit's perfect attendance record, achieved despite demands on leaders' time back home, shows how important the summit has been to leaders in managing domestic politics as well as international affairs.

In the deliberative domain, the leaders' public communiqués proliferated in length and breath, covering a broad and widening array of topics across the economic, social, and security domains. Yet their focus shifted significantly over the years (appendix C). Starting in 1997, global public health became a sustained, significant concern, as terrorism and weapons nonproliferation have been since 2002. In 2005, climate change was added to the list of priorities. Conversely, since 2001, financial crisis, macroeconomic policy, financial regulation, and international financial institution reform were dropped and almost disappeared. They briefly soared back in 2009 before plummeting again in 2010. The summit's democratic direction setting also increased, especially after 1989.

The G8's decisionmaking proliferated, especially since 1996, as measured by the number of precise, obligatory commitments that it made. Those commitments were largely and increasingly complied with by G8 members in the following year, until the next summit, when new commitments were made. Since

1996 compliance has risen rather steadily, to achieve a solid B grade. The United States, which had ranked among the lowest compliers from 1975 to 1989, soared after 1996 to stand among the most faithful compliers in the club. That suggests that the G8 had become a club that could bind even its most powerful members, including the United States of George W. Bush, which otherwise was inclined to taking unilateral action outside the G8 (Kirton, Larionova, and Savona 2010).

The G8 also developed its own global governance by increasingly institution-alizing itself. It created a broadening array of ministerial bodies, adding to its original finance and foreign minister ones (appendix D). But it stopped adding any after 2001 when, inspired by the anthrax attacks in America, it created the Global Health Security Initiative, with Mexico included but Russia left out. During the subsequent decade, the trade ministers' Quadrilateral, created in 1981, fell into disuse at the ministerial level, although the deputy ministers kept it intact. Different ministerial-level small groups of World Trade Organization members seemed better positioned to do the North-South deals needed to get the latest round of multilateral trade liberalization done. While several sporadic ministerial meetings for development, energy, health, and agriculture took place, they were never fully institutionalized. In 2010 no ministerial meetings were held beyond those for finance, foreign affairs, and development.

The G8's twenty-first-century preference was for a proliferating array of often short-lived official-level bodies. These often reached out to involve non-G8 states in creating a global network only loosely guided from the summit top (appendix E). This official-level institutionalization included the issue-specific Heiligendamm Dialogue Process among G8 and G5 countries, as equals, which lasted from 2007 to early 2010 (Cooper and Antkiewicz 2009). The major inno-vation in twenty-first-century institutionalization was the summit's connection on a more regular basis with an ever-broadening array of civil society communi-ties (appendix F). That broadening, appropriate for a body dedicated to open democracy and composed of all democratic polities, deepened the societal legiti-macy of the G8 club. In the lead-up to the summit in June 2010, many citizens participated in G8 governance on the inside, while almost none protested vio-lently outside or about the summit itself.

All of those achievements took place without the G8 acquiring any legal char-ter, council of ministers, secretariat, or stand-alone bureaucracy such as those of the European Union or UN. They therefore cast into considerable doubt the value of many of the standard proposals for G8 reform, based as they were on copying other international organizations and liberal institutionalist, legalized, hard-law logic (Ikenberry 1993; Kirton and Trebilcock 2004). At the same time, the G8's robust and rising record allows for evidence-based assessments of why the G8 performed so well, where and why it failed, and how it and similar insti-tutions such as the G20 should be constructed and operated in the years ahead.

The G8's Limitations, 2000–10

The G8 as a modern democratic concert succeeded when six largely system-level conditions existed (Kirton 1989, 1993, and 2004). First, successful global governance was demanded by a sequence of severe shocks that showed leaders how vulnerable their own major powers were—the modern equivalents of the French Revolution and Napoleon, which gave rise to the initial global concert, the Concert of Europe, in 1814. Second, the multilateral organizations established from the 1940s had failed to meet that demand, either because none of them were dedicated to shocks and vulnerabilities involving energy, integrated environmental issues, terrorism, crime, corruption, and other such concerns or because their legal charters, governance arrangements, and organizational culture prevented their fast, flexible, innovative response. Third, the G8 concert, containing only major powers, often had the globally predominant and internally equalizing capabilities to supply an effective response easily. Fourth, because the major power members shared common principles of open democracy—as distinct from the common anti-revolutionary convictions of those in the 1814 Concert of Europe—they were like-minded enough to agree on an effective collective response. Fifth, the leaders had high domestic political control, capital, continuity, competence, and commitment to the central issues, making it more likely that a well-tailored, effective agreement would be reached. Sixth, their constricted, controlled membership allowed them to be alone together as leaders in their cherished club, making effective collective action likely to arise. As a result of those six conditions, the G8 operated as a genuine club of equals where any and every leader could lead or follow, form flexible coalitions, and prevail in the end.

Changing Causal Conditions

With all of its successes, what went wrong for G8 governance as the twenty-first century arrived? Some who privilege human agency could point to the self-confidence and complacency of G8 governors collectively after they had won the cold war, liberated Kosovo, and watched globalization and America's "Goldilocks economy" bring prosperity to their citizens and much of the world. The arrival in 2001 of George W. Bush as president of the United States provided others with a convenient individual-level starting point to tell the story of how and why G8 governance went wrong, with climate change constituting the first chapter of this tale. Of particular importance here was Bush's decision, as host of the G8's 2004 summit, not to invite any of the G20-only countries, other than Turkey and South Africa, that France had started to involve in G8 summits as host in 2003.

Those who consider the largely system-level causes of G8 governance can better pinpoint how changes in the twenty-first century dragged the G8's performance down. Here the empirically proven concert equality model of G8 governance accounts for a considerable component of the change (Kirton 2004; Kirton, Larionova, and Savona 2010).

The first cause of successful G8 governance that the concert equality model highlights is the demand for global governance produced by severe shocks that show even the most capable countries that they are vulnerable to deadly threats arising from state and nonstate actors abroad and at home, threats that they cannot control without the assistance of their most capable colleagues abroad. Because leaders of the largest, most successful states can be slow learners, it often takes a second shock or successive shocks for them to respond in a rational way, as the G7's responses to the 1973 and 1979 oil shocks show (Ikenberry 1988). The concentrated, comprehensive, interconnected combination of shocks from 1971 to 1975 launched the G7 and its strong across-the-board performance during its early years. The twin 1979 shocks of the Iranian revolution and the Soviet invasion of Afghanistan turned the G7's focus more to political-security subjects during the 1980s. In the twenty-first century, the second Indian and then Pakistani nuclear shocks of 1998 and the terrorist shocks of 9/11/2001 and 7/7/2005 had a similar effect (appendix G). As no shocks of similar magnitude from finance and economics directly killed citizens in G7 countries or led to large human costs in many other countries from 2001 to 2008, G8 governance of those issues increasingly took a subordinate place. While some might have ideally expected or wanted the G8 to have predicted and prevented the 2008 financial crisis, concerts composed of long successful major powers that require consensus among all major power members are inherently slow-moving institutions that often require a severe shock, and a second severe shock, before they act. During the twenty-first century, the G8 devoted its energies to terrorism, where shocks came in steady succession, and to development and health, above all in Africa, where the largest number of human lives were being unnecessarily lost every day.

The second cause of successful G8 governance is the failure of the old multilateral organizations from the 1940s. Faced with the shocks from 1971 to 1975, it was clear to all that the International Monetary Fund (IMF), the General Agreement on Tariffs and Trade (GATT), the International Atomic Energy Agency/Non Proliferation Treaty (IAEA/NPT), and the UN Security Council (UNSC) Permanent Five (P5) had massively failed. Even the plurilateral Atlantic additions of NATO, the Organization for Economic Cooperation and Development (OECD), and the Kissinger-inspired International Energy Agency (IEA) of 1974 proved inadequate. Hence the leaders of the G7 had to directly produce the required global governance themselves, with Japan, Germany, Italy, and Canada fully in the front ranks.

Moreover, the architecture constructed "after victory" in 1945 had generated no multilateral organizations dedicated to energy, the environment, climate change, foreign direct investment, competition policy, transnational crime, or terrorism, forcing G7 leaders to invent them for themselves. Even where the biggest and best bodies existed, in finance and development in the IMF and World Bank, their formal character and organized culture prevented them from making the fast, flexible responses to new shocks that were required. Even in routine operations in their core competence, their professional staff's record of prediction and prevention often was poor (appendix H). However, when G7/8 leaders provided the highest-level political direction to their ministers, who largely controlled these institutions, their formidable resources could be innovatively mobilized to meet the challenges at hand (appendix I).

The G7/8's great success from 1988 to 2005 in relieving the debt of the deserving poorest countries shows that dynamic at work (Fratianni, Kirton, and Savona 2007). Yet during the twenty-first century, rising powers outside the G8, led by China, India, and Brazil, became increasingly dissatisfied with the international institutional arrangements defined in the distant past, especially as the shocks became newer and larger and the multilateral organizations, especially with their Eurocentric governance, ever more inadequate to cope with them.

The third cause is the globally predominant, internally equalizing capabilities of G8 members, starting with overall capability, which is best measured by GDP at current market exchange rates. Here the data show that the G8's global predominance has not seriously declined, due to an ever-expanding EU whose increasing supranational policy competence and character make it more like the G8 member states (appendix J). Moreover, while the G8's internal equality in capability depends heavily on exchange rate changes among its members, it has not seriously declined when the generally retreating United States and rising Russia are on their normal long-term growth paths. Yet during the twenty-first century, the G8's overall predominance without the EU steadily declined, its internal equalization stalled after 2005, and rising powers on the outside increasingly rose to rank above those within, with China surpassing Japan to take the second spot in GDP globally in August 2010 (appendix K). Thus, particularly in issue areas where the EU did not enjoy increases in its supranational competence and where the issue-specific capabilities of non-G8 members rose most rapidly, G8 performance declined.

The fourth cause is the common democratic commitment and character of the G7/8 members, a cause central to the club's creation, mission, and continuing like-mindedness at its core. While all G8 member polities have their democratic defects, the United States survived its initial Watergate crisis and far less serious ones, such as the effort to impeach President Bill Clinton and to recount Florida's votes in the 2000 presidential election. Japan in the 1990s changed its governing party through free and fair elections, then did so a second and a third time. And Russia arguably remains as committed to democracy in principle and in practice as it has been since Mikhail Gorbachev, the inventor of perestroika and glasnost, first sent his letter of de facto "surrender" on behalf of the Soviet system to the G7 leaders at their Paris summit in 1989. Above all, the expanding EU has added to the G8 many more democracies, some of them coming from previously undemocratic states. Yet in the twenty-first century the second generation of the post–cold war global democratic revolution has produced many more consequential democratic polities outside the G8/EU club (appendix M). Thus the G8 can decreasingly claim to be the world's leading, inclusive, democratic club, especially as the G20 since 1999 has had twice as many democratic members as the G8 does.

The fifth cause is the political control, capital, continuity, and competence of G8 leaders at home, which allows them to adjust to their fellow G8 partners abroad to forge collective solutions that their own citizens will accept. It also enables G8 governments to comply with their leaders' summit commitments to deliver results that work. During the 1970s, G7 leaders had these features in abundance, especially as so many former finance ministers in Germany, France, Japan, and Italy reached and remained in the leaders' ranks. Since then there have been long periods of continuity. But seldom have former finance ministers, business people, or economists become leaders. Starting in 1998 finance and foreign ministers ceased coming to the summit to help their leaders and to encourage them to focus on the economic issues that few leaders understood or enjoyed. The G8 summits after 1999 dealt decreasingly with most issues in the finance and economic domain (see appendix C). By 2010, there were few leaders with expertise in finance and economics within the G8, but more within the G20-only group (appendix N).

The sixth cause is the constricted participation that fosters the sense of being alone together in the top-tier club and the sense of global responsibility that such a social-psychological dynamic and self-definition of interest and identities incite. Here the G8's very slow, highly selective addition of full members had maintained that cohesion-inducing clubbiness through 1998, when Russia was admitted. But when the twenty-first century arrived no new members were added, while the proliferation of ad hoc, partial participants, often in changing configurations, increasingly lessened the leaders' time alone. By the 2010 summit, G8 leaders had only a day together, some of which was spent with their outreach partners on site. This clubbiness, commitment to common democratic principles, and the still-limited relative capability of each of the rising powers outside the G8 made the G8 reluctant to respond to twenty-first-century shocks by admitting new countries as full members of their summit club or by abandoning it altogether in favor of a new, difficult-to-negotiate, unproven club.

The Changing Systemic Context

Those who delve more deeply into the structure of the international system have the most compelling account of why G8 governance worked so well in the late twentieth century but faded when the twenty-first century arrived. For in an intensely globalizing world characterized by complexity, uncertainty, and the shock-activated nonstate vulnerabilities that it brought, connectivity replaced relative capability as the critical cause, systemic significance replaced major power as the key criterion of international rank and relevance, and the ability to listen and learn in an open horizontal network rather than control from a closed hierarchical club became the kind of global governance that worked. Thus at the apogee of its post–cold war achievements from 1997 to 1999, the victorious G8 was left to watch a poorly regulated property market in Thailand spread in just over a year to bankrupt the newest member of the G8 concert, despite the ability and willingness of the rich G7 members and their IMF to bail Russia out yet again. One month later, in September 1998, they watched again as this contagious crisis took down American hedge fund Long-Term Capital Management and with it, almost, the financial system of the so-called remaining "sole superpower," the United States.

G7/8 governors did have some sense of the changing system. Indeed, among the greatest successes of the G7/8 was its decision in 1999 to follow the vision of the finance ministers of its largest and smallest members, the United States and Canada, to create a G20 finance ministers' forum tailored to this new world. Among its greatest failures was its leaders' inability to foresee that, as on August 15, 1971, finance was but the first area in which new shocks from a new system would arise. On September 11, 2001, they brutally learned that there was much more. But they still largely confronted the cascading shocks at the summit level with their slowly changing concert club of old. Simply stated, several of the 9/11 hijackers had come from Saudi Arabia, but no governors ever had or would—after their sole appearance in 2003—come to the G8 summit to help combat terrorism at its source.

The G8 governors did start to invite ever more frequently an ever-enlarging array of nonmember countries and multilateral organizations to participate in an ever-expanding portion of their summits and of its ministerial and official bodies. Here the French had led, with the G7 leaders and France's invited guests dining simultaneously but separately at the 1989 summit and with the heads of four multilateral organizations joining the G7 for a post-summit lunch in 1996. In the twenty-first century, outside leaders were invited by Italy in 2001, Canada in 2002, and France in 2003. In 2003, China, India, Brazil, and many others came for the first time. George Bush followed a different formula for outreach in 2004, dispensing with China, India, and Brazil in favor of nations from the democratizing broader Middle East and North Africa.

Then in 2005 Britain's Tony Blair picked the formula that froze the G8 on its future path. He invited what became the Group of Five (G5)—China, India, Brazil, Mexico, and South Africa—to portions of the summit and to the ministerial Gleneagles dialogue on clean energy and climate change. In 2006, the novice Russian hosts were convinced to follow the G5 formula. The Germans continued in 2007, adding the official-level, issue-specific Heiligendamm Dialogue Process, which affirmed the equality of all thirteen members of the G8 and G5. The Japanese in 2008 took the next step, by holding as part of their G8 summit a leader-level gathering of the American-inspired MEM-17 on climate change. It still left the G20 members of Saudi Arabia, Turkey, and Argentina out.

To be sure, the G8 leaders at the time felt that they had little choice, as India and China signaled that they were reluctant to abandon their historic position as leaders of the developing world to join the "rich man's club." But the simple argument that all outside powers only wanted a larger club in which they were equal cofounders is too deterministic, given the way that rapidly rising powers were dynamically reconstructing their interests and identities in response to systemic, societal, and state changes during those years. Indeed, the leaders of both India and China eagerly accepted their first invitation to come to the G8, along with many others, as partial participants in 2003. They did so again in a much more restricted group of emerging middle-class countries in 2005. Hu Jintao's China also eagerly attended G7 finance ministers' meetings in October 2004 and October 2005, and, along with several other outsiders, several times afterward.

Therefore the more compelling conclusion is that the G8 failed to admit another individual country as a full, equal member of the G8 club. One disincentive for adding India may have been the G7's reluctance to accept Russia as a full member. Only in 2002 was Russia allowed to host a G8 summit, which it did in 2006. It was never admitted to the G7-centric Global Health Security Initiative, created immediately after the anthrax attacks in the United States in the autumn of 2001. Russia was never admitted as a full member of the G7 finance ministers' forum.

Amidst the innovations for inclusiveness, a stark fact stood out. Never were the rising powers, whose relevance was increasingly recognized, allowed to participate as full equals in all of the summit events to consider how all issues addressed at the summit could be combined in innovative ways. Even on July 7, 2005, when the invited leaders of China, India, Brazil, Mexico, and South Africa stood shoulder to shoulder with Tony Blair and his G8 colleagues to condemn the terrorist attacks on London that very day, such an impressive display of G13 solidarity on the central security issue did not inspire the G8 to upgrade the status of the G5 members in the club. The ultimate value of the summit as an international institution of leaders who alone can cover and coherently combine all issues in creative synergistic solutions, including terrorist finance, was thus withheld from the G8 and their guests.

The costs were poignantly seen elsewhere at the 2005 Gleneagles summit. Here the G8 leaders, at their lunchtime session with their G5 colleagues, launched an open, energetic, and educational discussion on trade. The leaders of the two great deadlocked poles, the United States and India, learned a lot from each other and their colleagues and seemed set to search for a solution to get the long overdue Doha Development Agenda done. As Gleneagles was designed to address the thematic trilogy of "debt, aid, and trade," that would have given the summit its third great success. But the lunch ended and the non-G8 leaders were sent away, before the spontaneous combustion that only leaders can produce could reach full force and deliver far-reaching results.

It could have unfolded differently. At the Toronto summit in 1988, the G7 leaders had foreseen the future by identifying in their communiqué a new process they labeled "globalization," with intensifying economic interdependence at its core. They concluded:

> Certain newly industrializing economies (NIEs) in the Asia-Pacific region have become increasingly important in world trade. . . . With increased economic importance come greater international responsibilities and a strong mutual interest in improved constructive dialogue and cooperative efforts in the near term between the industrialized countries and the Asia NIEs, as well as the other outward-oriented countries in the region. The dialogue and cooperative efforts could centre on such policy areas as macroeconomic, currency, structural and trade, to achieve the international adjustment necessary for the sustained, balanced growth of the world economy. We encourage the development of informal processes which would facilitate multilateral discussions of issues of mutual concern and foster the necessary co-operation (G7 1988).

Some thought that a rising China deserved a place in the G8. For the 2000 Okinawa summit the leaders of Japan and Germany tried but failed to bring in China and a few other Asian countries (Kirton 2001). By 2005 some thought that the time had come to add to the G8 concert the durably democratic and arguably major power India, in keeping with the G8's pure practice of admitting one major democratic country at a time and admitting it for good (Kirton 2005a). Yet what the Commonwealth had accomplished in 1947 by admitting a newly democratic India as a full member, Britain did not do in the G8 in 2005 nor earlier in 1998, when it let Russia in. In addition to its imperial history, which may have made it more difficult for Britain to consider India as an equal,

Manmohan Singh had become prime minister only the year before and was just starting his program of economic reforms to replace India's long-standing, sluggish, sometimes called "Hindi," rate of growth.

The greatest paradox and failure of G8 governance is that a concert that appropriately admitted Russia, its defeated enemy, never did so even for India, its more durably and deeply committed democratic partner, which had more relative capability and fewer nuclear weapons than Russia possessed in the summer of 1998. The G8 has never admitted as an equal member any of the former colonies of any of its members, apart from the very special cases of the United States and Canada, regardless of their rising relative capability and the democratic commitment, character, and stress-tested resilience that they may have demonstrated over many years. The G8 failed by its own criteria where India was concerned. With the sole exception of Canada and perhaps the United States, the G7/8 remained an ex-colonizers club. With the sole exception of Japan and Barack Obama's America, it remained a white and Christian as well as wealthy club. It did so even when the world as a whole and the G8 countries themselves were becoming far less so. The deadly al Qaeda terrorist attacks on the World Trade Center in 1993 and again in 2001 showed that more diverse soft power was needed to govern the new twenty-first-century world.

The second great global governance failure of 2005 came not at Gleneagles with its G8 plus G5 formula in July but at the United Nations at its Millennium Summit in September. There Canadian Prime Minister Paul Martin, who had thought from the start that the G20 should meet at the leaders' level, tried as a leader to hold such a meeting focused on the current concern with avian flu and health. All G20 leaders seemed willing except George W. Bush, whose prospective absence ensured that no such G20 summit was held. Given his experience at his first G8 summit in 2001, where he was constantly criticized by the prime minister of Belgium, President Bush did not like attending international summits, especially one where he would be criticized not just by his seven G8 colleagues but, in his estimation, probably by ones coming from lesser powers who could not understand the unique demands and responsibilities that a leader of a superpower faced.

As the G7 financial system and economy moved toward crisis, G8 leaders were unable to cope at their annual summit, which still was limited to about two days. Angela Merkel, the host in 2007, initially wanted to focus seriously on the global economy and regulating hedge funds. But given the resistance of her partners, led by the United States, she chose to use her scarce political capital to secure advances on climate change and let her finance and economic initiatives drop. At the 2008 summit in Japan, climate change, with the first MEM summit, again took pride of place. Only in 2009 in Italy, after the 2007–09 crisis had struck in full force and two G20 summits had been held, did finance and economics make a substantial comeback at the G8. But the summit emphasis was still on food security, at an outreach session involving about forty leaders on the summit's final day.

The G8's 2010 Muskoka summit was designed to deal only with development and security, leaving finance and economics to the G20 leaders' meeting in Toronto the next day. But the G8 leaders nevertheless started their summit with a private discussion of finance and economics, focused on the Euro-crisis, which had erupted in Greece the previous month. They also dealt with trade and investment and several other subjects shared with the G20. But their outreach contained none of the G5 except South Africa and none of the key G20 economic powers. As did the G7 finance ministers, the G8 leaders remained a useful leadership subgroup, or an insurance policy for the broader G20. Yet the G7/8's crisis-induced 2009–10 economic revival did little to repair their earlier failure to predict and prevent, their ongoing failure to focus on finance and economics, and their failure to expand to admit the rising economic powers as equals, especially as democracies such as India and now Korea moved toward becoming top-tier states.

Those failures also eroded the G8's governance capacity on its own core development and security agenda. The Muskoka G8 discussed Iran's nuclear program without the presence of all the powers that could impose financial sanctions against it, a notable contrast to the treatment of terrorist finance at the G20 finance ministers' meeting in 2001. The Muskoka G8 also dealt firmly with North Korea's recent act of aggression against the Republic of Korea, but it was left to Japanese prime minister Kan to carry the absent President Lee's case. On development, Korea did contribute to Canada's signature G8 initiative to raise money for Millennium Development Goals 4 and 5 on child and maternal health. But none of the other G20-only members, all absent from Muskoka, did.

The G8's Lessons for G20 Governance

From the G8's twentieth-century legacy and twenty-first-century limitations, several lessons for G20 summit governance stand out. The first is that the G20 should have a more comprehensive agenda. It should embrace at least the first-order, functionally linked, political-security dimensions of its existing agenda on finance, economics, trade, development, food security, disaster relief, climate change/energy, corruption, and terrorist finance. As the G8 in practice is dealing with several of these G20 subjects, there is little reason for the G20 not to reciprocate. Moreover, both bodies should deal with and link both domains explicitly, in the interest of effectiveness, transparency, and accountability. In short, the G20, like the G8 from its start, should become a club with a more comprehensive agenda, to unleash the unique power of leaders to make trade-offs, create synergies, and innovate.

To take just one example beyond the G20's existing "political" agenda of terrorist finance, money laundering, and corruption, the fossil fuel subsidy phase-
out commitment inevitably raises questions about the ensuing expanded reliance
on nuclear energy and thus nuclear proliferation, just as it has done in the G8
since 1977. There thus may be a case for G20 foreign ministers to begin meeting, for example, on the margins of the opening of the UN General Assembly,
if only to advance the MDGs and other commitments within foreign ministry
competence that the leaders in Toronto so recently affirmed.

The second lesson is to privilege openness as a unifying principle. That
applies in the social and political as well as in the economic sphere. It is the
source of the growing like-mindedness that will transform the G20 from a group
into a club. It builds on the principle of making globalization work for the benefit of all, including socially or politically excluded or underprivileged minorities
within the G20 member states. This principle, along with promoting financial
stability, has been the G20's core mission since its inception in 1999. It further
builds on the G20's repeated endorsement of the principles of transparency, free
flow of information, and rule of law (Kirton 2005b). It will reciprocally reinforce those principles in key G20 members calling for them (Yu 2005; Yang
2010). Indeed, as China's prime minister Wen Jiabao said in Shenzhen in late
August 2010, "Without the guarantee of political system reform, the successes
of restructuring the economic system will be lost and the goal of modernization cannot be realized" (Johnson 2010; People's Daily Online 2010). There is
good reason to believe that political openness and economic growth broadly go
together in mutually reinforcing ways over the longer term (Friedmann 2006).
There is a similarly strong case that political openness and social stability do
too. This is by no means an implicit invitation for the G20 to add to its agenda
explicit discussions of the political systems and practices, let alone human rights
records, of its members. It is rather a recognition that greater diversity will flour-
ish if diverse groups have greater social and political equality, within as well as
across G20 member states.

Regime effectiveness depends more on shared social purpose than on a preponderance of raw material power (Ruggie 1983). The principle of openness
will ensure the G20's effectiveness long after the crisis that created it has passed.
As the values of social and political openness have global appeal, their reinforcement will enhance the G20's legitimacy in the eyes of the "G172" citizens left
out. They therefore should guide the G20's policy prescriptions to its own members and outsiders and its choice of who should lead and join the group.

The third lesson is to open G20 governance to a broad array of civil society
communities, beyond the big business community, which now has a privileged
place. In an important move, in September 2010 the Canadian hosts called
the first meeting of G20 legislators to discuss food security. The Korean hosts

added the research-academic community for a pre-summit conference in Seoul in October 2010. But there is still a long way to go to catch up with the G8's record in bringing in civil society. Meetings of the media, first nations, and faith communities of the G20 countries would be an important next step (Hamilton 2010). Such civil society expansion would involve the global citizenry beyond G20 countries in global governance, in some cases more effectively than bringing their own state leaders to the G20 summit to speak on their behalf.

The fourth lesson is to improve the accountability of G20 governance. That requires going beyond inviting reports from the multilateral organizations that G20 members, and the G7 ones within them, largely control. It can be done by developing the mechanisms for self-monitoring of members' compliance that the G8 has instituted over the past few years. Independent compliance monitoring involving authoritative outsiders also has an important place.

The fifth, final lesson is to remain prepared to have longer and special intersessional summits, the latter as the G20 did in its first two years and as the G8 did to advance its core mission in 1985 and 1996. For the G20 these need not be only in response to financial crises, or indeed to crises of any kind. The demands of global governance are great and growing, well beyond the capacity of a single G8-only summit in the spring and a single G20 summit each fall. An intersessional G20 summit could be added to the scheduled G8 one, following Canada's Muskoka-Toronto model, in June 2010. And the annual G20 summit could be lengthened beyond its normal duration of less than a day to give leaders the time that they need to become a club that leaders lead.

References

Cooper, Andrew, and Agata Antkiewicz. 2009. *Emerging Powers in Global Governance: Lessons from the Heiligendamm Process.* Waterloo, Canada: Wilfred Laurier University Press.

Dobson, Hugo. 2004. *Japan and the G7/8: 1975–2002.* London: RoutledgeCurzon.

Fratianni, Michele, John Kirton, and Paolo Savona. 2007. *Financing Development: The G8 and UN Contribution.* Aldershot, U.K.: Ashgate.

Friedman, Benjamin. 2006. "The Moral Consequences of Economic Growth." *Society* 43, no. 2: 15–22.

G7. 1988. "Toronto Economic Summit Economic Declaration." Toronto [www.g8.utoronto.ca/summit/1988toronto].

Hajnal, Peter I. 2007. *The G8 System and the G20: Evolution, Role, and Documentation.* Aldershot: Ashgate.

Hamilton, Karen. 2010. "Inspired Leadership." In *G8-G20: The Canadian Summits,* edited by John Kirton and Madeline Koch. London: Newsdesk Publications.

Ikenberry, John. 1988. *Reasons of State: Oil Politics and the Capacities of American Government.* Cornell University Press.

———. 1993. "Salvaging the G7." *Foreign Affairs* 72 (Spring): 132–39.

Johnson, Ian. 2010. "Reform Talk in the Air before Key Meeting in China." *International Herald Tribune*, September 29, p. 1.

Kirton, John. 1989. "Contemporary Concert Diplomacy: The Seven-Power Summit and the Management of International Order." Paper prepared for the International Studies Association Annual Conference, March 29–April 1, London.

———. 1993. "The Seven Power Summit and the New Security Agenda." In *Building a New Global Order: Emerging Trends in International Security*, edited by D. Dewitt, D. Haglund, and J. Kirton. Oxford University Press.

———. 2001. "The G7/8 and China: Toward a Closer Association." In *Guiding Global Order: G8 Governance in the Twenty-First Century*, edited by John Kirton, Joseph Daniels, and Andreas Freytag. Aldershot, U.K.: Ashgate.

———. 2004. "Explaining G8 Effectiveness: A Concert of Vulnerable Equals in a Globalizing World." Paper prepared for the panel "Explaining G8 Effectiveness" at the Annual Convention of the International Studies Association, Montreal, Canada, March 17–20.

———. 2005a. "The Future of the G8." In *G8 Summit 2005: Mapping the Challenges*, edited by Maurice Fraser, pp. 187–89. London: Newsdesk.

———. 2005b. "Toward Multilateral Reform: The G20's Contribution." In *Reforming from the Top: A Leaders' 20 Summit*, edited by John English, Ramesh Thakur, and Andrew F. Cooper, pp. 141–68. Tokyo: United Nations University Press.

———. 2008. "Consequences of the 2008 U.S. Elections for America's Climate Change Policy, Canada, and the World." *International Journal* 64 (Winter): 153–62.

Kirton, John, Marina Larionova, and Paolo Savona. 2010. *Making Global Economic Governance Effective: Hard and Soft Law Institutions in a Crowded World*. Farnham, U.K.: Ashgate.

Kirton, John, and Michael Trebilcock. 2004. *Hard Choices, Soft Law: Voluntary Standards in Global Trade, Environment, and Social Governance*. Aldershot: Ashgate.

Kissinger, Henry. 1982. *Years of Upheaval*. Boston: Little Brown.

———. 1979. *White House Years*. Boston: Little Brown.

———. 1975. "The Industrial Democracies and the Future." *Department of State Bulletin* 73 (November 11): 757–64.

———. 1973. *Metternich, Castlereagh, and the Problems of Peace: 1812–1822*. Boston: Houghton Mifflin.

———. 1964. *A World Restored: Europe after Napoleon*. New York: Grossett and Dunlap.

People's Daily Online. 2010. "Shenzhen, Frontier of China's Reform." August 27 (http://english.peopledaily.com.cn/90001/90776/90882/7119613.html).

Putnam, Robert, and Nicholas Bayne. 1984. *Hanging Together: The Seven-Power Summits*. Harvard University Press.

Ruggie, John. 1983. "International Regimes, Transactions, and Change: Embedded Liberalism in the Postwar Economic Order." In *International Regimes*, edited by Stephen Krasner, pp. 195–232. Cornell University Press.

Yang, Yao. 2010. "The End of the Beijing Consensus: Can China's Model of Authoritarian Growth Survive?" *Foreign Affairs* (January/February).

Yu, Yongding. 2005. "China's Evolving Global View." In *Reforming from the Top: A Leaders' 20 Summit*, edited by John English, Ramesh Thakur, and Andrew Cooper, pp. 187–200. Tokyo: UNU Press.

3

The Impact of the G20 on Global Governance: A History and Prospective

NGAIRE WOODS

This chapter presents a short, analytical history of the G20 leaders' group. It examines the impact of the G20 on outcomes in international cooperation and its impact on the processes and institutions of global governance. The first part of the chapter traces the trajectory of the G20 across its first four meetings, highlighting the fact that after the initial "crisis committee" phase of the G20, the cooperation achieved by the group waned dramatically. The second part of the chapter examines whether the global agenda has been broadened or influenced by the inclusion of emerging economies. The third and final part of the chapter examines the prospects for the G20 looking forward, sketching out major areas in which the G20 needs to act as an agenda setter and orchestrator of global governance. To foreshadow the conclusions, the G20 is uniquely placed as an informal agenda-setting group to push forward global cooperation in four key areas: financial regulation, development assistance, exchange rates, and international institutional reform.

The Trajectory of the G20 Leaders' Group

The immediate precursor to the G20 leaders' group was an informal forum for discussion among officials from the G7 countries and a select group of "systemically significant" developing countries in the wake of the 1997 East Asian financial crisis. The G20 finance group emerged because it became clear (at least to some) that G7 discussions on dealing with the global crisis of 1997 needed to include countries that were not part of the informal G7 network, which had been driving policy in the International Monetary Fund (IMF) for a long time.

What impact did the G20 finance ministers' group have? Two studies of the group at work reveal much about its outcomes and processes.[1] In its early years it was a powerful forum for consensus building in crisis management. It forged consensus on a framework for debt restructuring (collective action clauses and voluntary standards) and on the need for IMF quota reform. That said, G20 finance group outcomes were not so different from those of the G7. During its early years, the G20 finance group's formal statements echoed those of the G7 finance group. It is true that as time passed that became less true; the group's positions and agenda became more distinct from those of the G7. However, the group's agenda also became less pressing. The influence of the G20 finance group declined—until the financial crisis of 2008 reminded people of the existence of an informal network that was more representative than the G8.

The life cycle of the G20 finance group suggests an interesting possible trajectory for the G20 leaders' group. The finance group sprang to life as part of crisis management at the global level. It may not have instantly produced outcomes that were different from those of the preexisting G7 group, but its composition sowed seeds of change for the longer term. It was a recognition of the shift in global economic power. It reinforced a growing concern about the anachronistic power balance in existing institutions of global economic governance. It created a blueprint for a grouping through which to broaden participation.

The G20 finance group was informal in the sense that it had no formal rules of membership, no formal authority to make rules, and no formal processes for making decisions or resolving disputes.[2] Those were also attributes of the G7 and G8 and G20 leaders' groups. This helps clarify what these groups do and do not do. They are not formal international organizations to which states have delegated power. This gives the G20 freedom to do other things, such as setting agendas, coordinating policies and distributing tasks across existing institutions, and building consensus on norms and knowledge.

2008 Crisis Committee of Leaders

When President George W. Bush called the first meeting of G20 leaders in November 2008, the failure of Lehman Brothers had shaken confidence in markets across the world. The sight of the leaders of the world's largest economies

---

1. See chapters 1 and 2 of Leonardo Martinez-Diaz and Ngaire Woods, *Networks of Influence: Developing Countries in Networked Global Order* (Oxford University Press, 2009).

2. For these reasons, Leonardo Martinez Diaz and I describe it as a network. See "The G20: The Perils and Opportunities of Network Governance for Developing Countries" at www.global economicgovernance.org.

meeting in Washington was reassuring to many. It was crucial to include emerging economies since leaders needed collectively to agree to stimulate domestic demand and not to use protectionism. Without the cooperation of China, India, Brazil, and others, the G7 countries could have found themselves agreeing to row against a tide that would overwhelm them.

The G20 leaders also agreed to work toward new global financial regulations. The 2008 agreement by the G20 leaders set out a work plan more detailed and practical than any G8 communiqué (reflecting, many would say, its roots as a group of finance ministers and central bank governors). On development, the G20 leaders reaffirmed the agreement reached at the Monterrey UN conference on financing for development. That said, the results of this agreement and the leaders' pledges to assist developing countries resulted in rather pauce outcomes.[3] The IMF and World Bank were to deliver the pledged funds, and those institutions needed time to rearrange their mechanisms for lending and to lend in ways that met their precautionary policies and safeguards. It is difficult to see that the broader G20 membership made a difference on this issue.

On institutional reform, the G20 leaders together voiced the need for more reform in existing institutions. The G20 (unlike the G8) specified the need for a broader membership of emerging economies in the Financial Stability Forum and for better collaboration between that body and the IMF. Here the addition of emerging economies clearly pushed institutional reform a little higher on the agenda. It had long been on the G8 agenda, but it had been taken forward at a glacial pace.

This first meeting of the G20 leaders set a new agenda with priorities for action and the beginnings of detailed instructions for international organizations. This agenda setting could not have been done in the IMF, the United Nations, the World Bank, or the World Trade Organization, not least because each of those organizations has some formal authority delegated to them by governments on condition that the power be used only in decisionmaking processes and structures. That condition makes the institutions difficult to use, to change, and to adapt at high speed. Existing institutions could not range across each others' mandates. Furthermore, a broader leadership group was needed to provide strategic direction to each of the international institutions and relate them to each other. The G20 highlighted both the need for an informal forum (such as the role played by the G7) and the need to broaden representation in such a forum.

The G20's most important impact on global governance was signaled clearly at the first summit. A new, broader, group was sitting in the cockpit of the global

---

3. See Ngaire Woods, "International Responses to the Impact of the Financial Crisis on Developing Countries," paper prepared for the European Parliament, 2009 (see www.globaleconomic governance.org).

economy, and that fact was widely picked up by the world media. The Indonesian press reported that "during the November 2008 Summit in Washington, D.C., the leaders of advanced economies stood on an equal footing with their emerging nations' counterparts addressing the global economic and financial issues candidly."[4] Al Jazeera reported that "if you go through the document, you see words like 'reform of financial markets,' 'transparency,' 'integrity'—it doesn't really amount to a hill of beans. . . . But what it does amount to is that we have seen for the first time under one roof . . . 20 of the key economic nations in the world. The crucial thing is that the emerging markets—the developing nations—are at the table as well."[5]

The London Meeting: A High Point in International Cooperation?

Armed with a substantive agenda (and the work plan created in Washington), the G20 leaders came to London in April 2009 to agree to a seemingly dramatic set of measures. Leaders promised to give the IMF access to some $500 billion in new resources, and they also agreed to support a new special drawing rights (SDR) allocation that would inject $250 billion into the world economy—what some would call global quantitative easing. They reaffirmed their commitment to refrain from protectionism. They agreed to work toward extending regulation and oversight to all systemically important financial institutions, instruments, and markets, including, for the first time, systemically important hedge funds. On development assistance, leaders called for at least $100 billion in additional lending by the multilateral development banks (MDBs) and promised $250 billion in support for trade finance. They also agreed to use additional resources from agreed IMF gold sales for concessional finance for the poorest countries, together with surplus income, to provide $6 billion in additional concessional and flexible finance for those countries over two to three years.

On institutional reform, the leaders agreed to establish a new Financial Stability Board (FSB) as successor to the Financial Stability Forum (FSF), including members of all G20 countries, FSF countries, Spain, and the European Commission. They agreed that the FSB should collaborate with the IMF to provide early warning of macroeconomic and financial risks and actions needed to address them. Leaders also committed to implementing the package of IMF quota and voice reforms that had been agreed in April 2008, and they called on the IMF to complete the next review of quotas by January 2011. In respect of the World Bank, the leaders committed themselves to implementing the reforms agreed in October 2008. They also agreed that heads and senior leadership of

---

4 . "Indonesia and the G20," *Jakarta Post*, April 3, 2009.

5. "G20 Agrees on Financial Action Plan," *Al Jazeera English*, November 15, 2008.

international financial institutions should be appointed through an open, transparent, and merit-based selection process.

The London G20 summit demonstrated that the G20 leaders could set a new cooperation agenda and create new mandates and institutions. That said, it was clear that implementation would rely on national governments and formally constituted international institutions. The role of the G20 was to set priorities for organizations.

The Waning of the "Crisis Committee"

In hindsight, the London summit was a high point of cooperation. However, it was accompanied by serious questioning in the media of whether the actions of the G20 leaders would match their words and pledges. Trade protectionism was scrutinized. The *Jakarta Post*, for example, wrote:

> The G20 Summit in London . . . saw the group vow their opposition to trade protection, specifically promising not to raise barriers to trade before the end of 2010. Five months have passed since then. The Global Trade Alert group has reported over 100 protectionist measures have been implemented by the G20 members over that period. The G20 has no sanctions it can apply to transgressors.[6]

Other journalists across the world picked up this theme, highlighting reports that seventeen of the twenty had used protectionist measures since they had pledged not to do so in Washington.

There also was skepticism about progress on financial regulation. The *Financial Times* wrote that "the emphasis on quantities rather than concrete agreements also serves to mask the big missing element in the communiqué: a new and binding commitment to specific measures to clean up the toxic assets of the world's banking systems."[7] In other reporting, the same newspaper noted that "the summit text included commitments to curb 'risky' bank bonuses, but offered little new on monetary policy or efforts to clean up bank balance sheets."[8]

On institutional reform, there was some progress. The emerging economies began to push harder for a greater voice in the IMF and World Bank. The G7 economies had as priorities financial regulation and a coordinated strategy on growth and stimulus, but they recognized they would need to concede on governance reform. That said, divisions within the G7 slowed negotiations on this. There were doubts about institutional innovations. *The Economist* questioned the role of the new FSB:

6. "What Is the G20 Really Fighting For?" *Jakarta Post*, October 19, 2009.
7. "Large Numbers Hide Big G20 Divisions," *Financial Times*, April 2, 2009.
8. "G20 Leaders Hail Crisis Fightback," *Financial Times*, April 3, 2009.

Collaborating with the IMF, [the FSB] is meant to ferret out macroeco-nomic and financial risks. But if it warns, who will listen? Imagine the scene in Congress in 2015. The economy is booming, but Americans cannot get mortgages because some pen-pusher in Basel says the banks are taking too much risk. The banks would be freed faster than you can say 'swing voter.'[9]

The Pittsburgh G20 meeting was far less dramatic than the meeting in Lon-don. As one report at the time suggested:

The Group of 20 leaders' summits, born in crisis less than a year ago, may be suffering from a return to normal times. Leaders arriving in Pittsburgh yesterday splintered into an array of differing priorities . . . the G20 is down to more nitty-gritty issues, making it more difficult to rally popular support. As a result, its unity is coming under strain, stoking concern that its accomplishments will shrink in scale.[10]

The G7 priorities were growth and pressing ahead with global financial regu-lation. The emerging economies' priorities were to push for further governance reform to give them more voice in the international financial institutions and to restart the Doha multilateral trade negotiations.

On financial regulation, leaders committed to developing by the end of 2010 internationally agreed rules to improve both the quantity and quality of bank capital and to discourage excessive leverage. They agreed to act together to raise capital standards, to implement strong international compensation standards aimed at ending practices that lead to excessive risk taking, and to improve the over-the-counter derivatives market, creating more powerful tools to hold large global firms to account for the risks that they take.

However, two opposing views of financial regulation had begun to emerge in the wake of the London summit. G7 countries with global financial sectors were pushing for global regulation. Emerging economies preferred a more nationally differentiated approach, expressed (subtly) by Rajat Nag, managing director of the Asian Development Bank: "My feeling is that countries, including China and India, would want to see financial regulations that are more comprehensive and transparent, but at a national level, I don't think anybody would want a supra-national regulator."[11]

The G20 as an institution had acquired legitimacy but attracted some criticism when it designated itself as "the premier forum for our international

9. "Spin and Substance; Buttonwood," *The Economist,* April 11, 2009.

10. "G20 Will Replace G8 as Global Economic Forum; World Leaders Near Agreement on New Banking Regulation," *Globe and Mail,* September 25, 2009.

11. "Indonesia Warns on Over-regulation," *Financial Times,* March 5, 2009.

cooperation" in Pittsburgh. Some smaller emerging markets not in the G20 club, such as Thailand and Chile, expressed annoyance.[12] Other non-G20 policymakers complained that they would henceforth be expected to comply with rules of which they might not even be notified, the G20 having no formal decisionmaking or reporting apparatus.

The outcome of Pittsburgh highlighted the beginning of a return to politics as normal. The real lifting work of the G20-inspired agenda needed to be taken up by international organizations and national governments. The G20's capacity had been to permit cooperation to be agreed, to set a stage on which it could be announced.

Challenges for a Global Steering Committee

The Toronto G20 summit, held in June 2010, highlighted three tensions for the G20. First, as an agenda-setting group, the G20 leaders' summit in Toronto achieved little. The agenda was riven with divisions among members, including a growing divide on the question of global or national economic regulation and coordination, which is to some extent a divide between industrialized and emerging economies. The summit was equally marked by a rift between the United States and Europe on whether to focus on stimulus spending or deficit reduction strategies. Greece's sovereign debt crisis had focused European politicians on deficit reduction as a way to ensure market confidence. The U.S. administration remained concerned about jobs and growth. The result was a fudge voiced as support for "growth-friendly" austerity measures and deficit reduction "tailored to national circumstances." In essence, wrote the *New York Times,* "the leaders were blessing their decision to go their own ways." The one issue on which there was agreement was institutional reform; the Toronto Summit endorsed a package of reforms that would result in a shift in voting power toward developing countries in the World Bank Group by a total increase of 4.59 percent since 2008.

Second, in the run-up to Toronto, the long-standing issue of China's exchange rate and U.S. concerns about it had reared up once again, and some saw that as dominating U.S. international efforts. That issue highlights the ongoing lack of an international cooperative mechanism to deal with exchange rate disputes, such as the return to an authoritative role for the IMF in exchange rates.

Third, the G20 Toronto summit attempted to be more inclusive than others. It was marked by a much wider participation of non-G20 countries, including Algeria, Colombia, Egypt, Ethiopia (NEPAD), Haiti, Jamaica, Malawi (African Union), the Netherlands, Nigeria, Senegal, Spain, and Vietnam (ASEAN). That reflected growing concerns that the G20 would make agreements without the

12. "Cosmetic Surgery? The Role of Emerging Markets," *The Economist,* October 3, 2009.

input of or information about non-G20 countries and without reporting back to them. How? Because the G20 was giving instructions to international organizations (such as the IMF) directly and thereby informally bypassing the properly constituted decisionmaking process of those organizations.

Has the G20 Been Influenced by Its Emerging Economy Members?

The G20 has included emerging economies in a leaders' group that has rapidly superseded the G8. But an underlying question that needs to be posed is whether the emerging economies have in fact influenced the outcomes of the G20. The first section of this chapter noted that the G20 finance ministers somewhat shadowed the G7 finance ministers, at least in the early years of the G20 finance group. By contrast, in the G20 leaders' group, the inclusion of emerging economies has been crucial to agreements on several core issues.

In the wake of the 2008 crisis, the global economy suffered a massive shock. Global trade and production shrank dramatically. Industrialized countries had as a first priority the goal of restoring growth and refraining from protectionist measures. Emerging economies were crucial to that; it took agreement from the high-growth economies such as China, India, Brazil, and Korea for the world economy to make a swift recovery.

Emerging economies also have been crucial in financial regulation. Members of the Basel Committee have subsequently reflected that the presence of China, India, and Brazil in the G20 has decreased the backsliding that might have occurred as some G7 members encountered opposition to regulation by their powerful global financial sectors. Having wrought the crisis, major financial sector actors were quick to recover profitability after the crisis, and they began to lobby against regulation with equal speed.

The participation of emerging economies in the G20 has had an interesting effect on institutional reform. Small incremental changes to voting power had already been under way in the IMF,[13] and the G20 (finance ministers and then leaders) has kept the issue on the agenda. It has also provided a forum for emerging economies to coordinate their own positions and thereby to bargain harder for changes. That has been most obvious in the negotiations on new arrangements to borrow, the credit lines offered by a group of countries to the IMF permitting it to lend more if necessary (and if the group of creditor countries agrees). In the aftermath of the crisis, emerging economies were reluctant to extend credit lines if they did not have a significant voice in when the credit lines could be activated. After robust negotiations, China, Brazil, Russia, and

13. Ngaire Woods, "Global Governance after the Financial Crisis: A New Multilateralism or the Last Gasp of the Great Powers?" *Global Policy* 1, no. 1 (2010), pp. 51–63.

India succeeded in pushing for an arrangement whereby the four of them could collectively veto the activation of the credit lines.[14]

The one issue on which emerging economies have left less of a mark in G20 decisions is development assistance and mitigating the impact of the crisis on developing countries. As a result of the addition of development to the G20 agenda at the Seoul summit, emerging market economies may now have more of a voice in shaping a G20 approach to the developing world.

An Agenda for the Global Steering Committee: Building on Lessons from the G20's History

The G20 has shifted the definition of legitimacy in global governance. A comparison of G8 and G20 communiqués highlights the growing marginalization of the G8 as an economic coordinating body.[15] Much of the 2009 L'Aquila communiqué merely reaffirms commitments made by the G20 in London and provides little in the way of new initiatives. The G8 communiqué issued in 2010 in Huntsville, Canada, addresses only the issue of trade (with a blanket statement to resist protectionism) and poverty reduction, which informs the crux of its content. The 2010 G8 communiqué is devoted entirely to matters of development (especially in sub-Saharan Africa), environmental sustainability, and international peace and security.

Korea's chairing of the G20 is a very significant development. As the first emerging economy to chair the global steering committee, Korea is underscoring an updated vision of the group's agenda, most obviously in its effort to put development high on the agenda.[16] That is important. Until now emerging economies and the G7 have been working in different parallel worlds on development,[17] and the G20 has a powerful, unique capacity to overcome that divide. At present G7 or "traditional" donors meet in the OECD/Development Assistance Committee (DAC) and also coordinate in various donor groups. Most important of all, they are seen by emerging economies as clinging to a common aid agenda

14. The politics of these negotiations is discussed at greater length in Woods, "Global Governance after the Financial Crisis."

15. See Ngaire Woods, "The G20 Leaders and Global Governance," October 2010 (www.globaleconomicgovernance.org/wp-content/uploads/Woods-2010-The-G20-and-Global-Governance.doc.pdf).

16. At the Toronto summit leaders agreed to create the High-Level Development Working Group, which would offer guiding principles on development to the G20 centered on growth, mutual accountability, outcomes, and systemic issues.

17. Ngaire Woods, "Whose Aid? Whose Influence? China, Emerging Donors and the Silent Revolution in Development Assistance," *International Affairs* 84, no.6 (November 2008), pp. 1205–21.

focused on social spending. A different view of development is propounded by China, Brazil, Korea (albeit an OECD member), India, Saudi Arabia, and other emerging donors, and their aid is increasing. In the past the traditional donors have tended to interpret new aid flows outside of their own rules and norms, such as those from emerging economies, as threats.[18]

The G20 presents an opportunity to open up a dialogue on equal footing, on neutral territory, between different kinds of donors. The Seoul summit gave general guidance to that endeavor by endorsing principles of development beyond the Millennium Development Goals (MDGs), highlighting assistance for growth and an infrastructural agenda that could permit developing countries to meet the MDGs in ways that depend less on ongoing assistance from Western donors.

In addition to development, there are three other items of unfinished business on which it is crucial that the G20 leaders act. These concern undertakings on which they have already embarked, and the G20 alone can deliver the envisioned outcomes.

Financial regulation is crucial. In 2008 industrialized countries—led by the United States and the United Kingdom—moved quickly to bail out their banks and to attempt to mitigate the damage wrought by their banks on the global economy. In turn, the banks recovered extremely quickly, having found new opportunities for high profits in their governments' crisis management and stimulus policies. The result is that the same banks that caused the crisis have now recovered, marshaled information and resources, and successfully returned to lobbying their governments to forestall or postpone regulation. They have been remarkably successful. Countervailing their efforts are emerging economy governments (which face different pressures) at the G20 table and public opinion (the Pew Foundation figures show very strong support, particularly in the United States and Europe, for stricter financial regulation).

The G20 is uniquely placed to bring together a balance of governments, some of whom are influenced by powerful financial sector interests and some of whom are influenced by industrial or other economic interests. It is also uniquely placed to orchestrate (and distribute tasks among) the large number of international organizations now involved in financial regulation, including the IMF, the FSB, the Bank for International Settlements, the World Bank, European regional institutions, International Organization of Securities Commissions (IOSCO), and the International Accounting Standards Board (IASB).

In spite of all this, the proposals for financial reform prepared for and by the G20 will need ongoing monitoring and vigilant oversight by G20 summits. There are a large number of issues—such as the "too big to fail" debate, bank capital and liquidity standards, and derivatives and shadow banking, among

18. Ibid.

others—that require continuing review and further reform. Much work remains to ensure that the new Financial Stability Board has the appropriately universal membership, clear mandate and authority, and staffing and capacity needed to be an effective instrument of financial reform enforcement.

The G20 needs to focus the attention of leaders on reinforcing efforts to take forward robust financial regulation, such as by agreeing to further more robust actions on financial regulation. The emergence of a "currency war" reminds us that the G20 leaders have not come to an agreement on exchange rates.[19] The Mutual Assessment Program (MAP) launched in earlier summits provides an important starting point for this. But this new form of surveillance will need teeth. There are still no agreed rules on exchange rates (or an agreed benchmark against which to measure whether they are fair or not), and further progress is required to strengthen the IMF's capacity and authority not just to conduct surveillance but to continue (within the organization) moving to strengthen a more multilateral approach to surveillance. In Seoul the G20 noted the importance of further progress on these issues.

Finally, institutional reform in the IMF and in the World Bank is proceeding in small increments and will continue so to do. Missing from the attention given to the shift in power toward emerging economies has been the question of how much of the price is being paid by developing countries. The head of the secretariat of the G24 (the intergovernment group representing developing countries in the IMF and the World Bank) has calculated that the lion's share of the shift in voting power is a shift from developing countries to emerging economies. That fact highlights that governance reform has long since fallen into a set of quid pro quo negotiations obsessed with relative power calculations among powerful countries. For that reason, a determination by G20 leaders to lift the debate is crucial. They might match their commitments to ensure equity for non-G20 members with actions on governance reform that do in fact ensure equity.

In Seoul further progress was made. But the G20 needs to move further to equip the IMF and World Bank to deal with twenty-first-century problems, ensuring at the very least accountable headships, effective representation, and instruments and staffing that permit the organizations to meet the collective action problems faced by members in all regions.

The G20's effectiveness has sprung from its informal, non-institutionalized form. The G20 has operated as an informal network, signaling the intent of powerful countries to cooperate, providing a stage on which they can commit to cooperate, and crafting jointly agreed (when possible) priorities for cooperation. What the G20 has not been—and cannot be if it is to be a nimble crisis

19. Guido Mantega, "Brazil in 'Currency War' Alert," *Financial Times*, September 27, 2010 (www.ft.com/cms/s/0/33ff9624-ca48-11df-a860-00144feab49a.html#axzz1If5lCEIA).

manager and agenda setter—is an institution that can implement. The task of implementing agreements made by G20 leaders falls to international organizations endowed with formal rules of membership, a formal decisionmaking process, and a formal authority to implement.

An effective global steering committee will need to travel light, convening with rapidity (as occurred in November 2008), unencumbered by rules and structures but inclusive enough to command a minimum of legitimacy. G20 leaders will need to find ways to ensure that as a group they do not ride roughshod over the interests of nonmembers (as they are doing on governance reform). They will need to ensure that the formal institutions to which they remit implementation (such as the IMF, the Financial Stability Board, and the World Bank) are fully representative and accountable, balancing the light, nimble flexibility of the G20 with the full legitimacy and authority of formal organizations.

4

The G8 and the G20: What Relationship Now?

GORDON SMITH

The leaders of the G20 countries made clear at their meeting in Pittsburgh in September 2009 that the G20 was the premier international forum for the discussion of economic issues. That was reaffirmed in Toronto. The G8, however, continues, with its next meeting scheduled to take place in France in 2011, the following meeting in the United States, and a meeting in the United Kingdom in 2013. Indeed, Prime Minister David Cameron has already spoken about what he sees as being on the agenda (essentially global security questions).

Important issues, however, remain. How does one define the limits of the international economic agenda? Does it matter whether both the G8 and the G20 address the same or very similar issues, development and climate change being two of the most important? Is the makeup of the G8 optimal to discuss nuclear proliferation in general or more particularly as it relates to Iran and North Korea? What about the regional situation in Afghanistan and Pakistan? Some argue for the need for a body in which like-minded countries can meet. Is that the G8? In what respect is Russia more of a mind with the other members of the G8 than a number of other G20 countries?

Underlying these questions is one that asks what the effect is of excluding certain countries from part of the summit process (I include the G8 and the G20 in "summit process"). We know what the effect was on the Outreach 5 (China, India, Brazil, Mexico, and South Africa) for the G8; the five leaders became increasingly irritated and eventually created a group of their own. If the G8 could caucus before more inclusive meetings, they asked, why could a G5 not do the same thing? Inadvertently, through its outreach process, the G8 in effect "created" the G5: the countries excluded from the main part of the discussion decided to meet separately to prepare and styled themselves the G5. There were meetings at the head of government and official levels. There was even a secretariat (or perhaps non-secretariat, in Barry Carin's terms). Are we going to generate the same outcome with the G20?

On July 7, 2010, the Chinese news network Xinhua circulated an interesting article written by Madhav Nalapat, an Indian university professor. Its publication followed on the G8 and the G20 meetings in Canada. While the article was written by a professor in India and circulated in the first instance by a Chinese official media organization, it would be well to assume that it reflects perceptions in at least both China and India. The sentiments are certainly understandable. Nalapat writes:

> Over the years, there has been a crescendo of voices from the US and the EU urging that large emerging economies such as India and China be "responsible stakeholders in the international system". . . . What is left unsaid is that such voices expect Delhi and Beijing to be responsible to Washington and Brussels. . . .
>
> When the G8 was expanded into the G20, it was expected that the new forum would set right the imbalance in global consultations on financial matters by ensuring that the voices of China, India and Brazil are heard before policy gets decided. In other words, just as the G7 became the G8, the G8 would become the G20.
>
> Instead, the G8 has continued, and has imposed a format whereby they meet in advance of the G20 summits and work out a common position that they then ask the other 12 countries to accept. The G8: G20 format has become a means to influence the big emerging nations to once again accept the policy leadership of the US and the EU, rather than being a forum to reconcile the needs of both the developed as well as the emerging countries.
>
> If the G8 continues, then the "G12" need to meet in advance of such get-togethers the way the G8 does, so as to seek to find common positions on global issues.
>
> Both the developed economies as well as the big emerging economies need each other for mutual benefit and common prosperity. Both need to work in harmony and conciliation. However, the present situation is that the G8 still seek to impose their views on the rest of the world.
>
> The developed world needs to accept that it can no longer dictate to the big emerging countries. They need to understand that a win-win solution means that both sides share both the pain and the gain.

The G8 needs to disband itself so that both developed and emerging countries can together work to resolve the problems facing humanity. Should it continue, then we need a G12.[1]

The last thing the world needs is a G12, but if we persist in excluding China and India and other major developing countries, that will be the result. The benefits of enlarging the G8 to the G20 will be lost. The sense of exclusion—dare I say deception—will be increased. As mentioned above, only a few years ago the G8 started meeting with a group originally called the Outreach 5. While certain leaders wanted to move quickly to a G13 in which everybody was treated equally, that did not happen. There was opposition from several quarters. The following quotations eloquently reveal how leaders of developing countries felt: "We are indeed of one mind . . . we can't be put in a situation where we are asked to join in the dessert and miss the main meal," said South African president Thabo Mbeki on October 17, 2007.[2]

Referring to the Heiligendamm summit, Indian prime minister Manmohan Singh stated: "We were not active participants in the G8 processes. In fact, the G8 communiqué was issued even before our meeting. . . . [In the future] we should get a chance to discuss issues of our concern . . . so that our point of view can be reflected in [the G8's] thought processes."[3]

Brazilian president Luiz Inacio Lula da Silva put it this way: "I make the case for the extended summit to become the core of a permanent forum where the developing and industrialized countries can transparently and representatively exchange their views on the issues that require a concentrated answer. . . . This will enable the intensification of multilateral action to make globalization show more solidarity and become less asymmetrical."[4]

Paul Martin, the former Canadian prime minister, observed from his experience at summits that "the image of Hu Jintao, the president of China, and Manmohan Singh, the prime minister of India—leaders of the two most populous countries on earth, quite possibly destined to be the largest economies on earth within our lifetimes—waiting outside while we held our G8 meetings, coming in for lunch, and then being ushered from the room so that we could resume our

1. Madhav Nalapat, "G8 Must Make Way for New System," Xinhuanet, July 7, 2010 (http://news.xinhuanet.com/english2010/indepth/2010-07/07/c_13387514.htm).

2. In Sholain Govender, "India, Brazil, and South Africa Hold Joint Summit," Emerging Minds Online, October 17, 2007 (http://emergingminds.org/India-Brazil-and-South-Africa-Hold-Joint-Summit.html).

3. In Praful Bidwai, "G8, G5, or G4? A Tough Choice for India," Financial Express Online, July 1, 2007 (www.thefinancialexpress-bd.com/more.php?news_id=2825).

4. Luiz Inácio Lula da Silva, In "Focus: The G8 and Me: A Personal Look at Globalization," DW-World, May 31, 2007 (www.dw-world.de/dw/article/0,,2542982,00.html).

discussions among ourselves, is one that stayed with me. . . . Either the world will reform its institutions, including the G8, to embrace these new economic giants, or they will go ahead and establish their own institutions."[5]

In fact, it appeared in 2007 that others agreed that the time had come to enlarge the G8. President Sarkozy of France stated on August 27: "I hope that, bit by bit, the G8 becomes the G13. Alongside economic consultations, the close cooperation between the most industrialized countries and the major emerging countries that is needed to combat climate change warrants this expansion."[6]

A few months later, on November 12, 2007, English prime minister Gordon Brown said that "to build not just security but environmental stewardship and prosperity free of global poverty, I want a G8 for the 21st century. . . . The G8 has to increasingly broaden to encompass the influential emerging economies now outside but that account for more than a third of the world's economic output."[7]

The situation changed with the creation of a G20 at the leaders' level in November 2008 in response to the international financial crisis. While G20 finance ministers and central bankers had been meeting regularly since 1999, it was concluded that the challenges were so great that they required leaders' engagement. The G8+5 format has effectively withered away. Now that there have been summits of twenty members, it would be very hard to go back to thirteen (some suggested it should be or should have been fourteen, adding Egypt so that a Muslim country would be present).

Already it is clear to G20 leaders that they must discuss and must be seen to be discussing development issues. If that does not occur, the G20 would be severely criticized by the poorer countries of the world. The G20 countries cannot promote growth just among themselves, forgetting those countries that do not have such dynamic economies. The United Nations negotiations on climate change will have as its next event a meeting in Durban, South Africa. The chances of success are very low. It is, in my opinion, only a matter of time until climate change is seriously discussed in the G20 context. The financial dimension already is being discussed.

The G8 has provided a means of coordinating global peace and security policies. Meetings occur at the level of foreign ministers and political directors twice a year, once in the spring in the lead-up to the G8 summit and again in September when the UN General Assembly meets. Recent discussions have focused on

5. Paul Martin, *Hell or High Water: My Life in and out of Politics* (Toronto: McClelland & Stewart, 2008).

6. Nicolas Sarkozy, "Speech by Nicolas Sarkozy, President of the French Republic, at the Opening of the Fifteenth Ambassadors' Conference," International Relations and Security Network (ISN), August 27, 2007 (www.ambafrance-au.org/france_australie/spip.php?article2501).

7. Gordon Brown, "Speech to the Lord Mayor's Banquet," November 12, 2007. Excerpts retrieved from www.acronym.org.uk/dd/dd86/86uk.htm.

security issues, in particular nonproliferation and the efforts of Iran and North Korea in the nuclear field, and there have been many discussions of terrorism and the situation in Afghanistan and Pakistan. There has also been work recently on the problem of dealing with failed and failing states, where terrorists find it easier to create bases because normal government authority no longer exists.

Similarly, the G8 has created a number of bodies at the official level. At the Huntsville summit in 2010 there was a report from a "conference of senior officials" on capacity building. There are a variety of other working groups of officials, including the Africa Clearinghouse (a number of African leaders have been to summits for a consultation in past years, and the practice continues), the Counter-Terrorism Action Group, the Peacekeeping/Peacebuilding Experts' Meeting, the Roma-Lyon Group (on international terrorism and crime), and the Global Partnership Working Group (on preventing terrorists or states that support them from acquiring or developing weapons of mass destruction). Finally, the G8 commissioned work from officials on enhancing the accountability of the G8.

But when one reflects on this agenda, what sense is there in having these discussions without China and India, at a very minimum, present? Is it true that there is some particular like-mindedness of the G8? And even if that is so, what are the effects of communicating that perception to other leaders? There is a lot of confused talk about "like-mindedness," but I would make two points. The first is that if one wants to break global deadlocks, one cannot deal only with like-minded states. If there is to be a positive outcome, one has to deal with those that have a stake sufficient to require that they be included. Second, it is far from clear that the members of the G8 have a greater degree of like-mindedness among themselves than they do with other members of the G20.

The G8 has run its course. I believe that its activities ought to be taken over by the G20. That could mean, for example, that G20 foreign ministers and political directors could meet as needed. The fact that the last G20 took place in Seoul makes the point. North Korea's nuclear program is, almost all would agree, a serious threat to international peace and security. South Korea and China are obviously essential components of any serious discussion of what is to be done. Both are members of the G20. Surely it makes no sense to limit high-level discussions of this key issue to the G8. President Sarkozy addressed the future role of the G8 in a major speech on August 25, 2010.[8] He said: "A word about the G8. Some have said it is condemned. Others believe it has a rosy future if it refocuses on security issues and its partnership with Africa." He then went on, rather cryptically: "The future will decide, and France intends to prepare this summit

8. Nicolas Sarkozy, "Speech by the President of the Republic, 18th Ambassadors' Conference, Elysée Palace, August 25, 2010 (www.ambafrance-ca.org/IMG/pdf/10-08-25-18th_Ambassadors_Conference.pdf).

carefully. It will allow leaders whose views are often very similar to discuss, as they did in Canada this past June, subjects of common interest and major political issues ranging from Iran to the Middle East peace process to Afghanistan." Note the words "often very similar."

Sarkozy continued: "The summit will also provide an opportunity to discuss the destabilization of Caribbean nations, West Africa and the Sahel by drug trafficking between Latin America and Europe. Together, we must cut off this drug route, help transit nations, and protect Europeans from this scourge. No doubt, in this context, we will have to raise the issue of the fight against al-Qaeda in the Sahelian strip between Mauritania and Somalia." One might think Mexico, among other G20 countries, would be an interested party to those discussions.

With respect to Africa, the French president stated: "The summit's other major theme will be the partnership with Africa, because the G8 alone represents 80 percent of international public aid." Yet it is China, a G20 country, that is now the largest source of private investment in Africa. President Zuma of South Africa has welcomed Hu Jintao, stating that Western donors press their political systems on the developing world but that the Chinese approach appears to have been very successful. So, in light of this sometimes conflicting evidence, where do we stand on the future of the G8, and what does this situation mean for France as the next G20 chair?

One lesson appears to stand out above all—when a critical global issue needs to be discussed at the leaders' level, the credibility of that discussion and its outcome rises significantly when the relevant countries are at the table. Accordingly, it was clear that the ongoing financial crisis could not be successfully addressed without the input of the major emerging economies, and the G20 summit sprang to life. A similar assessment can now be made with respect to a range of security issues and climate change: the key regional countries must be present, and the G8 simply is not representative enough. Indeed, recent experience strongly suggests that leaving countries out simply fosters resentment and unproductive bloc politics.

Second, the success of summits depends heavily on adequate preparation. The G20 summits have worked largely because the G20 finance ministers have met repeatedly since the mid-1990s. The habits of consultation and compromise have become ingrained, and practical agreements on the economic side have proved to be possible in remarkably short order (admittedly in crisis conditions). The same degree of preparation will be needed if the G20 takes over the security issue from the G8—and that would seem to argue for bringing the G20 foreign ministers into play as a separate body. If the G20 agenda is to expand, the groundwork must be done in advance, and the transition of security and climate change issues from the G8 to the G20 may take several years to accomplish. But the process of thinking this important change through must start soon.

I had hoped that President Sarkozy would decide against hosting a G8. In fact, retaining the G8 is a step backward for Mr. Sarkozy, as he was ready to enlarge, indeed to take the leadership in enlarging, the G8 to the G13/14. After all, what will the G8 discuss but issues such as nuclear proliferation, development, how to deal with failed states, and maybe climate change? Those issues are important for the entire G20 membership, not just or even particularly the G8. The geometry of power in the world has changed and so has the functional agenda of issues requiring the cooperation of key countries. How can we be surprised if the excluded twelve countries feel that they too must have their "pre-meeting"? Is this the way to manage our ever-increasing global interdependence?

The answer to the last question is clearly "no," and it is time to reassess the assertion that the G8 is more "like-minded" than the G20. A roadmap is necessary to take global governance from a restrictive G8 to a more inclusive and effective G20.

5

Turning the G20 into a New Mechanism for Global Economic Governance: Obstacles and Prospects

LAN XUE AND YANBING ZHANG

It is widely believed that the G20 summits have played a positive role in managing the global financial crisis since their inaugural meeting in Washington, D.C., in 2008, preventing a great global recession and fostering reform in international financial institutions. At the Pittsburgh summit in 2009, the G20 was officially defined as "the premier forum for international economic cooperation"[1] and was also given a role in promoting strong, sustainable, and balanced growth globally. Its success has generated further expectations from member countries. Many believe that the G20 has the potential to become the key mechanism of global economic governance as many non-crisis issues are brought into the agenda. For example, China's premier, Wen Jiabao, in a report to the People's Congress in March 2010, mentioned pointedly that "China will continue to use the G20 and other platforms to participate in the reform process of the global governance system and to safeguard the interests of developing countries."[2] That was the first time that the G20 was mentioned formally in the Chinese government's working report.

---

1. "Fact Sheet: Creating a 21st Century International Economic Architecture" (www.whitehouse.gov/the_press_office/Fact-Sheet-Creating-a-21st-Century-International-Economic-Architecture/ [September 3, 2010]).

2. Wen Jiabao, "Working Report to the People's Congress," 2010 (www.gov.cn/2010lh/content_1555767.htm [October 4, 2010]).

Now that the turbulent days of the global financial crisis have passed, the question is how to turn the G20 from a crisis management committee to a "global steering committee," as some suggested, that can serve as a genuine and effective mechanism of global governance. To be sure, the interests of members of the G20 are strong and the expectations of the global community are high. While people have been enthusiastic and optimistic about the future of the G20, there are also a number of key issues that must be dealt with properly to make the G20 truly a new mechanism for global economic governance.

We believe that the G20 still has a long way to go to play its due role in the post-crisis era. We can identify three key challenges to the group's capacity to become a genuine and effective mechanism of global governance. The first one is agenda setting. What are the core issues that the coming G20 summits should focus on so that tangible outcomes can be achieved to show their effectiveness in the short term? The second is the institutionalization of the G20 in the medium term. The third is the dynamics of the interactions among the major powers, which determines how the G20 will work in the long run. Obviously, these three challenges are interlocked, and all of them surfaced at the Seoul summit in November 2010.

The G20 and the Issue of Agenda Setting

At the Pittsburgh G20 summit in 2009, the leaders had clear ideas about what they should do in the two summits in 2010. Under the framework of strong, sustainable, and balanced growth, the first summit was designed to discuss how to regulate the mature part of the global economy and the second was supposed to focus on how to promote the development of the rest of world. The reform of the International Monetary Fund (IMF) and the World Bank was to be finished along with the two summits. It was also expected that there might be some breakthroughs in the institutionalization of the G20. For example, the year 2010 was described in the Chinese media as the year for the G20 to be institutionalized, before the Toronto summit.[3] However, things have changed quickly since the Pittsburgh summit.

First of all, the unsuccessful UN climate change conference in Copenhagen, the tension between the United States and China on the issue of currency valuation, the delayed reform of the IMF, and the continued running of the G8 in parallel with the G20, as insisted on by some G8 members, all seemed to cast some doubt about what could be achieved at the Seoul summit. In addition, in

---

3. "Yang Jiechi: This Year Is the Year for the G20 to Be Institutionalized, and We Hope All Parties Can Work Together" (www.chinadaily.com.cn/micro-reading/politics/2010-03-07/35178.html [September 3, 2010]).

2010 the UN summit on Millennium Development Goals (MDGs) in September, the East Asian summit in October, the APEC annual meeting in November, and the Cancun conference on climate change in November affected the Seoul summit in various ways. In other words, Korea faced many challenges in hosting a successful summit that could help the G20 to make the transition from a crisis management committee into a global steering committee.

At the same time, the global community also understands very well that institution building needs patience and focus. There may be many steps before the G20 turns from a crisis management committee to a steering committee for global economic affairs. The fact that the Seoul summit was the first G20 summit to be held outside G8 countries symbolizes a significant step in the evolution of the G20. It also highlights Korea's successful development experience and its recent effort to become a "global Korea." The Korean host has also made substantive contributions to the agenda setting of the G20 by presenting financial safety nets and development as the two new agenda items. As a representative of Korea's Presidential Committee for the G20 Summit has pointed out, economic development in developing countries is closely linked with economic recovery in the developed countries. By staying focused on global economic issues while expanding specific concerns to include not only those of a few member countries but also those of many others, the G20 will develop its institutional capabilities and accumulate credibility in its effort to become a true "premier forum for international economic cooperation."

One natural progression is to transform the G20 from a crisis management committee to a risk management committee for global economic affairs. The key point is that the best crisis management is crisis prevention. To prevent crises, risk management activities, such as identifying key risks or making investments to mitigate them, become paramount. However, the very nature of risk has made it almost impossible for us to deal with various risks effectively. The uncertain nature of risks means that while the investment in risk management must be made now, the payoff, which is uncertain, comes in the future. Our political system is organized with clearly defined terms. Very few political leaders would be willing to invest their resources to generate benefits whose credit may be given years later to others or even to their political opponents. Political incentives run against the logic of rational economic or risk analysis; that is probably why, although we have been taught many lessons by various financial crises, we still keep having them. So, one major global leadership vacuum is in risk management of global economic affairs, and the G20 can be a useful platform for filling it. The discussion on global financial system regulation is already moving in the right direction. Korea's proposal to add financial safety nets to the G20 agenda creates a new momentum for such an initiative.

The G20 and the Institutionalization Issue

There have been many discussions on the institutionalization of the G20. One challenge for the G20 is how to keep the delicate balance between being a forum for consultation and coordination on one hand and being an important decision making mechanism on the other. On the consultation and coordination side, there is already a dazzling array of regional and global governance summits, such as the Asia-Pacific Economic Cooperation (APEC), that already provide leaders of different countries with many opportunities to convene and consult. In addition, many other semiofficial and nongovernmental meetings, such as the World Economic Forum in Davos, also bring leaders together. The key is to make the G20 a platform that inspires and innovates, which requires informality and spontaneity. At the same time, if the G20 is envisioned as an important decision making mechanism, it should be equipped with the formal process, authority, and institutions necessary. Such a requirement is almost the opposite of the ones proposed previously. Dealing with such obvious contradictions is a challenge.

Another related issue is how to institutionalize the G20's linkages with the world beyond the G20, such as the existing global economic institutions and the nonmember countries and regional organizations. This part of institutionalization is probably as important as the part regarding operational issues. With respect to the existing global economic institutions, the most important include the International Monetary Fund, the World Bank, and the World Trade Organization (WTO). There are also several key UN agencies with concerns on a range of global economic issues. The 2008 global financial crisis has shown the limitations of the existing global economic institutions in preventing or tackling such a crisis. At the same time, it is also clear that those institutions are indispensible in restoring the global financial order. The general consensus, therefore, is that the Bretton Woods system established after World War II needs to be reformed but not thrown away. Its reform was part of the agenda on the Seoul G20 summit.

Given the G20's emergence as a new mechanism for global economic governance and the prominent role of existing global economic institutions, there may be great advantages for upgrading the participation of existing global economic institutions from just observing to participating in more institutionalized fashion. For example, it is possible to make it part of the formal agenda at the G20 summit to have the heads of the IMF, World Bank, and WTO give briefings on the work at these institutions and get feedback from the G20 leaders. The Seoul G20 summit seems to have made progress on this issue as well as on engaging with nonmember countries by inviting some of them to participate. These two arrangements can be further institutionalized.

There is also a need for the G20 to develop a culture and style of inclusiveness and cooperation in its institutionalization process. There are some common grounds that can become the basis for such a culture and style. For example, all the members of the G20 share the goal of finding solutions to global deadlocks to ensure global economic development and prosperity. All members recognize the current economic system as the basic foundation for global economic activities and want to preserve and improve it. Nobody wants to rock the boat. The developed countries come with experiences and capabilities but find it difficult to deal with global challenges alone; they also need the participation of major developing countries, working with them and developing trust. The developing countries come with the momentum of development but have many daunting domestic challenges that call for the experience and support of developed countries.

At the same time, the members of the G20 also need to recognize the differences among themselves, which are many, including differences in history, ideology, population, economic size (the largest economy is 50 times the size of the smallest), stage of development, political systems, and so on. It is unavoidable that each member will bring with it its unique understanding of and perspectives on global challenges. If we see these differences as baggage and want to work on them to develop a club of "like-minded" members, we may be wasting our precious time and energy and abandoning our true mission, which is to solve global deadlocks. Instead, we should take such differences as assets and explore how we can take advantage of them by turning them into complementarities. In other words, we should try to find common grounds to unite, instead of expanding our differences to divide.

One should not forget that each leader also faces very different domestic constraints. Take China for example. China is still in the midst of a major industrial and social transition. China is facing tremendous challenges in moving away from resource-intensive manufacturing and in accommodating the approximately 13 million people who are urbanized annually. China's per capita GDP is still around 100th in the world. Even if leaders share the same concerns on global issues and agree on the causes, the solutions that they propose could be very different. From a political perspective, perhaps the real merit of the G20 is that it can gradually build up global concerns and consensus among the major powers of the world in the long run.

The G20 and World Politics

That the G20 summits were born in the turbulent days of the global financial crisis means that in the era of globalization, a single state, even the most powerful one, cannot deal with major global challenges like the financial crisis of 2008 by itself; it also means that the existing global governance bodies, like the UN, the IMF, the World Bank and the G8, do not have sufficient capacity to do so either. At the same time, the different responses and performances of different countries also show that we still live in a state-centered world and that states are still the key actors in world affairs. Global governance is not "governance without governments";[4] it is bringing states together to work to manage global affairs. What has changed is simply which states and how many states can work together to make important collective decisions for the world.

States often work together to make collective decisions on public affairs. Sometimes they succeed, and sometimes they fail. But the reason for them to work together, either in the form of bilateral relations or in the form of multilateral relations, has always been the same: namely, their "enlightened self-interest,"[5] which was highlighted again by the G20 leaders in March 2010. The obstacle to the G20's becoming the key mechanism of global governance in the long term also lies there—that is, states often have different interests and disagreements. It is useful for us to examine what the perceived interests were that brought the G20 leaders together and what potential obstacles may yet paralyze the G20.

The G20 had existed for nine years as a platform for dialogue between the important developed and developing countries at the ministerial level before it was upgraded to the summit level in 2008. While one should never forget the tremendous contributions made by those individuals and institutions that made the transition possible, the perceived interests of major players also formed the basis of the G20 summit.

First of all, the G20 summits served the greatest interest of the United States in the most difficult days of the financial crisis. Before the crisis the United States was not interested in the idea of the L20 or the G20 summits because it had no intention of changing the existing global governance architecture, within which it served as the core, or hegemon. However, unlike the other financial crises that came after the breakdown of the Bretton Woods system in the 1970s, this crisis originated in the United States and soon spread to the whole world through the global financial markets.

The crisis brought home to the global community the weakness of the U.S. economic system. From the U.S. perspective, there was a need for institutional mechanisms that could help to deal with the crisis in the short run and save its global leadership in the long run. It was exactly in such a historical context that the G20 summit became a natural choice for the United States. Once the G20 summit came into being, it showed to the world that it filled a vacuum as a new mechanism

4. See James N. Rosenau, *Governance without Government: Order and Change in World Politics* (Cambridge University Press, 1992).
5. Joint letter from the G20 leaders, March 29, 2010 (www.whitehouse.gov/the-press-office/joint-letter-g20-leaders [September 3, 2010]).

for global economic affairs. The successful G20 summits in Washington and London gave the United States confidence in the role that such a platform could play—namely, as "the premier forum for international economic cooperation."

The second force that supports the G20 summit is the non-G8 countries within the G20. For the five major emerging economies—Brazil, China, India, Mexico, and South Africa—the G20 is certainly a better choice than the G8+5 framework. Under the G8+5 framework, the five countries did not share the same rights and status as the other G8 countries. The G20 summit provides them the opportunity to share the same status as the G8 countries so that their concerns and interests can be properly voiced and discussed. For the other six non-G8+5 countries—Argentina, Australia, Indonesia, Korea, Saudi Arabia, and Turkey—the G20 summit is even more desirable since it provides opportunities for them to have greater influence on the most important decisions in global economic affairs.

The third force that has enhanced the importance of the G20 in world politics is those countries that believe that they should be included in the G20. Since the G20 was defined as the premier forum for international economic cooperation at the Pittsburgh summit, some other countries have clearly shown their interest in joining in the G20 and have begun to lobby for their inclusion, which again is a good indication of the desirability of the G20.

However, there are also legacies and forces that the G20 must deal with carefully for it to become an effective mechanism for global economic affairs. One challenge is the relationship between the G8 and the G20. Some G8 countries are concerned that as more countries become involved, their role and influence may be marginalized structurally. It is likely that France or other European members of the G20 may use the chance to hold the G8 and G20 summits next year to propose their ideas of how to handle the relationship between the two groups.

The discussion in this chapter shows both the hopes and the challenges that the G20 faces in the post-crisis era. What we would like to highlight here is that the major challenge that the G20 faces in the long run is how to ensure compromise and cooperation among major powers. The stable relationships among major powers are still a key foundation of the G20. The G20 can certainly play an important role in serving as a platform to enhance mutual understanding and cooperation among major powers. While its major focus is on global economic affairs, the G20 can also provide opportunities for leaders to exchange their views on other international affairs, which may generate positive externalities for addressing some global challenges. As China's Wen Jiabao says, "dialogue is better than confrontation."[6] The G20 will also keep reminding world leaders

6. Xinhua News Agency, "Wen Jiabao Said Dialogue Is Better than Confrontation for the Sino-US Relationship," May 25, 2010 (http://news.xinhuanet.com/politics/2010-05/25/c_12140920. htm [September 3, 2010]).

of the existence of global public interest and of the fact that, as U.S. secretary of state Hillary Clinton said in Beijing last year, "When you are in the same boat, you should keep the peace on the crossing."[7]

Conclusion

The Seoul summit is a real milestone for the G20 not only because it was held outside G8 countries but also because through it the G20 is making the transition from a crisis management committee to a global economic steering committee. Agenda setting and institutionalization will continue to be challenges. In this short chapter we argue that the G20's agenda should be less ambitious at the beginning stage and should focus on economic issues. At the same time, we also suggest that the G20's linkages with existing economic institutions can be strengthened and the G20's engagement with nonmember countries can be enhanced. We are happy to see that the Seoul summit kept a nice balance between regulating the modern part of the world economy while galvanizing support to develop the rest. Seventy years ago, Schumpeter reminded us that "capitalism . . . is by nature a form or method of economic change and not only never is but never can be stationary"—it is "the perennial gale of creative destruction."[8] We hope the G20 can become an effective mechanism that helps the global economy to maintain dynamic growth and avoid devastating destruction.

7. "Hillary Clinton: Chinese Human Rights Secondary to Economic Survival" (www.telegraph. co.uk/news/worldnews/asia/china/4735087/Hillary-Clinton-Chinese-human-rights-secondary-to-economic-survival.html [September 3, 2010]).

8. Joseph Schumpeter, *Capitalism, Socialism, and Democracy* (London: Routledge, 1994 [1942]), pp. 82–84.

PART II

Financial Crisis and Regulatory Reform

6

Financial Sector Reform and the G20

PAUL MARTIN

The great strength of the free market is its ability to innovate; its great weakness is its tendency every so often to take innovation a bridge too far. Nowhere is that weakness more damaging than when it appears in the banking system, a system that depends almost entirely on the trust that we repose in it, even more so when that system knows no borders. That is why the moral hazard posed by institutions that violate that trust will eventually eat away at the very foundations of the global economy and that is why the reform of the financial system must be at the core of the G20's approach to the financial crisis.

Basel III has long since reported, but the question still remains: "Where do things stand?" Unfortunately, while progress has been made, it is not in proportion to the magnitude of the problem. For instance, the question of "too big to fail" has been punted. It must be resolved.

Presumably at some point this will be partially dealt with through various types of buffer capital and debt that can be bailed in, for we should not expect a finding that oversized institutions be broken up. That being said, it would not be too much to ask for the means whereby segments or divisions within a financial institution can be separately regulated and hived off if necessary. This means national resolution authorities and targeted bankruptcy laws will be required.

The simple truth is that while much time and money will be spent regulating large financial institutions, it should be self-evident that the real watchdog should be an institution's creditors, shareholders, and directors. If they are not prepared to protect their investment then they should bear the cost. Bankers, their shareholders, and creditors should be under no illusion. They must understand that a system whereby financial institutions take excessive risks and earn excessive profits while the world pays the bill for their failure is no longer on.

To its credit, the Basel committee did come down on the single most important banking issue that it had to deal with—the core equity, liquidity, and leverage standards for G20 banks themselves. What financial institutions need first and foremost is a solid foundation—an equity base that will allow for human lapse, one that can withstand the ravages of greed or the unexpected. However, while the committee has spoken, it was only after much delay and more than a little backtracking.

The debate over bank capital has focused primarily on the needed enhancement in the quality of tier-one capital and on a gradation of buffers bailing in creditors and a series of intermediaries. Some allege that this will result in restricted lending and an aborted economic recovery.

The Basel committee and a number of central banks, including Canada's, have effectively rebutted that allegation by providing analysis confirming that the negative consequences of enhancing bank capital would be minimal in the short term and the positive effects would be very beneficial in the medium and longer terms. Moreover, the Bank of Canada's analysis showed that the gains from improved bank capital will endure over time. In short, it is the gift that keeps on giving.

Thus the time has come to bring the debate to conclusion and to accelerate the process of the international harmonization of principles and rules. The Bank of Canada forecasts "that as a result of the crisis, cumulative foregone economic output from 2009 to 2012 will be 16% of GDP in Europe. Over the longer term it estimates the shortfall could grow to 40%." The report concludes with the following: "Financial crises are normally followed by financial repression; economic downturns, by increased protectionism. Without credible, coordinated financial reforms, we risk losing the open trading and financial system that has underpinned the economic miracle of recent times."[1]

The fact is, however, you do not have to read the gripping scribblings of central bankers to know that safer banks mean a stronger economy—it is common sense. In the last twenty years two bubbles burst in the United States: the dotcom bubble, which, while critical, was more easily absorbed and the bank crisis, which caused an economic downturn to mutate into a perfect storm. Why the difference? Why was the second bubble so much more serious? It was because a bank crisis is a crisis of confidence and trust, and nothing is more damaging to the economic system.

1. Mark Carney, "Bundesbank Lecture 2010: The Economic Consequences of the Reforms" (www.bankofcanada.ca/en/speeches/2010/sp140910.html).

It is in this context that I would point out that in establishing the new rules for bank capitalization, the Basel committee also set out a lengthy transition period for achievement. This is understandable at this crucial period in the economic recovery. Although truth be told, one might wonder whether a decade-long transition is not excessive. If sound bank capital is an absolute requirement for safety, should the world have to wait a decade before breathing a sigh of relief given what it has just been put through?

The lengthy transition period also raises another issue, one that is of even greater concern. When the Basel committee began its work, there was a concerted attempt to dilute its recommendations. It was successful, but not completely. It will be the G20's responsibility to ensure that the transition period is used as it is supposed to be used and not as a nine-year opportunity to reopen the battle for a further dilution of the rules, a battle perhaps more easily won when memories of the current crisis begin to fade.

Now so far, I have raised the issues of "too big to fail" and inadequate bank capital. These are only two of many issues ranging from the treatment of derivatives to the misallocation of credit that characterized the subprime fiasco that threatened the global system. Thus the last measure I would raise is the need for an international body whose primary goal is to protect against the rise of systemic risk across borders.

The basis of bank regulation must be sound national rules and standards. A single global regulator is unworkable. However, there are huge gaps in the global system, and the world needs a coordinator to monitor risk, capture the evolution of financial innovation and ensure the means of enforcement of the principles agreed to. Fortunately, the organization to do all of this has been created, at least in embryonic form; it is called the Financial Stability Board (FSB). However, its authority has not been determined, it is clearly understaffed, not enough countries are members, and it is far from certain that the members of the G20 will share sovereignty to the extent necessary to give the FSB tangible powers of enforcement.

In terms of authority and staffing, this is not the time for the G20 to underwhelm. What is required first is a monitor with the authority to prevent the contagion or systemic failure that results from regulatory capture at the national level. Never again must the world stand by, passive observers of the inability or unwillingness of national regulators to follow the trail of the private sector as it invents new ways of financial innovation beyond the reach of needed regulation.

What does this mean? To cut to the chase, it means that in the current crisis, in too many instances, national regulators did not understand the nature of the toxic assets that they were allowing to exist. For that reason the staff of the FSB has to be sufficient in number and of the highest quality and experience, and it also must be compensated commensurately, all so that it can at a minimum ring the world's warning bells.

Next, in terms of membership, the G20 leaders must not repeat the mistake of the G7 finance ministers a decade ago when they limited the membership of the FSB's predecessor, the Financial Stability Forum, to the G7 countries and a couple of others. Unfortunately, that appears to be exactly what they are in the process of doing. At the present time the Financial Stability Board's membership is limited to G20 members and four others. This is myopic. If the FSB is indeed to become the "fourth pillar" as it must, its membership has to be the same as that of the IMF and it should report to an executive board of its own.

Last, the FSB must have the capacity to enforce its rules. At the present time the means of enforcement being considered are peer review and public shaming. The first works—up to a point. The second will not. It is virtually impossible to shame a great power.

Whether enforcement occurs through a form of WTO-type sanctions or host country regulations that apply to banks from recalcitrant countries in such a way that the private sector itself insists that international standards be observed is open to debate. What must not be open to debate is that the application of the rules be mandatory. Surely we have learned something from the Financial Sector Assessment Program's sad experience with voluntary adherence over the last decade.

Now at some point someone is going to scream out that the establishment and enforcement of minimum rules across borders represents an unacceptable infringement on national sovereignty. Let me therefore close with the following. Coming to grips with what it takes to make globalization work requires a global consensus that cannot be squared any longer with the traditional exercise of sovereignty. The current definition was established in 1648, and it was all about rights and the parochialism of rigid borders. Surely if we have learned one thing from the financial crisis, it is that the definition of sovereignty must now include sovereign duties and the responsibility of nations to each other.

An effective FSB is not an infringement on national sovereignty. In fact, it is integral to the protection of sovereignty in the twenty-first century. For instance: when the U.S. and European financial players created toxic assets and sold them around the world to everyone's detriment, was that not an infringement on the rest of the world's sovereignty? Was the global recession itself not partially the result of the infringement on the sovereignty of every country that was affected by the failure of the European and American banking systems to exercise minimum standards of prudence? What has happened in Europe with its sovereign debt crisis is yet another instance of how the unthinkable can become real. In the last few months, financial markets have stripped away sovereignty's last remaining economic veneer from some of the oldest countries in the world.

More and more the issue is whether national governments are going to recognize their duty to their own citizens to adhere to international norms so that the fear of contagion ceases to be the sword of Damocles hanging over an increasingly integrated global system or whether the markets will make the decision for them.

In the same vein, the need to recognize sovereign duties becomes even more dramatic when we look at how quickly the global landscape continues to change. What the governments of the West must come to grips with is the reality that if they hide behind counterproductive arguments over sovereignty now, in the years to come, when the Chinese and Indian economies have penetrated global economies even further and they stumble, there will be no stimulus package big enough to rescue any of us.

The question has been asked, Why would we build an international model that has all of the market freedoms of our national economies but none of its protections? That is why we need global financial reform, and that is why the G20 must act.

7

G20 Financial Regulatory Reform: Current Status and Future Challenges

YUNG CHUL PARK AND SUNGMIN KIM

The recent unprecedented global financial crisis played a key role in making the G20 the premier forum for discussion of global economic issues. However, the objective of the financial regulatory reform pursued by the G20 is not to merely respond to the crisis but to reestablish the overall financial system to prevent the recurrence of such crises in the future.

The financial regulatory reform of the G20 began by reflecting on the deregulation movement that had been going on until the outbreak of the financial crisis. Basically, pre-crisis financial policies had generally pursued deregulation, based on the following two presumptions: the first was that competition would enhance the efficiency of financial systems by accelerating innovation in financial instruments and management; the second was that new financial instruments being developed would ensure a safer financial system through the diversification of risk.

Contrary to those presumptions, however, the financial system, relying for its stability mainly on the self-discipline imposed by the market, demonstrated great structural vulnerabilities during the global financial crisis. In the pre-crisis period, many countries had lowered their former regulatory barriers between commercial and investment banking activities so as to facilitate competition. Faced with fierce competition, however, financial institutions concentrated on increasing their size and took excessive risks in pursuit of higher yield, practices that expanded the systemic impacts of their failures. Meanwhile, the financial innovation that was expected to diversify risk actually made financial transactions more complicated and opaque, so that it became harder to detect the buildup of risks. The heavy reliance on leverage in asset management also exacerbated procyclicality, damaging the overall stability of the financial system. Furthermore, securitization and the development of derivatives markets facilitated growth of the shadow banking system, which lowered the effectiveness of financial supervision centered on bank regulations.

The structural vulnerabilities that surfaced during the recent crisis were not confined to the management of individual financial institutions but spread to include the financial system as a whole. In this regard, the G20 reform on financial regulatory reform must therefore be very comprehensive.

Against that backdrop, this chapter looks into the current status of G20 financial reform regarding capital and liquidity standards, the introduction of regulations on systemically important financial institutions, infrastructure improvements in the financial system, the macroprudential policy framework, and other issues. The chapter then focuses on some of the future challenges of the G20.

Current Status of Financial Reform

The recent global financial crisis triggered criticisms that the Basel II framework for bank regulation had failed to fulfill its role in crisis prevention. Financial institutions assessed as having sound capital adequacy experienced rapid deterioration in financial soundness and failure after the subprime crisis broke out, leaving much doubt as to the reliability of the Basel II capital standards.

Capital and Liquidity Standards

To improve the quality of capital and ensure that each item satisfies the definition of capital, the Basel Committee on Banking Supervision (BCBS) has developed measures to simplify and improve the transparency of capital structures while adjusting the levels of asset risk to reflect reality.

STRENGTHENING CAPITAL REQUIREMENTS

First, the quality of capital will be improved by the BCBS's new standard. Regulatory capital will consist of common equity and retained earnings for higher loss absorbency in times of shock, and non-common equity elements that used to be classified under tier 1 or tier 2 will have to satisfy separate entry criteria. Second, capital regulations will be strengthened so that capital adequacy ratios will be applied not only to total assets but also to individual items.[1] Third,

---

1. The ratios of total capital (tier 1 + tier 2), tier 1 capital, and the common equity components of tier 1 capital to risk-weighted assets should exceed X percent, Y percent, and Z percent, respectively.

tier 1 capital will consist mainly of common equity, including retained earnings, and a rigorous set of deductions and exclusions[2] from tier 1 capital will be introduced. Fourth, capital requirements will be raised for stocks, bonds, and other trading book items as well as for asset-backed securities, and differentiated risk assessments are now conducted on not only different products but also different counterparty risks.

To facilitate the expansion of capital in times of crisis, the BCBS is reviewing the capital that can be easily converted into common equity when financial conditions become difficult. At the same time, to improve transparency a leverage ratio will be introduced as a backstop to the risk-based capital requirement.[3] The new leverage ratio includes not only exposures from on–balance sheet but also off–balance sheet positions in order to correct the risk measurement errors of the Basel II framework and to reflect off–balance sheet transactions.

Introducing Global Liquidity Standards

Recognizing the fact that unstable funding structures lead to high levels of liquidity risk, the BCBS has proposed both short-term liquidity standards to enable financial institutions to withstand sudden capital flows during stressed funding conditions and mid- to long-term liquidity standards. The liquidity coverage ratio (LCR[4]) confirms the short-term resiliency of an institution's risk profile by ensuring that it has sufficient high-quality liquid resources to survive an acute stress scenario lasting for one month. The objective of the net stable funding ratio (NSFR)[5] is to promote resiliency over a longer time horizon by creating additional incentives for banks to fund their activities with more stable sources of funding on an ongoing structural basis.

Relieving Procyclicality

To enhance the countercyclicality of regulatory capital while encouraging banks to build up capital buffers in good times in preparation for future difficulties (table 7-1), the BCBS has established the following measures:

—*Relieving the procyclicality of minimum capital requirements.* The default rate using the "through the cycle" (TTC) rating system will be used instead of that of the "point in time" (PIT) rating system, to flatten the capital formula.

2. Twelve items, including deferred tax assets, goodwill, and other intangibles, were deducted from regulatory capital.

3. The leverage ratio is defined as the ratio against total capital exposure. Capital consists mainly of tier 1 capital, and total exposure implies the amount indicated on the balance sheet without any application of risk weights.

4. Highly liquid assets/net cash outflows over thirty-day time period ≥ 100 percent.

5. Available stable funding/required stable funding ≥ 100 percent.

Table 7-1. *Capital Requirements and Buffers*

Percent

Capital requirement and buffer	Common equity[a]	Tier 1 capital	Total capital
Minimum (A)	4.5	6.0	8.0
Conservation buffer (B)	2.5		
A + B	7.0	8.5	10.5
Countercylical buffer	0.0–2.5		

Source: Basel Committee on Banking Supervision.
a. Common equity after deductions.

—*Designating a capital conservation buffer.* A specific percentage of earnings will be designated as a capital conservation buffer that is fixed regardless of the economic cycle, to be used to absorb losses during periods of financial stress.

—*Applying a countercyclical capital buffer.* A countercyclical capital buffer is a variable buffer, applied in accordance with macroeconomic conditions, that has the effect of restraining excessive credit expansions during economic booms and preventing sudden credit contractions during economic busts.

IMPLEMENTATION SCHEDULE

The BCBS released the trading book package reforms in July 2009 and the improved capital and liquidity proposals in December 2009. Subsequently, a quantitative impact study (QIS) was conducted to specify the level of regulation and the macroeconomic impacts of the new prudential regulations as well as to analyze the long-term costs/benefits. The results were reported to the BCBS meeting.

The QIS results showed that the new capital and liquidity standards were likely to have great impacts on France, Germany, and Japan. In the short term, the stronger regulations were expected to lower GDP due to increased loan spreads and a reduction in the supply of loans. In the long term, however, the benefits outweighed the costs, as the expected loss of yield decreased with the lower frequency of bank crises. The benefits from this were higher than the loss of yield from higher loan interest rates.

Taking into consideration the need to differentiate regulatory deductions, leverage ratios, and liquidity standards among country-specific business models, the BCBS revised its December draft for regulatory reform and released a new package in July 2010. The final version of capital reforms was presented to the G20 Seoul summit in November 2010 after the draft version was delivered to the Financial Stability Board (FSB) and the meeting of G20 finance ministers and central bank governors in October 2010. At the Group of Governors and

Heads of Supervision (GHOS) meeting held on September 12, 2010, the BCBS confirmed the minimum capital requirements for each item (total, tier 1, and common equity) and the specific phasing-in arrangements. The regulatory items will be confirmed by the end of 2010 or the first half of 2011.

The phasing-in arrangements confirmed by the BCBS on September 12 are as follows: The minimum common equity and tier 1 requirements will be phased in between January 1, 2013, and January 1, 2015, while the total capital requirement will be fully applied from January 1, 2013. Twenty percent will be deducted from common equity each year from January 1, 2014, to January 1, 2018. The capital conservation buffer, composed of common equity, will be phased in between January 1, 2016, and January 1, 2019. It will be 0.625 percent of risk-weighted assets (RWAs) the first year, and this ratio will be increased each subsequent year by an additional 0.625 percentage point. Countries that experience excessive credit growth may consider accelerating their buildup of the capital conservation and countercyclical buffers.

In the case of the leverage ratio, after the supervisory monitoring period and parallel run period, final reviews and adjustments will be conducted with a view to migrating to a pillar 1 treatment on January 1, 2018.

Systemically Important Financial Institutions

Many systemically important financial institutions (SIFIs) avoided failure during the recent crisis thanks to government interventions that include capital expansion, deposit guarantees, and so forth. During the rescue process, however, losses were limited to their shareholders while most of their creditors were protected. The bailouts were based on policy judgments that SIFI failures would pose a risk of collapse of the entire financial system. However, they also spread the notion that governments have no choice but to rescue SIFIs when they fall into default, raising concerns about moral hazard.

The international discussions on regulating SIFIs, led by the FSB, are being conducted on the following three fronts: Reducing probability and impact of failure, improving resolution capacity, and strengthening financial infrastructure (table 7-2).

REDUCING THE PROBABILITY AND IMPACT OF FAILURE

The Macroprudential Supervision Group (MPG) under the BCBS is currently discussing capital surcharges, liquidity surcharges, large exposure restrictions, and measures to strengthen supervision. However, some argue that no additional regulations on systemically important banks (SIBs) are necessary, because the new Basel II accord will be more than enough to effectively resolve issues related to SIBs.

Table 7-2. *Regulatory Framework for SIFIs*

Objective	Policy measure	Institution
Reducing probability and impact of failure	Stronger prudential requirements Stronger supervision Limiting size and scope of institution	FSB SCSRC,[a] BCBS
Improving resolution capacity	Stronger contingency plans for individual institutions Improving cross-border resolution capacity	FSB CBCM[b]
Strengthening financial infrastructure	Facilitating use of central counterparties	CPSS,[c] IOSCO[d]

Source: Financial Stability Board.
a. Standing Committee for Supervisory and Regulatory Cooperation.
b. Cross-Border Crisis Management Group.
c. Committee on Payment and Settlement Systems.
d. International Organization for Securities Commissions.

The role of supervisory colleges, in which both the home and the host supervisors participate, is critical for the effective supervision of cross-border SIFIs. As of September 2009, supervisory colleges that are consultative working groups comprising home and host supervisors and that work together to ensure effective supervisory cooperation and coordination had been established for at least forty-three cross-border financial institutions. At the same time, to help both the home and the host supervisors ensure that the supervisory colleges work as effectively as possible, the BCBS released a consultative document on good practices for supervisory colleges in March 2010 and subsequently decided to also develop a more detailed implementation guidance.

The Standing Committee on Supervisory and Regulatory Cooperation (SCSRC) under the FSB is conducting an analysis of the adequacy of the business models and structures of financial institutions. In the meantime, on July 22, 2010, U.S. president Barack Obama signed the financial regulation reform act, with its main component, the Volcker rule, restricting the size and business scope of large financial institutions.

IMPROVING RESOLUTION CAPACITY

Developing effective tools and a framework for resolution of large complex cross-border financial institutions became an urgent issue following the bankruptcy of Lehman Brothers. Many complex economic and legal issues are involved in the bankruptcy of large complex cross-border financial institutions as they have the characteristics of both a cross-border company and a financial institution. Moreover, if a jurisdiction establishes a legal framework that strengthens the protection of its people's rights in resolving cross-border financial institutions, that may bring about much international conflict and cause severe financial market disruptions. In this context, the FSB and the BCBS are working to establish stronger contingency plans for individual financial institutions and measures to improve the cross-border resolution framework, both by the end of 2010.

The FSB is establishing a crisis management group for each major cross-border financial institution. The crisis management groups are formed of supervisors, central banks, and resolution authorities from the key home and host jurisdictions of the major cross-border financial institutions. They are tasked with developing recovery and resolution plans for each firm and assessing its resolvability. In parallel, the FSB is establishing contingency plans for individual institutions, enhancing the effects of the resolution frameworks in different jurisdictions, and improving the frameworks for resolution of cross-border financial institutions through its Cross-Border Crisis Management (CBCM) Working Group.

The Cross-Border Resolution Group (CBRG) under the BCBS has established ten recommendations for cross-border bank resolution in March 2010. The CBRG recommends establishing core coordination standards and signing memorandums of understanding (MOUs) with jurisdictions needing amendments of domestic law in order to develop a phase-by-phase arrangement for strengthening of cooperation.

In the meantime, the IMF has also released a report on measures to enhance coordination among supervisors for cross-border bank resolution in June 2010. The IMF proposes the development of a minimum level of common standards to ensure harmonization of national resolution rules; robust supervision by the home supervisors leading the resolution process; and principles for developing cross-border bank resolution frameworks that encourage host country authorities to accept the leadership of the home country authorities.

IMPROVING OVER-THE-COUNTER MARKETS

The market impacts of SIFI failures will be reduced by the clearing of over-the-counter (OTC) derivatives through central counterparties (CCPs). At the G20 Pittsburgh summit in September 2009, the G20 leaders agreed that all standardized OTC derivatives should be traded through exchanges or electronic trading platforms, with clearings carried out through CCPs by the end of 2012.

At the G20 Pittsburgh summit, the G20 leaders asked the FSB to integrate and adjust the various measures proposed for regulating SIFIs and to develop a final set of regulations. In line with this mandate, the FSB reported to G20 leaders at the November Seoul summit on measures for resolving the negative externalities caused by SIFIs. The FSB steering committee is in charge of comprehensive oversight and coordination of various discussions on the work related to SIFIs.

At its June 14, 2010, plenary meeting, the FSB proposed "constrained discretion" on the part of national supervisors in imposing capital surcharges on SIFIs. The principle of "constrained discretion" gives national supervisors a certain amount of discretion in imposing regulations on SIFIs while securing consistency among national policies. The FSB proposed the principle of constrained discretion on the basis of its judgment that while there is a consensus on the need for consistent standards, there is no "one-size-fits-all" solution.

STRENGTHENING FINANCIAL INFRASTRUCTURE

OTC Derivatives Markets. Credit default swap (CDS) transactions account for only 10 percent of total financial derivatives transactions around the world, but the bankruptcy of Lehman Brothers and the bailout of American Insurance Group (AIG) highlighted the risks of these types of transactions. When Lehman Brothers filed for bankruptcy, it had a US$150 billion CDS protection selling position. AIG also had a US$400 billion protection selling position, which was saved through a government bailout. Due to the recent fiscal turmoil in Greece, moreover, active discussions continue on whether to ban speculative CDS transactions and on how to secure transparency in the derivatives markets within the EU.

At the G20 Pittsburgh summit, the following two proposals were made to minimize the systemic risk when a counterparty in an OTC derivatives transaction files for bankruptcy. First, standardized OTC derivatives should use the central counterparties for clearing by the end of 2012. The process of direct clearing and settlement between two parties will be transferred to central counterparties (margins are required for stability of the clearing process) for indirect clearing and settlement (figure 7-1). Second, nonstandardized OTC derivatives should centralize trade information, including transaction volume, amount of exposure for each institution, and so forth by mandated reporting to trade repositories.

While international organizations are continuing their efforts to amend the relevant rules and regulations, the industry is also participating in the reform process, with commitments to expand the use of CCPs. Thirteen countries, including the United States, Europe, and Singapore, have been running CCPs and are now making full-fledged efforts to improve their infrastructures for better OTC derivatives trading.

Accounting Standards. The fair value accounting model for financial assets and the current system of loan-loss provisioning based on incurred losses increase procyclicality. At the same time, the complicated accounting standards of different countries reduce financial market transparency and hinder the efforts to converge toward a single set of global accounting standards.

Figure 7-1. *Central Counterparties for Derivatives*

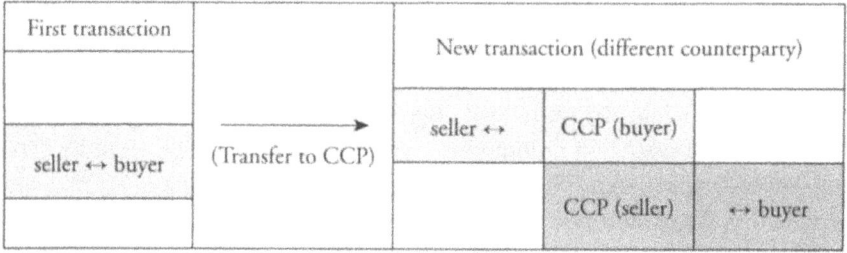

First transaction		New transaction (different counterparty)		
		seller ↔	CCP (buyer)	
seller ↔ buyer	(Transfer to CCP) →			
			CCP (seller)	↔ buyer

The efforts to strengthen accounting standards can be summarized as comprising two aspects: improving accounting standards and converging to a single set of high-quality global accounting standards. In this context, the International Accounting Standards Board (IASB) plans to release a revision of the International Financial Reporting Standards (IFRS) by the end of 2010 and to begin their obligatory application from 2013 onward. Many countries are also replacing their national accounting standards with the IFRS or are working hard to narrow the differences between the two standards.

At the G20 Pittsburgh summit, leaders requested that the International Accounting Standards Board and the Financial Accounting Standards Board develop a single set of global accounting standards by June 2011. At the G20 Toronto summit, however, the IASB and the FASB requested a six-month delay in that deadline for converging the accounting standards by the end of 2011.

Hedge Funds. Failures of hedge funds may not only damage their investors but also cause systemic shock to the financial market. However, hedge funds, like individual investors, are not subject to regulations, and that is a major blind spot of financial regulation. Basically small to medium-sized hedge funds cannot cause systemic risks on their own, but it is possible that they can bring about systemic risk through herding behavior. In fact, some people point to the herding behavior of hedge funds as one of the main culprits behind the financial imbalances during the recent financial crisis. G20 member countries are closing the gaps in opinion on making registration and information disclosure by hedge funds mandatory. In terms of more direct regulations, however, including capital and leverage requirements, major countries still hold greatly differing positions (the United Kingdom and the United States versus Germany and France).

As a first step, the G20 leaders agreed at the London summit on basic principles for requiring registration of hedge funds and their managers and for disclosure by them of information to be used for systemic risk assessments. At the G20 meeting of finance ministers and central bank governors in London in September 2009, there was agreement on continuing the efforts to close the gaps in hedge fund regulation although no decision was reached on any specific action plans. At the G20 Toronto summit, leaders agreed to sustain efforts to strengthen regulation and oversight of hedge funds in order to enhance the transparency of their operations. The FSB was mandated to review the status of implementation of the previous G20 agreements in each member country and to report the results to the meeting of the G20 finance ministers and central bank governors in Washington in October 2010.

In the meantime, in an effort of international financial organizations, the International Organization of Securities Commissions (IOSCO) published its "Hedge Funds Oversight: Final Report" in June 2009, proposing principles to regulate the registration and disclosure of hedge funds, prime brokers, and banks. The IOSCO is now reviewing the implementation of its principles in each country. In February 2010, the IOSCO published an agreed template for the global collection of hedge fund information, enabling the collection and exchange of consistent and comparable panel data by regulators and other competent authorities and facilitating international supervisory cooperation in identifying any possible systemic risks posed by this sector. In addition, in May 2010, the IOSCO released a set of principles for cross-border regulation and supervisory cooperation to enable national authorities to conduct effective supervision of hedge funds. In line with that, the BCBS is reviewing ways of addressing counterparty risks of companies dealing with hedge funds to strengthen their risk management.

Compensation. The current compensation practices in financial institutions reflect for the most part short-term performance, and that has been criticized as a key factor behind the global financial crisis because it encouraged excessive risk taking. In March 2010, the FSB released the findings and conclusions of the peer review of implementation of the principles and standards[6] endorsed by the G20 leaders at their summits in London in April 2009 and Pittsburgh in September 2009. In its "Thematic Review on Compensation: Peer Review Report," the FSB noted that the principles and standards are well reflected in the regulatory and supervisory frameworks of member jurisdictions.[7] It also added some recommendations, however, and urged member countries to work toward complete adherence.[8] It is critical to sustain the efforts of supervisory institutions and financial institutions in developing efficient linkages between risk and achievement.

Credit Rating Agencies. Inadequate risk assessments by credit rating agencies and investors' overreliance on their ratings were criticized as being among the

6. Financial Stability Board, *Principles for Sound Compensation Practices and Implementation Standards* (2009).

7. Sixteen of twenty-four countries have reflected the FSB principles and standards in their regulatory and/or supervisory approaches, and four countries are planning to reflect them shortly.

8. Financial Stability Board, *Thematic Review on Compensation: List of Recommendations* (2010).

reasons behind the recent financial crisis. National and regional initiatives are ongoing to strengthen oversight of credit rating agencies (CRAs), based on the IOSCO CRA Code of Conduct Fundamentals, and the IOSCO plans to report on whether there are differences in implementation among countries. Countries are planning to introduce supervision and/or regulations on CRAs, with a focus on improving the disclosure of ratings methods or processes, preventing conflicts of interest, and differentiating among credit ratings for structured products.

Meanwhile, the BCBS and the FSB are preparing measures to reduce the use of ratings in the process of financial institution regulation. The BCBS is working to address a number of inappropriate incentives arising from the use of external ratings in the regulatory capital framework.[9] The FSB will examine the risks to financial stability related to the official use of ratings as well as possible options and next steps for addressing those risks.

Macroprudential Policy Framework

Recently, discussions on the macroprudential policy framework have come to the fore as it was recognized after the recent financial crisis that focusing merely on the soundness of individual financial institutions, through microprudential policy, is insufficient for responding effectively to systemic risk. The discussions on macroprudential policy began because of the fact that systemic risk was not managed appropriately before the eruption of the financial crisis, despite the severe financial imbalances indicated by excessive leverage buildups and signs of asset price bubbles.

The issues discussed at the G20 regarding a macroprudential policy framework can be classified into three categories: developing systemic risk indicators and policy instruments based on time series data; establishing the criteria for judgment of the systemic importance of financial institutions, markets, and products; and conducting early warning exercises (EWEs).

To monitor and assess systemic risk based on time series data, indicators for systemic liquidity risk, margins and haircuts, leverage, and so forth and policy instruments are being developed. In the cross-sectional aspect, criteria including size, substitutability, and interconnectedness are being established to judge the systemic importance of institutions, markets, and products. As for the EWE, it reviews the accumulation of global imbalances, financial system vulnerabilities, and so forth in order to provide warnings when necessary. The EWE therefore

---

9. Insufficient risk assessments within banks themselves; over-production of "good ratings" by CRAs; and Cliff effects in capital requirements. For example, if the risk weight is 100 percent for a BB- rating and 350 percent for a B+ rating, the exposure of securitization will centralize on BB-. In other words, if the credit rating falls one step, the risk weight increases exponentially by 250 percentage points.

focuses its analysis on tail events and cross-border spillovers that can develop into systemic threats.

In accordance with the G20 leaders' agreement at the London summit, the BCBS, the Committee on the Global Financial System (CGFS), and the Bank for International Settlement (BIS) are developing liquidity and leverage indicators and instruments such as countercyclical capital buffers and developing criteria for determining the systemic importance of financial institutions, markets, and products. Furthermore, the FSB, the BIS, and the IMF submitted their report entitled "Guidance to Assess the Systemic Importance of Financial Institutions, Markets and Instruments: Initial Considerations" to the meeting of the G20 finance ministers and central bank governors at St. Andrews, following the mandate agreed on by the leaders at the G20 London summit. Regarding the EWE, the FSB and the IMF, on the basis of their bilateral agreement and at the request of G20 leaders at the London summit, conducted two EWEs, in April and October 2009, and reported the results to the International Monetary and Financial Committee (IMFC) meeting. The FSB and the IMF will conduct two EWEs each year on a regular basis and make confidential reports on the results to the IMF board of directors, FSB member countries, and the IMFC as necessary.

Other Issues

BURDEN SHARING

Many countries used government funds to bail out insolvent financial institutions during the recent global financial crisis, and they have subsequently had to cope with serious fiscal burdens. At the G20 Pittsburgh summit, the G20 therefore raised the necessity of financial institutions sharing the burdens of those bailouts and of any future government interventions and agreed to develop burden-sharing measures. In addition, at the meeting of the G20 finance ministers and central bank governors in April 2010, the IMF proposed a financial stability contribution (FSC) and a financial activity tax (FAT) as burden-sharing measures. The FSC would be a levy to cover the fiscal cost of any future government support to the financial sector. It would be paid by all financial institutions, but the base of the levy would be limited to non-core deposits, which are riskier than others and not subject to deposit insurance.[10] The FAT would be levied on the tax base of the sum of profits and remuneration in order to discourage excessive risk taking on the part of financial institutions and to enhance fair taxation. At the G20 Toronto summit in June 2010, leaders reaffirmed the significance of preparing burden-sharing measures and agreed that countries should take approaches that fit their own circumstances but that comply with

10. Assets (including some off–balance sheet items); capital; insured liabilities.

the following principles: protecting taxpayers, reducing risks from the financial system, protecting the flow of credit in both good and bad times, taking into account individual countries' circumstances and options, and helping promote a level playing field.

As the IMF submitted its final report[11] on burden-sharing measures and leaders reached agreement on its basic principles at the Toronto summit, countries were expected to develop measures that fit their own conditions in the latter half of 2010.

Non-Cooperative Jurisdictions

Hedge fund transactions through tax havens and off-shore financial centers were also seen as a problem leading to the financial crisis. Insufficient prudential regulations and information led to limited detection and management of the risks imposed by hedge funds that set up paper companies in off-shore financial centers.

To protect the global financial system and prevent tax leakages, the G20 initiated discussions on non-cooperative jurisdictions (NCJs) in the areas of exchange of information on taxation and anti–money laundering/combating the financing of terrorism (AML/CFT). At the G20 London summit, leaders requested that the relevant institutions conduct peer review processes and assessments to ensure full compliance with global standards on taxation, anti–money laundering, and combating the financing of terrorism. The OECD Global Forum will be conducting a three-year survey on jurisdictions to see whether they have implemented the internationally agreed tax standards and will report its findings to the G20 meetings. The G20 initiated peer reviews of tax havens from March 2010 and will deliver its first report on this issue by the end of 2010. The Financial Action Task Force (FATF), through its public statement on February 18, 2010, released a list of countries that pose serious risks to the global community due to their defective systems for AML/CFT.

The FSB and Its Role in Strengthening Standards Adherence

In the process of pursuing financial regulatory reform to prevent recurring crises and to develop effective crisis responses, the G20 agreed on the need for establishment of an international cooperation group. As a result, the Financial Stability Forum (FSF) was expanded and re-established as the Financial Stability Board with a broadened mandate to assess the vulnerability of the financial system, to establish global standards, and to review the status of compliance by member countries.

---

11. International Monetary Fund, *A Fair and Substantial Contribution by the Financial Sector: Final Report for the G-20* (2010).

The FSB published its Framework for Strengthening Adherence to International Standards in January 2010 to ensure the consistent implementation of international financial standards and has been evaluating the level of adherence of member jurisdictions to those standards. The FSB framework comprises three parts: leading by example; FSB peer reviews; and promoting global adherence to standards. Since its establishment at the G20 London summit, the FSB has participated in the G20 meetings in order to give progress reports on the processes of standard implementation in member jurisdictions and the standard setting bodies (SSBs).

Although the FSB was established at the G20 London summit, there is no systematic framework under which the FSB files regular reports to the G20 other than during G20 meetings. As part of its efforts to strengthen its function, the FSB proposed the establishment of regional groups, to be composed of non-FSB members as well, at the "Korea-FSB Financial Reform Conference: An Emerging Market Perspective," held September 9, 2010, in Seoul. One local FSB member and one non-FSB member will be selected as co-chairs of each regional group.

This measure is seen as part of the FSB secretariat's efforts to develop new work areas for the FSB out of concern that its role will weaken after the completion of financial regulatory reform discussions. One new work area for the FSB is supporting the building of capacity in countries with less-developed financial markets. The establishment of the regional groups is one part of its plan for carrying out that work.

Future Challenges

G20 financial regulatory reform is being pursued in four directions: strengthening the resilience of individual financial institutions; reducing systemic risks; reducing incentives for excessive risk taking; and eliminating regulatory blind spots. The G20 has put many efforts into financial regulatory reform in collaboration with the FSB, the BCBS, and the IMF, and its efforts led to achievements at the November 2010 Seoul summit, which is significant in the following respects.

Significance of the November Seoul Summit

First, the Seoul summit was the first at which a global response to the crisis was finalized. The G20 leaders agreed on the specific levels and phase-in periods for the new capital and liquidity standards. Up until now, financial crises have mostly been tackled locally, by reforms of the financial and economic systems of the individual countries affected. The recent crisis, however, after originating in the United States, spread out to include not only European but also Asian countries, in line with the interconnectedness of economies around the globe and the substantial amount of financial transactions now made worldwide. Under those circumstances, countries' policy measures need to be coordinated in order to effectively overcome the crisis and prevent the practice of regulatory arbitrage.

Second, the financial regulatory reform pursued by the G20 at the working level was endorsed by the G20 leaders at the Seoul summit, which increases the likelihood of implementation in each country. As the recent crisis arose from structural problems in the financial system as a whole, development of a comprehensive response is inevitable. This calls for the endorsement of member nations' leaders to ensure its implementation. The importance of leaders' endorsement can be highlighted by the fact that the Basel II framework, a nonbinding agreement, has not yet been implemented by all countries, even though it was agreed ten years ago.

Future Challenges of the G20

In order for the G20 to play a leading role in making the global financial system safer and in creating a more resilient global financial order, three critical conditions need to be satisfied. First, for the G20 to maintain its status as a premier forum, the chair countries must continue to show strong leadership. The United Kingdom, the 2009 G20 chair, showed great leadership in coordinating member countries' measures to reach adequate solutions in response to the recent global crisis. The G20 financial regulatory reform is still far from complete. There are also concerns that some countries may not adhere to the agreements, using lagging domestic economic conditions as an excuse. The G20 chair countries must therefore continue to show strong leadership. They need to play a leading role in developing a common vision for financial reforms in the future by consulting experts in various countries and effectively mobilizing the resources of international organizations, including the FSB, the IMF, and the BIS.

Second, it is important to develop a strong implementation plan and a loop for provision of feedback. New capital and liquidity standards were agreed on at the Seoul summit, and that is indeed a great achievement. But they are undoubtedly still only the beginning of the financial regulatory reforms that will come in the future. They are also a minimum set of standards, and their application is at the discretion of each country. Each country will have to strengthen its financial regulations in a way that best serves its own financial system. And the G20 should work to make sure that a level playing field is maintained and take whatever complementary measures are necessary to do so. In this regard, it is essential that we have an effective feedback process. For example, if there is a regulatory gap in terms of compensation practices between G20 member countries, despite their adherence to the same set of implementation principles, financial talents may transfer from areas with stronger regulation to those with weaker regulation.

The G20 must therefore ensure that a level playing field is established to prevent such results. Moreover, the FSB must conduct regular reviews on the implementation processes in G20 member countries and report the results to the G20.

Third, the G20 must sustain its efforts to prevent financial crises in the future. The financial regulatory reform by the G20 is based on countries' experiences in the recent crisis. Every crisis is different, however, and future financial crises may arise from areas that were perhaps overlooked in the current response. Korea has therefore proposed the establishment of a macroprudential policy framework and financial regulatory reform, from an emerging market perspective, as new G20 agenda items.

As part of the G20's efforts to prevent recurrence of a financial crisis, President Sarkozy of France recently announced that France, as the 2011 G20 chair, will focus on tightening the regulation of commodity derivatives and reforming the international monetary system, in consideration of how vulnerable emerging economies can be to large amounts of international capital flows. Through the recent financial crisis, Korea learned that a greater volume of international reserves and flexible exchange rates are not sufficient for alleviating foreign exchange market tension caused by a global crisis. Consequently, the Korean experience clearly presents a strong case for the establishment of robust financial safety nets at the global level. Given the remarkable expansion in the scale of international capital flows and the large quasi-fiscal costs accompanying the maintenance of huge volumes of foreign exchange reserves, self-insurance by means of international reserve accumulation is obviously not a sustainable solution.

More efforts should therefore be focused on improving the existing financial safety nets and on further diversifying instruments to tackle countries' temporary liquidity problems. It should be mentioned that the issue of moral hazard needs to be appropriately addressed in that process. It should also be emphasized that there is no one-size-fits-all solution, since each country's preference for each instrument will depend on its own circumstances. Consequently the feasibility of various other instruments needs to be explored. Such tools could include the expanded use of swap arrangements between central banks and the greater integration of regional arrangements, such as the Chiang Mai Initiative with the work of the IMF.

8

The G20 and the Challenge of International Financial Reregulation

JACQUES MISTRAL

Toronto, the fourth G20 summit, delivered few tangible results in the field of financial regulation despite the fact that financial regulation has been possibly the most important part of the agenda of the G20 meetings since their beginning. Following the collapse of Lehman Brothers in September 2008, the word was that "the global problem raised by the financial crisis had to find a global solution." Leaders agreed that reinforcement of regulations, their global harmonization, and their strict enforcement were necessary to bring more stability to the financial sphere. Among the forty-seven items mentioned in the Washington communiqué, no less than thirty-eight were devoted to detailing the main aspects of the new would-be international financial regulation.

In the spring of 2010, many of those issues looked seriously entangled. Just to recall the mood in Toronto, the negotiations of the Basel committee regarding bank regulations were stagnating, the deadline for accounting standards convergence had just been postponed, and no agreement could be concluded regarding an internationally coordinated taxation of banks. Not to speak of a vanishing European voice due to the chaotic answer of the Eurozone to its sovereign debt crisis. While the final communiqué in Toronto repeated previous commitments, the statement also recognized that "countries should be free to examine a range of policy approaches." Does that return to national solutions mean that the G20 is already *passé?*

What a difference two years make! When meeting in Washington and London, leaders clearly had to manage pressing and common challenges, and they did that successfully. Now, as President Sarkozy observed in a speech devoted to the future French presidency of the G20, the G20 faces a bifurcation. Either the G20 continues as a crisis management instrument or it makes a significant step forward into effective policy coordination. That cannot mean pure and perfect convergence in the ongoing process of reregulation. "One size fits all" does not work for fundamental reasons. What we should ambitiously work for is a "workable convergence." Will the reregulation processes now at work in the United States and in the EU deliver better regulation or fall into either complacency or overregulation? Are the reforms on both sides of the Atlantic sufficiently converging?

This chapter is organized as follows. Starting from market failures in the first section, I emphasize in the second the trade-off between financial risks and rewards. I explore next the conditions of international convergence in a multipolar world, with special emphasis on recent European decisions. The prevention of systemic risk and the reinforcement of bank regulation and supervision are then discussed as feasible accomplishments following the G20 decisions on bank regulation and supervision. For the future, the agenda will raise more treacherous questions, such as the treatment of systemically important financial institutions (SIFIs) and derivatives. Finally I discuss alternative views regarding the convergence of accounting standards and the leveling of the playing field for investment banking and other capital markets intermediaries. The conclusion discusses the chance to make the financial system safer and calls for summits not only to capitalize on existing results but to give a fresh momentum to the global reregulation process.

What's the Matter with Financial Market Failures?

The crisis has brought to the forefront a number of pitfalls in financial markets, behavior, remuneration, regulation, and supervision. A few words about our understanding of the crisis are useful to set the stage. There is a considerable degree of consensus between the two sides of the Atlantic regarding the origins of the crisis, which can be most easily encapsulated in two words, "excessive leverage."

How did we arrive at this debt disaster? First, there were macroeconomic causes: monetary policy has been too lax for too long; global imbalances have canceled any sense of discipline and allowed unlimited accumulation of debt. Second, there were microeconomic causes—financial innovation and lax supervision—followed by a series of secondary causes: ratings agencies, procyclical accounting standards, unregulated monolines, excessive profitability targets, wrong incentives, and so forth.

Markets failed; that is now broadly accepted. Financial deregulation and ineffective supervision figure among the causes and casualties of the crisis. For two years now, we have been asking "What was it about the financial system that wasn't self-correcting"? Two different answers can be offered to this question. Although the differences between them are seemingly small, they have very important policy consequences.

Many understand the wreckage to be a failure of a systemic nature: too much procyclicality, inadequate oversight, and the ideology of self-regulation. According to this view, the financial industry has grown too large; a smaller and safer industry would be in the interest of more stable growth. Its policy implication is that the future belongs to stronger regulation and supervision backed by rigorous macroeconomic policies oriented toward medium-term sustainability. If not offering a definitive solution, this would clearly have a key role in bringing back discipline to finance.

Others, less risk averse, are mainly pondering a broad failure of judgment that has been amplified by failure of supervision. It is human nature that banks learned to play the system skillfully! According to this view, trying to eradicate the failings of human nature could prove more damaging than useful: regulation may lead to serious unintended consequences. Its policy implication is that there are good reasons to think that the expansion of finance remains one of the better engines of economic growth; at the end of the day, risk taking is the very source of economic progress and should not be discouraged.

Having to respond to the public anger about the financial crisis, the G20 summits had little opportunity to ponder these nuances, which are not only analytical but also cultural in nature. Leaders had to act bravely and cooperatively. In terms of broad principles, they embarked on a ride of reregulation. Months of negotiations later, it is obvious how different agreeing on principles and broad objectives is from writing and enforcing rules and commitments. The uncomfortable truth is that regulation is not a straightforward avenue.

The Trade-Off between Risks and Rewards

The term "financial regulation" usually refers to a cluster of interrelated policies aimed at ensuring proper functioning of the financial system. Parts of the regulations are, or should be, similar to those enacted in other industries regarding the protection of consumers, the safe design of products, and the provision of appropriate information to the public. But finance is different in very important aspects. International financial regulation does not obey the same logic as that, for example, embedded in international trade agreements and institutions. "Free trade is good," and it has been (within regulatory limits reflecting food security concerns) pursued as such, but what about finance? Capital flows are good too, but finance regularly triggers crises: more than trade, finance needs rules. There is tension underlying financial liberalization. Free trade means going forward on a linear axis; free capital movements immediately expose a trade-off between risks and rewards. Getting a financial international agreement is much more demanding than liberalizing trade.

Until the 1970s, financial regulation developed almost exclusively at the national level. The first big pieces of international regulation started with the work of the International Accounting Standards Committee in 1973 and of the Basel Committee on Banking Supervision in 1974. Coordination among securities regulators developed in1983 under the auspices of the International Organization of Securities Commissions. Finance ministers and central bankers developed their cooperation according to different formats—G5, G7, G10, and finally G20 in 1999. Also in 1999, the Financial Stability Forum was inaugurated and the IMF started assessing national and supervisory frameworks through the Financial Sector Assessment Program (FSAP). Looking to the results, this program, despite its apparent activism, proved dramatically inefficient in detecting and preventing a global systemic crisis. Does that mean that international financial regulation is inevitably lagging the course of the real financial life?

One point, frequently made by the activists of financial liberalization, is that financial regulation today has weaker foundations than, say, trade or macroeconomics because it only recently turned into a major policy concern. That is a half-truth. Liberalization, the major policy concern in finance during the last decades, has been backed by a very strong theoretical argument, efficient market theory. Huge efforts have been made to turn academic research into policy recommendations. Where does the idea of "soft regulation" of finance come from, where does the idea of "transferring risks to those most able to bear them" come from, and where did the idea of relaxing capital standards because financial institutions were "more able to gauge risks than before" come from if not from a powerful conceptual framework turned into an ideological and political force?

That government intervention is harmful, that fair value is the quantitative incarnation of reason, and that securitization is the secret of risk evaporation have never been a result of science; rather, they represented one side of economic realities that had been for a period of time carefully manufactured into sort of a religious belief. Now we have to live with the legacy of this faith-based strategy. The trade-off between risks and rewards had been grossly tilted toward the minimization of risks and the overvaluation of rewards. It is now time to choose another point on this trade-off, but which one? Market failures are well recognized, but governments are poorly equipped to back their efforts toward financial reregulation. The efficient market theory brilliantly inspired a homogeneous vision of global finance, but it is now broken; without an equivalent theory for a time of reregulation, the world that we inherit is heterogeneous.

Don't Expect Pure and Perfect Convergence
of International Reregulation

History suggests that international regulatory harmonization could be a (relatively) simple task in one situation: when one country plays a prominent role, when financial activity is described according to a consensual view, and when the policy recommendation is to dismantle obstacles to the free circulation of capital. After the 1930s, the United States initially enjoyed global leadership with innovations like deposit insurance, securitization, and accounting standards enacted by the Roosevelt administration and subsequently adopted in other countries; reversing the trend, the United States powerfully acted during the last three decades to extend the use of financial innovations, to broaden the horizon of global finance, and to oppose foreign proposals to reduce its procyclicality. This period is over not only because the crisis has its origins in the United States but for a more fundamental reason. In a world that is becoming multipolar, it is time to think more seriously about the difficulties of international policy cooperation.

The world is no longer the bipolar world of the cold war or the brief unipolar one that followed the fall of the Berlin wall. "Multipolarity," for sure, is a suggestive word rather than a rigorous analysis, but the word undeniably captures something important. By the way, the G20 has been celebrated precisely for bringing the global summits in line with the present geopolitical realities. What about the implications of multipolarity for finance? The geography of modern finance has been organized following a London/New York axis. Germany and Japan became first-class industrial powerhouses but never dislodged—and never tried to dislodge—the Anglo-American financial preeminence. That preeminence certainly remains, but the big picture is now evolving into something much more complex.

First, the center of gravity of global finance is moving eastward. The emerging countries' share of the top 100 listed banks has surged from practically nothing to one-third of the world total, a significant part of it reflecting the rise of Chinese institutions. A similar picture emerges when one looks at global financial centers, of which Hong Kong, Singapore, and Tokyo (and Shanghai tomorrow) rank at the top of the league. The combination of deleveraging in the West and wealth accumulation in Asia will certainly reinforce this trend. That still does not translate into Asian countries playing a major role in the global financial policy debate. Emerging economies consider the financial crisis to be a Western mess. They are not reregulating in the Western style but rather holding their cards, and that does not contribute to making the world of global finance flat.

Second, continental Europe is looking for emancipation. Its financial culture and financial structures are different from those of the City or of Wall Street. A distinguished observer of European financial realities recently characterized Europe as the combination of a port, the city of London, oriented toward the ocean and a vast hinterland, continental Europe, each strongly interconnected with the other. In many aspects, continental Europe only reluctantly adopted the mantra of self-regulated efficient markets. Recall the harsh words of German officials going so far as to qualify American bankers as "locusts." More important, Europe appeared disarmed when facing the financial crisis. A more unified financial single market had been recognized for years as a desirable goal, but despite the creation of the euro, action remained timid and delayed due to conflicting national interests. After the crisis, public anger meant that inaction was no longer an option.

Europe in a Multipolar Financial World

For the EU, the clouds of the spring of 2010 have cleared. After months of delay, due to the political bickering following the installation of a new parliament, a new European Commission, and new European institutions, lawmakers and governments finally agreed in September to a radical overhaul of the patchy system of financial oversight, which should be definitively endorsed in 2011. Besides the new Systemic Risk Council, the new regime will rely on three new European supervisory authorities (ESAs) for banks (located in London), markets (in Paris), and insurance (in Frankfurt). This decision is a new example of a European tradition to use every crisis as an opportunity. The creation of such agencies, though opposed by national governments, was considered necessary to really organize EU-wide financial activities. Their creation out of three preexisting pan-European committees is a logical consequence of the crisis. On paper, the supervisory structure is a wise balance of national and EU-wide responsibilities. The main task of European agencies will be to set standards and rules, day-to-day supervision remaining with national authorities.

What are the differences with the past? The new ESAs are formal European institutions made up of the heads of the twenty-seven national supervisory authorities; they will make their decisions by simple or qualified majority voting even if they extend the tradition of the previous committees to work mainly by consensus so as to bring everyone on board. The ESAs will have binding powers in certain circumstances, in particular in case of "emergency situations," but they cannot enforce decisions that have budgetary implications: if facing a financial crisis, the market authority could temporarily ban certain products but the banking authority could not order a bailout. The size of the agencies will be modest (say, 100 people for each; the British FSA, in comparison, has 3,000), and they willingly will depend on significant member state input. All of this is a sensible, harmonized rulemaking process that is definitely needed for better functioning of the European financial industry and markets; it is also a subtle shift of power to Brussels.

Multipolarity eventually changes the behavior of the main actors. A multipolar world is one in which you simultaneously face asymmetry between the West and the rest and between the United States and the EU. In the past, for example, EU institutions were instinctively working on the basis of free market and internationalist considerations because those were the drivers of intra-European harmonization. The dynamics are changing as more political objectives are now, as everywhere in the world, fed into the debates; that in particular reflects the increased role of the European Parliament.

This European reaction is a striking demonstration of what we have to expect when entering a heterogeneous and multipolar world. The G20 is not the expression of a global political constituency; beyond the summits, decisions are made in Washington, Beijing, Brussels, and other capitals where, as we know, "all politics is local." Reregulation lies in the hands of domestic constituencies; that inspires a widespread reluctance to delegate formal powers to a supranational entity. Differences in financial industry structures also make uniform rules meaningless and unreachable. There is nothing like an ideal harmonization of legislations; the G20 has to engineer a "workable convergence." In November 2010, two years after the Washington G20 meeting in November 2008, two major changes in the financial landscape—the adoption of Basel III rules and the creation of systemic risk boards—were endorsed at the Seoul summit.

A Stronger Banking Sector

The crisis has demonstrated the importance of strengthening the resilience of the banking industry by implementing tougher rules on capital and liquidity. The package prepared by the Basel committee has been delivered in time after detailed consultations (see chapter 7 in this volume). It is very comprehensive and addresses these issues by improving the level and quality of capital for credit institutions as well as developing a framework for liquidity risk. The main elements of the proposal—which were adopted at the Seoul summit—are, first, to improve the quality of capital constituted especially under tier 1 and to introduce capital buffers to increase the loss-absorption capacity of banks; second, to rely on a non-risk-based leverage ratio as a supplementary measure to the Basel II risk control framework in order to curb excessive balance sheet growth; and third, to introduce a range of measures like forward-looking provisioning to mitigate the inherent procyclicality of the financial system.

Does all this rise to the challenge? Heated debates have flourished with regard to the impact of the proposed rules on financial institutions and on the real economy. The industry loudly cried folly and emphasized the depressive consequences that these exaggeratedly pressing rules would have on credit allocation and growth. That argument seems to fit with a polarized recovery: robust for large corporations but fragile for small business and households. Corporate debt markets suffered severely during the recession but have recovered as credit spreads have narrowed; by contrast, small businesses continue to face difficulties and frequently resent an inadequate access to credit.

Quantitative studies have been conducted to assess the impact of the proposed rules. They did not produce a complete consensus, but it seems fair to say that disinterested observers thought that the impact was clearly exaggerated by the industry, that the effect on price would be moderate (0.25%) and the consequences for growth limited and more than offset by the benefits of greater systemic stability. And at any rate, banks have been given until 2019 before the new rules apply in full force—an extraordinarily extended period of time for this transition!

The argument of the industry must also be reconsidered in light of the crisis. In the recent past, "easy credit availability" has constantly fueled rhetoric in favor of light capital requirements, which in turn meant a more leveraged banking sector. That was the beginning of the very sloppy argument that made us believe that a global financial industry as big as possible was indispensable for the future growth of the world. The argument cannot be considered anymore as common wisdom!

All in all, the Basel package represents a sensible compromise, offering elements of increased security without being heavy handed. There are nonetheless two troubling elements. The first is the basis of the argument itself. Higher capital requirements are necessary, but are they sufficient to prevent future crises? That remains inconclusive for a simple reason—namely, that the five largest U.S. financial institutions subject to Basel capital standards that either failed or were forced into government assisted mergers (Bear Sterns, Washington Mutual, Lehman, Wachovia, and Merrill Lynch) each had regulatory capital ratios ranging between 12 percent and 16 percent before they were shut down. They not only respected the regulatory minimums but were rightly considered well capitalized.

A second aspect possibly did not receive sufficient scrutiny. Basel III, like its predecessor, allows the big and complex global banks to use their internal risk models as key determinants of capital requirements. There are two arguments for that, of which one is flawed and the second dramatically flawed. The first is that "banks are more able than regulators to devote more resources to sophisticated methods [of building risk models]." True enough, but at what price for the quality of supervision? The second is that "banks have a strong incentive to get the exercise right." We now know how fragile that assumption is, especially for the most audacious and risk-prone institutions. In sum, there are good reasons to think that risk-modeling methods are now better than they were, but there are more reasons to be skeptical that the basic flaws and bias have been corrected. The Basel committee concluded that the benefits outweigh the costs—and above all, that there was no clearly superior approach.

The Basel committee has, in short, concluded a complex agreement in a short period of time, which is good news for its future work. The compromise, with the above-mentioned limits, offers the chance of a level playing field even if several countries, among them the United States and Switzerland, might find it not demanding enough. That would be sort of a reverse controversy, with the United States willing to adopt more stringent regulations than continental Europe! Some will conclude that, in the current context, harmonization efforts might lead only to weak global standards. That is an unnecessarily cynical argument. Anyway, Congress will always follow its own way—and the adoption of any Basel agreement in Washington remains an open question. With many others, I would finally consider the Basel proposals as an example of a workable convergence.

On top of that, it is possible to argue that many aspects of financial stability policy can be effectively tackled at the national (or regional) level. The international activity of large banks is typically less than one-fourth of their total business, Europe being an exception due to the financial single market and consequently to a higher level of cross-border integration. Outside Europe, it is not clear that even multinational groups require internationally uniform supervision. BNP Paribas, CITI, HSBC, or Santander illustrate that international synergies can arise from the leverage of technological know-how or better management of customer relations even with locally capitalized and funded retail subsidiaries that are subject to slightly different supervisory standards.

Preventing Systemic Risk

The financial crisis has demonstrated that safe banks are a necessary but not sufficient condition for ensuring a safe financial system. Deep and complex interconnections between financial intermediaries are the source of risks of a systemic nature. The key to preventing financial crises is the establishment of a process to identify and monitor vulnerabilities that threaten financial stability. It is easy to remember in the past decades a lot of situations— Mexican and many other debt crises, failures of savings and loans, dotcom and housing bubbles—in which such a process would have been more than desirable. In brief, the historical record is not encouraging in this regard.

Could it be different this time? At the risk of proving irremediably naïve, we are tempted to think that the short answer is yes. The true question relates to political will, but the task is not unmanageable, with the idea of weaknesses accumulating before the crisis being, at least for now, widely shared. Imbalances and risks have first to be recognized, rather than denied as we have too frequently witnessed during the last decade; they have thus to be calibrated in terms of their potential adverse effect on the economy. That is both more important and more difficult. This process is a continuous one of information gathering, technical analysis, and synthetic assessment. It should be systematic and comprehensive in nature, monitoring both the macro- and micro-aspects. We have witnessed the political will to meet these challenges.

Are EU and U.S. reforms appropriately designed? Will they prove to be up to the task? Credit should be given at the moment to the reforms adopted on both sides of the Atlantic. Prominent among other policy bodies, new institutions have been created to face the unique nature of systemic risk. In Europe, the new actor is called the Systemic Risk Board; in the United States, it is the Systemic Risk Council. Both will comprise policy officials, central bankers, and members from regulatory and supervisory bodies; the chair is held by the Central Bank in Europe and by the Treasury in the United States.

There is a debate about the effectiveness of both arrangements. In both cases, participants represent different interests and are subject to different public and private influences; that is the nature of the game, and consensus will not be easy to achieve. It can be argued that the U.S. solution relies exclusively on federal officials so that once consensus is reached, each agency has the authority to implement decisions. That solution can be effective enough if consensus can be reached; however, the experience of the past decade invites a cautious assessment in that regard. The EU board is sometimes wrongly characterized as a "reputational body," but it has real if less direct power than its American counterpart. More important, it is chaired by the independent and powerful European Central Bank.

In short, the distinctions between the American and European solutions for coping with systematic risk are of second order. Both the Systemic Risk Board and the Systemic Risk Council are reliable frameworks for tracking and preventing financial excesses. Experience suggests that coordination between the two will be satisfactory in the case of "standard" financial turbulence. Things would be tenser if a more severe situation arose (for example, another major banking crisis, a sovereign default threat, or a mix of both or divergence regarding the pursuit of quantitative easing). In such a case, issues could be elevated to the G20 level. The final answer would depend on the degree of consensus regarding the risk-reward balance of the financial outlook and on the political will to act accordingly and cooperatively. There is no known solution—as we already witnessed, in particular about the size of the stimulus package—to oblige convergence and overcome diverging political priorities regarding the use of budgetary and monetary rescue instruments.

The conclusion is that, when meeting in Seoul in November 2010, the G20 and the financial bodies acting under its guidance had reason to believe that they had done a good, even if partial, job. Looking forward, is this a sufficient reason for hope? Or will the forthcoming summits face more treacherous issues? We now explore some of them.

A Safer Financial Industry? "Too Big to Fail" and Derivatives

Another major vulnerability of the system is the question of "too big to fail." In the United States, several big financial firms, now called "systemically important financial institutions" (SIFIs), faced insolvency. As the Lehman failure demonstrated, that was posing a threat to the whole system. Government intervention was needed, as it was in previous financial crises, but the government did not have the tools to do the job. U.S. authorities had to provide bridge loans to sponsor mergers, to extend Federal Reserve funding, and to recapitalize these institutions with an unprecedented amount of taxpayers' money. Europe too faced similar risks in the United Kingdom and Ireland. On the continent, individual banks suffered, sometimes severely, without endangering the system.

The question raised by SIFIs is at the heart of modern finance. These institutions have grown in a way that put them outside the very logic of capitalism, which is to reward success by profits and to punish failure by bankruptcy. There cannot be a proper functioning of the whole system if such an important part of the economy is able to withdraw itself from market discipline. Solutions have been debated, and a report was submitted to the G20 by the Financial Stability Board.

If capital requirements alone are not up to the task, what other solutions can be implemented? The first is to ensure that governments have the special resolution authority to act so that there is an alternative to a massive bailout of failing firms. That is now part of the Dodd-Frank bill in the United States. One sensitive part of the scheme is to design the resolution process in a way that supports market discipline. Punishing the failures means the possibility of wiping out all of the stakeholders—the shareholders first but also the management and creditors. Whether these threats would be sufficiently biting to discourage imprudent behavior remains an open question. It would consequently be appropriate to have other tools. One of them would be a requirement to prepare wind-down plans, also called living wills, which would ensure the supervisory authority that a failure could be resolved without producing uncontrollable spillover effects; another policy would be simply to impose explicit size limits. A powerful economic argument backs the latter solution: there is no clear evidence that increasing size is always a source of improved efficiency. The debate should consequently be framed in a political economy context and raise the question of the excessive power accumulated by the SIFIs.

By enormously extending the sources of moral hazard that this crisis has already created, inaction regarding SIFIs would be a sure recipe for cooking up the next big crisis. Taking into account competitive or strategic considerations, one clearly sees that there is no national solution to the issue; confronting "too big to fail" could be one of the most important tests of the political will concentrated in the G20.

Markets also can have a systemic impact if they are insufficiently transparent, thereby leading to mispricing of risk and laying the basis for destabilizing adjustments; that was the case in the credit default swaps (CDS) market. Efforts to reform the CDS market are focused on making the market more transparent and reducing counterparty exposure. Consensus has emerged that over-the-counter markets need to be moved to central counterparties or subjected to additional requirements. Where such central clearing mechanisms existed before the crisis, payments flowed smoothly and defaults were handled well. Looking forward, it is important nonetheless to act carefully so that the benefits of multilateral counterparty netting are not offset by the concentration of operational risk inherent in such big institutions.

The future extent of securitization will depend crucially on how regulation is formulated. New regulations have already constrained some of the more complex products, but securitization benefits for economic growth should be secured by creating a secure environment for long-term investors (insurers, pension funds, and so on), which need to be convinced that the abuses that occurred in the run-up to the crisis are definitely under control. Incentives should be designed in a way that promotes a stricter view of the credit supply, which implies that originators will keep a significant share of credit on their books. On the other side, should regulations be designed and applied too strictly, originators may well find it uneconomical to originate loans, thus restricting unnecessarily the usefulness of securitization. Facing this trade-off—and with the lessons from the previous financial boom and bust all too clear—policymakers should, preferably, err on the side of caution.

The two previous sections suggest that when meeting in Seoul, the G20 was right to commend the progress made with the Basel capital framework and the systemic prevention schemes; however, the G20 cannot stop at that point because other major sources of financial instability have not been corrected. Due to their global nature, the questions of "too big to fail" and the organization of derivatives markets remain on the agenda, and they will not find a proper solution without a strong endorsement by the leaders.

Extending Capital Integration and Preventing Future Crises: Nonbanks and Accounting Standards

The argument in this chapter is that the world needs reregulation to prevent the repetition of the recent financial crisis and that reregulation has been and deserves to be powerfully promoted by the G20. This network (G20, IMF, FSB, Basel) has the capacity to do a lot to assess the financial outlook and the accumulation of systemic risks, to set authoritative standards and monitor the reasonable convergence of regulatory practices, and to fix the SIFIs and derivatives issues. On the other hand, we have also recognized that reregulation increases the risk of mutually incompatible policies, which could cause competitive distortions. That is why we should not expect perfect convergence and instead be happy with a "workable convergence." However, some crucial regulatory concerns, such as the SIFIs, can be addressed only at a global level. The future G20 summits have a difficult task in pushing the reregulatory agenda forward while ensuring the sustainability of financial integration. Will the process develop smoothly? Or will we see divergent views about the priorities?

The intrinsic logic of capital markets is to continue their process of global integration. Reregulating banks will be a boost to capital markets and other nonbank financial intermediaries. But experience clearly suggests that the transfer of financial flows from strictly regulated banks to less regulated capital markets and other nonbank financial intermediaries would bring new sources of risk and instability. Extending global capital market integration and preventing future financial crises could thus appear as conflicting goals and prove to be more difficult vehicles for delivering the fruits of a workable convergence. Two examples illustrate that point.

First, with banks more constrained, nonbanks are bound to thrive. Lower leverage within the banking sector will likely result in greater demand from those able to do so to access credit through capital markets. Because of higher capital requirements, risky credit will likely shift out of the banking industry to the nonbank financial system. Intermediation outside the banking system is going to grow, and capital market intermediaries will forcefully ask for more extensive freedom of action to seize new profit opportunities. How will regulation adapt to oversee the risks in this sector? Financial institutions like private equity or hedge funds are similar to banks in that they also have high leverage and potential asset-liability mismatches.

The industry will lobby policymakers to agree that such risk shifting is a condition of growth and that it is acceptable as long as it remains outside a well-protected banking system. However, it remains unclear how to avoid the development of another shadow banking system, operating under insufficient transparency and prone to building another form of systemic risk. Experience suggests that there are no unbreakable borders between different parts of the industry. Contagion is a basic lesson of the previous crisis, and it would be prudent to act accordingly. Nonbanks should consequently be subjected to bank-like regulation and supervision. Another important question is whether these institutions should be eligible—and under what conditions—for the same protections provided to deposit holders and to central banks' liquidity support. The answer to these questions depends, more than the ones discussed in the previous sections, on the very structure of the industry in different nations, as will be manifest in the case of investment banking.

Contrary to the traditional business of banking, the activities of nonbanks and investment banks are more internationally integrated, and they require more uniform rules. This issue cannot be treated independently of the structure of the financial industry and of the politics that frame those structures. In the United States, the Glass-Steagall Act, in response to the anger of those whose savings had been ruined by greedy bankers, decided on the separation of retail and investment businesses. This theme has made an important comeback with the so-called Volcker rule. There is reluctance in Europe—where the structure of the industry is based on the concept of "universal banks"—to follow the same route. In this debate, Europe is being accused of trying to protect its champions, but there are much more serious reasons.

The recent crisis suggests that Glass-Steagall–style regulation offers only weak protection since the excesses of the shadow banking system and of the investment banks have been powerful enough to draw the whole system into the abyss. It can even be reasonably argued that the separation of investment banks is radically counterproductive because they are offered the greatest latitude of action: their supervision relies only on a market authority like the SEC. That proved radically inadequate not only because the SEC was insufficiently staffed or in some cases captured by the industry but because the surveillance of complex financial institutions cannot be bestowed exclusively on the market authority. On top of that, there is an element of irony in the fact that the surviving U.S. investment banks survived the crisis thanks only to their rapid transformation into financial holding companies, thereby opening the umbrella of the Federal Reserve. It is audacious in such a context to argue that the European investment banking business located within universal banks enjoys a competitive advantage; the reverse is true. Without public rescue, American investment banking would have disappeared and now be ready for a refreshing start from scratch. The separation of investment banking, in short, has low appeal in Europe, and there is little to recommend convergence at any price on this issue.

Second, capital markets need consistent financial information. That is a clearly desirable goal, but it could also fuel a serious transatlantic rift. First, a lot of issues deserve to be taken into consideration by the G20 and its regulatory network, and those issues could be other examples of a workable convergence. Current risk-disclosure practices could certainly be improved; lessons could be drawn, for example, from the stress tests conducted in both the United States and the EU and those exercises integrated into a more coherent framework. The public supervision of rating agencies remains very much unconvincing; that calls for new initiatives, which should be as converging as possible. Surprisingly, audit firms have remained off the radar screen despite the fact that the Sarbanes-Oxley Act produced a transatlantic uproar after granting extraterritorial competence to U.S. authorities; designing a stronger international body should be part of the agenda.

That said, everyone knows that a more painful hurdle lies on the way toward "better" financial information, fair market value at any price. There is no issue where the theme of procyclicality is more provocative. Prematurely recognizing unrealized capital gains, it can be said, is the mother of all financial excesses. There is no issue where the intellectual candor of a financial body has been more deeply and systematically captured by the industry. Raising the lessons of the crisis, the London summit took the initiative to ask the International Accounting Standards Board (IASB) and the Financial Accounting Standards Board (FASB) to deliver convergence of their standards in June 2011; that hope has been (indefinitely?) postponed by the FASB. There are few reasons to believe that Europeans would accept convergence at a price that would be a return to what is considered a key ingredient of the crisis. Convergence of accounting standards is a worthy objective as long as the content and quality of the standards are designed to increase convergence, not volatility. Could this turn into another real transatlantic divergence?

The Task Ahead for the G20

Two years on, international reregulation has not gone as far as many, overwhelmed by the crisis and subdued by the strong wording of the G20 original communiqués, had expected. The danger of overreaction has definitely been avoided. Today, investment banks and investment bankers are back at the top; profits and bonuses, courtesy of public policies, not of "talent," are booming; and the nonfinancial economy continues to suffer. Has the chance to make the system safer been lost?

It would be premature to conclude that the process has slipped into complacency. Governments and regulators have started to do some of the things that might have averted the previous crisis. The pledges made by the initial G20 have had reasonable success given the obstacles to coordinated action in a multipolar and heterogeneous world. Governments have also been cautious not to worsen the prospects of a weakened financial system. But many of the basic mechanisms that concurred in the financial meltdown have remained untouched, and much more clearly remains to be done. Governments and central banks have not forgotten the crash and its consequences for their budgets and balance sheets, and far from seeing the financial industry as "God in action," the public could easily call for more action by governments. To avoid the risk of irrelevance, the G20 has little choice but to go further with respect to derivatives, "too big to fail," the shadow banking system, and accounting standards. The G20 has not lost its raison d'être and must push its agenda as far as convergence is feasible. That will not occur without a new political impetus.

9

Bank Regulation in Africa: From Basel I to Basel II and Now at a Crossroads

VICTOR MURINDE

The regulation and supervision of banking is a very topical issue, especially with respect to African economies, which have small banking units (for example, microfinance banks in Chad and Ethiopia) and large wholesale banks (for example, investment banks in Botswana and Namibia) but tend to offer a limited range of financial instruments, predominantly deposits and loans. As highlighted in Kasekende, Mlambo, and Murinde (2010), commercial banks continue to dominate the financial sector in Africa and nonbank financial institutions play a negligible role, except for public sector provident funds. In many African countries, capital markets remain peripheral as a vehicle for raising capital. However, as banking systems expand and offer a wider range of financial instruments, as in South Africa, Kenya, and Nigeria, among other large economies, how should bank supervision and regulation respond? Consider this from Adam Smith:

> Though the principles of the banking trade may appear somewhat abstruse, the practice is capable of being reduced to strict rules. To depart upon any occasion from those rules, in consequence of some flattering

I would like to thank Martin Brownbridge and Yves Kouame for comments on an earlier version of the paper that was presented at the African Economic Research Consortium (AERC) Senior Policy Seminar (SPS-XII) held in Mombasa, March 22–24, 2010. I am also indebted to Andy Mullineux and Kups Mlambo for constructive conversational comments on the ideas in this paper. However, as usual, I am responsible for any cantankerous errors.

speculation of extraordinary gain, is almost always extremely dangerous, and frequently fatal to the banking company which attempts it.[1]

In modern parlance, the above dictum mimics some elements of "narrow banking": the creation of banking institutions focused on the traditional functions, namely deposit taking from individuals and small and medium-sized enterprises (SMEs) and payment systems for institutions (see Kay 2009). The transition in bank regulation in Africa takes us back to the period before Basel I, then to Basel I, and then on to Basel II. Basel II has been problematic for Africa, as is argued further on, and recently the bank regulatory waters have been muddied by the financial crisis, which was generated outside Africa.

The crises in Asia, Mexico, Russia, and the North Atlantic region cannot be attributed simply to monetary issues or subprime mortgages; they were the result mainly of contagion effects exacerbated by weak regulatory environments (see Han, Lee, and Suk 2003; Sharma 2001; Jackson 1999; Sojli 2007; Goodhart 2008; and Mizen 2008). Although the latest crisis affected banks globally more than any crisis in the past, the serial occurrence of these crises seems to suggest that regulators must do something fundamental to stop the recurring cycle (see Brunnermeier and others 2009), especially for developing economies, which are most vulnerable to contagion but have no "voice" in the architecture of bank regulation.

In addition, the financial crisis exposed the inadequacy of the Basel rules. As Kay (2009, p. 7) observed: "Basel capital adequacy rules proved worse than useless." Globally, capital adequacy rules not only failed in their objectives but also generated "regulatory arbitrage," involving an explosion of asset securitization and the use of off–balance sheet vehicles intended to evade the rules. So, given the global financial crisis and some criticisms of Basel II, Africa is at the crossroads of bank regulation, contemplating where to go next. As observed in Brownbridge and Kirkpatrick (2002), the key questions for policymakers are related to specific methods of bank regulation and supervision that work best in existing economic environments. This is the challenge for Africa today: to try to recover from the financial crisis, encumbered with Basel II, which lost its credibility during the financial crisis, and to aim for regulation that will encompass specific features of banking, such as microfinance institutions and credit to SMEs.

This chapter highlights key trends in bank regulation in Africa, especially the transition from Basel I to Basel II, and hazards a conjecture on the future path for an effective regulatory regime for African countries. The rest of the chapter encompasses four sections. The first section presents a holistic perspective

---

1. Adam Smith, *The Wealth of Nations*, Book V, Part III (1776) (Oxford University Press), p. 820.

of bank regulation in terms of flow of funds and bank regulatory framework. It shows that bank regulation not only revolves around financial intermediation but also involves institutional, legal, and political environments. The second section highlights the evolution of the banking revolution in Africa, including the transition from Basel I to Basel II. The challenges facing bank regulation and supervision in Africa, now at a crossroads, are discussed in the third section, and some recommendations are proposed in the fourth and final section.

A Holistic Perspective of Bank Regulation: Flow of Funds

We invoke the flow-of-funds framework to underpin the role of bank regulation in ensuring the functionality of banks and capital markets in relation to households, companies, the government, and the external sector, in the sense that a "main function of the flow of funds accounts is to reveal the sources and uses of funds that are needed for growth" (Klein, 2000, p. ix). Importantly, in this framework banks matter if they are well regulated.

It is argued that bank regulation ensures timely receipt of accurate information and use of that information in the flow-of-funds transactions that take place in an economy, mainly involving exchanges of assets and liabilities. These transactions generate flows of funds from one agent to another and from one sector to another. In table 9-1, flow-of-funds accounts show net transactions in financial instruments among the key economic sectors (Green and Murinde 1998). Each row (i) represents an asset, and each column (j) a sector. Each cell (i,j) in the matrix shows net purchases (+) or sales (–) of asset i by sector j during the unit time period. The row sums of the matrix are zero as net purchases of an asset must equal net sales, and each column (j) sums to the jth sector's surplus or deficit—that is, its net acquisition of financial assets (NAFA). When households and companies make consumption and investment decisions, changes in the stocks of assets and liabilities are tracked through identities, which state that the current stock is equal to the sum of the previous period's stock; net flows into or out of the stock through transactions; changes in valuation (capital gains or losses); and depreciation of the preexisting stock. Net flows into or out of a stock correspond to entries in the flow-of-funds account for any given sector. Entries for nonreproducible assets such as land reflect flows (purchases and sales) that do not enter into the current account. However, one sector may sell land to another to augment its funds in order to purchase other assets. Intangible assets are also included in any complete representation of flow of funds (Green, Kirkpatrick, and Murinde 2005).

The behavior of banks in response to a regulator or any other agent may influence the portfolio behavior of the household sector and the company sector and the role of flow of funds in interest rate determination.[2] Hence, flow-of-funds models seek to explore why agents in a particular sector hold specific assets and why the agents choose to substitute assets in their portfolio. Also, as shown in Moore, Green, and Murinde (2006a, 2006b), stochastic policy simulations within a flow-of-funds model can shed light on the type of banking sector reforms that influence outcomes for households, companies, banks, and government. As Fleming and Giugale (2000) emphasizes, a key advantage of the flow of funds is that it imposes internal consistency on analyses and forecasts and provides an exposition of the complete financial implications of policy or other changes. Hence, the framework in table 9-1 revolves around the banking sector, but this sector can play its role only when it is well regulated and when there is financial stability.

In the context of bank regulation, the flow of funds provides a holistic perspective on the implications of effective regulation and supervision. First, the framework underpins the sources and uses of funds in the household, company, and banking sectors, on one hand, and the foreign sector, on the other. The bank sector provides financial intermediation from the household sector to the company sector. Financial instruments (such as deposit and loan interest rates), financial reforms, and bank regulation influence the size of intermediation. Therefore, in a flow-of-funds context, the main implication for bank regulation is the centrality of the financial intermediation role, so there must be a stable source of funding for all types of banks, including commercial banks and investment banks. For example, it is very important for banks to maintain adequate capital ratios to avoid liquidity and solvency risks. If commercial banks ignore the basic principle of the deposits ratio and over-rely on money market financing, liquidity crises may soon occur in banks once market confidence is lost. The crisis may be further complicated by the loss of market confidence through compounding liquidity problems, as in the recent financial crisis. Further, from a holistic perspective, the framework of bank regulation must encompass the main sectors in the flow of funds indicated in table 9-1. Barth, Caprio, and Levine (2006) provides a framework for bank regulation that covers the institutional issues.

The public-versus-private-interest view of regulation presents two contending theories of bank regulation (see Barth, Caprio, and Levine 2006). However, the overall regulatory framework also recognizes the key roles played by the institutional environment, political factors, and legal considerations.

In the case of the public interest theory, bank regulation seeks to protect and benefit the public at large as consumers of banking services. That requires that regulation aim to secure innovative and good quality services at low prices through the promotion of competition (Kay 2009). This view is based on the

---

2. See, in particular, Green and Murinde (1998, 2004, 2005).

Table 9-1. *Flow-of-Funds Accounts Showing Net Transactions in Financial Instruments among the Key Economic Sectors*

Account	Household sector H	Company sector P	Banks sector B	Government sector G	Foreign sector F
1. *Income–expenditures*					
1.1 Income (Y)	Y^H	Y^P			
1.2 Taxes (T)	T^H	T^P		T^G	
1.3 Consumption (C)	C^H	C^P		C^G	C^F
1.4 Investment (I)	I^H	I^P		I^G	I^F
Net acquisitions (S)	S^H	S^P		S^G	S^F
2. *Assets and liabilities: balance sheet accounts*					
2.1 Capital (K)	K^H	K^P		K^G	K^F
2.2 Loans (L)	L^H	L^P	L^B	L^G	
2.3 Domestic money (M)	M^H	M^P	M^B	M^G	
2.4 Foreign money (R)				R^G	R^F
Net worth (W)	W^H	W^P	W^B	W^G	W^F

Source: Modified version of table 3-1 in Green and Murinde (2005), p. 75.

argument that markets are prone to fail. In theory, unregulated banking markets can yield undesirable results, such as financial crises. The work by Nobel laureate Joseph Stiglitz (2001) is consistent with the public interest view of bank regulation. Stiglitz's main message is that credit markets fail to operate optimally when all parties to a transaction do not have the same level of information (the problem of "asymmetric information"), leading to undesired outcomes, which could be improved, in theory, by government regulation.[3] Hence, the argument is that effective bank regulation can foster the development of a properly functioning banking system, which can have positive effects on savings, intermediation, and economic growth. Bank regulation aims to improve intermediation efficiency; protects banks from negative externalities, such as financial crises; and protects the public from loan sharks and Ponzi schemes, for example.

The private interest view, or the Chicago theory, suggests that regulation does not protect the public at large but only the interest of specific groups. The Nobel laureate George Stigler (1983) argues that in practice some regulations protect

3. Broadly, there are three types of market failure in banking: fraud; systemic risk; and information asymmetry.

firms, organizations, and professional and occupational groups instead of the general public, which they were intended to protect. Stigler's view causes some economists to be a bit skeptical about the ability of regulators to correct market failure. In general, it cannot be taken for granted that governments will act in the interests of society as a whole. Governments may act at the behest of interest groups or firms, taking actions that enrich them, or they may act for the benefit of government employees or policymakers (see Barth, Caprio, and Levine 2006; Barth, Caprio, and Levine 2004; and Beck, Demirgüç-Kunt, and Levine 2006).

In practice, the relationship between the government and the central bank in African countries has been largely umbilical. Bank regulation serves to ensure the survival of the government (the sovereign), to finance the government, and sometimes to finance cronies or wealthy individuals who have familial, political, or corrupt connections in the government. Governments and their cronies have a "grabbing hand," and political leaders look more to their personal interests than to the interests of the public. Perhaps it is plausible to argue that in the context of Africa, although the weight of the public interest and the weight of the private interest in bank regulation vary over time, there is reasonable evidence to support the private interest view in some cases. That suggests that central banks that have very strong supervisory powers will attract political interference and possibly corruption. Indeed, Barth, Caprio, and Levine (2006) finds that domestic political factors shape bank regulations and their effectiveness.

It is useful to distinguish between microprudential and macroprudential regulation.[4] The former relates to factors that affect the stability of an individual bank or financial institution, while the latter refers to factors that affect the stability of the financial system as a whole, such as systemic problems. It follows that the nature and stance of microprudential regulation tend to be influenced by bank-specific characteristics, such as size and leverage, but they may also be influenced by how strongly the bank is linked to the rest of the banking system. In the case of macroprudential regulation, changes in the business cycle may influence changes in bank performance, so macroprudential regulation is required to reduce the adverse effects of the cycle on bank performance and the banking system in general. It has been proposed that countercyclical capital charges provide the way forward for future bank macroprudential regulation (see Brunnermeier and others 2009 and Jefferis 2009). According to Brunnermeier and others (2009), regulators should increase the existing capital adequacy requirements

4. The two are consistent with the "twin peaks" model in Taylor (2009), which sets out two fundamental objectives for financial regulation. The first is to ensure the stability and soundness of the financial system, or "systemic protection", while the second is "consumer protection," or protecting individual depositors, investors, and policyholders to the extent that they cannot reasonably be expected to protect their own interests.

(based on an assessment of inherent risks) by two multiples; the first is related to above-average growth of credit expansion and leverage, while the second, on capital charges, should be related to the mismatch in the maturity of assets and liabilities (for example, including adjustments to mark-to-market accounting).

However, since the global financial crisis erupted, it has been argued that a review of macroprudential regulation should encompass the broader aspects of financial services regulation, such as depositor protection or deposit insurance, and the safety of the payment system. Depositor insurance schemes raise funds through levies on other authorized firms. While these funds usually are not sufficient to cover the failure of large banking institutions, or a banking crisis, they are adequate for small deposit-taking institutions, so that the costs of bank failure are not passed on to the general public. Government bailouts of "too big to fail" banks in the global financial crisis (in the United Kingdom and the United States but hardly in Africa) have created a problem whereby taxpayers act as unpaid insurers of most transactions in wholesale banking.

Overall, in the holistic context of the flow of funds (table 9-1) and the framework of bank regulation, it may be argued that if bank regulation is weak or poorly implemented, sectoral outcomes will suffer and the standard of living may be seriously retarded. This is worrying in the sense that if African countries get bank regulation and supervision wrong, asset creation will suffer, intersectoral flows of funds will stagnate, savings and investments will slow down, the government sector may crowd out the private sector, and, consequently, particularly low living standards will languish. The question is this: "What is the 'right' bank regulation and supervision regime for African countries?" Should African regulators apply the Basel II standards simply because "rich countries do it"?

Evolution of Bank Regulation in Africa and the Transition from Basel I to Basel II

It can be argued that the regulation of banks in Africa has evolved through three overlapping phases. The first was the pre-1960s colonial phase. Colonies and territories were served by currency boards, the precursors of central banks—for example, the East African Currency Board (1919–66) and the West African Currency Board (1912–68). The regulation of banking was mainly controlled from abroad. For the most part, commercial banks were foreign owned, and the banks were regulated by the home country (Kirkpatrick, Murinde, and Tefula 2008). On the whole, regulation did not address public interest issues. For example, there was widespread market failure, and local entrepreneurs could not access bank credit. The entrepreneurs were presumed to lack adequate business acumen, good credit histories, and acceptable collateral (see Hyuha and Ddumba 1992 for an example from Uganda). Rather, the type of bank regulation that existed seems to have perpetuated the status quo, thus pointing to an aspect of regulatory failure in the context of bank intermediation among local entrepreneurs.

In the second phase—post-independence 1960s and 1970s—national central banks replaced currency boards and assumed limited bank regulation, in addition to issuing national currencies and introducing monetary policy. Importantly, the new central banks intervened to address market failure by launching state-owned development banks (notably, agricultural development banks, industrial development banks, and cooperative banks) to finance specific sectors. At the pan-African level, the African Development Bank was established in 1964 to finance long-term development projects. Further, in the 1970s regulation was invoked to effect nationalization; some countries (for example, Uganda and Tanzania) introduced state-owned commercial banks, mainly by nationalizing foreign banks. Governments used the banks to direct credit to local entrepreneurs (Brownbridge and Harvey 1998). However, the banks experienced principal-agent problems, especially when managers were political protégés and credit was allocated through political peddling (testimony to the private interest view of bank regulation discussed previously). Consequently, banks suffered bad loans from government-owned agricultural and manufacturing enterprises. In Ghana, for example, 47 percent of nonperforming bank loans in 1977 were attributed to government enterprises (Brownbridge and Harvey 1998, p. 64). Corruption and fraud also contributed to banks' impaired loan portfolios. Although the state-owned banks were technically insolvent in some countries, there was no banking crisis in terms of banks closing down or depositor runs on banks. The banks remained liquid and operational because they had a government guarantee.

The third phase, the Basel regime, includes the transition from Basel I to Basel II. When Basel I, also known as the 1988 Basel Accord, was initiated by the Basel committee in 1988 and enforced by the Group of Ten (G10) in 1992, the emphasis was on a set of minimal capital requirements for banks in order to address credit risk. Bank assets were classified and grouped into five categories according to credit risk, carrying risk weights of zero (for example, home country sovereign debt), 10, 20, 50, and up to 100 percent. It was required that banks with an international presence hold capital equal to 8 percent of their risk-weighted assets. African countries were not among the architects of the Basel Accord but, like most other countries, they adopted, at least in name, the principles prescribed in Basel I. However, the efficiency with which the Basel I principles were enforced in Africa, and even within G10 nations, varied considerably. African countries left Basel I because it became apparent that the regulatory regime was no longer fit for its purpose. For example, the diagnosis and prediction of bank failures using capital requirements and early warning systems were increasingly becoming a key concern for bank regulators. Maimbo (2002) notes that bank failures in Zambia in the mid-1990s brought into question the ability of the central bank to diagnose the financial condition of banks or to act promptly to implement corrective action. However, it appears that in the transition from Basel I to Basel II, African countries jumped from the frying pan into the fire. For example, Basel II does not address the key financial risks faced by banks operating in African countries, specifically the local banks, which are instrumental in financing SMEs, and microfinance banks, especially when there are too many of them to regulate effectively.

Because of the limitations of Basel I, the Basel Committee on Banking Supervision revised and extended the 1988 Basel Capital Accord to form Basel II. Basel II has three pillars: pillar 1 on minimum capital requirements; pillar 2 on the supervisory review process; and pillar 3 on market discipline (see, among others, Cornford 2008). The first pillar is structured around Basel I *credit risk* considerations, but it develops more extensive procedures for computing minimum bank capital requirements for *market risk* and regulatory capital requirements for *operational risk*.

The requirements for minimum regulatory capital for credit risk are calculated using two approaches, namely the standardized approach (SA) and the internal ratings–based approach (IRBA). The SA measures credit risk based on external credit assessments provided by external institutions, such as credit rating agencies (for example, Moody's, Standard & Poor's, and Fitch Ratings) or export credit agencies. The version of SA that is most used is the simplified standardized approach (SSA), which relies on only one of the simplest options available under the SA. The IRBA has two versions: the foundation version (FIRBA), by which banks calculate the probability of default on the basis of their own ratings but rely on bank supervisors for measures of the other determinants of credit risk; and the advanced version (AIRBA), under which banks estimate their own measures of all the determinants of credit risk, including stated loss and exposure.

Pillar 1 has been amended to enable banks to set minimum capital requirements for market risks, which may arise from adverse changes in interest rates, exchange rates, and the prices of stocks and financial instruments and could affect a bank's portfolio of tradable assets. Two alternative ways are used to set minimum capital levels for market risk: banks may use their internal risk management model (IM), or they may use a standardized methodology under which capital requirements are estimated separately for different categories of market risk.

There are three options with respect to regulatory capital requirements for operational risk, from the simplest to the most sophisticated. The simplest is the basic indicator approach (BIA), whereby the capital charge is a percentage of a bank's gross income; the next is the standardized approach for operational risk (SAOR), whereby the capital charge is the sum of the percentages of a bank's gross income from specified operations or, alternatively, for two of the main bank operations, namely retail and wholesale banking, of the sum of the percentages of loans and advances; and the most sophisticated is the advanced measurement approach (AMA), whereby banks estimate the required capital using their own internal system for measuring operational risk.

The second pillar sets rules for supervisory review of capital adequacy. It focuses on enhancing official supervisory practices and ensures that supervisory agencies have the power to scrutinize and discipline banks. The rules covered by pillar 2 include those setting supplementary levels of minimum regulatory capital for risks that are not covered at all or are covered inadequately by pillar 1. The third pillar envisions greater market discipline of banks through policies that force banks to disclose accurate, transparent information.

In general, considerable debate surrounds the validity of these pillars. Barth, Caprio, and Levine (2006) presents a comprehensive database on banking regulations of more than 150 countries. It offers the first comprehensive cross-country assessment of the impact of bank regulation on the operation of banks and assesses the validity of the Basel committee's influential approach to bank regulation. The authors' research, conducted at a time of heated debate on Basel II, throws some light on the three main pillars. For example, with respect to pillar 1, the evidence does not suggest that capital regulations have a significant impact on bank development, efficiency, stability, or corruption. This finding is attributed to the harmonization of national capital regulations, which makes it difficult to establish a relationship between capital regulations and bank performance. However, the lack of clear evidence on the beneficial effects of current capital regulations may reflect the inadequacy of the Basel I capital regulations and the need for implementing Basel II, or it may well be the case that banks tend to evade capital regulations.

Regarding the second pillar of Basel II, the authors found that strengthening official supervisory powers tends to make things worse, not better. Unless the country is in the "top ten" in terms of development of its political institutions, the evidence suggests that strengthening official supervisory powers hurts bank development and leads to greater corruption in bank lending without any compensating positive effects.

Regarding the third pillar, on market discipline, the authors found that regulations that require information transparency and that strengthen the ability and incentives of the private sector to monitor banks tend to promote sound banking. Barth, Caprio, and Levine (2006) concludes that strengthening capital standards or empowering supervisors does not boost bank efficiency, reduce corruption in lending, or reduce banking system fragility. Rather, what is more promising than regulations, which often tend to translate into discretionary abuse, is to introduce reforms that place far more emphasis on policies that promote market discipline, such as requirements for disclosure and transparency in the banking sector, as well as on better private sector monitoring of banks (see also Barth, Caprio, and Levine 2006; Barth, Caprio, and Levine 2004; and Beck, Demirgüç-Kunt, and Levine 2006).

In addition, the global financial crisis has provoked some questions on whether the existing bank regulatory systems are "fit for purpose." The argument is that the regulation of banks must do more than instill best practices among bankers or converge regulatory capital to prudential capital. Brunnermeier and others (2009) observes that current bank regulatory systems are imperfect because they implicitly assume that the whole banking system can be made safe by simply trying to ensure that individual banks are safe. However, banks and other financial institutions try to make themselves safer by behaving in ways that collectively undermine the system. For example, an individual bank may try to sell an asset when the price of risk increases, but if many banks act in a similar manner, the asset price will collapse, forcing institutions to take further steps to rectify the situation and leading to generalized declines in asset prices and enhanced correlations and volatility in asset markets. This type of endogeneity of risk is more pronounced when there is a common denominator such as a financial crisis, which destabilizes banks individually and engenders bank fragility (a perverse effect, contrary to the intended result of "financial stability").

There is also the issue of the role of ratings agencies in Basel II. The global financial crisis has shown that granting regulatory significance to ratings by private agencies for Basel II was a disastrous mistake; it stimulated extensive regulatory arbitrage. The widespread consensus is that these ratings should no longer play any role in financial services (see Kay 2009). The agencies should not be regulated; their role instead should be to inform investors in the marketplace instead of regulators.

It is not surprising that progress with Basel II in Africa has been rather slow. In a survey on how countries are progressing with the adoption of Basel II, Cornford (2008) found that as of mid-2008 only twelve of a total of seventeen countries in Africa that responded to the survey intended to adopt Basel II.

The dynamics and status quo of African countries also are interesting. As shown in table 9-2, the results obtained by Cornford (2008) suggest that not many more African countries had been converted to adopting Basel II by 2008 than had been in the initial survey conducted by the Bank for International Settlements (BIS 2004). In terms of pillar 1, the results in the table show that the African countries that responded to the survey intended to adopt the SA for credit risk and the BIA for operational risk, which is consistent with earlier surveys in 2004. But there seems to be an increase in the percentage of countries intending to introduce both the SA and the FIRBA for credit risk and the BIA and the SAOR for operational risk by 2009. The same finding is obtained with respect to pillars 2 and 3. The figures in table 9-2 also show that a higher percentage of African countries intended to introduce pillars 2 and 3 by 2009,

Table 9-2. *Intention to Adopt Various Pillars by African Country Respondents to Survey on Basel II*[a]

Pillar 1		Percentage intending to adopt, by approach	
Credit risk	Standardized approach (SA)	Foundation version of the internal ratings–based approach (FIRBA)	Advanced version of the internal ratings–based approach (AIRBA)
2007	17	0	0
2009	58	25	8
Operational risk	Basic indicator approach (BIA)	Standardized approach for operational risk(SAOR)	Advanced measurement approach (AMA)
2007	17	17	0
2009	42	33	17

Pillar 2	Percentage intending to adopt
2007	25
2009	75

Pillar 3	Percentage intending to adopt
2007	17
2009	75

Source: Cornford (2008, p. 5).
a. Percentage intending to adopt (of the twelve African countries that responded).

which suggests a widespread tendency by the respondents to prioritize the implementation of Basel II with respect to strengthening supervisory capacity and disclosure standards.

There are many reasons why most African countries have been slow in implementing pillars 2 and 3, namely limitations on supervisory capacity; lack of historical data, which is a big problem for the adoption of the IRBA as well as for risk-based supervision and capital management more generally; and problems regarding transparency and financial reporting. However, the data in the table imply that most respondents perhaps did address those problems, given that there was an increase in the percentage of countries intending to adopt the FIRBA for credit risk and pillars 2 and 3 by 2009. Of course, caution must be exercised with these results. A response rate of 32 percent (seventeen of fifty-three countries) is not impressive for generating an African position, and while the survey reports up to 2009, a more recent survey is required to update this information.

In order to identify a clear direction at the crossroads, future research on Africa should explore the determinants of bank supervisory and regulatory choices in selected groups of African countries. Current knowledge seems to suggest that countries with more open, competitive, democratic political systems that have effective constraints on executive power tend to adopt an approach to bank supervision and regulation that relies more on private monitoring, imposes fewer regulatory restrictions on bank activities and the entry of new banks, and has less of a role for government-owned banks. By contrast, countries with more closed, uncompetitive, autocratic political institutions that impose ineffective constraints on the executive tend to rely less on private monitoring, impose more restrictions on bank activities and new bank entry, and create a bigger role for government banks. These findings underscore the difficulty in deriving uniform, global best practice guidelines.

Africa at the Bank Regulatory Crossroads?

African countries were encouraged to adopt Basel II with no empirical evidence to support its adoption. So, when the debate focuses on Africa, there are three main questions. First, does Basel II suit the needs of African banks? Second, the biggest challenge to African banks and regulators is the measurement and management of credit risk, but how can Africa have bank supervisors who have state-of-the-art risk-modeling skills if they are not given the accompanying higher compensation? Third, what do African banks need?

There is also the question of whether the central bank is still the supervisory authority in African economies. As shown in table 9-3 (updated from Barth, Caprio, and Levine 2006), with respect to central bank authority there are three main categories of African countries: the group of countries where the central bank is the only regulatory and supervisory authority; the group of countries where there are multiple bank supervisors, including the central bank; and the group where the central bank is not the supervisory authority and a quasi-autonomous agency may be the supervisory authority. It is interesting that the majority of African countries fall in the first and third categories, which represent polar cases of the public-versus-private issue in bank regulation in Africa. Hence, although it appears from table 9-3 that in many countries, especially those in column 1, central banks are less prone to regulatory capture than quasi-autonomous agencies, it may well be the case that the institutional form matters less than the governance mechanism.

Globally, bank regulation has become merely one component of financial services regulation, and a range of the regulatory functions that used to be the responsibility of self-regulating agencies have been nationalized and are performed by public agencies. Examples include regulation of stock exchanges and the control systems of banks. The information on Africa in table 9-3 seems to point to the same development, which is not ideal because the regulatory functions that have been nationalized elsewhere in the world are not more effectively performed by public agencies. As noted in Kay (2009), the main issue is whether

Table 9-3. *Bank Supervisory Authority, Various African Countries*

Central bank is the only supervisory authority	Multiple supervisory authorities exist, including the central bank	Central bank has no supervisory authority
Botswana	Morocco	Algeria
Burundi	Nigeria	Benin
Egypt		Burkina Faso
Gambia		Cameroon
Ghana		Central African Republic
Kenya		Chad
Lesotho		Côte d'Ivoire
Libya		Gabon
Namibia		Guinea Bissau
Rwanda		Madagascar
South Africa		Mali
Sudan		Niger
Swaziland		Senegal
Tunisia		Togo
Uganda		
Zimbabwe		

Source: Barth, Caprio, and Levine (2006), updated.

the greater power of enforcement that a public authority has offsets the informational disadvantage experienced by an external regulator.

In addition, it should be taken into consideration that the global crisis broke during the transition from Basel I to Basel II for many African countries, thus complicating a process that already was rather slow, mainly because of resource constraints and data requirements. The global financial crisis has, therefore, raised a question: how does Africa adopt the very tools that proved impotent in the face of the global financial crisis?

Concluding Remarks: The Way Ahead

In general, it is useful to recognize why it was necessary to move from Basel I to Basel II and also what the international regulatory system offers for banks globally. In addition, it is important to note three further points: First, BIS has no legislative authority, thus Basel II constitutes a set of recommendations for national regulators to tailor the Basel II pillars to their country's needs for bank regulation and supervision. Second, Basel II is not "one size fits all"; it tries to meet different risk requirements by different countries, as can be seen from the options available under pillar 1, for example. Third, the Basel committee has attempted to offer a consultative process throughout the transition from Basel I to Basel II. For example, the current consultation is about strengthening the resilience of the banking sector and the international framework for liquidity risk measurement standards, and monitoring and input would be required from country regulators and the public. However, Kay (2009, p. 9) sums it up very well:

> The lesson of the failure of the Basel accords is not that the regime should be elaborated beyond the 400 pages of text in the current accords. It is that the whole system should be swept away, and the responsibility for capital adequacy and risk management be put back where it belongs—in the hands of the executive of banks, who should then carry heavy and exclusive responsibility for failure of control. There must be a better way. There is. It involves a combination of tighter, but more narrowly focused, regulation and a larger role for competition and market forces.

African countries must leave the crossroads for an alternative model of bank supervision that virtually amounts to Basel III. The current framework (Basel II) has always been controversial, but the global financial crisis provides the basis for Africa and other developing countries to come out with a strong voice and tell the Basel committee to start over again. Importantly, the "voice" has to be convincing, so it behooves all of us, policymakers and researchers alike, to produce watertight evidence as to how and why the bank regulation dilemma in Africa has to be addressed by a new standard. The evidence should address the following areas:

— *Access for Africa to the G20 meetings* in Korea in November 2010 was an important landmark because Africa was represented and participated in the development agenda of these meetings. Malawi and Ethiopia were invited to the G20 Seoul summits, as chair of the African Union and the NEPAD (New Partnership for Africa's Development), respectively. This action recognized that while the G20 goes beyond the initial G8 in membership and mandate, Africa and other lowest-income countries are still excluded from participation and agenda setting in the G20 as well as from directly shaping the intensity of the debate on procedures and policy strategies for the key development challenges. The G20 has to show that the transition from G8 governance of the world marks a genuine step forward. The G20 cannot be dominated by twenty countries that, although they represent the bulk of GDP, do not represent most of the world's population, which resides in the world's poorest countries—countries that are striving for development opportunities, including adequate financing.

—The most immediate action now relates to *Africa's voice in post-crisis bank regulatory reform*—that is, to securing Africa's access to, and voice in, the ongoing international architecture of bank regulation in terms of the proposed enhancements of the Basel II framework and the framework for adherence to international standards by the Financial Stability Board (FSB). The financial crisis severely tested the Basel II framework, which integrated traditional bank lending and capital market activities—especially during the transition from Basel I to

Basel II—in many African countries, which are now virtually at a crossroads. Although the crisis has slowed the momentum of regulatory reform in Africa, it has not derailed ongoing work. But the rules of the regulatory game are changing globally, and African countries are articulating what they need from the new bank regulation architecture. It is useful to note that Africa had no say in past regulatory reforms and that recent reforms of international regulatory bodies also leave African countries virtually voiceless (for example, Africa has only one of the forty-four institutional memberships in the FSB). The African Development Bank (AfDB) and African Economic Research Consortium (AERC) commend the African Committee of 10 (C-10), which represents African finance ministers and central bank governors, as an effective representation in the ongoing work of Basel reform and the innovations in the FSB. The C-10 is active post-crisis and represents the best efforts by African countries to deal with the peculiarities of financial regulation and the countries' development financing agendas. It is hoped that the AfDB, as secretariat of the C-10, would facilitate Africa's inputs into the discussion on banking regulation reforms coordinated by the FSB and the Basel committee.

—The other important next step is toward enhancing *Africa's role in sharing information for transnational regulation*. Africa takes this role seriously, which arises from cross-border supervision to reduce information asymmetry and nonconvergence of national and international regulation, especially where large foreign banks are heavily involved in small, poor economies. Specifically, Africa cannot effectively regulate foreign bank subsidiaries without strong information sharing with home regulators. Here, the key to effective cross-border supervision is to ensure information symmetry by sharing data between home- and host-country supervisors and to ensure cooperation by exploring mechanisms such as memorandums of understanding (MOUs). As a lead, the United States should sign MOUs to share information among U.S. and host-country African supervisors. This point arises from research evidence that shows that cross-border banking in Africa is growing in importance (involving, for example, foreign banks from Europe, the United States, and India and intra-African banking groups from South Africa, Nigeria, Kenya, Morocco, and so forth). The point also arises from the experience in Africa: before the financial crisis, Africa was repeatedly hit by the collapse of global banks (BCCI, Meridien) due to inadequate home-country regulation, poor communication of problems by regulatory authorities, and attempts by banks to hide problems in bank branches in low-income countries, including Africa. Also, past African banking crises have been exacerbated by the export of bank capital to tax havens.

—Another key issue relates to *risk weighting in the design of new regulatory architecture*. The financial crisis exposed the unreliability of risk weights produced by the key rating agencies (S&P, Moody's, and Fitch Ratings) as a market-discipline component of bank regulation. Bank risk was undervalued. Post-crisis, the issue of regulating credit rating agencies to avoid exacerbating financial instability is on the table for discussion, especially in African countries that do not have the capacity to generate their own risk-rating metrics. A key unresolved issue is how to measure and assign risk weights to the mix of banking services, both in small and large banking markets. Specifically for Africa, regulation needs to allow for flexibility in remodeling risk-weighted assets, especially where foreign banks dominate; for example, giving project finance a higher risk weight than residential mortgage lending may influence how credit is allocated in the real economy and hence address the issue of making access to finance easier in Africa. African researchers should continue to look into this issue and produce prototype models, information notes, and policy briefs in order to inform the ongoing discussions within the C-10 and the broader international forums.

—Should African central banks jettison (the encumbering) supervisory function or recast it—that is, in the context of table 9-3, where should each country be able to attain effective regulation? In this setting, can governments oversee supervision without interfering with the independence of monetary policy? This is an interesting idea for further research.

—What institutional, political, and legal settings favor effective bank regulation and supervision in Africa? Barth, Caprio and Levine (2006) provides striking evidence from data across the world that strengthening the discretionary powers of prudential supervisors in countries with weak institutional environments leads to a lower level of bank development, greater corruption in lending, and banks that are less safe and sound. The message to policymakers in Africa is that *what is "best practice" for advanced countries may not work for developing countries*. In the African context, following the Basel II recommendation, strengthening of supervisory powers has to be accompanied by substantial progress in institutional development.

—With respect to the structure and dynamics of the interbank market in specific African countries: how does this market work? Barth, Caprio, and Levine (2006) concludes that regulation works best when it facilitates market forces. Hence, the most relevant part of pillar 3 of Basel II for Africa is the interbank market. Bank regulatory policies that enable private markets to better monitor banks and that encourage private actors to "discipline" banks are associated with desirable outcomes: specifically, the interbank market provides the market discipline component of regulation, in addition to its apparent role in managing liquidity and hence monetary policy. Studies that document the microstructure of the interbank market in Africa (for example, nature of participants, prices, quantities, information arrival, transaction costs, and so forth) and how the market is evolving are very timely. Moreover, this market is most strategic in maintaining interbank confidence. One lesson from the financial crisis is that when the interbank market in the United Kingdom and United States went comatose, government intervention could not resuscitate the market.

—What aspects of microprudential and macroprudential regulation work best, separately or jointly, in specific case studies in Africa? Barth, Caprio, and Levine (2006) finds that the number of countries that set up their central banks as the sole bank supervisory agency (sixty-nine) was about the same as the number of those that did not provide the central bank with any supervisory power (sixty-one). Hence, the central bank is not always the supervisory authority. Quasi-autonomous bank regulation and supervision is good for Africa, to minimize the "private interest view" of regulation. Effective bank regulation and supervision should take on the microprudential role, mainly through "market discipline," and the macroprudential role of financial stability to reduce systemic risk through a quasi-government agency. Would this approach resolve the "too big to fail" problem, as many large banks are emerging in large African countries? To be of any value for banks in African economies, a new regulatory regime must encompass this dual role.

—What types of information asymmetry characterize the banking market in Africa? The lesson from Stiglitz (2001) is that the nature of information asymmetries matters; hence there is a role for the public view of regulation. If the agents in the banking market have the same level of information, or "symmetric information," the central bank does not have to intervene in the market. However, in Africa, information asymmetries are more pronounced in specific banking areas, such as microfinance institutions. It is not possible to regulate effectively all microfinance institutions in countries where there are too many; because of that, they pose the greatest prudential risk to their customers, as noted in Brownbridge and Kirkpatrick (2002). Identification of information asymmetries should help in generating a consolidated set of core principles for regulating microfinance institutions, including tools for monitoring unsafe and unsound practices and exit policies.

—Simplicity does it: the "narrow banking" model for Africa? As implied by the Adam Smith dictum, sometimes human nature tends to take very complex models such as Basel II as the most effective when, in fact, what is required is a simple formula. In instances where the banking systems are very simple and basic, why do we need value-at-risk (VaR) models for which we cannot collect the data, let alone run the model competently? The narrow banking model, as explained in Taylor (2009), is likely to keep depositors' funds safely tucked away from rogue traders (those who chase some flattering speculation of extraordinary gain), increase competition, and refocus regulators on protecting retail customers and essential services from the fallout of failures such as those that characterized the outbreak of the global financial crisis. So, essentially, the narrow banking model breaks up the banks into the category of banks that accept retail deposits and access the payment system and the "casino" category for financial markets. More important for Africa, narrow banking might facilitate lending to SMEs.

—The payment systems in Africa comprised the most likely casualty in case of bank contagion during the global financial crisis. The payment systems in most African countries are mainly unregulated and are driven by banks in the OECD whether they use real time gross settlement (RTGS), the batch payment system (for example, BACS), the credit card system (usually VISA and Mastercard), or the cash system. Innovations, such as M-PESA in Kenya, which is a mobile phone–based payment system, should be self-regulated.

—There is also the issue of *contingent funds for future financial crises*. In particular, the issue is that African countries are not in a position to finance large bailout plans in the event of major bank failures. One proposal under discussion is to introduce a financial transactions tax on bank balance sheets in order to build a fund against the contingent liability that could arise when banks fail. The proposal may be appealing to Africa for two reasons. First, for African economies the option of bank bailouts is not only inadequate but also infeasible. Second, Africa recognizes the need to be part of the international harmonization of financial transactions taxation in order to eliminate the possibility of banks getting involved in regulatory arbitrage and tax arbitrage, especially by global banks that are too big to fail and may threaten the stability of banking systems in small economies.

In conclusion, it is useful to highlight at least five main choices for African countries in the Basel III era. First, many African countries have transitioned their regulation from Basel I to Basel II, but post-crisis the countries are stuck at a crossroads. Going back to Basel I is not an option, and there is no point trying to maintain the status quo of Basel II when the quo no longer holds status; moving toward Basel III, albeit cautiously, is therefore the only option that remains. Second, the central banks of African countries must remember that because they were never involved actively in the architecture of Basel III and because Basel III is not a case of "one size fits all," it is imperative to review the Basel III recommendations—primarily in order to decide on the key aspects that must be incorporated in their bank regulatory frameworks. Third, most of the emerging themes for Basel III are merely tangential to the concerns of developing economies. In particular, while there are real concerns with developing risk management frameworks for identifying, measuring, and mitigating potential risks, one key lesson from the failure of Basel I and Basel II in Africa and elsewhere is that the proposed Basel III regime must go beyond market risk concerns: it must represent development-enabling regulation.

For example, in African countries, where microfinance and financing of small and medium enterprises are core activities in efforts to break away from poverty, simple regulatory tools for microfinance banking not only ensure banking stability but also reinforce social protection mechanisms for the poor and vulnerable in the process of economic growth. Fourth, an important cross-cutting element in Basel I, II, and III is capital adequacy. But it is useful to note that many African countries already have exceeded the Basel III enhanced capital requirements by building extra buffers to enable banks withstand financial stress. For this matter, the regulators must observe the possible trade-off between capital adequacy and intermediation, so that any higher capital standards are not achieved at the expense of the lending ability of banks, given the role of loan creation in the growth process. The danger is that banks may move away from growth-enhancing portfolio decisions, such as making loans, to other earning assets, such as government securities. Fifth, African countries should buy into sharing of information and coordinated enforcement of rules to mitigate the specter of regulatory arbitrage—a major occurrence under Basel I and Basel II.

References

Bank for International Settlements (BIS). 2004. *The Implementation of the New Capital Adequacy Framework in Africa.* Basel: Bank for International Settlements.

Barth, J. R., G. Caprio Jr., and R. Levine. 2006. *Rethinking Bank Regulation: Till Angels Govern.* Cambridge University Press.

———. 2004. "Bank Regulation and Supervision: What Works Best?" *Journal of Financial Intermediation,* vol. 12, no. 2: 205–48.

Beck, T., A. Demirgüç-Kunt, and R. Levine. 2006. "Bank Supervision and Corruption in Lending." *Journal of Monetary Economics,* vol. 53, no. 8: 2131–63.

Brownbridge, M., and C. Harvey. 1998. *Banking in Africa: The Impact of Financial Sector Reform since Independence.* Oxford: James Currey Ltd.

Brownbridge, M., and C. Kirkpatrick. 2002. "Financial Regulation and Supervision in Developing Countries: An Overview." *Development Policy Review,* vol. 20, no. 3: 243–45.

Brunnermeier, M., and others. 2009. *The Fundamental Principles of Financial Regulation.* Geneva and London: ICMB and CEPR.

Cornford, A. 2008. "Introduction to Basel 2: The Current State of Play." Paper prepared for the G24 Technical Group Meeting, September 8–9, UN Headquarters, Geneva.

Fleming, A. E., and M. M. Giugale. 2000. *Financial Systems in Transition.* Singapore: World Scientific.

Goodhart, C. A. E. 2008. "The Background to the 2007 Financial Crisis." *International Economics and Economic Policy,* vol. 4, no. 3: 331–46.

Green, C. J., and V. Murinde. 2005. "Flow of Funds: The Relationship between Finance and the Macroeconomy." In *Finance and Development: Surveys of Theory, Evidence, and Policy,* edited by C. J. Green, C. H. Kirkpatrick and V. Murinde. Cheltenham: Edward Elgar.

———. 2004. "Flow of Funds: Implications for Research on Financial Sector Development and the Real Economy." *Journal of International Development,* vol. 15, no. 8: 1015–36.

————. 1998. "Modelling the Macroeconomic Policy Framework for an Emerging Market Economy." *The Manchester School of Economic and Social Studies*, vol. 66, no. 3: 302–30.

Green, C. J., C. Kirkpatrick and V. Murinde. 2005. *Finance and Development: Surveys of Theory, Evidence, and Policy*. Cheltenham: Edward Elgar.

Han, K. C., S. H. Lee, and D. Y. Suk. 2003. "Mexican Peso Crisis and Its Spillover Effects to Emerging Market Debt." *Emerging Markets Review*, vol. 4, no. 3: 310–26.

Hyuha, M., and J. S. Ddumba. 1992. "Financial Decline in Uganda." Paper presented to the Uganda Economics Society, Makerere University, Kampala, November 20.

Jackson, K. D. 1999. *Asian Contagion: The Causes and Consequences of a Financial Crisis*. Boulder, Colo.: Westview Press.

Jefferis, K. 2009. "The New World of Banks, Governments, Regulation, and Supervision: Viewpoints from African Central Banks." Unpublished paper.

Kasekende, L., K. Mlambo, and V. Murinde. 2010. "A Comparative Overview of Bank Regulatory Experiences and Impact on Bank Competition and Intermediation Efficiency in Africa." African Economic Research Consortium, Senior Policy Seminar-XII, Mombasa, March 22–24.

Kay, J. 2009. *Narrow Banking: The Reform of Banking Regulation*. London: CSFI.

Kirkpatrick, C. H., V. Murinde, and M. Tefula. 2008. "The Measurement and Determinants of X-Inefficiency in Commercial Banks in Sub-Saharan Africa." *European Journal of Finance*, vol. 14, no. 7: 625–39.

Klein, L. R. 2000. "Preface." In *Financial Systems in Transition*, edited by A. E. Fleming and M. M. Giugale. Singapore: World Scientific.

Maimbo, S. M. 2002. "The Diagnosis and Prediction of Bank Failures in Zambia, 1990–98." *Development Policy Review*, vol. 20, no. 3: 261–78.

Mizen, P. 2008. "The Credit Crunch of 2007–2008: A Discussion of the Background, Market Reactions, and Policy Responses." *Federal Reserve Bank of St. Louis Review*, vol. 90, no. 5: 531–67.

Moore, T., C. J. Green, and V. Murinde. 2006a. "Financial Reforms and Stochastic Policy Simulations: A Flow-of-Funds Model." *Journal of Policy Modelling*, vol. 28, no. 3: 319–33.

————. 2006b. "Portfolio Behavior in a Flow-of-Funds Model of the Household Sector." *Journal of Development Studies*, vol. 41, no. 4: 675–702.

Sharma, S. 2001. "The Missed Lessons of the Mexican Peso Crisis." *Challenge*, vol. 44, no. 1: 56–89.

Sojli, E. 2007. "Contagion in Emerging Markets: The Russian Crisis." *Applied Financial Economics*, vol. 17, no. 3: 197–213.

Stigler, G. J. 1983. "Nobel Lecture: The Process and Progress of Economics." *Journal of Political Economy*, vol. 91, no. x: 529–45.

Stiglitz, J. E. 2001. "Principles of Financial Regulation: A Dynamic Portfolio Approach." *World Bank Research Observer*, vol. 16, no. 1: 1–18.

Taylor, M. W. 2009. *Twin Peaks Revisited: A Second Chance for Regulatory Reform*. London: CSFI.

PART **III**

The G20 Framework:
Rebalancing the Global Economy

10

Global Imbalances and the G20

KEMAL DERVIŞ

There is a new argument that the Great Depression was partly triggered by the Bank of France buying and hoarding huge amounts of gold.[1] Whatever its merits, this explanation draws attention to the fact that behavior determining the levels of foreign exchange reserves and current account and trade surpluses is at the heart of international macroeconomic interdependence. In 1944, Keynes, thinking of the international monetary system to emerge in the postwar period, held firmly to the opinion that countries with current account surpluses should be asked to adjust as much as countries with current account deficits. In practice, that has never been the case. One reason is, of course, that running out of foreign exchange reserves is a much more immediately threatening predicament than having an overflow of them is.

True, a country could let its exchange rate depreciate, but because of balance sheet effects—the fact that parts of the banking and corporate sector will have more liabilities than assets denominated in foreign exchange—and the decline in purchasing power due to the higher domestic price of imports, a loss in the value of a currency imposes more immediate costs on a country than an appreciation. So adjustment incentives are asymmetric. Countries with increasing current account deficits are usually forced to adjust by restricting domestic demand, while surplus countries are not forced to pursue expansionary domestic policies to reduce their surplus. Of course if reserves are not sterilized, there will be an

1. See Irwin (2010).

expansion of the money supply, but reserves can be sterilized and surpluses can perpetuate themselves for a long time without leading to domestic price increases and real appreciations that would eliminate the surpluses.

Global current account imbalances have been central to the debates surrounding the G20 process and to the leaders (L20) meetings themselves. The fact that some key current account imbalances increased substantially during the run-up to the crisis was an obvious trigger of the debate. The Chinese surplus and the U.S. deficit reached record levels in the 2005–07 period. Beyond those statistical facts, there are two underlying reasons for the emphasis on and concern about global imbalances.

First, many observers view the large inflow of liquidity that financed the current account deficit of the United States in the pre-crisis years as a key cause for the excessive leverage and risk taking that increasingly characterized the American financial sector. Many see a strong link between those large capital inflows and the extraordinary expansion of balance sheets in the financial sector as well as the development of the new "off–balance sheet" shadow banking system.[2] Without all that liquidity, risk taking and leverage would not have been so easy and the build-up of problems in the financial sector would have taken more time, perhaps allowing regulators a better opportunity to catch up with what was going on and intervene before it was too late.

Second, increasing trade deficits are a channel through which fiscal stimulus undertaken by one country can leak across borders to stimulate demand elsewhere rather than at home. In the global setting, when fighting recession or even depression is a priority, a kind of prisoner's dilemma and free-rider problem affect fiscal policy. It is in the interest of an individual country to have other large countries engage in fiscal stimulus—thereby creating demand for its own exports, which leads to greater production at home—while not itself incurring the longer-term cost of a larger burden of public debt. At the onset of the worldwide recession, there was a danger that major countries would wait for others to stimulate demand, protecting their own fiscal position while hoping to benefit from the expansionary policies of others. That was, in fact, the situation in the winter and early spring of 2009, when the world economy had hit rock bottom and when there was an urgent need to inject demand into the world economy. The London meeting of the L20 and the preparations that led to it can rightfully be credited with having made a key contribution to overcoming the free-rider problem and having facilitated a more coordinated and global fiscal expansion, with countries such as Japan and Germany, reluctant at first, joining the United States and China in what ended up as a simultaneous and strong worldwide expansionary fiscal policy.

2. See, for example, Brender and Pisani (2010) for a well-articulated version of this view.

There are, of course, other reasons for and benefits of global policy coordination—for example, the benefits from some degree of harmonization of financial sector prudential regulations and supervision. But the global imbalances debate has been closely linked to the interaction of liquidity flows into the United States and the leverage buildup there and, even more, to the need for global fiscal policy coordination. The latter has now entered a new phase, in which the increasing debt burdens in many advanced countries are focusing attention on the need for a gradual but differentiated fiscal retreat. Those that do have fiscal space should not retreat early or by too much, making it easier for those that are truly and immediately threatened by public debt concerns to adjust without devastating consequences on output and employment.

The Seoul summit faced a fiscal coordination challenge that is comparable in magnitude to that of the London summit. While the threat of an outright worldwide depression that existed at the time of the London summit has receded, thanks in part to the policies facilitated by the London summit, the threat today is that the recovery will lose steam and unemployment will remain stubbornly high in many countries. Moreover, a threat that was not strongly perceived at the London summit—and not even at the Pittsburgh summit—has added itself to the threat of prolonged recession in the advanced countries: the threat of rapidly climbing public debt to GDP ratios in many advanced countries and the risk of sovereign debt default in a few of them. Fiscal policies and their interdependence—which arises from the leakages from or complements to domestic effective demand that trade and current accounts balances represent—therefore are at center stage in the G-20 process.

Views on the Nature of Global Imbalances

While global imbalances have been a key topic for economists and policymakers in recent years, reflecting the unprecedented expansion of imbalances in the pre-crisis years, there are different appreciations of their fundamental long-term role in the world economy. Some economists emphasize that globalization of the world economy should be expected to lead to a reduction of "home bias" in the allocation of savings, with asset holders diversifying their portfolios across increasingly open national borders. This view of global capital flows emphasizes that there is no particular reason why net capital flows should be close to zero and, by implication, why current accounts should be in balance. Capital will and should flow from lower-return areas toward higher-return areas and from areas where savings are plentiful toward areas where savings are scarcer. According to that view, imbalances reflect a more efficient worldwide allocation of capital.[3]

3. See, for example, Greenspan (2007).

The opposite view is that global imbalances reflect not the unfettered and efficient working of global financial markets but both excessive precautionary demand for reserves and a mercantilist growth strategy by some emerging market economies. As countries try to self-insure against the type of private capital flow reversals experienced by many, for example, during the Asian financial crisis of the late 1990s, they run large current account surpluses to accumulate foreign exchange reserves. Many of the same countries also want to use net foreign demand in the form of an export surplus to add to their own domestic effective demand in order to boost their growth performance and accelerate domestic job creation. When these macroeconomic motives and policies are driving the sign and size of current accounts, capital may well flow in directions not determined primarily by relative real returns at the project level.

It would seem that during the past decade at least, the second view of current account determination explains most of the developments observed. Real returns to investment in China, for example, remained high, and yet China ran a very high current account surplus.[4] Much of the counterpart of the current account surplus came in the form of official reserve accumulations rather than in the form of private capital movements. In fact, China imports net private capital, as should be expected given the high returns available, but those imports have been more than compensated for by reserve accumulation. Official precautionary and mercantilist motives also explain current account behavior in much of the rest of Asia and, to a lesser degree, in other emerging market economies.

That does not mean, of course, that the view that globalization is likely to lead to a reduction of home bias in asset allocation is invalid. This consequence of globalization is likely to become more visible over the long run, just as globalization has led to an increasing share of trade in GDP. Developments so far, however, have been driven at least as much by official macroeconomic policy objectives as by purely private asset allocation decisions. It is those policy objectives and the manner in which they are being pursued that will be at the heart of the G20 process.

Rebalancing in the Global Context

At the time of the London and Pittsburgh summits in 2009, the main challenge appeared to be to ensure that a coordinated expansion of fiscal policies took place, of a size sufficient to compensate for the collapse in private demand triggered by the financial panic and coordinated enough that the countries that expanded would not face leakages abroad that would frustrate their efforts. The world went into the crisis with a very large U.S. current account deficit; large

---

4. On returns to capital in China, see Bai, Hsieh, and Qian (2006).

deficits in some smaller economies, such as Spain; and very large surpluses in China, Germany, some of the oil exporters and, to a lesser degree, Japan. But what appeared desirable, given the threat of a real global economic collapse, was an overall fiscal expansion, including in the United States despite its existing current account deficit. Within the framework of such an overall fiscal expansion, it was desirable that the "dosages" encourage a post-crisis rebalancing of the world economy. The argument was that if macroeconomic policy in the United States were to be more expansionary than the policy mix in the substantial surplus countries, imbalances in current accounts would rise further, leading to potential future instability. If, on the contrary, surplus countries expanded more strongly than deficit countries, there would be greater overall stability and better global growth performance.

The situation in the fall of 2010 was somewhat different. The imminent threat of a global economic collapse had receded. On the other hand, it is clear that in the advanced countries, recovery is not ensured. The emerging markets are so far maintaining strong growth performance, but there is little doubt that a persistent slowdown in the advanced economies will impact that performance.[5] Moreover, particularly after the Greek crisis, a lot of attention has focused on the public debt dynamics in the advanced economies, with a difficult dilemma having developed between the need to protect the recovery and the need to slow down or reverse increasing ratios of public debt to GDP. The global "balancing" problem for Seoul did not come in the form of a question of how much each country should expand its fiscal policy, as it did in London. Several questions have now arisen. Who can afford to and should maintain an expansionary stance and for how long? Who should reverse gears and by how much? What do such differentiated adjustments imply for the structure of current account balances that G20 policymakers should try to target?

Moreover, at a deeper level, the question of the efficacy of fiscal policy also is arising. Conventional wisdom seems to recommend a continuation of short-term expansion accompanied by announcements of medium-term consolidation, particularly in the world's largest economy, the United States.[6] But there are issues with this "sequencing" approach. Economic actors will react, to a large degree at least, to the entire dynamic fiscal package that they expect. In the United States, for example, a prolongation of the tax cuts enacted in 2001 and 2003 will be evaluated with other changes in tax policy, including an announcement that taxes will be raised in one or two years, at least if that announcement is credible. To what extent announced future policy changes impact today's behavior may be debatable, but once the question is posed in that way, most

5. On this, see the IMF's most recent *World Economic Outlook* (www.imf.org).
6. See, for example, Blanchard and Cottarelli (2010).

agree that expectations about the future will have some impact and that therefore it is not so easy for fiscal policy to follow a short-term expansionary impulse
and at the same time establish medium-term consolidation.[7]

Global Rebalancing

First, it is important not to reduce the global rebalancing problem entirely to a
problem between the United States and China. The U.S. deficit and the Chinese
surplus are no doubt very important when it comes to analyzing the structure of
demand in the world economy. Given the need for the household sector in the
United States to deleverage and to increase its very low saving rate, a reduction
in the U.S. deficit should be a medium-term objective, since U.S. public sector deficits will also have to decline for debt management and fiscal reasons. A
decline in U.S. net imports will subtract from world aggregate demand, and the
world thus needs a source of net demand expansion elsewhere. China is an obvious candidate because its trade and current account surplus has been large and
because it has been encouraged by government policies such as reserve accumulation and policies favoring corporate profits as well as private savings.

It would not be constructive and realistic, however, to focus all the attention
on China, first because the Chinese growth model cannot change overnight, nor
should it. While very competitive Chinese exports, benefiting from the low value
of the yuan, pose a challenge to many competitors, Chinese growth has also
been beneficial for the world economy, creating a strong demand for machinery
and commodity exports from other countries. A very sudden and large appreciation of the Chinese currency could create large excess capacity in the Chinese
tradable sector, reduce employment, and cause a substantial slowdown in the
Chinese growth rate.[8] That would not be in the interest of world growth. Second, there are significant surpluses elsewhere. Japan has been running a consistent surplus over many years, and so do some other East Asian countries. The oil
producers run large surpluses most of the time. And, last but not least, Germany
has been running an important surplus.

The most desirable "rebalancing" would therefore be one whereby, over the
2011–12 period, the U.S. deficit declines to 2 or 3 percent of U.S. GDP; the

---

7. For a recent analysis of fiscal policy in a dynamic context, see Leeper (2010). The study was
written within a strong "rational expectations" theoretical framework—a framework that is less
convincing after the great crisis of 2008 than it seemed before—but it does provide a strong argument that rather than annual budgets alone, it is the "path" of fiscal policy over time, at least over
the near term, that is likely to determine behavior.

8. For an analysis of how past appreciations have affected growth rates in a large sample of
economies, see IMF (2010a).

Chinese surplus declines from its record pre-crisis level of close to 10 percent of GDP to 4 or 5 percent of GDP; the Gulf oil exporters run a surplus in the range of 6 to 8 percent of GDP, not more; and Germany reduces its surplus to less than 2 percent of GDP. In addition, the developing countries, most of which are still in great need of capital and many of which have reduced their foreign debt to quite manageable levels in relation to their GDP and exports, should and could import more capital, running somewhat larger current account deficits, in many cases on the order of 3 or 4 percent of GDP.[9]

The G20 should encourage such a "gentle and global" rebalancing. It requires coordination of macroeconomic policies of all systemically important countries within the framework of the "strong, sustainable, and balanced growth" objective and the "mutual assessment process" as well as measures to protect the developing and emerging market economies from the excessive capital volatility of the past and the "sudden stop" crises, which had huge social, economic, and political costs.[10] It is only by providing developing countries with accessible precautionary finance from the International Monetary Fund and stable long-term capital flows from the development banks that the desire to accumulate excessive reserves and the mercantilist tendencies observed in the past decade can be moderated. The new package of IMF financial instruments adopted recently by the IMF board is a big step in that direction, as it expands access to precautionary finance.[11] Long-term net lending from the development banks remains wholly inadequate, however, despite a significant increase during the crisis, as capital increases have been very timid.[12] The G20 should bless the new financial instruments of the IMF, recommend their effective use, and work toward a further increase in the size of the IMF, ideally through another allocation of special drawing rights (SDRs). But it should also decide to review again the lending capacity of the development banks and open the way for further increases in their capital, with contributions that reflect the new realities of the world economy, not just past ratios. Such support for the Bretton Woods institutions and their regional counterparts is an essential instrument for global rebalancing. An expanded and proactive role of

9. For an early scenario along those lines, see my Per Jacobbsen lecture given at the annual meetings of the IMF and the World Bank in Istanbul in October 2009 (Derviş 2009).

10. On the costs of capital flow volatility and crisis, see, for example, Griffith-Jones, Ocampo, and Stiglitz (2010).

11. See IMF (2010b) for the description of the expanded flexible credit line (FCL) and the new precautionary credit line (PCL).

12. Net lending of the development banks is projected to be below 5 percent of total net flows to developing countries. World Bank, *Global Economic Prospects*, June 2010 (http://go.worldbank. org/OE8NEB3JP0).

the Bretton Woods institutions will also require real progress and "rebalancing" in their governance structures.[13]

To some limited degree the scenario described above seems to be unfolding. The Chinese surplus, after a steep decline in 2009, is likely to be at less than half of its record pre-crisis high in 2010. The surpluses of the oil exporters have also declined. The German surplus remains large, although there are signs of stronger import growth in Germany too. In some developing countries such as Brazil, which was not a net importer of capital before the crisis, a substantial current account deficit has appeared. The Indian current account deficit has also grown from very small to moderate. The U.S. current account deficit has declined, although not by as much as was expected, and the decline is taking place in the context of a weaker economy. If the economy were to pick up, as one hopes, the U.S. current account deficit could increase rapidly again (see table 10-1). These developments point to a fragile and insufficient rebalancing in need of support from coordinated actions and policies by the G20 countries.

The Public Debt Challenge

Another, related area that presents a key challenge but also an opportunity for the G-20 process is the search for the most desirable public debt management policies. Fiscal policies have spillover effects in the context of current accounts and global rebalancing, as discussed. They also have spillover effects and present the risk of contagion in the context of sovereign debt concerns. The world experienced such contagion in the context of the Greek debt crisis in the spring of 2010. The revelation that Greece's fiscal deficit was much higher than the government previously reported focused attention on Greek public debt dynamics, which spread to concern over Portuguese, Irish, Spanish, and even Italian debt, sending sovereign risk spreads for these countries soaring and even raising doubts about the survival of the euro. This illustrated how concern over one country's public debt can spread and cause as general crisis, including another banking crisis, as sovereign bonds have an important place in the assets of many financial institutions.

This "externality" relating to fiscal policies that should be of concern to the G-20 is the mirror image of the free-rider problem that was so prominent in London. Then, there was the danger of not enough countries participating in a global fiscal expansion. Today, given the generalized worries about public debt dynamics and the shift in the political atmosphere, particularly in the United

---

13. The latest initiative by the United States to encourage a reorganization of constituencies and a more balanced representation of various regions and groups of countries on the IMF Board of Governors should be welcomed by the developing countries. Also see Eichengreen (2004) on the "new Bretton Woods" and its role in global imbalances.

Table 10-1. *Current Account Balances and Projections*[a]

Billions of U.S. dollars

Economy	Current account balances							
	2008	2009	2010	2011	2012	2013	2014	2015
Emerging Asia	527	453	399	444	500	598	726	887
China	436	297	270	325	394	494	621	778
India	−25	−36	−44	−50	−54	−53	−53	−53
GCC	257	75	101	124	140	153	169	187
Japan	157	142	166	133	135	130	126	122
United States	−669	−378	−467	−400	−420	−466	−524	−602
Euro area	−101	−51	21	57	56	56	46	23
Other advanced economies	30	51	82	45	35	37	45	45
Other EMDEV economies	6	−52	−56	−106	−134	−139	−137	−160
World (error)	211	217	202	297	310	369	442	489
Memo item								
Germany	246	163	200	196	182	173	161	145
Russia	104	50	70	62	47	44	37	33
Spain	−156	−81	−72	−65	−64	−62	−63	−66
United Kingdom	−44	−24	−50	−49	−45	−36	−32	−32

Source: International Monetary Fund, *World Economic Outlook,* October 2010 (www.imf.org).

a. Emerging Asia includes China, Hong Kong, India, Indonesia, Republic of Korea, Malaysia, Singapore, Taiwan, Thailand, and Vietnam; GCC (Gulf Cooperation Council) includes Kuwait, Oman, Qatar, Saudi Arabia, and United Arab Emirates; other advanced economies include those classified as such by the IMF; and EMDEV (emerging and developing) economies include newly industrialized Asian economies (Hong Kong, Korea, Singapore, and Taiwan).

States, there is the danger of a generalized fiscal contraction, despite high unemployment, leading to a further slowdown in the pace of the recovery in the advanced countries.

There should be, of course, serious concern about public debt dynamics, which have already added close to 20 percentage points to the ratios of public debt to GDP in many advanced countries over the last few years and which could send debt-to-GDP ratios to levels that surely would put serious upward pressure on public borrowing costs and crowd out private investment (see table 10-2). But there is huge diversity in the fiscal space of countries in the G20 group and more generally across the world. China continues to have a strong fiscal position, as does Korea. Some of the other emerging countries have to

Table 10-2. *General Government Debt and Projections*[a]

Percent of GDP

Economy	2007	2008	2009	2010	2011	2014	2015
Advanced economies (average)	72.9	78.7	90.6	97.8	102.0	108.6	110.2
Canada	65.0	69.7	82.5	83.3	82.0	74.2	71.2
France	63.8	67.5	77.4	84.2	88.6	94.3	94.8
Germany	65.0	65.9	72.5	76.7	79.6	82.0	81.5
Greece	95.6	99.2	115.1	133.2	145.2	146.1	140.4
Italy	103.4	106.0	115.8	118.6	120.5	123.9	124.7
Japan	187.7	194.7	217.7	227.1	234.6	247.7	250.0
Portugal	63.6	66.3	77.1	86.6	91.8	97.1	98.4
Spain	36.1	39.7	55.2	66.9	75.6	89.8	94.4
UK	44.1	52.0	68.2	78.2	84.9	90.7	90.6
US	62.1	70.6	83.2	92.6	97.4	106.4	109.7
Emerging and developing economies (average)	36.9	35.2	38.0	38.0	37.6	35.7	34.2
Brazil	65.2	64.1	68.9	67.2	65.1	58.9	54.1
China	20.5	16.8	18.9	20.0	19.8	19.7	17.5
India	79.2	77.0	80.8	79.0	77.8	70.3	67.3
Mexico	38.2	43.3	44.9	44.5	44.1	42.4	42.4
Russia	8.5	7.9	9.0	8.1	9.1	10.0	13.0
Turkey	39.4	39.5	45.5	44.5	44.3	43.9	43.5

Source: International Monetary Fund, *Fiscal Monitor*, May 2010 (www.imf.org).

a. Gross debt as a percent of GDP; advanced and emerging and developing economies include those classified as such by the IMF.

be more careful about their debt dynamics, but most of them are not facing an immediate public debt threat. Among the advanced countries, on which concern is focused, there is great variation. Germany, for example, has more fiscal space than Italy. Outside the G20, Greece, Portugal, and Ireland clearly have acute problems, and while those economies are small, sovereign default concerns about them could create serious contagion, as we saw in the spring of 2010. Ten-year sovereign swap spreads differ by many hundreds of basis points, with the spreads for Greece, Ireland, and Portugal in an 8 to 10 percent crisis range. Germany, the United States, Japan, and the Netherlands, on the other hand, can borrow at record low cost.[14]

14. See Blanchard (2010).

This diversity in fiscal space requires a differentiated approach to fiscal consolidation over time. The worst scenario would be to undertake an abrupt global retrenchment in a herd-like fashion. Instead, what the G-20 should achieve is a carefully calibrated package of fiscal policies, differentiated by country and mindful of the fragile nature of the recovery and the stubborn unemployment problem.[15] The relative success achieved in London when countries committed themselves to a broad fiscal expansion must be followed by a commitment to careful, moderate, and differentiated consolidation.

Conclusion

In conclusion, two additional points deserve emphasis. First, it is going to be important to look at fiscal policies as packages of revenue and expenditure measures as well as at structural reforms in a dynamic setting. Communities, citizens, economic actors, and markets will react to the packages, not to individual measures. The "timing" discussion sometimes appears to imply that if government cuts taxes today and announces that it will raise them next year, consumers (and investors) will spend more today and spend less next year. Instead, most consumers will look at the announced path of taxes, at least in the near term, and try to adjust to that path. If the tax increases announced for next year outweigh the immediate tax decreases, consumers will restrict their spending immediately. One does not have to be a strong believer in Ricardian equivalence or in the rational expectations model of economic behavior to think that, at least over a horizon of a few years, economic actors will consider the likely path of fiscal policy and adjust to that path, rather than behave year by year looking only at policies in effect in the current year. The motto "stimulate now, consolidate tomorrow" therefore is somewhat misleading.

The real challenge is for each country to choose a dynamic fiscal package that reflects national circumstances, including longer-term structural measures, but then for the G-20 to calibrate the national dynamic approaches into an appropriate global package that takes into account the externalities and spillover effects. Doing so can only be a process, and the Seoul summit could not "solve" the problem in one stroke. Dynamic calibration will be difficult to achieve, and it may require a more careful look at the distribution of income too, which in some countries has become massively concentrated at the top, posing structural challenges to sustainable and broad-based growth in effective demand.[16] Nonetheless, the G-20 process will be judged a major success in the future if it can

15. On this, see also IMF and ILO (2010).
16. On income distribution issues and their potential interaction with macroeconomic policy challenges, see IMF and ILO (2010) as well as Rajan (2010).

help get the world a step closer to such an approach, which would anchor expectations, avoid panic, continue to support recovery, and yet encourage a gradual shift back to private demand as the key driver of growth.

Second, as the discussion above indicates, the coordination challenge goes beyond the G20 group as such. What happens in Greece or Ireland has systemic effects, despite the small size of those economies. That is another reason why the G20 process should be one that strengthens and energizes overall multilateral cooperation within the IMF and the other multilateral organizations, not one that replaces multilateralism. The G20 countries represent a huge part of the world's GDP and population. They can reach agreement and take initiatives that will have a determining influence on the world economy. But countries outside the G20 also are full members of the international community, and some of them can have systemic impact. On macroeconomic issues, the IMF, with its nearly universal membership, will be critical in helping structure and implement international economic cooperation. For it to be able to do that, the governance reforms and governance "rebalancing" that are under way have great urgency.

References

Bai, Chong-En, Chang-Tia Hsieh, and Yingyi Qian. 2006. "The Return to Capital in China." *Brookings Papers on Economic Activity* (Fall): 61–88.
Blanchard, Olivier. 2010. Keynote address at "Prospects and Dangers for the Global Economy." Georgetown Center for Business and Public Policy, Georgetown University, September 23 (http://cbpp.georgetown.edu/118171.html).
Blanchard, Olivier, and Carlo Cottarelli. 2010. "The Great False Choice: Stimulus or Austerity." *Financial Times*, August 11 (www.ft.com/cms/s/0/ea8e8acc-a57b-11df-a5b7-00144feabdc0,s01=1.html).
Brender, Anton, and Florence Pisani. 2010. *Global Imbalances and the Collapse of Globalised Finance*. Brussels: Center for European Policy Studies.
Derviş, Kemal. 2009. "Growth after the Storm." Per Jacobsson lecture, delivered at the Annual Meetings of the IMF and the World Bank, Istanbul (www.brookings.edu/speeches/2009/1004_global_economy_dervis.aspx).
Eichengreen, Barry. 2004. "Global Imbalances and the Lessons of Bretton Woods." *Economie Internationale* 100: 39–50.
Greenspan, Alan. 2007. "Balance of Payments Imbalances." Per Jacobsson lecture, delivered at the Annual Meetings of the IMF and the World Bank, Washington, October 21, 2007 (www.perjacobsson.org/lectures/102107.pdf).
Griffith-Jones, Stephany, José Antonio Ocampo, and Joseph E. Stiglitz. 2010. *Time for a Visible Hand*. Oxford University Press.
International Monetary Fund (IMF). 2010a. "Rebalancing Growth." *World Economic Outlook*. April.
———. 2010b. "IMF Enhances Crisis Prevention Toolkit." Press release no. 10/321. August 30 (www.imf.org/external/np/sec/pr/2010/pr10321.htm).

International Monetary Fund (IMF) and International Labor Organization (ILO). 2010. "The Challenges of Growth, Employment, and Social Cohesion." Discussion document for joint ILO-IMF conference held in cooperation with the Office of the Prime Minister of Norway, Oslo, September 13 (www.osloconference2010.org/discussion paper.pdf).

Irwin, Douglas A. 2010. "Did France Cause the Great Depression?" Working Paper 16350. Cambridge, Mass.: National Bureau of Economic Research.

Leeper, Eric M. 2010. "Monetary Science, Fiscal Alchemy." Paper prepared for the Federal Reserve Bank of Kansas City's Jackson Hole Symposium, *Macroeconomic Policy: Post-Crisis and Risks Ahead*, Jackson Hole, Wyoming, August 26–28 (www.kansas cityfed.org/publicat/sympos/2010/2010-08-16-leeper-paper.pdf).

Rajan, Raghuram. 2010. *Fault Lines: How Hidden Fractures Still Threaten the World Economy*. Princeton University Press.

11

The Political Economy of Global Rebalancing and the Role of Structural Reforms

PIER CARLO PADOAN

As the global crisis moves away from its immediate, emergency phase, the international community is turning to longer-term issues. The challenge is to build a global policy framework that can maximize the benefits of international collective action and put the global economy on the path to stronger and more sustainable and balanced growth. This challenge presents two, interrelated aspects: an economic one, which consists of identifying the policy mix at the global and national levels that is needed to move toward the "optimal scenario" of stronger and more sustainable and balanced growth, and a political economy one, which would facilitate and strengthen the incentives for countries to take the policy actions that lead to the optimal outcome. This chapter looks at both aspects and explores in particular the role that structural reforms can play in achieving the optimal scenario in both advanced and emerging market economies.

The Economics of the Framework

The purpose of the G20 framework is to achieve growth that is strong, sustainable (fiscally, environmentally, and socially), and balanced (with respect to external current account position) through a combination of macroeconomic,

The opinions and analysis reported in this paper are my own and do not necessarily reflect those of the OECD or its member countries.

exchange rate, and structural policies. It takes into account that different country groups have different policy priorities, which reflect both different national preferences and the different positions of their national economies vis-à-vis the global system. From this point of view, the G20 countries are classified in the following four groups: advanced economies, emerging market economies, countries having a current account surplus, and countries having a current account deficit. This classification leads to the identification of different policy packages for countries belonging to the different groups that, if adopted, would lead the global economy to an optimal scenario—one that is superior in terms of growth, employment, and fiscal and external sustainability to a scenario in which national policies do not take into account spillover effects on other countries.

Simulations by the IMF (with OECD inputs) identify such an upside scenario as part of the mutual assessment process that underpins the G20 framework for growth. Simulations by OECD support this result (see figure 11-1). In the upside scenario, different policy actions tend to reinforce each other. As an illustration, consider that in the OECD scenario analysis the fiscal consolidation required to stabilize debt-to-GDP ratios in OECD countries would reduce the size of global imbalances—measured as the GDP-weighted sum of countries' absolute saving-investment gaps (in relation to GDP)—by about one-fifth. If, in addition, surplus countries, both advanced and emerging, were to deregulate their product markets and China were to raise public health spending by 2 percentage points of GDP (without taking any offsetting budget measures) and deregulate its financial market, global imbalances would decline by twice as much. On the other hand, while fiscal tightening would also contribute to a narrowing of intra–Euro area imbalances, the size of the effect would be more muted. Reducing employment protections in Spain, Portugal, and Greece would only slightly reduce the overall size of intra–Euro area imbalances, although the saving-investment gaps of the three countries would narrow considerably. In what follows, I concentrate on the role that structural policies can play in moving toward the optimal scenario. Structural reforms can improve the collective policy outcome through their impact on growth, fiscal consolidation, and current account imbalances (through the saving-investment gap).

Impacts of Structural Reforms on Potential Output

OECD analysis of the impact of structural reform on potential output—through labor productivity and utilization (average hours worked and employment)—has focused on a number of policy areas, including product and labor market regulations, tax policy, and human capital.[1] These areas have featured prominently

---

1. This section is based on de Mello and Padoan (2010a).

Figure 11-1. *Alternative Scenarios Illustrating Growth, Debt, and Imbalances*

Policy simulations (2016–25 average)

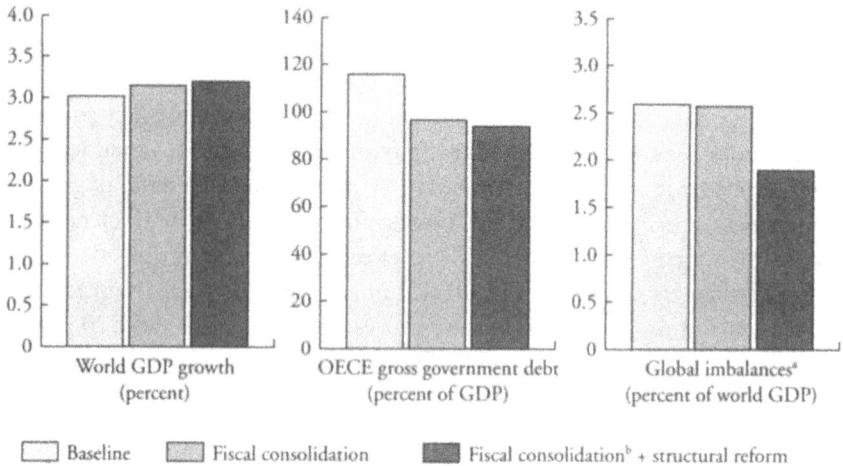

Source: OECD, *Economic Outlook*, no. 87 (May 2010).

a. A summary measure of global current account imbalances is constructed as the absolute sum of current balances in each of the main trading countries or regions.

b. Fiscal consolidation including exchange rate response.

among the structural priorities identified in *Going for Growth*, the OECD flagship publication on structural policy surveillance—which now includes Brazil, China, India, Indonesia, and South Africa—since it was launched in 2005. Because actions in different policy domains are interconnected and often mutually reinforcing, policy initiatives to raise labor productivity will also likely have an influence on utilization, and vice versa.

The impact of different structural policies on GDP per capita can be gauged by using simulated "multipliers" for the average OECD country (table 11-1). The multipliers can be reported for unit changes in different policy items, such as a reduction in the average replacement rate of unemployment benefits by 10 percentage points, and for one-standard-deviation changes in policies to allow for comparability across policy instruments. The multipliers can also be simulated over a ten-year period and at steady state to shed light on the time horizon required for different reforms to come to fruition.

On the basis of the simulated multipliers, it appears that the policy levers that are most effective in raising GDP per capita in the long term are related to education, particularly reforms aimed at lifting the average number of years of education of the adult population and improving the academic performance of

Table 11-1. *Average Effects of Unit Reforms on GDP per Capita Average across OECD countries*

Percent change

Reform	Definition of "unit" shock	OECD average	OECD standard deviation	Simulated effect (unit changes)		Simulated effect (one-standard deviation changes)	
				After 10 years	Steady state	After 10 years	Steady state
Labor market policies							
Average replacement rate	−10 ppt.[a]	27.2	11.0	1.9	3.0	2.0	3.2
Employment protection legislation (EPL)	−1 index point	2.2	0.8	0.3	0.4	0.2	0.3
Maternal leave weeks	+10 weeks	27.0	20.5	0.1	0.2	0.2	0.3
Childcare benefits	−0.1 ppt.	0.6	0.1	0.0	0.0	0.0	0.0
Childcare support	+0.1 ppt.	0.6	0.1	0.0	0.0	0.0	0.0
Standard retirement age	+1 year	64.3	2.3	0.2	0.3	0.3	0.6
Implicit tax on con-tinued work	−10 ppt.	26.9	19.9	0.2	0.4	0.4	0.8
Average weekly normal hours and overtime	+1 hour	44.3	4.7	0.1	0.1	0.4	0.4
Taxation							
Average tax wedge	−10 ppt.	30.0	9.9	3.3	5.2	3.1	5.0
Marginal tax	−10 ppt.	32.4	9.5	1.1	1.1	1.1	1.1
Product market regulation							
Gas	−0.1 index point	3.3	1.1	0.1	0.1	1.1	1.0
Electricity	−0.1 index point	1.8	1.3	0.1	0.1	1.0	1.2
Road	−0.1 index point	1.6	1.4	0.1	0.1	1.5	1.3
Rail	−0.1 index point	3.6	1.5	0.1	0.1	1.5	1.4
Air	−0.1 index point	2.0	1.6	0.1	0.1	1.7	1.5
Post	−0.1 index point	3.0	0.5	0.1	0.1	0.4	0.4
Telecommunications	−0.1 index point	1.6	0.9	0.1	0.1	0.9	0.9
Overall	−0.1 index point	2.5	0.8	0.73	0.67	5.7	5.1
Human capital							
PISA score	+10 points	496	21.4[b]	0.1	2.0	0.3	4.1
Average years of schooling (16–24 cohort)	+1 year	12.6	1.0	0.6	8.1	0.6	8.3

Source: Sebastian Barnes and others, "The GDP Impact of Reform: A Simple Simulation Frame-work," OECD, January 18, 2011 (www.oecd.org/officialdocuments/publicdisplaydocumentpdf/?cote=ECO/WKP(2011)3&docLanguage=En).

a. ppt. = percentage point.
b. Excluding Mexico and Turkey.

high school students, as measured by PISA scores of fifteen-year-olds. In addition, steady state effects are strong for reform of tax systems (a cut in average tax rates), employment protection legislation (a reduction in average unemployment benefit replacement rates), and enactment of pro-competition regulations in product markets. Other reforms, such as raising the standard retirement age, reducing the implicit tax on continued work at older ages, and cutting marginal tax wedges, can also have a significant growth dividend.

The time that it takes to reach the steady state differs across policy areas. Labor market and tax reforms are assumed to work relatively fast, especially reforms affecting hours worked. By contrast, productivity-enhancing reforms converge toward steady state productivity levels at a slower pace. Although human capital reforms have a strong steady state effect on GDP per capita, these reforms take a long time—around fifty years—to become effective for all cohorts and even longer to have their full effects on GDP per capita.

Structural Reforms and Fiscal Consolidation

The structural reforms recommended in *Going for Growth* are directed at improving long-term levels of GDP per capita.[2] However, while many of the reforms can be implemented in a fiscally neutral manner, most have important side effects that could improve or worsen fiscal balances. This is of particular importance given the large post-crisis fiscal deficits. Against that background, this section examines the extent to which various structural reforms to boost long-term output may have co-benefits for public budgets.

Efforts to consolidate the public finances can be aided in many cases by implementation of structural reforms. Historical experience suggests that fiscal consolidation is more likely to be achieved through cuts in spending than by raising taxes, possibly because consolidation demonstrates commitment and strengthens the credibility of the consolidation strategy.[3] Also of relevance for the role of structural reform in fiscal consolidation are structural measures that raise potential output through higher labor utilization, which are likely to contribute more to fiscal consolidation than measures that work through the productivity channel. On the expenditure side, higher employment is often associated with lower public spending on benefits, while such benefits generally adjust to productivity gains.

Overall, six stylized categories of structural reforms can be distinguished depending on their effect on fiscal positions—positive (directly or indirectly) or negative—and on whether they boost long-term GDP per capita by raising

2. This section is based on OECD (2010).
3. See, for example, Alesina and Ardagna (2009) and Guichard and others (2007).

employment or productivity (table 11-2).[4] Four of the categories could contribute to both raising long-term living standards and consolidating public budgets. These include reforms that would enhance fiscal positions either directly, by reducing public spending, or indirectly, by gradually increasing tax receipts through higher productivity and, especially, higher employment.

Global Imbalances

Global imbalances, measured as the sum in absolute terms of the current account positions of the world's major countries and regions, nearly halved in the aftermath of the global crisis after reaching a post–World War II high of over 5 percent of world GDP in 2008.[5] But they are widening again, as the world economy recovers from the post-crisis recession and output gaps close. Large global imbalances are not necessarily undesirable, to the extent that they reflect increased financial integration and a more efficient allocation of global savings across countries. But past experience shows that current account reversals following rising global imbalances can be sizable. Structural reforms can significantly mitigate the size of global imbalances and make them more sustainable.

Ongoing OECD analysis shows that structural policies can influence the saving and investment decisions of firms and households—and hence the current account balance—through a variety of different channels.[6] To the extent that households attempt to smooth consumption over time, any reform that temporarily affects the growth of income or the real rate of interest should temporarily influence the saving rate of households. Moreover, policies may affect the precautionary saving behavior of households by altering the level of uncertainty that they face and the mechanisms that they have at their disposal to insure themselves against adverse events. The investment rate, in turn, should be influenced by all policies that affect the cost of capital and/or the return on investment projects. Due to the wide range of different channels and the complex interactions among them, the sign and the size of the link between structural policies and saving and investment remain largely an empirical question.

Empirically, saving and investment rates are significantly influenced by macroeconomic conditions, many of which are affected by structural policy settings. In particular, policies that foster productivity growth also boost saving

4. The classification of reforms according to whether they primarily raise employment or productivity is stylized and reflects the main channel through which they are expected to increase GDP per capita. In practice, however, a number of reforms, such as a relaxation of anticompetitive regulations in product markets, can have both employment and productivity effects.

5. This section is based on OECD (2010).

6. See OECD (2011).

Table 11-2. *Fiscal Impact of Various Types of Growth-Enhancing Structural Reforms*

A. Reforms that directly improve fiscal positions	
Employment-enhancing reforms	**Remove schemes undermining incentives to work.** Restrain access to disability and sickness benefits schemes. Reduce unemployment benefit levels and/or duration. Phase out early retirement schemes and/or increase legal retirement age.
Productivity-enhancing reforms	Improve public spending efficiency, in particular in health care and education. Reduce the scope of state control. Reduce public subsidies (support for agricultural producers/energy subsidies). Reduce housing subsidies. Implement taxes on negative externalities such as pollution (for example, carbon emissions pricing/green taxes).

B. Reforms that improve fiscal positions only indirectly	
Productivity-enhancing reforms	**Relax product market regulation.** Ease entry restrictions in nonmanufacturing sectors. Reduce barriers to entrepreneurship. Reduce barriers to trade and foreign direct investment **Implement revenue-neutral changes in tax structure.** Increase the share of consumption and property taxes and reduce the share of corporate and labor income taxes. Broaden the tax base and cut the tax rate.
Employment-enhancing reforms	**Relax employment protection legislation.** Reduce legal minimum wages where high and/or for specific groups. Relax product market regulation.

C. Reforms that are likely to weaken fiscal positions at least in the short run	
Employment-enhancing reforms	Increase public spending on active labor market policies. Reduce the tax wedge on labor income.
Productivity-enhancing reforms	Increase public spending on innovation, education, infrastructure. Reduce international trade barriers (tariffs).

Source: OECD (2011).

and investment in the medium-to-long run. The results point to a negative net impact of productivity-enhancing reforms on the current account position. Similarly, the empirical analysis suggests that policies that reduce the user cost of capital also boost the investment rate. Insofar as such policies work through a reduction in the real rate of interest, they also reduce the saving rate, so they should worsen the current account position. Also, policy reforms that involve changes in public revenues and expenditures and are not fiscally neutral will alter a country's total saving rate and thereby its current account, because Ricardian equivalence holds only partially.

There is also some evidence that structural policies have an influence on saving and investment on top of any impact that works through changes in macroeconomic conditions. First, there is evidence that higher social spending (in particular on health care) and more generous unemployment benefits are associated with a lower saving rate and a lower current account balance, most likely reflecting lower precautionary saving by households. Second, stricter employment protection legislation (EPL) appears to be associated with lower saving rates, but only in countries where unemployment benefits are low. Stricter EPL also appears to raise the investment rate, at least in OECD countries, possibly through greater substitution of capital for labor. Third, there are some indications that removing competition-unfriendly product market regulation boosts investment, though that effect is likely to be only temporary. Fourth, financial market deregulation tends to lower the saving rate in emerging market economies. Fifth, firm- and sector-level evidence suggests that a lower tax burden on firms boosts business investment and thereby weakens the current account.

The empirical analysis also gives some insights into potential links between structural policies and the saving and investment rate, which may be less potent. In particular, while deregulated financial markets could in theory strengthen the current account effects of other reforms by facilitating consumption smoothing, they are not found to alter the impact of other policy reforms on the saving and investment behavior of private agents. Also, there is weak evidence that structural policies influence the speed at which firms and households adjust their saving and investment behavior to changes in macroeconomic conditions.

The analysis suggests that a number of structural reforms that are desirable on efficiency and/or welfare and equity grounds would be associated with a reduction of global imbalances by narrowing the gaps between domestic saving and investment in several major economic areas. In particular:

—Developing social welfare systems in China and other Asian economies would fulfill an important social goal in its own right and reduce the need for precautionary saving, thereby moderating these countries' large current account surpluses.

—To the extent that high saving rates in surplus countries are related to demographic developments and reforms that cut the ratio of retirement benefits to wages earned (replacement rates), reforms to improve the sustainability of public pension schemes in light of population aging by delaying retirement could help to reduce those surpluses.

—The removal of policy distortions that encourage consumption, such as tax deduction of interest payments on mortgages in the absence of symmetric taxation of imputed rent, could help increase household saving in a number of countries.

—In several countries, removing competition-unfriendly product market regulation could encourage higher capital spending. The empirical analysis suggests, for example, that aligning the level of economy-wide product market regulation in Japan and Germany with OECD best practices could raise private investment in those countries by 0.6 and 0.7 percentage points of GDP respectively in the short run.

—Financial market reforms that raise the sophistication and/or depth of financial markets may relax borrowing constraints in emerging market economies and thus help to reduce the high saving rates observed in some of them. For example, if China implemented reforms that raised its financial reform index to be up among the bottom half of indexes of OECD countries, the total saving rate could drop by about 3.75 percentage points of GDP.

Implications for Capital Flows

Structural and macroeconomic measures aimed at reducing saving-investment gaps could have important implications for capital flows.[7] While imbalances can be reduced through appropriate policies, they will not be (and indeed should not be) completely eliminated. Such policies would have implications for the direction and composition of flows of capital between surplus and deficit countries. While a fully fledged analysis is beyond the scope of this chapter, a few stylized facts can be highlighted. For example:

Fiscal consolidation will be much needed in several countries as a result of a massive build-up of government debt related to the global crisis. A reduction, over the years, in the rate of growth of the supply of government bonds in (mostly advanced) countries that currently have high debt and/or budget deficits could therefore lead to a rebalancing of capital flows from surplus to deficit countries toward corporate bonds, equity, and/or foreign direct investment, which could enhance growth. Of course, for such a rebalancing to take place, the effects on demand for riskless assets (government bonds) and private sector

---

7. This section is based on de Mello and Padoan (2010b).

securities of changes in the rates of return on those assets would need to be taken into account (see Caballero and Krishnamurthy 2009).

Greater exchange rate flexibility in emerging market economies that currently have large current account surpluses could also lead to a change in international capital flows. In the event of a revaluation of their exchange rate parities, surplus countries whose currencies are currently pegged or tightly linked to the U.S. dollar would no longer need to accumulate large amounts of international reserves in the form of U.S. government bonds. To the extent that lower demand for U.S. bonds was matched at least in part by rising investment in corporate bonds, equity, and foreign direct investment (FDI) in deficit countries, a combination of fiscal consolidation in deficit countries with greater exchange rate flexibility in surplus countries could enhance growth.

Structural reform to lift global potential output after the crisis could have potentially strong effects on the composition of capital flows, especially if reform was combined with fiscal consolidation in deficit countries and greater exchange rate flexibility in emerging market economies with large current account surpluses. For example, initiatives that could lead to higher household savings in the United States would affect the size and composition of insurance and pension fund portfolios. Liberalization of entry restrictions in sheltered sectors in surplus countries, such as Germany and Japan, could create opportunities for foreign investment in those countries. Reforms in emerging market economies with large current account surpluses aimed at reducing household savings (by strengthening social safety nets) and/or corporate savings (through financial market reform) would increase the attractiveness of investing in such countries, thus limiting capital outflows toward advanced economies.

The Political Economy of the Framework

The previous discussion leads to the conclusion that there are economic policy strategies at the country and global levels that can deliver the upside scenario. However, that requires a cooperative approach to policy setting and implementation among G20 countries. Achieving a cooperative, superior solution is at the core of the mutual assessment process, which takes place within the G20 framework and which implies that countries share their policy programs and adjust them to take into account their collective dimension. This implies looking at the conditions that lead to international cooperation. The literature on international cooperation indicates that global economic and financial stability (provision of global public goods) is best obtained in a "hegemonic" structure (under single-country leadership). But effective global governance is also possible "after hegemony"—that is, with multiple leaders. This is the framework case based on the mutual assessment process. Historical experience (and theory) suggests that there are conditions for effective governance under multiple leadership that generate the right incentives for collective action.[8] Those conditions are the following: actors (countries) must have a long-term policy horizon; actors must be willing to adjust their preferences and policies; and actors have to engage in repeated interactions to establish mutual trust and enhance the credibility of international institutions.

So the question is whether or not the G20 process satisfies those conditions. This is not a trivial point if we recall that there have been several cases of failure to cooperate under multiple leadership. A recent failure in multi-country governance relates to the attempt to deal with global imbalances before the global crisis broke out. As is well known, the issue of addressing global imbalances (which many see as the macroeconomic environment that led to the crisis) had been on the policy agenda for several years. The policy assignment was well understood and endorsed by the G7 (for example, the Doha declaration), but policies were not delivered, which indicates that incentives for collective action were not strong enough, possibly also due to the absence of pressure from a crisis.

Is it different today? Are there, in the current situation, incentives that are strong enough to lead to a cooperative solution? Let us briefly look at the three conditions. The G20 process seems to be characterized by a long-term policy horizon, the first condition. The agenda of the G20 has moved from emergency response during the acute phase of the crisis to the identification and implementation of a long-term growth strategy. The G20 framework, by definition, casts the policy discourse into a long-term horizon. This element could be further strengthened if the G20 included in its agenda issues such as how to move toward "new sources of growth" and a fresh approach to development issues. The exit from an acute crisis may weaken the momentum toward taking collective action, but on the other hand, as countries have to face the "deep scars" of the crisis—such as lower potential output and prolonged unemployment—the incentives to adopt long-term policy strategies may increase.

The second condition deals with the willingness of countries to adjust their policy preferences and commitments to achieve a common goal. This issue is common to all policy domains but may appear as especially problematic in the area of structural policy. Such policies are "country specific," as they reflect differences in national preferences, economic structures, and institutions. In addition, they have traditionally been considered to belong to the domain of "domestic policies" because, until recently at least, the impact of such policies on other economies had not been fully understood. The discussion above shows that the impact of structural reforms on other countries and on the performance of the global economy can be relevant and that well-designed structural measures do provide a tangible contribution to the global policy scenarios.

8. See Padoan (2007).

The issue then arises of how to identify country priorities in the structural policy domain (also given the fact that the menu of structural policies is quite large and diversified). *Going for Growth* is a tool to identify (five) priorities for each country through use of quantitative performance and policy indicators to select the first three priorities, in areas where performance and policy weaknesses coincide; and use of country-specific expertise to identify the remaining two priorities. In the context of the G20 framework, national priorities can be identified also by taking into account the impact of domestic policies on the rest of the world—most notably, but not exclusively, through their effect on saving-investment gaps and current account imbalances.

Let us conclude with the third condition: repeated interaction among countries to build confidence and mutual trust and at the same time to strengthen institutions. There are elements that suggest that such interaction will continue and reinforce itself over time, also thanks to the G20 framework. Let me mention two of those elements. The G20, in its leader configuration, is a young institution bringing together a set of quite diverse countries. This implies that all countries can see themselves as contributing to the establishment of a new body rather than just joining something that was in place beforehand. That should enhance their sense of ownership in the whole group. Second, the very broad coverage of the G20 economies in the global economy implies that policy action taken by the group will have a truly global impact, thus enhancing the benefits of cooperative outcomes.

Finally, international organizations can support the process by strengthening all three conditions. They can assist countries in assessing the implications of their policy strategies and the consequences of adopting different policy mixes, pointing out the benefits of a longer time horizon (also because an international organization's assessment is not biased by domestic political cycles). They can facilitate the identification of priorities that take into account both domestic and international goals, thus facilitating the adjustment of preferences, if needed. They provide an instrument for repeated policy interaction and ensure that confidence building continues through formal and informal networking. Last but not least, international organizations can further strengthen collaboration among themselves, as they are currently doing in the G20 process, by exploiting their comparative advantages and the division of labor. That collaboration, in turn, strengthens and facilitates the G20 country interaction.

Conclusions

The G20 framework is a novel policy tool that has an economic and a political economy function. The economic function is to identify a mix of macroeconomic, exchange rate, and structural policies, diversified across countries according to the different positions each country holds in the global economy, that permits achievement of a "superior" outcome in terms of growth, sustainability, and balance. The political economy function, which is somehow less considered in the policy debate, is to facilitate cooperation—that is, the adoption of the "appropriate" set of policies needed to move toward the "superior" scenario.

This chapter shows that an optimal (upside) scenario is indeed possible, if the appropriate policy mix is adopted. It examines in some detail the impact that well-targeted structural policies can produce in terms of higher growth, fiscal consolidation, and smaller global imbalances. It also argues that the G20 framework can be instrumental in fulfilling the conditions needed for international cooperation under multiple leaderships, which is reflected in the G20 process. Finally, it argues that international organizations can support this process in a significant way by playing a stronger and more coordinated role.

References

Alesina, R., and S. Ardagna. 2009. "Large Changes in Fiscal Policy: Taxes versus Spending." Working Paper 15438. Cambridge, Mass.: National Bureau of Economic Research.

Caballero, Ricardo J., and Arvind Krishnamurthy. 2009. "Global Imbalances and Financial Fragility." Working Paper 14688. Cambridge, Mass.: National Bureau of Economic Research (January).

De Mello, L., and P. C. Padoan. 2010a. "Promoting Potential Growth: The Role of Structural Reform." OECD Economics Department Working Paper 793. Paris: Organization for Economic Cooperation and Development.

———. 2010b. "Are Global Imbalances Sustainable: Post-Crisis Scenarios." OECD Economics Department Working Paper 795. Paris: Organization for Economic Cooperation and Development.

Guichard, S., and others. 2007. "What Promotes Fiscal Consolidation: OECD Country Experiences." OECD Economics Department Working Paper 553. Paris: Organization for Economic Cooperation and Development.

OECD. 2010. *Going for Growth*. Paris.

———. 2011. *Going for Growth*. Paris.

Padoan, P. C. 2007. "Political Economy of New Regionalism and Global Governance." In *European Union and New Regionalism*, edited by M. Telò. Aldershot, U.K.: Ashgate.

12

G20 Framework for More Sustainable and Balanced Growth

HYEON WOOK KIM

There is little question that the recent global financial crisis was caused by weak risk management in large financial institutions combined with failures of financial regulation and supervision and that global imbalances did not trigger the crisis. However, global imbalances were an integral part of the globally low interest rates and large capital inflows into advanced economies that fostered the buildup of leverage and creation of riskier assets that led to house price bubbles in the U.S. and European countries. Although the crisis was not created inevitably from global imbalances, there was a connection, and we cannot deny the role of global imbalances in the crisis.

That is why more emphasis needs to be placed on global imbalances in considering the prospects for the global economy in the post-crisis era and determining what measures can mitigate obstacles to the resumption of growth. Priority must be given to policies that will prevent future financial crises, and those policies should focus on measures to unwind global imbalances and prevent their recurrence.

As we all know, the G20 nations committed themselves to promoting the rebalancing of the world economy. They have since been engaged in a framework exercise to ensure strong, sustainable, and balanced growth of the world economy (hereafter referred to as the G20 framework), not just working on recovery from the global financial crisis. The G20 governments agreed on a set of national and international policy choices for that purpose at the Seoul summit in November 2010.

Role of the G20 Framework

Considering the features of global imbalances in the 2000s, it would not be difficult to see the G20 framework as a truly desirable channel for the discussion of policies by the international community. First, in contrast to previous episodes in the 1980s, the global imbalances of the 2000s have had a group of emerging markets rather than advanced countries as the counterpart of the United States. The current global imbalances therefore should be viewed as truly global, and it would be very difficult to resolve them by utilizing policy coordination only among advanced countries like the G7. In that regard, the G20 provides a perfect venue for those countries to talk about current and future policies for rebalancing the global economy.

Second, global imbalances in the 2000s were much greater in terms of size than previous ones, and the recent global crisis reminded us that the large trade surpluses and deficits that had characterized the global economy could no longer be tolerated. Global rebalancing is critical to achieving sustained and balanced growth and preventing renewed financial instability. The strategy for global rebalancing should focus on reallocation of global demand from deficit countries to surplus countries: surplus countries need to stimulate domestic demand while countries with considerable deficits need to strengthen their competitiveness and increase private savings. Such a huge-scale reallocation of global demand cannot be achieved in the short run, and the problem of global imbalances cannot be rectified in one or two strokes of policy. At the same time, it points to the need for a coordinated mechanism to design an optimal international policy mix that would have the intended impact within a reasonably short period of time and to oversee the global rebalancing process from a long-term perspective. In that respect, the G20 framework can be considered as the most well-established candidate for such mechanism.

Third, because global balances in the 2000s also have deep roots in structural problems such as inadequate social insurance, rigid labor markets, and poorly developed banking sectors in emerging markets and some advanced economies,[1] it should be recognized that international policy coordination for global rebalancing requires ongoing national structural reforms. Structural reforms are very important in the G20 framework discussion as they are one clear way that the potential growth of countries can be enhanced globally, particularly when countries seem to

---

1. Those problems cannot be resolved by exchange rate adjustments in the short run since they do not originate from exchange rate misalignment. A primary lesson from the experience of global imbalances in the 1980s is that correcting the structural problems of economies in the long run is not a matter that can be dealt with by macroeconomic or exchange rate adjustments but one that requires fundamental changes through structural reforms.

have exhausted their macroeconomic policy capacity to cope with the crisis. The sustainable growth of the global economy cannot be achieved without the commitment of its nations to a wide range of complex structural reforms.

Structural reforms are often politically difficult to implement. The upfront costs are generally obvious, such as job losses in particular sectors of the economy, while the longer-term gains are harder to identify at the outset. However, every crisis provides opportunities for reform, and this one is no exception. With the discovery of new engines of growth after the crisis, the national policy priority in developing countries is shifting to structural reform. It is clear that there is need to improve the quality of Asian emerging market economies since their growth may not be sustainable under the pre-crisis growth model. Urgent attention should be given to structural problems in Asian emerging markets; otherwise global imbalances will re-expand and impede long-term growth. Structural problems have to be dealt with by national governments, but they will be made more tractable through international cooperation. Therefore, the G20 framework can play a role in effectively communicating the benefits of structural reforms. In addition, Asian emerging market countries have experience in "making reforms happen" to advance national growth strategies. The national commitment of those countries to the G20 framework is also important to achieving the sustained recovery of the advanced economy as well as global rebalancing.

Remaining Issues for the G20 Framework

To draw more comprehensive action plans and to elicit policy commitments for rebalancing the global economy, more concrete understanding and agreement among national governments on the objectives of the G20 framework are needed. One example is the "strong growth" that the G20 framework aims for. Contrary to "sustainable growth" and "balanced growth," which can be easily substantiated with the pre-crisis problems of the unbalanced global economy, "strong growth" might not appear to go well with other objectives. In envisioning a new landscape in the post-crisis global economy, the pre-crisis state, which could be said to be characterized by overheated demand, overleveraged financing, and asset price bubbles, is clearly not the picture that we desire to see. It would have been more appropriate to have objectives that focus on longer-term issues—for example, "*more* sustainable and balanced growth."

In the April 2010 meeting of G20 finance ministers and central bank governors, the short-term meaning of "strong growth" was clarified to mean "to close current output and employment gaps in G20 countries as soon as possible."[2]

---

2. The medium- and longer-term meanings of "strong growth" were also announced, but it seems that they simply rephrase the ultimate goals of "sustainable growth" and "balanced growth."

However, the possibility of misperception of or inconsistency between short-term and longer-term objectives will still exist unless the positions on output or employment gaps in G20 countries are clearly and cautiously addressed. For example, as the uncertainty surrounding the global economy appears to grow along with bumpy and uneven signals of global recovery, there are increasing calls for another round of U.S. policy actions to boost domestic demand. If the U.S. Federal Reserve responds with a resumption of quantitative easing, that may depress the value of the dollar—although that would not be the intended effect—so such a move may help reduce global imbalances. However, if the potential GDP of the United States has decreased due to the crisis and thus the output gap already has closed, it is more likely that a policy response to boost domestic demand in the United States would worsen the imbalances. Similar risks of re-expanding global imbalances will continue to exist in other advanced deficit economies as long as the short-term meaning of "strong growth" remains as an objective of the G20 framework.

Concerns on the conflict between short- and long-term objectives also apply to the debates on fiscal consolidation. While the series of fiscal tightening and consolidation measures introduced by countries with large fiscal debts will promote sustainable growth of the global economy by reducing the possibility of fiscal crisis, they are also perceived as slowing down the recovery from the crisis. However, as recovery seems evident in many economies around the world, it is time to focus on the longer-term perspective. While it may be too early for fiscal consolidation in a few countries with slower rates of recovery, it is never too early for governments to develop and set out credible, multi-year fiscal consolidation strategies. Massive fiscal debt and the uncertainties associated with them lead to decreases in market confidence, yielding low private consumption, and they will not be any help in achieving long-run global growth. Therefore, obtaining market confidence in the fiscal consolidation plans announced by some advanced countries with huge fiscal debts will be the top priority for global policymakers.

It is also necessary for the G20 framework to clarify its policy stance regarding the yuan-dollar exchange rate adjustment, and its stance should be shared with international financial markets. It is surely not the first time that the world economy has had such significant imbalances.[3] This time is not much different in the sense that it has become fashionable again to blame the exchange rate policies of surplus countries, especially China, for those imbalances. As China ran a huge current account surplus despite its fast-growing economy and rising

---

3. The most prominent episode was in early 1980s, when widening current account positions led to intensive international coordination with concrete policy commitments under the G5/G7 Plaza (1985) and Louvre (1987) agreements focusing on exchange rates.

oil prices, its rapid accumulation of official foreign reserves was considered an indicator that exchange rates were misaligned. In economic theory, it is correct to argue that the flexibility of the exchange rate scheme will help China to cope with its internal problems, such as inflationary pressures and the possibility of asset bubbles, by strengthening monetary policy independence. Also, it will most likely help global rebalancing.

However, adjusting the exchange rate alone may not be adequate to attain global rebalancing. In addition, the exchange rate issues are more complex and intractable than acknowledged. Considering that the yuan exchange rate is just one of the many causes of global imbalances, the magnitude of the yuan appreciation needed will depend on how much correction of other problems takes place. Also, there is no clear evidence that exchange rate adjustment is an effective tool for global rebalancing. Before the financial crisis, for example, the U.S. dollar depreciated substantially and the yuan appreciated by approximately 15 percent, but no major correction in the global imbalance took place. Therefore, if the yuan alone has to bear the burden, it is not difficult to imagine that the yuan will have to appreciate substantially, by much more than 15 percent or even 30 percent. In that event, the volatility and uncertainty of international financial markets will increase, and the risks involved may be much bigger than it would be worthwhile to take. And, it seems political to discuss the exchange rate when it comes to dealing with the Chinese yuan, whose appreciation would be considered a threat to maintaining employment levels in the country.

Therefore, a G20 framework approach that emphasizes the importance of exchange rate flexibility without specifying a timeline for adjustment or the degree of adjustment needed would be appropriate. But, there is more to be done. There are still widespread expectations of yuan appreciation, and the uncertainty regarding exchange rates has been increasing, which may induce unnecessary government intervention in other Asian foreign exchange markets. And, as can been seen from the Japanese experience in the late 1980s, there will be growing political resistance to structural reform when the external pressures of currency appreciation get stronger, especially in the export-driven developing countries. Therefore, rather than keeping silent on this issue, it would be better for the G20 framework to admit the limitations of exchange rate adjustment in the short run and to announce that, although it is recommended that the Chinese government allow the gradual appreciation of the yuan, the orderly implementation of structural reforms is more important for the sustainable growth of the Chinese economy as well as for global rebalancing.

Meanwhile, to increase the usefulness of the G20 framework, policy recommendations should focus on specific countries and they should be relevant and possible to implement at the country level. The policy options agreed at the

Toronto summit were based on groups of countries facing similar circumstances. However, given that economic policies are ultimately implemented by individual countries, policies designed for a group of countries may be inappropriate for some countries in the same group. For example, Japan and Germany, whose fiscal debt situations are extremely different, are both in the group "advanced surplus countries." Among the Eurozone countries, some are included in "advanced surplus countries" and others in "advanced deficit countries," so that it is difficult to understand the premise of the macroeconomic policy mix on which the recommended monetary and exchange rate policies are based. In particular, structural reforms need to reflect country-specific characteristics in terms of economic structures, institutional settings, and social preferences. There should be no unified formula for structural reform measures, and each member country must take the lead in designing and implementing reform strategies tailored to their individual needs and circumstances.

Last, an appropriate system for evaluating the performance of the G20 framework with a sufficiently long-term horizon should be devised. After the announcement of the framework, global imbalances, which appeared to have peaked in 2006–07, seemed to have narrowed in the aftermath of the current global crisis. China's current account surplus of $426 billion in 2008 fell by 33 percent to a surplus of $284 billion in 2009. The Middle East, which as a region ran a surplus of $348 billion in 2008, witnessed a drop of 90 percent to just $35 billion in 2009. Over the same period, the U.S. current account deficit of $706 billion dropped by over 40 percent, to $418 billion. However, concerns about global imbalances have not gone away. In fact, trade imbalances are widening again. The U.S. trade deficit increased to $49.9 billion in June 2010, the biggest increase since October 2008. In July 2010, one month later, China recorded a $28.7 billion trade surplus, the biggest since January 2009. For the time being, the widening trend in global imbalances may continue in the course of global recovery, especially when countries with a relatively slower recovery implement additional policies boosting domestic demand.

In addition, some of the structural reforms expected in the emerging economies, especially those in East Asia, will take many years—possibly more than five or ten years—to be implemented and to bring about the intended materially significant reallocation of demand. That means that the G20 framework will have to allow some time for the policy measures to be implemented in order to lay the foundations for sustainable and balanced growth of the global economy. Therefore, the global community should be cautioned not to evaluate the performance of the G20 framework on the short-term horizon and to recognize that the problem of global imbalances cannot be rectified in the short run. Definite impacts of international coordination will appear only over a reasonably long period of time.

International Policy Coordination

To conclude, I would like to reemphasize the importance of continuing international policy coordination. The global community has succeeded in protecting the world economy from falling into the "Great Depression 2.0" by adopting unprecedentedly coordinated stimulus policies. However, the response to the crisis also reminds us that there is ample room for the policy coordination mechanism to be improved. For example, the pressing fiscal problems of some European countries could have been alleviated if neighboring countries with fiscal capacity had done more.

In addition, the cooperation witnessed in the days of crisis may prove difficult to sustain as the crisis recedes and governments exit from their stimulus policies. No universal restrictions can be put on the speed of the exit strategy and fiscal consolidation of individual countries, and the global community should continue to discuss strategies tailored to meet the economic conditions of each country and their spillover effects. In order for each government to carry out correct policies, accurately understanding global economic conditions is of great significance. The sharing of information on macroeconomic conditions and the policy stance of individual countries therefore is especially important to global cooperation.

The arithmetic of global imbalances is not unfavorable to the world economy, but coordination to deal with the issue is not easy to achieve. It may be impeded by the collective action problem. The success of the G20 framework exercise depends critically on effective collaboration among countries, which requires each government to be convinced that rebalancing policies will be conducive to its national economy. The basic principle of policy coordination is that prescribed policy changes should be those that are in a country's best interest as well as in the global interest. By the same token, it will make the most sense for the G20 framework to develop a package of common measures that produce desirable changes in themselves but also contribute to global rebalancing.

The Seoul G20 summit demonstrated that global economic cooperation will continue to be effective in the long run. Adequate communication mechanisms should be ensured to discuss the G20 framework beyond the summit and its long-run final outcome. Communication is necessary to deal with the integrated nature of the policy challenges facing most countries, and it will also contribute to strengthening public and market confidence.

13

Rebalancing the World Economy: The G20's Potential Role

PEDRO S. MALAN

Once upon a time there was the Great Moderation (GM). And the GM evolved into the Great Complacency (GC). And the GC evolved into the Great Credit Crunch (GCC), which evolved into the Great Global Crisis (GGC). And the panic about the implications of the GGC led to thea Great Fiscal and Monetary Expansion (GFME), which overcame the panic and avoided a major global recession. But the GFME came a bit too late. The crisis had already carved very deep scars in the financial and the real sectors of the key industrial countries.

"No crisis like this has a simple or single cause, but as a nation, we borrowed too much and let our financial system take on irresponsible levels of risk." So wrote U.S. secretary of the treasury Tim Geithner in March 2009. As we know, the complacency that led to the crisis was not at all restricted to the largest economy in the world. In my view, it had four main pillars.

The first was complacency about the sustainability of the prevailing large global imbalances, which continued to grow. The second pillar was complacency about the bubble in asset prices, especially in housing. The third was an excess of confidence in central banks' ability to "solve" the crisis by sharply reducing interest rates. And last—but by no means least—there was undue complacency about the capacity of "balkanized" systems of regulation and supervision of financial institutions to do their job.

The first three were widely discussed. The fourth barely, if at all. And from there came the truly big surprises. The combination of these complacencies, we now know, proved terrible in generating the conditions for a crisis and its effects on the levels of economic activity and employment. Despite the exceptional fiscal and monetary response, the consequences will be with us for years to come in terms of slower growth and high unemployment in rich countries.

That will be true not only in rich countries but in all countries, developed and developing, that have large "twin deficits" (fiscal and current account); a high debt-to-GDP ratio; a large proportion of their debt held abroad or denominated in foreign currencies or in a currency that the country uses but does not issue (like the euro); an uncompetitive supply side; rigidity in their fiscal regimes; and high and rising age-related government spending. There are several countries in such a situation. As the historical experience suggests, following a major financial crisis, government finance, obliged to respond to the crisis with further and larger commitments of public resources, may face abrupt and deep deterioration.

Recovering sustainable global growth depends on pulling off two rebalancing acts, as Olivier Blanchard, IMF's chief economist, rightly points out. One is the shift from public to private domestic demand in countries that have several of the characteristics listed above. For all of them, there is a need—in some cases, a very urgent one—to address medium- and long-term structural fiscal issues. That is especially true for the G20 countries, which formally approved as the "highest priority" the need "to lay the foundations for strong, sustainable and balanced growth." There can be no such thing in countries with unsustainable fiscal situations over the medium and longer term. A strong convergence of views within the G20 on this subject would be most important to enhance its role in international coordination.

The other "balancing act" is "across countries," between domestic and external demand. There are national, regional, and global aspects of the issue that make it, as the recent experience has demonstrated well, very hard to move ahead using a policy-oriented approach. In the rest of this chapter, I will try to explain why we should not give up entirely on the issue of rebalancing demand. On the contrary, there is, I think, a glimpse of hope—and a role for the G20.

Why is it so difficult to move forward in this second rebalancing act? As is well known, one of the main pillars of the Great Complacency was the supposed sustainability of a pattern of global imbalances without reductions in the rate of growth of domestic spending (and/or exchange rate depreciation) in the main deficit countries: the United States as primus inter pares, but also the United Kingdom, Spain, Australia, France, Italy, and Greece, to name a few. The counterpart of the deficits were the surplus countries: China, as primus inter pares, but also Germany, Japan, Netherlands, Russia, Norway, Saudi Arabia, Switzerland, and Sweden. For some of them, in principle, some combination of increase in domestic demand and/or exchange rate appreciation would have helped to achieve an orderly adjustment of the large—and growing—global imbalances. As Herbert Stein's joke goes, "If a situation cannot be sustained, it won't be."

The IMF tried to engage the relevant countries in a process of multilateral consultations prior to the Great Credit Crunch, but it led nowhere—in part because the Great Complacency was there and many people, including professional economists, did not see a problem with the fact that the United States had a 6 percent GDP current account deficit. As a proportion of U.S. total assets, this is about 1.5 percent of GDP. What is the problem if foreigners (households, firms, and governments) are willing to buy 1.5 percent of U.S. assets for a while? The second reason why multilateral consultations led nowhere is that the Great Crisis concentrated the hearts, minds, and nerves of policymakers around the world. The global imbalance discussion took a back seat to the pressing issue of how to avoid a major financial crisis. The third reason is that current account surpluses and deficits each have a domestic counterpart in terms of the net financial position of their respective relevant domestic sectors (families, firms, governments). And their net position may differ widely from country to country, depending, for example, on the degree of leverage of the financial institutions that intermediate borrowing by, and lending to, families, firms, and governments.

But there are additional, fundamental reasons why it is so difficult to move in this area: the discussion about whether the deficit or the surplus countries have the main responsibility for the adjustment (whether the need is real or perceived) has been with us since the breakdown of the gold standard—and it has never been solved satisfactorily. Why? Because it would have required a much higher degree of international cooperation (at least among the relevant players or currency areas) than we have seen so far. To have deficit countries blaming surplus countries (or one of them) or to have surplus countries blaming deficit countries (or one of them) would simply not do. But we have to try, once again, because there is truly no alternative but to constructively engage the relevant countries or areas in a meaningful set of interactions—not to achieve a consensus (too big a word) but to try to achieve a higher degree of convergence than we have achieved so far. Since convergence is currently rather low, progress at the margin could have some meaning and establish a basis for taking the next steps. As the Chinese say: "One should cross a river by feeling the stones with your feet"—but by always moving ahead.

The G20 was born in a crisis (1997–98), and its importance was renewed in another crisis (2007–09). It now meets also at the level of heads of state and/or government. The G20 role and its influence would depend largely on its capacity to see itself and to be seen by others as an evolving arrangement, a living experience, a flexible, open, and adaptive forum, able to engage in ongoing interaction with many international bodies and institutions—such as the IMF, the World Bank, and the regional development banks—and with new bodies such as the Financial Stability Board. In this connection, it is very important that the G20's voice should be raised loud and clear against protectionist measures, unilateral actions, and beggar-your-neighbor policies.

But the G20 and those who believe in its role should never lose sight of the fact that behind the G20 are governments, usually the same governments that are present in the several international bodies mentioned above. Governments, of course, have to handle their own domestic, their own regional, and their own global interests. Such is life. But when push comes to shove, the effectiveness, influence, and role of the G20 will be no greater than the governments behind it agree that they want them to be. The fact that the Great Complacency, like the Great Moderation, is over and the very worst of the Great Crisis is behind us may open new opportunities for achieving a higher degree of convergence through international cooperation that is within the reach of the G20.

PART IV

The G20 and Development

14

Bringing Development into the G20: Overarching Themes

HOMI KHARAS

The G20 is the self-appointed "premier forum for international economic cooperation." As such, it seeks to be a steering committee for the global economy, born of a need to fight the Great Recession but with larger aspirations: to avoid crises and establish a foundation for strong, sustainable, and balanced growth. The nineteen countries of the core group represent some 80 percent of global GDP, suggesting that the G20 has sufficient economic mass to provide collaborative, coordinated responses to shape the global economy.

Why should a global steering committee care about development? There is a moral and strategic economic rationale that other groups like the G8 have also found compelling. From a moral perspective, sustainable, inclusive global growth cannot continue without correcting ever-larger divergences in per capita income. For example, the mean income in sub-Saharan Africa fell from 1/17 that of the United States in 1980 to 1/44 in 2009. "Strong, sustainable, and balanced" global growth is not consistent with so many countries being left so far behind. At the same time, developing countries have a significant role to play in the growth and rebalancing of the global economy. There is a need to increase global aggregate demand, and in today's world two sources of that demand are consumer demand from the middle class in large, dynamic emerging economies and demand for investment in infrastructure across the developing world.

Strong development is seen as a core strategic and security imperative by many G20 countries. However, fifty years after the UN's "development decade" of the 1960s, there is an appreciation that development is a complex phenomenon with no single path to success. The Washington Consensus, the East Asian model, and the newly formed Beijing Consensus all have their adherents, so within the G20 there is unlikely to be agreement on a single best approach to development. Unlike the G7 (a like-minded group of countries embracing private-sector-led market economies), the G20 countries are very diverse. Can they agree on actions that deliver tangible results on development?

In this chapter, I argue that by taking up development as a topic, the G20 helps to build its inclusiveness, legitimacy, and institutionalization as a group concerned with long-term issues rather than a firefighting group. By choosing selected themes in development, it can achieve tangible results that will bolster its credibility and reduce the friction that arises from its democratic deficit.

Why Was Development Chosen as a Topic for the Seoul Summit?

Korea's chairmanship of the G20 in 2010 represented an opportunity to bring development issues into the policy discussion on the global economy. As the only G20 country that has successfully transitioned from poor to rich since World War II, Korea offered a unique perspective on international cooperation and partnerships in development. Development and poverty reduction continue to be the principal preoccupations of many Asian leaders; by taking up the development agenda, which is a high priority for all developing countries, Korea was able to make the G20 leaders' meeting a much more inclusive event that is relevant for the whole world.

The November G20 summit was the second of three high-profile international meetings on development: the United Nations High-Level Plenary Meeting on the Millennium Development Goals, September 20–22, 2010, New York; the G20 Leaders Summit, November 11–12, 2010, Seoul; and the Fourth High-Level Forum on Aid Effectiveness, November 2011, Busan.

The G20 should be seen as a way of connecting major international gatherings, ensuring consistency of messages and a focus on results. The UN Millennium Development Goals meeting has concluded that leaders remain committed to achievement of the goals and that renewed efforts are warranted. Hence, it was appropriate for the G20 Seoul summit to have specific proposals for the next steps to take on at least a portion of this agenda and to broaden the dialogue beyond aid to include a variety of instruments for supporting economic growth in developing countries. Similarly, the Seoul G20 communiqué's call for fresh approaches to aid and development provides encouragement for the development ministers who will reconvene in November 2011 in Busan to discuss the follow-up to the Paris Declaration and the Accra Agenda for Action on Aid Effectiveness.

International aid and development cooperation now has a track record of working on the basis of multi-year programs, and that fits well with the G20 desire to address longer-term structural issues in the global economy. The UN Millennium Development Goals set global targets through 2015, and the Fourth High-Level Forum on Aid Effectiveness should seek to develop new targets and principles for improving aid effectiveness, building on the progress achieved toward the Paris Declaration targets.

Is Development a Suitable Topic for G20 Leaders?

One of the most significant outcomes of the Pittsburgh summit in 2009 was the agreement to implement a framework for strong, sustainable, and balanced global growth. Many have construed that as a way of focusing on the U.S.-China current account imbalance, which, in the eyes of some, contributed to the buildup of toxic assets in the advanced economies. But that is too narrow a view: the framework serves to multilateralize the discussion of imbalances, both in terms of number of countries and, potentially, in terms of the scope of the issue. In past episodes of global current account imbalances, developing countries have played important roles in the global adjustment process, and there is every reason to think that there are substantial advantages to having them doing so again now. For example, when oil-exporting countries raised prices and ran large current account surpluses in the mid-1970s and again in the early 1980s, the petrodollars were recycled to finance current account deficits in developing countries like Brazil and India. But imbalances go well beyond current account deficits. They exist in access to energy, food security, carbon emissions, financial stability and resilience, health and education outcomes, and wealth.

Some social imbalances have been spelled out in the UN Millennium Development Goals (MDGs) and specific targets adopted to remedy matters. A key idea is that global collective action is essential to resolve global imbalances. The framework for strong, sustainable, and balanced growth thus provides a useful entry point for considering a range of global development issues.

Narrowing the Scope of the Development Agenda for the G20

The G20 cannot reasonably be expected to take on the whole array of development issues. Instead, it must concentrate on a few items that fit the economic and financial focus of the group. Yet it must also recognize that development is multifaceted and requires an interlinked set of policy interventions. Balancing the need for focus and achievable results with the desire to be broad and inclusive is a delicate task.

One way to narrow the agenda is to develop and agree on a set of principles or overarching themes to guide the inclusion of development issues in G20 agendas. The following list could be a starting point for discussion. The G20 members could agree that development issues would be taken up in the future only if doing so

—helps to promote strong, sustainable, and balanced growth

—requires international cooperation and collective action

—results in concrete and tangible results

—reinforces the legitimacy and relevance of the G20 in the eyes of non-G20 countries.

By applying those principles, the G20 would be able to differentiate its consideration of development from the G8 approach. It would signal a paradigm shift in the global debate on development (see table 14-1).

First, by linking development closely to the framework on strong, sustained, and balanced growth, the G20 would automatically shift the focus of the discussion from aid, welfare, and poverty reduction toward growth, opportunity, and development. Doing so would recognize the positive growth momentum in many poor countries, including those in Africa, that existed prior to the crisis and explore how it can be sustained. It would encourage a discussion of global structural transformation, such as the likely evolution of manufacturing and commodity exports. All developing countries can participate in such a debate to identify for themselves the opportunities in globalization and act accordingly. The G20 would also be able to discuss systemic risks and actions needed to shield developing countries from the worst impact of external shocks. In this way, the development discussion could link with other elements of the G20 agenda, such as the discussion on safety nets and financial stability.

Second, the G20 should act only when collective action is called for. For example, the macroeconomic scenarios that are being developed based on G20 member policy submissions have implications for the flows of trade and finance for development. Alternative scenarios, more supportive of development, may be feasible—for example, coordinating fiscal consolidation strategies or external balance of payments adjustments. A broad discussion of development options, with emphasis on coherence among trade, finance, investment, migration, and aid policies rather than on just the quantity of aid, would be a useful step forward. One example of the principle of policy coherence and collective action being put into practice is the establishment of the G20 Financial Inclusion Experts Group, which has a commitment to improve access to financial services for the poor at the same time as new regulations for financial safeguards are being developed under Basel III.

Third, the principle of focusing on tangible results is one that emphasizes concrete actions rather than grand announcements. Too often, G8 announcements have been made with great fanfare but with limited follow-up. Aid outcomes for 2010 are the latest disappointment, given the expectations raised following the Gleneagles commitments. The G20 should focus on concrete actions. That

Table 14-1. *Differentiating the G20 and G8 Approaches to Development*

Principle	G20 approach	G8 approach
Strong, sustainable, and balanced growth	Focus on growth Global structural transformation Systemic risk management	Focus on welfare/poverty Country structural adjustment Mitigate impact of shocks
Need for collective action	Coherent policies toward development	Focus on aid
	Model good practices	Define homogeneous standards
	Reduce free-riding through dialogue and common understanding	Enforce global rules
Tangible results	Implementation focus (templates/ scorecards)	Announcement focus
	Common accountability framework	Ad hoc accountability mechanisms
	Significant legacy agenda	Fresh agenda each meeting
Legitimacy and relevance to others	Reform governance of international financial organizations	Influence agenda of international financial organizations
	Middle-income and low-income development issues	Low-income focus, especially Africa
	Involve regional organizations	Invite specific countries

Source: Author's illustration.

in turn presupposes that the groundwork has been done in advance so that any new initiative can be implemented in a timely fashion. In that regard, the establishment of the G20 High-Level Development Working Group is a significant institutional step, but it could be strengthened if integrated with the finance minister process. The bulk of the G20 agenda already is devoted to discussing the legacy of prior meetings, and that is how it should be in an institutionalized setting. Because the G20 summit will rotate among so many countries, leaving the agenda open would risk a series of ad hoc initiatives aimed at grand announcements rather than results. Having a template and scorecards along with a common accountability framework permits the G20 to take a consistent approach to development over time.

Fourth, the principle of legitimacy and relevance implies that the discussion should focus on topics that benefit all (or most) developing countries, middle income and low income alike, including topics such as the activities of the international financial institutions. That contrasts with the strong emphasis on Africa that has emerged from the G8. It would position the G20 to act as a steering committee for the world rather than for just a small group of countries. To reinforce that image, it would be useful for the G20 to involve regional organizations in the developing world in their discussions. The C10, for example, has already organized itself as a representative body for Africa in G20 discussions.

Putting Principles into Action: A Priority Development Agenda

A number of development topics that are consistent with these principles can be regarded as priorities for G20 consideration. At the aggregate level, it would be useful for the G20 to understand the implications of its collective policies on growth and poverty reduction, based on an analysis by the World Bank and macro scenarios of the IMF. Discussion could include global demand and prospects, finance, trade, commodity prices, and adequate provision of global public goods. It would assess growth poles and bottlenecks among emerging economies, South-South linkages, prospects for public and private capital flows, and global fiscal, inflation, sovereign debt, and commodity price risks. Such an assessment would provide all countries with a common framework on risks and opportunities in the global economy that can be used in developing national strategies.

Specific sectoral and cross-cutting development topics should also be included in the agenda. The development process involves accumulating human and physical capital, building institutions and policies to use them efficiently, and leveraging market opportunities. A variety of tools besides aid are needed to support development in a coherent way. What is important is to have a menu that recognizes the totality of this process, from which recipient countries can choose according to their priorities. The menu should have some continuity over time, but it does not have to be static. Other issues could be added. For example, energy security and climate change and its financing are major issues for development, but consensus has not yet developed to the point that concrete action is likely to be forthcoming at the G20. These issues also have their own processes, such as the United Nations Framework Convention on Climate Change, and it is important for the G20 to support and complement these processes rather than act as a substitute or alternative forum.

A menu of important development topics that are ready for discussion now could include the following:

INFRASTRUCTURE

Infrastructure remains one of the key bottlenecks to development, and significant financial resources are required to implement the vast backlog of necessary projects. A G20 initiative, building on regional studies, could help provide a systematic review of country and cross-border infrastructure needs (such as the World Bank maps of what is required to complete effective infrastructure networks in Africa) and promote new forms of public-private partnerships to generate the resources required. Some countries are setting up specific infrastructure funds as a way to mobilize new loans. Because infrastructure projects offer several possibilities for securitization of revenue, the potential for infrastructure bonds is significant. The amounts could be increased further through securitization of a portion of aid in order to have a larger pool of resources representing an advance commitment to major infrastructure investment in coming years. The G20 could also encourage international financial institutions to review the concept of "fiscal space" to identify where there may be room for greater public sector infrastructure spending, especially in countries with access to capital.

HUMAN RESOURCE DEVELOPMENT

Learning, especially early child and primary education, is at the heart of development. Studies increasingly show that it is the skills learned at school, not the years of education, that determine economic success, both at the individual and the country level. That has long been recognized in Asia, and Asia's commitment to quality education has been a major factor in its ability to grow rapidly. Having a well-educated labor force also helps reduce vulnerability to external shocks and facilitates a low-cost structural transformation of the labor force when necessary. Current international initiatives emphasize access to schooling rather than quality. Access is improving, and progress has been good on achieving the MDG on primary school completion and on gender parity in education. But learning levels are low: in Mali, 94 percent of second-grade students cannot read a single word; in Uganda, half of third-grade students cannot do so. The need for international and national action on improving the quality of education is fundamental to achieving balanced global growth.

Given its importance to development, there is a need for collective action to share experiences on how to improve education quality and on effective tools to benchmark and monitor the learning of literacy and numeracy skills. It may be appropriate for leaders to consider a new Global Learn to Earn initiative. Many G20 members (including developing country members) already support education as donors; several have participated in early grade reading assessments and so have experiences to share in using such tools. A multilateral Global Learn to Earn initiative would involve collaboration between the G20 and other national governments, making it a truly collective endeavor.

Such an initiative would differ from the traditional "vertical fund" in that it would embrace many types of support in addition to aid, such as capacity strengthening, South-South cooperation, and knowledge sharing. New quality-measurement tools like early grade reading and math assessments and national educational accounts or assessment systems offer an opportunity to measure results and sharpen accountability.

TRADE

Developments in trade negotiations and avoidance of protectionism as well as movement of workers and remittances are critical for development. Several G20 members have already adopted duty-free, quota-free access for the least developed countries, and others may be encouraged to move in that direction, embodying the principle of modeling good practice. Aid for trade is another area where the G20 can help, providing both the soft and the hard infrastructure necessary to facilitate the movement of goods from factories and farms to ports and helping countries link to global and regional supply chains. The G20 should take care not to substitute its own deliberations on trade for the formal negotiation process taking place under the Doha Development Round.

PRIVATE INVESTMENT AND JOB CREATION

Jobs are perhaps the top priority for most developing countries, yet they are not explicitly covered by the MDGs. The G20 could signal its commitment to job creation in the developing world by reviewing the rules and regulations governing investment. Promoting cross-border investment and the application of science and technology to development issues will lead to more jobs in recipient countries, but it needs to be done in a prudent fashion. There is the danger of starting a "race to the bottom" as countries seek to ease the cost of doing business through across-the-board deregulation. A G20 understanding of the costs and benefits of regulation in different environments could help countries compete for investment in a healthy way.

FINANCE FOR DEVELOPMENT

The rules for financial stability and new financial regulation have been largely developed by the Financial Stability Board, but developing countries face major issues with access to finance as well as with the stability of financial systems. Several global issues remain unresolved: the desirability of some form of Tobin tax or other innovative financing modalities; the quantity and quality of official development assistance (ODA) in an environment of weak fiscal balances; and possibilities for leveraging ODA through public-private partnerships. The G20 already has formed expert working groups to develop proposals relevant for developing countries on inclusive and innovative finance, including finance for small and medium enterprises.

A further issue faced by developing countries is the volatility of official and private financial flows. It has created, in part, the need to accumulate large amounts of foreign exchange reserves in some countries to mitigate its effects, but such practices are likely to be globally inefficient. The G20, through its representation in international financial institutions, can play a significant role in developing systems to help stabilize net financial flows, through safety nets and other countercyclical arrangements. For low-income countries, financial volatility can come about through procyclical aid flows, another phenomenon that deserves G20 attention. In some instances, developing countries themselves have instituted capital controls restricting private inflows to avoid volatility, but in so doing they have unwittingly cut themselves off from a growing pool of philanthropic private capital available at highly concessional terms (for example, for microfinance).

Food and Energy Security

Food and energy price spikes have been severe, and they have resulted in significant development setbacks in recent years. Their impact can be reduced by developing better safety nets for vulnerable households in developing countries, but that requires effective delivery institutions that may be beyond the reach of many countries. A more direct approach is to reduce commodity price volatility directly, possibly through the use of insurance and forward markets by global institutions. For example, the World Food Program currently buys all its food on spot markets, but its needs are greatest when food prices rise sharply. There could be scope for efficiency gains by reviewing such practices. Also, there are no modalities at present to regulate export restraints. These, as is well known, accentuate the volatility of prices on international markets. The World Trade Organization could be called on to review such practices. Improving agricultural development and small-holder productivity is another major initiative to improve global food security. The new Global Agricultural and Food Security Program, set up under G20 auspices, provides a number of options for innovative finance and new public-private partnerships to support country-led programs.

Governance

Stronger institutions that reduce the scope for corruption and provide assistance on tax reform to increase domestic resources for development can also be addressed through collective action by the G20. Tax avoidance and illegal capital flight cost developing countries billions each year, with transfer pricing a particularly troublesome practice. Programs like the stolen assets recovery initiative require global collaboration to deny stolen assets a safe haven.

Knowledge Sharing and Learning

Few developing countries have agencies dedicated to evaluating their development projects and programs. Aid recipient countries cannot get transparent access to data on who is doing what in their countries in terms of development cooperation. Without transparency, the concepts of country ownership and mutual accountability, both keys to aid effectiveness, cannot be satisfactorily

Table 14-2. *Menu of Development Topics*

Topic	Principle			
	Growth	*Collective action*	*Tangible results*	*Relevance*
Infrastructure	Market connectivity and job creation	Multi-stakeholder financing	Increased volume of resources for infrastructure investment, including regional projects; review of "fiscal space" assessments by international financial organizations	High priority for all developing countries
Quality education	Raise quality of human capital	Sharing of cost-effective experiences in raising quality; early grade international benchmarking	Global Learn to Earn initiative	High priority for all countries
Trade	Improve competitiveness	Multilateral liberalization	Support aid for trade; duty-free, quota-free access for least developed countries	High priority for all countries
Private investment	Job creation	Benchmarking global economic competitiveness	Innovative public-private partnerships to share risk	Most relevant for countries with foreign direct investment appeal
Finance	Inclusive and innovative finance	Avoid free-riding on debt forgiveness; ambitious aid targets; reduce volatility in finance through better global regulation	Predictable finance; multilateral development bank capital increases; international financial organization concessional replenishments; developing country "voice" and governance improvements in international financial organizations	Emerging and middle-income economies
Food and energy security	Raise small-holder productivity; supply chains; private sector involvement	Agricultural research; develop export quota modalities	Global agriculture and food security program	Low-income countries
Governance	Stronger domestic institutions	International rules for tax havens, transfer pricing	Assistance with recovery of stolen assets	All developing countries
Knowledge sharing and learning	Knowledge for development	Sharing of development implementation experiences	South-South cooperation; support for evaluation of public spending	All developing countries

Source: Author's illustration.

implemented. The G20 membership includes the most comprehensive group of aid donors in the world; therefore it is the appropriate forum for taking responsibility to advance this agenda. The G20 should also link its development agenda with other forums like the Fourth High-Level Forum on Aid Effectiveness in 2011 and the United Nation's Development Cooperation Forum.

The list above is indicative of a menu-driven approach to the G20 development agenda. The G20 should agree on such a list (or a modified version) and then review progress and the need for action before each meeting. The idea of a menu approach is to adopt a limited set of topics to be followed over several meetings, to maintain continuity and focus, and to avoid leaping from topic to topic. Not all topics will require leaders' input and discussion, but leaders should be alerted to progress on each topic and invited to discuss options when expert groups have determined that additional action is required. Table 14-2 illustrates how the four principles would apply to the topics proposed in the menu.

Not all items need to be discussed by leaders at every meeting. For example, food security has already been taken up in Pittsburgh and a new global program to promote food security was launched in April 2010. Perhaps no further discussion by leaders would be warranted other than of ways to encourage additional countries to join and of monitoring of implementation under the program. Some items may not be sufficiently developed, in terms of tangible results or programs, to be taken up at a leaders' meeting, and those items could be postponed until the time is right. Complex proposals, such as those on how to use insurance and futures markets to stabilize commodity prices, could be examples.

The Seoul Development Consensus and the Multi-Year Action Plan for Development go a long way toward establishing a menu approach to development consistent with the overarching themes of G20 engagement. In implementing this agenda over time—and it is admittedly very broad—the core principles of engagement need to be kept in mind. Specific G20 programs on development should be

—oriented toward economic growth and based on implementation of the Framework for Strong, Sustained, and Balanced Growth

—a sign of a paradigm shift in the international debate on development compared to the G8

—founded on the collective action of the G20

—a mechanism for expanding the G20 role to one that includes all regions and countries, including low-income countries

—a way of establishing the credibility of the G20 by producing tangible results

—appropriate for an institutionalized body taking up the long-term challenges facing the global economy.

15

Laying the Foundation for a Long-Term G20 Work Program on Development

SIMON MAXWELL

Korea took an important step in placing development firmly on the agenda of the G20 summit in November 2010. A Working Group on Development was established at the Toronto meeting in June 2010 and brought forward specific proposals in Seoul. Although the subject will receive additional prominence, development has been an important thread throughout all of the G20 summits, including London, Pittsburgh, and Toronto.[1] There are strong links and many cross-references between the G20 process and others, including, among others, the G8, the UN Millennium Development Goals summit, the trade talks, and the climate change talks. The argument can roughly be summarized in a ten-point program, as follows:

—There are still many poor people in the world.

—The financial crisis made poverty worse, and the poor are subject to significant other shocks and adverse trends, not least climate change.

—Growth in developing countries is an essential element of poverty reduction, and it will also contribute to global recovery.

---

1. For the leaders' statement from the London summit, see www.wcoomd.org/files/1.%20Public%20files/PDFandDocuments/Highlights/G20_Final_London_Communique.pdf; for the statement from the Pittsburgh summit, see www.pittsburghsummit.gov/mediacenter/129639.htm. For the Toronto Declaration, see http://canadainternational.gc.ca/g20/summit-sommet/2010/toronto-declaration-toronto.aspx?lang=eng.

—Special urgency is needed to tackle lagging Millennium Development Goals (MDGs), hence the G8 maternal and child mortality initiative and the recurrent references to food security, among others.

—Aid is an essential part of the solution, hence the importance of tracking and meeting official development aid (ODA) pledges.

—Aid should be administered by a well-functioning international system, hence support for the aid effectiveness agenda and the emphasis on reform of the multilateral system (UN, Bretton Woods institutions, MDBs).

—Equitable trade rules and a well-managed financial system provide essential underpinning of an open and market-led economy, hence Doha, the Financial Stability Board, and other elements of financial sector reform.

—A climate deal also provides essential underpinning, hence positive references to the United Nations Framework Convention on Climate Change.

—Private sector and private financial flows are important.

—The G20 is a good forum to provide leadership and coordination in pursuit of development goals.

In reading the declarations and communiqués, it is important to resist the temptation to think that financial stability and other global macroeconomic questions (including imbalances) are not development issues—they are. To illustrate, consider the twenty-point "charter" produced in advance of the Toronto meeting by a group of researchers under the auspices of the U.K. Overseas Development Institute (box 15-1). This list of points relevant to "crisis-resilient and transformative growth" in low-income countries includes items on fiscal and monetary stimulus policies, trade, fossil fuel subsidies, and exchange rates.

Despite the convergence of concerns, it is worth saying that there sometimes seems to be a disconnect between the various sections of the communiqués—or perhaps, better put, a difference of emphasis. Over the 2008–09 period, financial stability, fiscal stimulus, and exit strategies have unsurprisingly dominated the G20 agenda—perhaps at the expense of what might be considered a traditional development agenda. The creation of the Working Group on Development can be considered an important step to rebalance the agenda.

For the short term, the Working Group on Development looks likely to prioritize those parts of the traditional development agenda that are growth related, growth being the core economic area in which the G20 might have a comparative advantage. The key pillars include infrastructure; private investment; human resource development; trade; financial services; food security; and knowledge sharing.[2] Proposals will be made in each of those areas.

2. Ahn (2010).

Box 15-1. *G20–Low-Income Countries Twenty-Point Charter for Crisis-Resilient and Transformative Growth*

The G20 is to recommit to the framework of strong, sustainable, and balanced growth and follow core policies in order to achieve that goal, including the following:
—Deficit countries are to increase savings (for example, the United States).
—Europe is to consolidate its budgets and engage in structural reforms to boost growth.
—Emerging economies are to revalue the exchange rate (for example, China).
—Emerging economies are to boost domestic demand by raising social safety nets ensuring that households save less.
—Germany and Japan are to provide greater incentives for their companies to invest.

LICs are to provide plans and benchmark their efforts to promote transformative growth by
—Building productive capacities and fostering productivity change
—Promoting economic diversification and competitiveness
—Promoting private sector development
—Providing energy and road infrastructure and responding to the challenges of development in a carbon-constrained world
—Investing in good-quality and appropriate human capital to improve labor productivity
—Ensuring and improving technological capacity to adopt new and implement old technologies
—Streamlining governance and bureaucracy.

The G20 is to consider the effects of its core economic policies on LICs and, where appropriate, make its policies more developmentally friendly in areas such as the following:
—Exiting fiscal and monetary stimuli in a developmentally friendly way
—Appropriate financial regulation that takes into account the capital needs of poor countries
—Rebalancing the global economy, using reserves for global growth, and promoting flexible exchange rates.

The G20 is to consider the policy coherence and effects of its external policies on growth in LICs in areas such as the following:
—Aid to address global challenges and transformative growth—aid for trade (AfT), for example—supporting technical change and infrastructure and filling the skills capabilities gap
—Provision of global financial liquidity, stimulating financial inclusion and investing international reserves for global growth
—Providing incentives for outward FDI to LDCs and support for SEZs drawing on local capabilities
—Promoting open trading rules
—Removal of fossil fuel subsidies.

Source: Te Velde (2010).

A Changing Development Agenda in the Longer Term?

In the longer term, it will be necessary also to review the integrity and robustness of the development narrative. Consider, for example, these four points:

—Most poor people now live in middle-income countries that may not need aid rather than in low-income countries that definitely do; of the remainder, many live in fragile states, where aid is difficult to disburse and where a different approach to development may be required.

—Many developing countries have bounced back from the recession more quickly than developed countries and have higher rates of growth; some of them have done that, at least in part, by apparently ignoring Washington Consensus strictures on open economies and free markets.

—Despite their rhetoric, many developed countries have become less committed to development, as traditionally defined, with consequent erosion of their commitment to increased levels of ODA.

—Global issues have become major drivers of development policy, leading to a reallocation of financial and political capital away from country-led development programs and toward engagement with regional and global public goods; however, it is not axiomatic that that signifies an equal enthusiasm for multilateralism.

The Challenge of the New Geography of Poverty

First, the geography of poverty has changed, with implications for development policy. The majority of the poor now live in middle-income countries. That is partly because some countries containing large numbers of poor people, including India and China, have now become middle-income countries (MICs), but there are many other new MICs.[3] A study by Andy Sumner summarizes the situation as follows, with data for 2007–08 (see table 15-1):

> In 1990, 93% of the world's poor people lived in poor countries—meaning low-income countries (LICs). . . . Three-quarters of the world's approximately 1.3 billion poor people now live in middle-income countries (MICs) and only about a quarter of the world's poor live in the remaining 39 low-income countries, largely in sub-Saharan Africa. This is then a startling change over two decades and it implies there is a new "bottom billion" who do not live in fragile and conflict-affected states but largely in stable, middle-income countries.[4]

3. Sumner (2010) lists twenty-seven post-2000 MICs, including Cameroon, Côte d'Ivoire, Pakistan, and Vietnam.
4. Sumner (2010).

Table 15-1. *Global Distribution of the World's Poor by Country Type,*
2007–08[a]

Million (percent)

Country type	Fragile and conflict affected	Not fragile or conflict affected	Total
Low income	156 (12)	214 (16)	371 (28)
Middle income	144 (11)	813 (61)	957 (72)
Total	300 (23)	1,027 (77)	1,329 (100)

Source: Sumner (2010).
a. Numbers have been rounded.

Should middle-income countries receive aid? If so, how much and of what type? Donors are often somewhat ambiguous in their answers to those questions. In its 2001 middle-income strategy, for example, the U.K. Department for International Development (DFID) argued that

middle-income country governments must lead the fight against poverty in their own countries. The main effort of the international community should be directed towards improving the broader policy environment, including reducing barriers to trade and improving the international financial architecture. . . . [A]lthough less significant in overall terms, official aid flows will remain substantial for the foreseeable future. These need to be better targeted, better coordinated and more effective. Technical assistance has a particularly important part to play.[5]

The first statement implies a reduction in aid; the second implies continuation of aid but with a change of composition toward technical cooperation (and, as evident from the full text, a shift from grants to loans). It is not irrelevant that certain middle-income countries—India, for example—have strong historic links with the United Kingdom and strong expatriate communities living there. Reducing aid is not an easy choice for U.K. ministers to make.

Table 15-1 shows that 23 percent of the poor live in fragile states, about half in low-income countries, and half in middle-income countries. It might be thought that the case for aid to low-income fragile states is unambiguous. However, as is well known, spending money in fragile and conflict-affected states is not easy, except perhaps in the humanitarian sphere. By definition, governance and government systems are weak, authority is often disputed, and aid can lubricate rather than impede conflict.

5. DFID (2001).

A narrative is thus waiting to be written on development, one that will be very difficult for the development community to handle. If middle-income countries do not need aid and if aid is hard to spend in fragile states, what is to be done with all the money pledged at successive summits and UN meetings? Some donors may argue that it is less important to fulfill past promises.

How Strongly Does the G20 Hold to the Washington Consensus?

A second issue is the shift in economic dynamism to the East and South and the development models that pertain. There is a marked difference in expected GDP growth rates in 2010–11 between Europe, the United States, and Japan, on one hand, and the rest of the world on the other, including especially most of Asia, Latin America, and Africa. That is not a new phenomenon. The share of global GDP that arises in Asia in particular has risen to over one-third.

The G20 has argued for an open and market-led economy, and it would be convenient if differential rates of growth could be explained by reference to a particular economic model—for the sake of argument, the Washington Consensus model. In fact, an active debate is under way about development models.[6] The G20 has reflected one set of views, concluding in April 2009 that "we believe that the only sure foundation for sustainable globalization and rising prosperity for all is an open world economy based on market principles [and] effective regulation."

On the other hand, other observers have given more emphasis to the role of the state and to the importance of public expenditure. Thus, reporting to the UN General Assembly, the Stiglitz Commission argued in 2009 that "the ideas and ideologies underlying key aspects of what has variously been called neo-liberalism, market fundamentalism, or the Washington consensus doctrines have been found wanting."[7]

These concerns are reflected in the work of organizations like the UN Conference on Trade and Development (UNCTAD). A contribution by UNCTAD, for the Trade and Development Board meeting in May 2009, concluded that "developing countries need to continue to address income inequality and to invest more in education, training, trade-adjustment assistance, health care, community development and tax policy."[8] Similarly, the International Labor

---

6. For further discussion, see Maxwell (2009).

7. See paragraph 136, *Report of the Commission of Experts of the President of the United Nations General Assembly on Reforms of the International Monetary and Financial System* (www.un.org/ga/president/63/interactive/financialcrisis/PreliminaryReport210509.pdf).

8. See www.unctad.org/en/docs/cicrp1_en.pdf.

Organization has agreed on the Global Jobs Pact, focusing on protecting employment, delivering public services, and building social protection for all.[9] The pact has been referenced by the G20.

My own take has been to focus on the capability of countries, not just to recover the status quo ante but to prepare their economies and societies for the next big wave of change and challenges, some of which can be thought of as risks and some of which (like technological breakthroughs) can be thought of as opportunities. If countries wish to rise to these changes and challenges, they will need to invest in the pillars, or drivers, of competitiveness—for example, in higher education and training, technological readiness, and innovation. They may also need to adopt an active industrial policy, including protection in some cases; see, for example, the exchange on this between Justin Lin and Ha Joon Chang.[10]

Development in a Downturn

The third issue is about the commitment to development among the traditional aid donors and its implications for aid architecture. Despite repeated declarations at summits, there is evidence that some countries are resiling from commitments and that others are reorienting aid away from traditional MDG expenditures toward, for example, supporting foreign policy objectives in places like Afghanistan.

The latest estimates of aid volume for 2010, provided by the Development Assistance Committee of the OECD (figure 15-1), show a likely deficit of over $US10 billion compared to the Gleneagles commitments. A review of European commitments by CONCORD and AidWatch concludes that

all evidence indicates that 2010 will not see significant improvements. According to official estimates, 2010 aid levels are expected to reach a maximum of 0.46% of the GNI, far from the 0.56% collective target and over €11bn short in terms of funding. Most of these shortfalls will be consequence of insufficient funding by Italy (€4.5bn), Germany (€2.6bn) and France (€800m).

Official aid figures, however, fail to capture the reality of European aid flows. In 2009, European countries reported €3.8bn of inflated aid

9. See www.ilo.org/global/What_we_do/Officialmeetings/ilc/ILCSessions/98thSession/pr/lang--en/docName--WCMS_108456/index.htm.

10. See DPR Debate, "Should Industrial Policy in Developing Countries Conform to Comparative Advantage or Defy It? A Debate Between Justin Lin and Ha-Joon Chang" (www.econ.cam.ac.uk/faculty/chang/pubs/DPRLin-Changdebate.pdf).

Figure 15-1. *DAC Members' Net Official Development Assistance (ODA),*
1990–2009, and DAC Secretariat Simulations of Net ODA to 2010

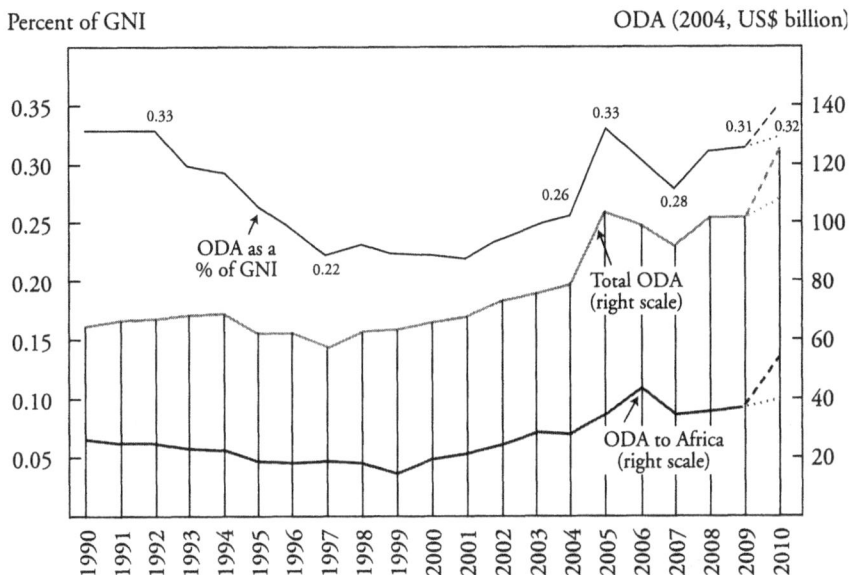

Percent of GNI   ODA (2004, US$ billion)

Source: OECD, April 14, 2010 (www.oecd.org/document/1/0,3746,en_21571361_37949547_449
86561_1_1_1,00.html).

Note: Dashed line indicates the growth-adjusted trajectory envisaged at Gleneagles. Dotted line
indicates estimates based on reported intentions or current 2010 budget plans made by DAC members.
Dotted line for Africa indicates a Secretariat estimate of likely actual spending.

as ODA, or almost 8% of the total figure. A breakdown of the data shows
that €1.4bn was debt cancellation, €1.5bn student costs and almost €1bn
was spent on refugees in donor countries.

Once inflated aid is discounted from the officially reported ODA figures, aid levels drop to 0.38% of European GNI. If EU Member States
continue the current trend and once inflated aid is discounted, EU countries will fall €19bn short of their promises in 2010. This is a significantly
larger amount than the €11bn shortfall official figures predict.[11]

There are genuine dilemmas for aid donors in defending aid volumes at a
time of recovery from recession and of severe public expenditure constraints.
Even in countries where public opinion has been strongly supportive of development, the likelihood of severe public expenditure cuts may lead to erosion of

11. Concord and AidWatch (2010).

support. For example, the results of a recent U.K. panel study published by the Institute of Development Studies at the University of Sussex show that more than half of the population supports aid to poorer countries, but that 63 percent believe that aid should be cut as part of efforts to reduce the budget deficit—this at a time when aid budgets have formally been ring-fenced.[12]

Faced by such pressures, governments may reduce aid or use the aid budget to cover a wider set of commitments than in the past. It would be surprising, for example, if European donors, at least, were to spend a smaller share of the aid program on refugees or students than in the past; those expenditures are formally accountable as ODA, but they do not represent transfers to developing countries. More is likely to be spent in support of foreign policy objectives (without violating the rules of the Development Assistance Committee of the OECD on what counts as aid, although those rules may come under scrutiny—for example, to allow more spending on security). A particular concern is whether aid funds will be used to meet climate commitments, including the Copenhagen commitment to spend up to $US100 billion a year on mitigation and adaptation by 2020. Although some donors have pledged to ensure that no more than a certain percentage of aid is spent on climate matters (the previous U.K. government led by Gordon Brown specified 10 percent), the evidence is that a good part of "fast start" finance is not additional but is being drawn from aid budgets.[13]

Donor governments can also be expected to frame development as being about making the world safer for their own populations, combining a moral case with self-interest. That was the case, for example, of a U.K. white paper of 2009, which talked about development in terms of common interest:

> For many, the moral imperative to end poverty is reason enough to act. As the world becomes richer and more sophisticated, we increasingly have the means to end poverty, and our excuses for failing to do so are becoming progressively more threadbare. But in the 21st Century, development is not merely a moral cause, it is also a common cause. The success and security of other countries profoundly affect our own success and security. Justice, security and prosperity are indivisible: none of us can fully enjoy them unless we all do. Building Britain's future and building our common future go hand in hand.[14]

12. Henson and Lindstrom (2010).

13. See, for example, www.faststartfinance.org/; for a discussion of additionality, see www.odi. org.uk/resources/details.asp?id=4931&title=climate-finance-additionality-definitions-implications.

14. See www.dfid.gov.uk/documents/whitepaper/building-our-common-future-print.pdf.

Shifting from National to Regional and Global Issues

Finally, it may seem perverse to say so in the wake of the New York summit on the Millennium Development Goals, but there are good grounds to think that the development agenda will increasingly be driven by regional and global issues rather than the more traditional concern with poverty reduction programs at the country level. Indeed, that is not surprising, given the preceding analysis: middle-income countries are expected to tackle poverty with limited help from rich countries; global issues are high on the agenda of groups like the G20; and rich countries must "sell" development as being part of investment in making the world safer. Current concerns include climate; food security; water supplies; pandemics; financial contagion; drugs; crime; and nuclear proliferation. These topics have been highlighted in many reports, including the report of the Task Force on Global Public Goods.[15]

The link between global issues and the Millennium Development Goals is partly through goal 8, which has been regarded as a very weak goal, containing a number of somewhat unrelated targets and indicators (box 15-2). A better structure is needed, one that sets outcome targets, as do some other MDGs. For example, when it comes to trade, it would be interesting to specify not just the characteristics of a system, as in target 8a (see box 15-2), or that levels of tariffs should be monitored, but rather to provide specific numbers for average tariffs—or in the case of agriculture, for producer support.

An important issue for the G20 is the extent to which a new emphasis on global public goods will encourage a commitment to multilateralism. On one hand, it might be thought that an emphasis on global issues is necessarily multilateral. On the other hand, recent evidence (trade, climate) illustrates the difficulty of maintaining momentum and reaching solutions. In work on the European Union, Gavas, Johnson, and Maxwell characterized the choice as being between cooperation on one hand and consolidation on the other; they have also explored the conditions under which cooperation or consolidation is more likely, as in table 15-2.[16] Their research among opinion leaders in Europe showed that there was a strong preference in the European context for cooperation, in the sense of setting international norms, and rather little (in the development field) for consolidation. Thus, instruments like the European Consensus on Development or the Code of Conduct on Division of Labor were favored, but channeling a greater share of aid through the European Commission was not. It would be interesting to ask similar questions in a G20 context.

15. See www.ycsg.yale.edu/activities/collaborations_taskforce.html.
16. Gavas, Johnson, and Maxwell (2010).

Box 15-2. *Millennium Development Goal 8:*
A Global Partnership for Development

Target 8a: Develop further an open, rule-based, predictable, nondiscriminatory trading and financial system
Includes a commitment to good governance, development and poverty reduction; both nationally and internationally

Target 8b: Address the special needs of the least developed countries
Includes tariff and quota free access for the least developed countries' exports; enhanced programme of debt relief for heavily indebted poor countries (HIPC) and cancellation of official bilateral debt; and more generous ODA for countries committed to poverty reduction

Target 8c: Address the special needs of landlocked developing countries and small island developing States through the Programme of Action for the Sustainable Development of Small Island Developing States and the outcome of the twenty-second special session of the General Assembly

Target 8d: Deal comprehensively with the debt problems of developing countries through national and international measures in order to make debt sustainable in the long term.

Indicators for Targets 8a, 8b, 8c, and 8d

Official development assistance (ODA)
8.1 Net ODA, total and to the least developed countries, as percentage of OECD/DAC donors; gross national income
8.2 Proportion of total bilateral, sector-allocable ODA of OECD/DAC donors to basic social services (basic education, primary health care, nutrition, safe water and sanitation)
8.3 Proportion of bilateral official development assistance of OECD/DAC donors that is untied
8.4 ODA received in landlocked developing countries as a proportion of their gross national income

More generally, research on collective action in the international environment suggested that success required a combination of an enabling social environment and rational self-interest—a mutually reinforcing mix of culture and calculus. That led to a nine-step program for improved collective action:

—Keep the core group small.

—Develop trust-building measures from the beginning.

—Use the same core group for as many issues as possible in order to keep transaction costs down and benefit from what economists call economies of scope.

—Make it awkward or embarrassing not to cooperate. Leaders themselves can do this, but civil society plays an important role.

—Choose the right issues: the ones where all the players have something to gain and something to lose.

8.5 ODA received in small island developing States as a proportion of their gross national incomes

Market access
8.6 Proportion of total developed country imports (by value and excluding arms) from developing countries and least developed countries, admitted free of duty
8.7 Average tariffs imposed by developed countries on agricultural products and textiles and clothing from developing countries
8.8 Agricultural support estimate for OECD countries as a percentage of their gross domestic product
8.9 Proportion of ODA provided to help build trade capacity

Debt sustainability
8.10 Total number of countries that have reached their HIPC decision points and number that have reached their HIPC completion points (cumulative)
8.11 Debt relief committed under HIPC and MDRI Initiatives
8.12 Debt service as a percentage of exports of goods and services

Target 8e: In cooperation with pharmaceutical companies, provide access to affordable essential drugs in developing countries
8.13 Proportion of population with access to affordable essential drugs on a sustainable basis

Target 8f: In cooperation with the private sector, make available the benefits of new technologies, especially information and communications
8.14 Telephone lines per 100 population
8.15 Cellular subscribers per 100 population
8.16 Internet users per 100 population

Source: UNDP, "Goal 8: A Global Partnership for Development" (www.undp.org/mdg/goal8.shtml).

—Choose, for example, genuine global public goods, which look like an especially good bet.

—Start to think about positive incentives.

—Apply, perhaps as a last resort, the lesson that collective action is often most successful when the costs of defection are high. More aid may be a carrot, less aid a less palatable but equally effective stick.

—Set up institutions to manage these interactions and relationships.[17]

The G20 has demonstrated a strong commitment to a culture of cooperation. How strong has it been in creating positive and negative incentives for changed behavior?

17. See www.odi.org.uk/resources/download/469.pdf.

Table 15-2. *Conditions under Which Consolidation or Cooperation Is More Likely*

Consolidation more likely	Cooperation more likely
Exclusive competence	Shared competence
High spillover	Low spillover
Narrowly defined areas of collaboration	Broadly defined areas of collaboration
Binding rules of international cooperation	Soft law
Consensus-based decisionmaking	Majority decisionmaking
Similar member states interests, preferences, and policy positions	Heterogeneous member states interests, preferences, and policy positions
Equal power distribution	Unequal power distribution
Shared norms	Lack of shared norms

Source: Gavas, Johnson, and Maxwell (2010).

A Mission Statement for the G20?

The G20 may or may not want to take on new issues, depending on how it defines its remit and on how it answers three questions. First, the G20 must decide whether its primary concern is with crisis management or long-term issues. Its recent history has been dominated by the need for a global response to the financial crisis—and the severity of that crisis provided a justification for upgrading the meetings from the finance minister to the leader level. However, crisis-related finance issues, like bank regulation, are a traditional concern of finance ministers, and heads of government may prefer to take a wider view. For example, food, energy, climate, and development are legitimate long-term concerns. The G20, on this reading, is concerned with long-term global issues—with helping to manage the global commons on which we all increasingly depend.

Second, the G20 will need to decide whether to limit itself to economic issues or take a wider view. Its history is economic: the G20 was originally established, under the leadership of Paul Martin of Canada, as a forum of finance ministers. The urgency of tackling the global financial crisis has kept it tethered in that arena. Should it now spread its wings? An obvious extension is to the economic aspects of global issues like climate change. Some would like the G20 to take further steps—for example, into nuclear proliferation and other security issues. Does it then displace the G8? Some would like it to, although the two will run side by side, at least until the French presidency in 2011 (see chapter 4 in this volume.) The most likely outcome is that the G20 will take on a broad range of issues.

That raises a third question, about the relationship of the G20 to other bodies. It may well be the case that the G20 contains two-thirds of the world's population and accounts for 85 percent of global GNP, but it cannot replace institutions that offer representative voice to the G-172, which are not included in the G20. This problem is not exactly solved by inviting nonmembers to the meetings, even representatives of bodies like the African Union. The lesson seems clear. The G20 can provide a forum for consultation and coordination, a platform for consensus building, and a mechanism for mutual accountability, but it should see its role as supporting, not supplanting, the institutions of global governance.

The G20 should see itself as a body that deals with global issues, both long and short term, economic and noneconomic; that works responsibly and respectfully with other institutions; and that recognizes that it is a forum for consultation as much as a vehicle for taking decisions and launching initiatives. This is a worthy field on which leaders can engage. The vision is one that implies a mission statement for the G20. An ambitious but appropriately modest mission statement could be the following:

> Our vision is of a secure, fair, and sustainable world, one that supports the well-being of all the world's people and the planet that we share. We work together for this better world by sharing our ideas, collaborating on the development of specific proposals, and holding each other to account. Our role is to support effective, accountable, and representative global institutions.

Conclusion: A New Narrative on Development

The G20 could operate within the parameters of its past engagement, roughly following the ten-point program outlined at the beginning of the paper and focusing in the first instance on growth. Alternatively, it could open new issues for discussion and contribute to reframing of the development agenda. It could also create a new framework for multilateralism. A new ten-point program might look something like the following:

—Poverty reduction and human development are essential moral goals—and they also provide the essential underpinning of security in both rich and poor countries. Human security is a global public good.

—Aid is essential, especially in the relatively small number of low-income countries, in which about a quarter of global poverty is found.

—Middle-income countries also need some aid, but of a different kind, especially in the form of loans and technical cooperation.

—Fragile states need special help, some of which may be financial but some of which will be political, diplomatic, and even in some cases military.

—Development strategies will be country specific, but all countries need to invest in their capability for growth, particularly in the health and education of their citizens and in a business environment that reduces transaction costs, supports technical change, and encourages innovation.

—Successful development also requires a managed engagement with the global economy, including with respect to measures that enable sustained development of the private sector.

—Both developed and developing countries need to work together to strengthen the international environment for development. A new and improved goal 8 is a top priority, with unambiguous outcome indicators.

—The difficulty experienced in reaching global deals on topics like trade and climate illustrate the need for a new commitment to multilateralism.

—The G20 is a good forum to provide leadership and coordination in pursuit of development goals.

—The G20's primary purpose should be to support effective, accountable, and representative global institutions.

References

Ahn, Choong Yong. 2010. "To Remain Relevant, the G20 Needs Seoul's Development Agenda." *Global Asia* 5, no. 3 (Fall).

Concord and AidWatch. 2010. "Penalty against Poverty: More and Better EU Aid Can Score Millennium Development Goals." Brussels.

Department for International Development (DFID). 2001. "Middle-Income Countries Strategy." London.

Gavas, Mikaela, Deborah Johnson, and Simon Maxwell. 2010. "Consolidation or Cooperation: The Future of EU Development Cooperation." Discussion paper. Bonn: German Development Institute (www.die-gdi.de/CMS-Homepage/openwebcms3. nsf/(ynDK_contentByKey)/ANES-875B3N/$FILE/DP%206.2010.pdf).

Henson, Spencer, and Johanna Lindstrom. 2010. "Aid to Developing Countries: Where Does the U.K. Public Stand? Results and Analysis from the U.K. Public Opinion Monitor." Institute of Development Studies, University of Sussex, September.

Maxwell, S. 2009. "From Crisis Management to Long-Term Prosperity: The Role of the Commonwealth." Paper presented to Commonwealth Finance Ministers' Meeting, Limassol, Cyprus, September 30–October 2. Commonwealth Secretariat, London (www.simonmaxwell.eu/images/stories/fmm095%20%20from%20crisis%20 management%20to%20long-term%20prosperity%20-%20the%20role%20of%20 the%20commonwealth.pdf).

Sumner, A. 2010. "Global Poverty and the New Bottom Billion: What If Three-Quarters of the World's Poor Live in Middle-Income Countries?" Institute of Development Studies, September (www.ids.ac.uk/index.cfm?objectid=D840B908-E38D-82BD-A66A89123C11311F).

Te Velde, Dirk W. 2010. "The G20 Framework for Strong, Sustainable, and Balanced Growth: What Role for Low-Income, Small, and Vulnerable Countries?" London: Overseas Development Institute, June (www.odi.org.uk/resources/download/4905.pdf).

16

The G20 and Development:
From Financial Stability to Sustained Growth

JOMO KWAME SUNDARAM

The ascendance of the G20 to holding summit meetings at the leaders' level (L20) seized on the urgent need to address the world economic meltdown triggered by the subprime mortgage crisis in the U.S. housing market, in 2007. Although the G20 finance ministers and central bank governors group was established back in 1999 following the Asian financial crisis, with the Great Recession of 2008–09 it has evolved into what it calls the premier forum for discussion among major industrial and emerging market countries of key issues related to global economic stability and growth.

During its first year, the L20 was quite successful in leading and coordinating some crucial international aspects of crisis management. However, the recent preoccupation with large public finance deficits and the reduced sense of urgency following the tepid, uneven, and fragile recovery since mid-2009 threatens to undermine its earlier success. There is concern that because recovery remains fragile and uneven, uncoordinated austerity-based (rather than growth-based) fiscal consolidation in major economies will precipitate a double dip recession. What's more, the current policy preoccupation with deficit reduction threatens official development assistance (ODA) already pledged. Earlier calls for internationally coordinated financial regulation, curbs on executive remuneration, and taxation of financial institutions and transactions are not expected to result in much progress in the near future. The threat of regulatory arbitrage once again undermines internationally coordinated strengthening of regulation at the national level.

At the same time, existing development crises emanating from the Great Recession are further compounded by climate change as well as food and fuel price hikes, threatening achievements in reducing poverty and hunger. Climate change adversely affects poor and vulnerable groups and countries disproportionately more than others. Hence, the Korean initiative to put development on the G20 agenda was timely, appropriate, and laudable. The G20 can do the most good by adopting and advancing the financing for development (FfD) agenda agreed to in Monterrey in 2002 and by ensuring that financial system reform is consistently countercyclical, developmental, and inclusive.

The Millennium Development Goals and Development

The United Nations has been associated for decades with development, and it is important to differentiate between the internationally agreed development goals that have come out of the summits and conferences since the 1990s and the Millennium Development Goals (MDGs), which were the focus of the MDGs summit in September 2010. The summit's assessment of the MDGs suggests that there has been some progress, but that it has been uneven. There have been important setbacks with the recent multiple crises, but the MDGs remain achievable, although some specific targets may not be met.

The overriding emphasis on the importance of official development assistance in achieving the MDGs by 2015 has drawn its fair share of criticism. In recent decades, international development has been consigned to ministries or departments of international development cooperation with limited authority to disburse limited resources for ODA and technical cooperation. And ministries in developing countries that address development issues are often not present at international negotiations affecting development that are held at the UN and elsewhere.

The MDGs' focus on social targets was largely a response to growing inequality, reductions in government spending, especially social provisioning, and the failure of the influential, if not hegemonic, Washington Consensus to accelerate economic growth. Instead, the consensus urged market liberalization and anti-inflation measures, with little regard for distribution and welfare beyond temporary targeted social safety nets during crises. In response to criticisms, structural adjustment programs (SAPs) were replaced by country assessments based on ostensibly country-owned poverty reduction strategy papers (PRSPs), most of which lacked any serious employment generation strategy to reduce destitution. Critics have claimed that the PRSPs are thinly disguised SAPs, often drafted for rather than by developing country governments.

An important element of the MDGs commitment has been the focus on international cooperation associated with goal 8, expanding and strengthening international partnerships, on which there has been very uneven and limited progress. Over the last decade, the amount of ODA delivered has been less than half the target first established in 1971. There has also been little progress on addressing related problems of aid effectiveness, predictability, volatility, and fragmentation. Especially troubling has been the difficulty of getting delivery on commitments already made—including, for instance, the G8 commitments on enhancing food security made at the l'Aquila summit in 2009.

Despite repeated commitments to conclude the Doha round of trade negotiations, the likelihood of achieving a truly developmental outcome is far from ensured. While a few countries, mainly in East Asia, have been able to accelerate their industrialization through improved market access, earlier trade liberalization has resulted in deindustrialization in most developing countries. National food insecurity is on the rise, with many countries in Sub-Saharan Africa having been transformed from net food exporters in the 1980s into net food importers more recently. Aid for trade (AfT) is supposed to be additional to existing ODA commitments; consequently, there is concern that aid diversion for AfT is intended to induce developing countries to accept what is on offer in the Doha round regardless of the adverse longer-term implications for development. Concessions to the least developed countries (LDCs)—such as providing 100 percent duty-free and quota-free market access—have been held back for similar reasons, even though it will take years for most LDCs to be able to develop new productive capacities and take advantage of such concessions.

Despite recent development-related UN summits, there has been little progress on many long-standing concerns, including the absence of an agreed framework to accelerate sovereign debt workouts. Although global efforts to achieve the MDGs have helped spur progress in dealing with the heavily indebted poor countries (HIPCs), there is still no proper sovereign debt resolution framework; that has become painfully obvious with the broad range of countries recently hit by sovereign debt problems, including not only poor countries but also middle-income as well as some wealthy countries.

There has also been relatively modest progress on lowering the prices of essential medicines, enhancing technology transfer, and improving access to new technology, so crucial not only for essential medicines, but also for increasing smallholder food production as well as addressing climate change mitigation and adaptation.

Some Key Lessons for Addressing Development Challenges

In order to enhance economic growth as well as stability, there is certainly an urgent need for a consistently countercyclical as well as developmental macroeconomic policy framework and institutions. That has to be achieved largely at the international level. Development requires dynamic structural change that is sustainable and equitable, as demonstrated by the Northern European and Northeast Asian experiences. There is also renewed recognition of the need for development strategies that are truly nationally owned and for greater national policy space to accelerate development. International assistance is also required to ensure affordable social protection, even for some of the poorest economies, especially to achieve the MDGs, address inequalities, and overcome social exclusion.

Below I list some important lessons, learned over the recent decades, about reducing global poverty and substantially improving living conditions around the world:

—National ownership of development strategies, with sufficient fiscal policy space, is a fundamental principle to be respected and ensured by the international community.

—One-size-fits-all policies and programs that are adopted without considering context and circumstances are bound to fail.

—Sustained and equitable growth, which requires dynamic structural change, is crucial for making substantial progress in reducing poverty.

—Macroeconomic policy should be developmental, supporting the growth of real output and employment, instead of being narrowly focused on low inflation, balanced budgets, and current account deficits. Making public investments, managing capital flows, and supporting agriculture as well as small and medium-sized enterprises are crucial for strong, sustained, and balanced development.

—A universal social protection floor can help maintain and regenerate livelihoods, particularly for the disadvantaged and vulnerable. Universal social provisioning is affordable, even for the poorest countries.

—Addressing inequalities and social exclusion is critical. Inequality and social exclusion limit the contribution of growth to poverty reduction and attainment of the other MDGs.

—Lack of adequate, consistent, predictable financial support and a coherent, predictable policy environment at the national and international levels are major constraints.

—There is an urgent need to ensure more supportive international frameworks for trade, taxation, and technology, especially for climate change mitigation and adaptation, to sustain inclusive long-term development.

—Sufficient, predictable, and well-coordinated financing for development and budget support should include ODA, philanthropy, debt relief, and new financing sources.

UN-G20 Complementarities: Legitimacy, Inclusiveness, Effectiveness

Although the G20 is a more inclusive policy forum than the G7/G8, it is still an ad hoc arrangement, a self-selected, informal group. Some claim that limited membership is necessary for effective action. But more than one-third of the world's people and 85 percent of its countries have no effective voice in the G20. It lacks the legitimacy of the United Nations, an inclusive charter-based organization. Nonetheless, the G20 represents a large portion of the global economy. Thus, the G20 and the UN can and should play complementary roles in ongoing recovery and reform efforts; for both bodies, legitimacy and effectiveness need not be mutually exclusive.

Taking into account the global context as well as lessons from the UN experience, the following suggestions can prove vital to addressing the G20 development agenda:

—Prudential risk management, including capital controls (both the IMF and the World Bank now support this goal, which is in fact a sovereign right under the IMF's Articles of Agreement, VI).

—Enhancement of both fiscal and policy space to ensure consistently countercyclical macroeconomic policies—not only in recessionary conditions, but also in boom times—to minimize dangers due to bubbles, manias, and panics.

—Development of an alternative macroeconomic policy framework for productive employment creation and sustained growth.

—Development finance for investment and technology development to accelerate structural change.

—Inclusive finance to promote and support productive economic activities largely ignored by or overcharged by existing credit facilities—for example, smallholder agriculture and small and medium-sized enterprises.

—Greater international tax cooperation for enhancing revenue and fiscal space for all countries.

—More efficient, equitable, and effective debt workout mechanisms for more predictability to ensure less disruption and to enhance fiscal and policy space.

—International economic governance reform to reflect the changed global economic balance while ensuring more equitable voice and participation, thereby enhancing inclusiveness and legitimacy.

What Can the G20 Do?

First and foremost, we all need to ensure a strong, sustained, and balanced global recovery. With that broad goal in mind, a number of actions can be recommended to achieve various objectives, as follows:

Rebalancing the Global Economy

Over the past decade, developing countries have been financing the external deficits of major industrial countries. Much of those transfers have taken the form of investment of foreign exchange reserves accumulated by developing countries for protection against external shocks. A reversal of this pattern is needed.

—The G20 should help to redress the global imbalances through reforms to the global reserve system. That would reduce the need for massive reserve accumulation by individual countries for self-protection, facilitate greater pooling of reserves at the international level, and substantially increase the world's capacity to deploy international liquidity—such as special drawing rights (SDRs)—to deal with balance-of-payments crises and enhance resources for sustainable development financing.

Facilitating Financial Transfers

The achievement of the internationally agreed development goals, including the MDGs, will require much larger financial transfers to developing countries. Developing countries must have adequate and predictable access to flows of ODA and multilateral financing (concessional and non-concessional). Crisis-induced budget deficits and fiscal consolidation among larger G20 members must not lead to cuts in their aid budgets.

—The G20 should improve aid effectiveness, outlined in the 2005 Paris Declaration and 2008 Accra Agenda. The G20 should also examine how those mechanisms can be supplemented with more innovative measures to improve access to additional finance for climate change mitigation and adaptation as well as aid for trade.

Facilitating Investment

The financial crisis led to a sharp but brief fall of private capital flows to developing countries, followed by the resumption of hot money flows to emerging markets. But real investment trends remain tepid, with added concerns about the risk of investment protectionism in response to the crisis. At the Toronto summit, G20 leaders emphasized the importance of enhancing foreign investment opportunities and avoiding new protectionist measures.

—G20 members should help mobilize private investment through the multilateral development banks and by promoting increased bilateral and multilateral cooperation with developing countries.

Ensuring Countercyclical Prudential Regulation

Surges in short-term capital flows to emerging economies may generate inflationary pressures and destabilize currencies and financial markets. Appropriate prudential regulation and measures are needed to restrict the impact of excessive capital inflows on national economies. Greater consideration should be given to restricting international capital mobility—for example, through the use of international taxes or national capital controls—to reduce the risk of financial crises.

—G20 members should support and develop guidelines for countercyclical capital account management to limit excessive foreign capital inflows in boom times, and to limit capital flight during crises.

Ensuring External Debt Sustainability

The external debt situation of many developing countries has deteriorated because of falling trade, remittances, and capital flows and the increased volatility of commodity prices. Many "post-completion point" HIPCs still have debt burdens well above the thresholds used for their debt write-off. As a result, other low-income countries and several middle- and even high-income countries have found their difficult debt situations exposed.

 —*The G20 should help expedite the development of a fair process for working out sovereign debts that takes into account the interests of both debtors and creditors in order to reduce the costly uncertainty and disruption associated with sovereign debt crises.*

Ensuring Inclusive and Development-Oriented Financial Sectors

The recent Basel III agreement to require banking institutions to more than triple core tier-one capital ratios from 2 percent to 7 percent by 2019 is said to be necessary for ensuring financial sector stability. However, it does not address the continued dangers posed by the persistence of the shadow banking system and the dangerous procyclicality of such ostensible safeguards. Moreover, it is likely to raise the cost of credit and further constrain financial inclusion and development financing. The ongoing financial regulatory and supervisory reforms may thus inadvertently impede economic growth, especially in developing countries. Financial regulation in developing countries should instead promote both financial stability and inclusion.

 —*In this connection, the G20 Toronto Declaration agreed to strengthen developing countries' efforts to develop inclusive finance, especially to support small and medium-sized enterprises.*

Enhancing Domestic Resource Mobilization

Illicit financial flows, especially those related to tax evasion, constitute an enormous drain on the resources of both developing and developed countries. The linkages between tax evasion and other illegal international activities, such as money laundering, terrorism, and drug trafficking, underscore the urgency for more effective international responses.

 —*The G20 should support the creation of an intergovernmental commission for international tax cooperation to build on the work of the UN Committee of Experts on International Cooperation in Tax Matters, which has proposed a code of conduct on cooperation in combating international tax evasion.*

Completing the Doha Development Agenda

 —*The G20 should provide stronger leadership and make more tangible contributions to enhance the development impact of the Doha Round of trade negotiations in order to expedite its conclusion.* In the meantime, the G20 should explore other means of improving market access for developing countries, including the early and effective implementation of duty-free, quota-free access for the least developed countries.

Facilitating Trade

Many developing countries need assistance to facilitate trade and to improve their trade-related infrastructure and productive capacities and capabilities. Much more needs to be done to improve the quality and quantity of AfT, which should remain additional to ODA commitments. At the Toronto summit, G20 leaders committed themselves to maintaining the momentum for AfT.

—*The G20 should ensure that AfT also goes to developing countries, especially the LDCs, to enhance their international competitiveness and foster economic growth by strengthening their productive and export capacities and capabilities.* It should also compensate them for lost tariff revenue and productive capacities due to trade liberalization.

Global Green New Deal

In early 2009, the UN secretary-general advanced the idea of a Global Green New Deal (GGND) for simultaneously tackling the problems of global economic recovery, climate change mitigation, and other related developmental challenges. Soon after the crisis exploded in late 2008, the secretary-general proposed that the GGND address, in a coherent way, the multiple crises. It is useful to recall U.S. president Franklin Roosevelt's New Deal of the mid-1930s, which contributed not only to output recovery but also to jobs recovery. Renewable energy is now generally acknowledged to have much greater potential for job creation than fossil fuel energy.

There is now a broad consensus that significant amounts of "green investment," much of it upfront, will be needed to address climate change mitigation as well as adaptation and the challenges to environmental sustainability. However, the global financial crisis will have long-lasting implications for financial flows to developing countries, particularly as capital becomes scarcer and more expensive at a time when financing needs, such as for "green infrastructure," are expected to increase.

—*The G20 should adopt the GGND framework for sustainable and balanced recovery and facilitate financing of green investment.* That would require global cross-subsidization and large-scale public investment to attract private investment—for example, through international feed-in tariffs to promote renewable energy provision.

Following years of easy credit and overinvestment before the crisis, the world now faces underutilized overcapacity in most profitable economic sectors and hence an understandable reluctance for the private sector to invest. That is precisely why special arrangements and public investments are needed to induce the large-scale investment that can generate renewable energy and mitigate global warming. Public investments do not necessarily crowd out private investment, as has often been presumed; in fact, public investments are often vital to induce badly needed private investments, through public-private partnerships. Such investments will also put late-comer developing countries on a renewable energy path, thus ensuring that their development will not exacerbate global warming.

Only well-coordinated cross-border public investments can fund the needed green public goods and induce complementary private investments. G20 coordination support will ensure not only a more sustainable economic recovery, but also a more equitable recovery. It will also advance the international community's efforts to address global warming, food security, and development challenges together.

Concluding Remarks

A historic opportunity is upon us. If we do not urgently address these issues, we will miss a crucial window for fundamental systemic reform—the "Bretton Woods moment"—offered by the crisis. Fifteen years after the 1929 crash and the beginning of the Great Depression and toward the end of World War II, leaders from forty-four countries (including twenty-eight developing countries) met at the United Nations Conference on Monetary and Financial Affairs at Bretton Woods for three weeks. They created the IMF and the International Bank for Reconstruction and Development (IBRD) as part of a yet-to-be-established UN system to lay the grounds for postwar reconstruction, postcolonial development, and the unprecedentedly long period of sustained growth and job creation that followed, referred to as the postwar Golden Age. Such a rare opportunity to address long postponed systemic reform has come again, with G20 leaders uniquely positioned to rise to this historic challenge. But in order to do so adequately, the challenge of policy coherence must be met and the agenda must shift from monetary and financial stability alone to broader systemic and sustainable developmental challenges.

The emphasis on aid disbursement for social objectives, said to have been encouraged by the focus on achieving the MDGs, has recently given way to a more pragmatic—and less ideological—approach to accelerating economic growth, reflected, for example, in the recommendations of the World Bank-based Growth Commission. A renewed emphasis can be seen on the need to create conditions more conducive to accelerating economic growth, including infrastructure provision.

The G20 growth framework seeks to ensure that growth is characterized by inclusiveness and resilience, both of which are necessary for sustainable and equitable development. The G20 initiatives for economic recovery successfully facilitated monetary and fiscal stimuli while limiting protectionism of different types. The working and expert groups set up by the G20 finance ministers are addressing important challenges, including financial inclusion, not addressed at Bretton Woods. However, actual progress on financial reforms suggests there is still much work to be done to ensure future monetary and financial stability, to enhance arrangements to prevent and manage crises, and to ensure that financial institutions and arrangements will finance accelerated growth and employment creation.

As the G20 started off as an initiative of finance ministers, the United Nations contributions on financing for development are probably most useful and relevant. Most relevant in this regard is the 2002 Monterrey Consensus on FfD. The Monterrey initiatives involved six areas, including domestic resource mobilization, and the need for enhanced international cooperation on taxation is especially important in this regard. The other FfD areas include international trade, capital flows, aid, debt, and systemic issues.

The G20 can play a critical leading role in enhancing FfD initiatives, and some of its own initiatives thus far demonstrate its potential. For example, the London summit decision to emit SDRs provided additional liquidity and resources for the IMF. Further SDR emissions can not only supplement international liquidity; they can also be countercyclical and developmental and become the basis for an alternative reserve currency system.

17

Infrastructure and Development: A New Area for International Cooperation

SERGIO BITAR

I would like to put forward that the time has come to include infrastructure on the international policy agenda of developed nations in support of growth in developing countries. Based on extensive experience accumulated during Chile's democratic governments, from 1990 to 2010, I illustrate the impact that a sound infrastructure plan has on growth and equity and how developed countries and companies can invest and build partnerships with the public sector and private local firms. New ideas for economic development should be addressed by the G20. The G20 must operate "as a premier market place for development paradigms" (Lim 2010, p. 71).

Infrastructure as a Vital Part of Development Policies

Economic policies and instruments aimed at higher economic growth are usually dispersed or applied in segments. They reflect different settings and circumstances, and countries lacking a coherent strategy and a systemic vision usually pay the price down the road. In the recent past, the proposals most frequently made by international organizations and developed countries to less developed ones concerned inflation control, reduction of fiscal deficits, and flexible rates of exchange. Those proposals also preached a reduction in the functions and the size of the public sector and the freeing up of market forces.

A different set of policies has now been designed to pursue social objectives—poverty reduction, basic housing, health, and education. On the growth and

investment side of international cooperation, in addition to aid, trade exceptions, and incentives for foreign investments, new instruments have gained relevance: innovation, technical assistance, free trade agreements (FTAs), and public-private partnerships in infrastructure.

However, what is still lacking is a better understanding of the interaction
between the different approaches and a way to link and integrate them into one
framework and thus achieve sustained development. As Colin Bradford points
out, "21st century challenges are horizontal, characterized more by linkages than
their isolation from other issues" (Bradford 2010, p. 43). To be successful, then,
infrastructure policies and plans also must work together.

Infrastructure's Impact on Development

Building infrastructure contributes enormously to economic growth and equal
opportunities. It facilitates export expansion by increasing productivity, lowering
transport costs, and creating new connections with areas suitable for agriculture,
mining, and tourism. It also helps to reduce marginality, a major cause of poverty, by connecting new and rural areas by land, sea, rivers, and air. In addition,
it facilitates regional integration and social inclusion by providing easier access to
education, health, water, electricity, and markets for small firms. New ventures,
investments, and employment soar.

Studies show a clear and positive correlation between growth and investment
in roads, ports, airports, dams, and water systems (Rozas and Sanchez 2004;
Machicado 2007; and Cipoletta, Perez, and Sanchez 2007). In most cases—in
Latin America, Asia, and Europe—research demonstrates that the correlation is
higher in the early or middle stages of a country's economic development.

However, these two effects of infrastructure—growth and equity—are often
unnoticed, not emphasized enough in political debates or given priority by
international organizations, in spite of their high multiplier effect. Such a weak
perception of the importance of infrastructure must be corrected in order to gain
the political support needed for a persistent and stable level of investment.

Lessons from the Chilean Experience

The Chilean case (1990–2010) is a useful and successful example. Investments
in infrastructure confirm a positive link with growth, territorial integration, and
the competitiveness of main export activities. The continuity and stability of
policies and projects during a span of two decades proved fruitful.

The military dictatorship (1973–89) left the country with a high deficit in
public works, among other flaws. The new democratic government had to deal
with consolidating democratic procedures and human rights, reducing inflation

and unemployment, attracting foreign capital, and reducing poverty. The development strategy that was devised to address those issues—which was followed by four successive governments—was named "Growth with Equity."

Export growth was enhanced by a series of free trade agreements (fifty-seven agreements were in operation in 2010), and as a result, new markets were available for our exports. But exporting required a rapid improvement in infrastructure. The long distances from Chile to large markets made it imperative to reduce transportation costs, create greater capacity, and improve the quality of services. Moreover, our development strategy had a priority: to play an active role in the South Pacific by offering good infrastructure services and free trade agreements for trade and investment between Asia and South America. Chile's free trade agreements with China, Korea, and Japan on one hand and Argentina, Brazil, and other Latin American countries on the other require good infrastructure and efficient logistics—in addition to supportive customs, financing, and security arrangements, strict anticorruption norms, and the right, proactive attitude for achieving results. Chile's membership in APEC (whose 2004 meeting took place in Santiago) reinforced the commitment to expand toward the Pacific. New laws including incentives to attract foreign firms to take advantage of our FTAs with Asian countries were passed in order to transform Chile over the long term into a "platform" for drawing companies that produce goods and services for the international market.

Meanwhile, a number of Latin American nations have developed a major plan comprising large projects to connect different countries through roads, electric facilities, and oil and gas pipelines. The IIRSA initiative (Initiative for the Integration of Regional Infrastructure in South America), which was created in 2000 in Brasilia and includes twelve countries, has helped to design a new vision for Latin American integration. IIRSA has identified 514 projects (forty-seven large groups of projects) with an estimated investment of $69 billion (see www.iirsa.com).

In Chile, public investment in infrastructure expanded after 1990, but the need exceeded the available resources by far. To accelerate growth and increase equity, the government required more resources. Besides public financing, two other sources could provide funds—international financial organizations (World Bank, Inter-American Development Bank, Corporacion Andina de Fomento) and private capital. The government decided to resort to the latter by enhancing public-private partnerships.

Between 1993 and 1998 three bills were sent to and then revised and approved by Chile's Congress. The first law established new procedures and formulas for granting long-term concessions to private firms for the building and operation of public works, in particular interurban and urban highways and airports, supervised by the Ministry of Public Works. The initial success of those initiatives led to a new stage, in which the same model was used to build jails, dams, hospitals, and public buildings and even to plan a very large tunnel through the Andes to connect Chile and Argentina. In that case, both countries have had to harmonize their concession laws.

In a short period of time, highway and airport services were upgraded. The first law was improved in 2010, taking into consideration the criteria suggested by the OECD (OECD 2007). The state was also able to free its resources in distant regions, connecting areas with comparative advantages in agriculture, mining, and aquaculture. In addition, toll roads had a progressive effect on income distribution because they were paid for by resources extracted from those who used cars instead by fiscal income from all citizens.

The second law concerned ports. It allows private capital to invest in and manage ports through a long-term agreement, while infrastructure will stay in the state's hands. Public bidding attracted many Chilean and foreign companies, and our capacity and productivity grew.

The third law concerned water. The state owned several water supply plants located in various parts of the country. By law, the state granted concessions to private companies to operate those plants and build others and defined strict regulations to ensure water supply and quality and to decide prices. As a senator, I participated in the discussions to put enough safeguards in place to ensure efficiency, consumer protection, and a transparent system for defining prices and resolving controversies. The system has worked. Subsequent adjustments have been made to include sewage treatment in cities and to expand underground rainwater channels in cities.

In 2010, over 99 percent of the Chilean population had access to potable water and over 95 percent had treated waste water in urban centers. These figures rank among the highest in the world. A positive effect was reflected in health indexes and agricultural production. Public funds became available for investing in rural areas, dams, and flood protection.

With regard to energy, private companies are operating in the generation, transmission, and distribution of energy under a regulatory system to ensure investment as well as efficient and sustainable production through a price calculation procedure. At the same time, a new law was passed in order to provide incentives for investing in renewable energy.

These laws, procedures, and institutions created to ensure coordination allowed Chile to advance rapidly. Private investment, mostly foreign, contributed with almost 30 percent of total financing in public works between 1995 and 2010. Furthermore, thanks to such private flows, the government liberated resources to build smaller projects favoring low-income families around the nation.

Infrastructure expansion resulted from a national plan. Success depended and will depend in the future on consensus building. This approach was embodied in "Chile 2020: Infraestructura para el Desarrollo [Chile 2010: Infrastructure for Development]," a January 2010 report issued under my direction by the Ministry of Public Works (www.mop.cl/2020).

Preconditions for a Successful Infrastructure Program

The implementation of a systematic infrastructure program requires a more advanced level of economic and institutional development. At least five preconditions should be in place to ensure success:

—*A shared political decision* based on the conviction that human capital (education) and physical capital (infrastructure) are the two pillars on which the future must be built. The public sector should focus on both, from a long-term perspective. That requires a global view and a commitment shared by both principal national forces—the government and opposition parties—to lend continuity to a set of projects and strategies through different administrations. Moreover, developed countries must commit themselves to increase financing from international financial institutions for infrastructure projects.

—*A responsible economic policy* that ensures stability, reduces ups and downs, prevents fiscal deficits, and applies flexible exchange rates. Inconsistencies or fluctuations in public investment constitute the worst adversary for infrastructure projects, which are the first to suffer when fiscal cuts occur. In the Chilean case, monetary and exchange policies were taken in harmony with fiscal measures. Public debt decreased from 70 percent to 7 percent of GDP between 1990 and 2010. The creation of the Economic and Social Stabilization Fund (financed by the increase in copper prices) enabled better macromanagement, low inflation, and financing of public initiatives in the midst of the international crisis to sustain employment.

—*Laws and institutions* that build confidence among local and foreign investors, covering the need for an independent and efficient judiciary, a sound procedure for resolving disputes, transparency of all bidding processes, a clear anticorruption stance and measures to combat it, and, finally, a specialized government unit made up of capable professionals who can design, negotiate, and supervise infrastructure works.

—*A solid and duly regulated banking system* that can ensure that major infrastructure programs have access to private financing. After a rough financial crisis in the 1980s in Chile, new regulations were established. Today the Chilean banking system shows high capital ratios and provisions, and it was not infected with toxic assets. Such solidity is an advantage for infrastructure development. First, the banking system is able to provide short-term financing for construction and, second, it has the capacity to transform short-term credits into a bond system to cover the fifteen to twenty years needed to finance concessions.

—*A long-term plan* that transcends one administration and is followed by the next. Such a process requires the active participation of regional actors as well as local participation and technical support. It should be revised every two to four years to introduce the necessary adjustments.

It is worthwhile to explore, in addition to the five preconditions, why infrastructure projects do not seem to be of great relevance in public debates and political proposals. It is also important to seek ways to extend support for such projects, both nationally and internationally. In my experience, it is feasible to increase public perception of the importance of infrastructure when there is a clear political commitment. Sustained efforts to provide and share information with the public, members of national legislatures, and major stakeholders are needed to highlight the importance of infrastructure projects for development and equity in their respective regions. A change in perceptions requires a narrative that can stand over the long term. As projects affect specific areas and communities, it is essential to foster partnerships with regional governments to jointly define projects and provide financing while simultaneously creating opportunities for citizens to participate in the preparation of plans.

One should bear in mind that major investments in roads, dams, airports, and generation plants, among others, are carried out far from cities and are not easily seen by the population at large. Neither do they benefit lower-income groups directly, since members of those groups often do not use cars, much less airplanes. For them especially, clear explanations are needed about the positive effects of infrastructure projects in their daily lives. Moreover, in order to avoid conflicts, governments must have nationwide programs that include most areas and cities, establish regional balance, define priorities, and make real benefits known to those involved—for example, the benefits of connectivity for growth, of water systems for health and agriculture, of ports and airports for exports, and of tourism for opportunities for small firms and employment.

Finally, I think that evaluation of infrastructure projects in general tends to minimize the benefits and must be reviewed. Usually, such evaluations measure only time savings and exclude collateral innovations such as the creation of new ventures, improvements in quality of life, and easy and rapid access to public services, education, and health. In the case of cultural or ecological tourism, proposals for special programs, which normally are more expensive, are discarded when expected traffic creation and spending by tourists are underestimated.

On the international side, the possibility of attracting foreign companies to invest in infrastructure in developing and emerging countries will depend on the preconditions described previously, but additional factors may help. A government counterpart of private firms, with high technical standards and the administrative authority to make decisions and solve problems, will be invaluable. The promotion of the main projects among potential investors will also favor a positive response.

Moreover, in the early phases, foreign investors may require additional guarantees or ensured minimum income until the concession system gains stability.

In Chile, the experience has been successful. Spanish firms took the lead, followed by builders and concession managers from Italy, Germany, Sweden, and Mexico. All of them had extensive experience in their countries of origin, so they were familiar with the kind of business they were involved in. Along the road, some of them failed while others consolidated and expanded. More recently, Italians and Colombians took over some Spanish firms. When Chile called for bids to build hospitals, firms from France and Brazil presented offers, sometimes as consortia made up of different companies.

The benefits for Chile have exceeded costs. Organizational expertise and technology were transferred, and Chilean companies learned from them. Partnerships soared. Banks and services from the countries of origin follow the companies. Officials from other governments, primarily Latin American but also Eastern European, came to observe this experience and the workings of our system. International companies also learned and transferred the knowledge that they acquired abroad.

When business is sound, with clearly outlined laws and procedures in place, governments can explain their aims and thereby attract investors. This approach can now be enhanced by governments of developed countries that are willing to search for new avenues of international cooperation.

Time for International Cooperation in Infrastructure

The time has indeed come to give priority to infrastructure in development plans and projects.

—Actions must transcend aid and trade exceptions. Infrastructure is an essential factor for growth, enhancing exports, increasing productivity, and improving the well-being of low-income families.

—Developed countries (and also emerging ones) can actively promote the participation of national and regional financial institutions as well as their large firms in financing and bidding for new projects. Banks and pension funds are and will be more involved in the future in such initiatives. Large contractors and companies that operate concessions can associate with their local counterparts and transfer their knowledge and management expertise.

—A synergetic combination of public funds, international financing, and public-private partnerships (PPPs) could be designed specifically for different countries, in accordance with their level of development and multiyear plans.

—PPPs are a new and specific form of foreign investment. Banks can agree to long-term financing with governments based on guarantees like minimum income for new concessions.

—Many countries (Chile and Korea, among others) show positive performance in PPPs. They can offer technical information and share their institutional and legal experiences to attract investment to other developing countries, helping them to create a regulatory system that facilitates the building of trust for a promising public-private partnership. OECD (2010) reports a vast variety of best practices. Such factors are worth considering when thinking about new global initiatives to attain a "strong, sustainable, and balanced growth," as stated in the G20 framework.

References

Bradford, Colin. 2010. "Pragmatic Leadership for the 21st Century." In *The New Dynamics of Summitry*, edited by Colin Bradford and Wonhyuk Lim. Seoul: Korea Development Institute.

Cipoletta, G.., G. Perez, and R. Sanchez. 2010. "Políticas Integradas de Infraestructura, Transporte, Logística: Experiencias Internacionales y Propuestas [Integrated Infrastructure, Transport, and Logistics Policies: International Experiences and Proposals]." Santiago, Chile: CEPAL (May).

Lim, Wonhyuk. 2010. "Sharing Knowledge for Development." In *The New Dynamics of Summitry*, edited by Colin Bradford and Wonhyuk Lim. Seoul: Korea Development Institute.

Machicado, Carlos. 2007. "Macroeconomic and Welfare Effects of Public Infrastructure Investment." Corporación Andina de Fomento. Caracas, Venezuela (November).

OECD. 2007. *Principles for Private Sector Participation in Infrastructure* (Paris: 2007).

———. 2010. *Dedicated Public-Private Partnership Units* (Paris: 2010)

Rozas, Patricio, and Ricardo Sanchez. 2004. "Desarrollo de Infraestructura y Crecimiento Económico [Infrastructure Development and Economic Growth]." Santiago, Chile: CEPAL (October).

18

Sharing Knowledge for Development

WONHYUK LIM

Composed of advanced industrial nations and leading developing countries, the G20 provides a great opportunity to approach development issues from new directions. Whereas advanced industrial nations regard their own development as an achievement of the past and tend to take an aid-centric approach to international development, leading developing countries consider development a current policy challenge for themselves as well as for other developing countries and tend to adopt a growth-centric approach. In addition, leading developing countries are playing an increasingly important role in providing official development assistance (ODA) and setting up programs to share their own development experience and knowledge through South-South cooperation. Interaction between advanced industrial nations and leading developing countries within the G20 is bound to lead to intellectually stimulating and influential discussions on what really works for development. The G20 can serve not only as "the premier forum for international cooperation" but also as a premier marketplace for development approaches and practical case studies based on the actual experiences of its member countries. Toward that end, in cooperation with international organizations, the G20 should establish an interactive search-and-match platform to share knowledge for development and to set up a network of officials and experts who have an intimate knowledge of the challenges of development.

Alternative Development Paradigms

Development may be conceptualized as a result of synergies between enhanced human capital and new knowledge involving complementary investments in physical and social capital. The fundamental policy challenge is for the state to work with nonstate actors and markets to address innovation and coordination externalities while minimizing negative government externalities. Certainly, through incompetence and corruption, some governments may create more problems than they solve, but "getting the government out of the way" does not help resolve innovation and coordination externalities. Instead of dismissing the state from the outset, it would be more constructive to examine what needs to be done to increase competence and reduce corruption on the part of the state as it deals with innovation and coordination externalities (Lim 2011).

Although there are multiple approaches and paths to development (Rodrik 2007), there are basically two alternative development paradigms at the conceptual level. Differences in the two largely reflect differences in assumptions about the relative magnitudes of innovation and coordination externalities on the one hand and negative government externalities on the other. The first paradigm emphasizes the importance of having the right institutional framework and regards liberalization as key to development. The second paradigm focuses on the challenge of detecting and mitigating constraints as they emerge and argues that capacity building is critical to development. Sabel (2004) calls the first paradigm the "endowment" view and the second paradigm the "bootstrapping," or evolutionary, view of development. Yanagihara (1992) refers to the first paradigm as the "framework approach" and to the second as the "ingredients approach."

According to the endowment-framework paradigm, economies with "appropriate endowments" tend to grow and those lacking such endowments (or their functional equivalents) do not. Examples of appropriate endowments include cultural values and institutions regarded as being conducive to growth. According to this paradigm, the state should focus on getting the institutional framework "right" and then get out of the way. In other words, the state should release market forces and let enterprises and individuals play the game. The assumption underlying this liberalization agenda is that the state will generate large negative externalities if it tries to go beyond setting up the institutional framework and that free enterprises and individuals can adequately resolve innovation and coordination externalities. Moreover, there is an implicit assumption that the "right" institutional framework is universal.

In contrast, according to the bootstrapping-ingredients paradigm, the development challenge is not so much to get growth to start by adopting big-bang reforms as it is to sustain it by developing problem-solving networks to detect and mitigate constraints as they emerge. Developing countries frequently lack markets and institutions that advanced industrial nations take for granted, and the state should facilitate growth by supplying the missing ingredients, which are often characterized by externalities. According to this development paradigm, the key is for a country to retain ownership of its development and progressively expand its own capacity to add value and respond to shocks, even as it actively learns from and engages with the outside world. The assumption underlying this capacity-building agenda is that negative government externalities such as corruption can be contained and that the state should play an active role in addressing innovation and coordination externalities. Moreover, this paradigm tends to emphasize the importance of conducting experiments tailored to the local context rather than importing a set of institutions assumed to be universally applicable.

These differences in conceptualization lead to differences in policy prescriptions. The Washington Consensus, for instance, is based on the endowment-framework paradigm and advocates liberalization, privatization, and stabilization. In contrast, drawing from their own development experience, East Asian countries tend to subscribe to the bootstrapping-ingredients paradigm and emphasize the state's active role in progressively developing local capabilities (World Bank 1993). The Millennium Development Goals are also guided by the bootstrapping-ingredients paradigm, but they do not offer concrete policy guidelines on how to achieve poverty reduction and human development. These different approaches and paths to development potentially offer a large body of case studies from which developing countries can draw lessons.

Knowledge-Sharing Landscape

Emerging evidence indicates that the sharing of development experience and knowledge among peer practitioners can greatly contribute to local capacity development and ownership. A number of national governments and international organizations are engaged in this effort. In today's multipolar global economy, knowledge sharing no longer takes place only in the form of North-South cooperation. A growing number of developing countries are engaged in South-South cooperation. Also on the rise is triangular or trilateral cooperation, typically involving an international organization as an intermediary between two development partners.

Among international organizations, the UN's Special Unit for South-South Cooperation (SU/SSC) has provided leadership for many years. The World Bank, for its part, has set up the South-South Experience Exchange Trust Fund (SEETF), which is designed to respond to the needs of reformers in low-income countries by connecting them to policy experts from developing countries. The OECD has also developed a methodology for knowledge sharing among member countries. In addition, multiple international organizations have been strengthening their roles in facilitating the exchange of development experience and knowledge, including by operating platforms like the Global Development Learning Network (GDLN). Also, some international organizations have been using information collection and dissemination as an accountability mechanism, combined with something as simple as text messaging to reach the general public. The World Bank, for instance, has been making good use of "crowd assessment" and "dual-track ICR (implementation, completion, results)" to communicate directly with customers and assess and improve the effectiveness of its programs.

Among national governments, Germany's Federal Ministry for Economic Cooperation and Development (BMZ) commissions its implementing organizations to carry out financial and technical cooperation to provide assistance to developing countries. Japan is also actively engaged in knowledge sharing and recently introduced the Japanese model of quality and productivity improvement, *kaizen*, to Ethiopia and other African countries (GRIPS Development Forum 2009). Established in 2004 in cooperation with the UNDP, the International Poverty Reduction Center in China (IPRCC) promotes South-South cooperation— for example, sharing its experience in agricultural development with Tanzania.

Korea's Development Experience and Knowledge Sharing

Korea has been especially active in knowledge sharing, drawing from its own development experience (see appendix). Korea's dynamic development experience over the past half-century has been a source of fascination for development specialists and a source of inspiration for other developing countries eager to extract lessons that they can apply even if they cannot exactly replicate Korea's experience. Sharing Korea's development knowledge and tailoring policy advice to the needs of developing countries may be the greatest gift that Korea can offer the world.

Since launching its Knowledge Sharing Program (KSP) in 2004, Korea has provided policy consultations to twenty-four countries on topics ranging from development planning to crisis management. The Korean government sends out demand surveys to potential partner countries through its embassies and tailors its consultation projects to meet the needs of those countries. Former high-ranking government officials are directly involved in the policy consultations to share their intimate knowledge of development challenges. They describe in detail the decisionmaking process and pepper their descriptions with interesting anecdotes; they empathize with government officials in developing countries; and they complement the analytical work of policy experts and specialists who have extensive experience in their fields. The government officials and practitioners effectively pair up with their counterparts in development partner countries to work jointly on pressing policy challenges and share development knowledge in the process. This knowledge-sharing exercise is much more effective than a "one-size-fits-all" or template approach in discovering what really works for development. Furthermore, in a number of cases, policy consultations have led to substantive follow-up projects. For instance, a knowledge-sharing project on export development for the Dominican Republic (Lim 2009) subsequently led to a concessional loan program for a trade center and a technical assistance program to help establish the Dominican Export-Import Bank.

G20 Knowledge-Sharing Platform and Network

As national governments and international organizations increasingly engage in sharing development experience and knowledge, there is increased need for coordinated efforts to deal with two problems. First, the search-and-match mechanism for connecting demand with supply leaves much to be desired. There is no interactive knowledge-sharing platform that allows "customers" to compare and contrast various development case studies that interest them and permits "providers" to showcase their expertise and offer technical assistance. Second, inadequate funding prevents some low- and middle-income countries from sharing their experience and knowledge with potential development partners. For many developing countries, the OECD's "best practice" may be less relevant than the "promising experiments" of their peers, but resource constraints may impede useful South-South or triangular cooperation. These shortcomings represent areas where G20 intervention may be justified given its core objective of "strong, sustainable, and balanced growth" through international economic cooperation.

To optimize the search-and-match mechanism and to maximize the effectiveness of development through knowledge sharing, the G20 should consider a two-stage process in which a central platform would offer practical information through development case studies in the first stage and development partners would get together to craft tailor-made cooperation programs in the second stage. The G20 should also provide support so that low- and middle-income countries can share their experience and knowledge with their peers—for instance, through triangular cooperation managed by international organizations.

For this interactive knowledge-sharing platform to work, it is imperative that "customers" be able to select from a broad menu of options offered by "providers" to pinpoint the specific expertise that they need (a la the i-Phone model). A customer country should no longer have to contact various national governments and international organizations and assess the relevance of their experience for its needs in an ad hoc fashion. For instance, a developing country interested in obtaining practical advice on operating a free economic zone (FEZ) should be able to compare and contrast various case studies on FEZs offered by other countries. Once this customer country finds the best match for its needs, it should be able to contact the provider country and work together to craft a tailor-made cooperation program, with support from the G20 and international organizations if necessary. For instance, a country like Ghana might feel that it has a great deal to learn from Malaysia—an ethnically diverse, medium-sized country that has successfully diversified and upgraded its economic structure (Breisinger and others 2008)—and then contact Malaysia for practical advice on FEZs through bilateral or trilateral cooperation.

A system operator should manage the knowledge-sharing platform and work with national governments and international organizations to enrich its content and functionality. The system operator should take stock of existing platforms that facilitate the exchange of development experience and knowledge and create a "map" of the platforms with a view toward integrating them. Although the question of who plays the role of system operator may lead to a serious turf battle among institutions with a high stake in knowledge-sharing programs, the G20 should select the system operator based on merits. As an interim measure, the G20 may launch pilot platforms in specific areas such as vocational training and tax administration.

In addition, the G20 should establish a Knowledge Sharing Corps, or a network of officials and experts with an intimate knowledge of development challenges. They should work with their counterparts in development partner countries to discover jointly what works in the local context. This could complement the "Gray Peace Corps" proposed by Jagdish Bhagwati, which would hire large numbers of doctors, engineers, and scientists from aging industrial nations to deal with skill shortages in developing countries (Banerjee 2007, p. 96).

Appendix. Korea's Development Experience

Korea's development took place through the joint discovery and upgrading of comparative advantage. To promote development, the government and the private sector made joint efforts to address innovation and coordination externalities. The government shared the investment risks of the private sector and provided support largely based on performance in competitive global markets. The reinforcement of successful experiments through the feedback mechanism of performance-based rewards led to dramatic changes over time. Korea retained ownership of its export-oriented industrialization and progressively developed its own capabilities even as it actively engaged in external interaction to learn from and trade with the outside world. Committed to social cohesion, Korea pushed

This appendix is from Lim (2011) and Winters and others (2010), a paper commissioned by the Presidential Committee for the G20 Summit of Korea, available at www.sussex.ac.uk/economics/research/workingpapers and http://cid.kdi.re.kr/cid_eng/public/report_view.jsp?pageNo=1&pub_no=11569.

ahead with a coordinated program of trade, industrial, and human resource development to generate rapid, resilient, and shared growth.

Mitigating Downturns

Over the past fifty years, Korea experienced only two years of negative growth (1980 and 1998). Even as Korea embarked on its export-oriented industrialization in the 1960s, it made serious efforts to raise agricultural productivity to achieve food security and to narrow the urban-rural income gap to maintain social cohesion, mainly through the Saemaul Undong (New Village Movement). Flexible adjustment played a critical role in mitigating the impact of external shocks such as the oil price shocks of the 1970s. Macro policy discipline, in turn, provided a countercyclical buffer to mitigate downturns in the wake of the 1997–98 Asian economic crisis and the 2008 global financial crisis. In the wake of the 1997–98 crisis, Korea strengthened prudential regulation to safeguard financial stability and increased its international reserve accumulation to insure itself against sudden capital flow reversals. Korea's experience with financial sector development, in fact, illustrates the importance of having a set of institutions to monitor and discipline corporate management and highlights the risks of implementing asymmetrical market liberalization.

Raising the Underlying Growth Rate

International trade helped Korea to discover its comparative advantage and alleviate coordination failures; overcome the limits of its small domestic market and exploit scale economies; learn from good practices around the world and upgrade its economy; run a market test of government policies and corporate strategies; and devise performance-based reward schemes.

While relying on global markets, Korea made conscious and concerted efforts to move into higher-value-added areas along the value chain by making complementary investments in human capital and infrastructure. The government established mechanical/technical high schools as "centers of excellence" in each province, offering full scholarships to poor but talented young students. Universities were called upon to select one specialized engineering field, related to a nearby industrial complex if possible, and to develop an academic program to teach students in that field. Korea also invested in power, transport, communications, and water infrastructure to facilitate economic growth and human development. Improving infrastructure management required reform of state-owned enterprises.

Korea provides a prime example of the virtuous cycle involving economic growth and human development. Although Korea was one of the poorest countries in the world in the 1950s, it invested its limited resources in promoting universal primary education. Investing in people was not enough by itself to promote growth in the absence of complementary industrial and trade developments, but it provided the basis for Korea's initial take-off in the 1960s. Korea's rapid growth, in turn, facilitated human development and poverty reduction. Korea's human development index (HDI) rose at an average annual growth rate of 0.97 percent over the 1980–2007 period—the fastest rate of improvement among eighty-three "very high" and "high" human development countries, as classified by the UNDP.

Overarching Factors

The political economy changes triggered by the student revolution of 1960 and the military coup of 1961 proved critical to Korea's subsequent containment of corruption and establishment of merit-based institutions. Korea also made extensive efforts to narrow the knowledge gap with the outside world. The overarching factors of institutions and governance and access to knowledge provided the basis for Korea's rapid, resilient, and shared growth.

References

Banerjee, Abhijit Vinayak. 2007. *Making Aid Work.* MIT Press.
Breisinger, Clemens, and others. 2008. "Accelerating Growth and Structural Transformation: Ghana's Options for Reaching Middle-Income Country Status." IFPRI Discussion Paper 00750 (Washington: International Food Policy Research Institute).
GRIPS Development Forum. 2009. *Introducing KAIZEN in Africa.* Tokyo: GRIPS.
Lim, Wonhyuk. 2009. *Export Development for the Dominican Republic.* Seoul: Ministry of Strategy and Finance and Korea Development Institute.
———. 2011. "Joint Discovery and Upgrading of Comparative Advantage: Lessons from Korea's Development Experience." In *Postcrisis Growth and Development: A Development Agenda for the G-20*, edited by Shahrokh Fardoust, Yongbeom Kim, and Claudia Sepulveda. Washington: World Bank, pp.173–226.
Rodrik, Dani. 2007. *One Economics, Many Recipes: Globalization, Institutions, and Economic Growth.* Princeton University Press.
Sabel, Charles F. 2004. "Bootstrapping Development: Rethinking the Role of Public Intervention in Promoting Growth." Paper presented at the Protestant Ethic and Spirit of Capitalism Conference, Cornell University, Ithaca, New York, October 8-10.
Winters, L. Alan, and others. 2010. "Economic Growth in Low-Income Countries: How the G20 Can Help to Raise and Sustain It." Seoul: Korea Development Institute (www.sussex.ac.uk/economics/research/workingpapers and http://cid.kdi.re.kr/cid_eng/public/report_view.jsp?pageNo=1&pub_no=11569).
World Bank. 1993. *The East Asian Miracle: Economic Growth and Public Policy.* Oxford University Press.
Yanagihara, Toru. 1992. "Development and Dynamic Efficiency: 'Framework Approach' versus 'Ingredients Approach.'" Translated and published in *Japanese Views on Economic Development: Diverse Paths to the Market*, edited by Kenichi Ohno and Izumi Ohno. London and New York: Routledge, 1998.

PART V

The G20 and the System of International Institutions

19

IMF Legitimacy and Governance Reform: Will the G20 Help or Hinder?

THOMAS A. BERNES

The global financial crisis coincided with and was preceded in some degree by an IMF crisis. The IMF crisis, which involved the relationship between the G7 and the IMF, was in part a result of neglected governance issues, particularly on the part of the G7. Those issues still exist, and they need to be addressed by the G20; if they are not, they will fester again. The question becomes whether the G20 will be a help or a hindrance in addressing the issues of IMF legitimacy and governance.

The G20 has described itself as the premier forum for international economic cooperation. The IMF sees itself as the premier institution for international economic cooperation. The underlying question is what the real difference is between the premier forum and the premier institution. The G20 is a self-appointed, informal group with no secretariat and no legal framework. It was born of the recognition that the G7 no longer reflected economic reality in today's world. The IMF is a formal, universal, treaty-based organization, and its members have obligations to it. Prior to the economic crisis in 2007–08, the IMF was increasingly being seen as ineffective in its mission by many and lacking in evenhandedness by the emerging markets, in part because of the role that the G7 grew to play behind closed doors and in part because most of the membership of the IMF felt that they did not have a say in its management and policy work. That view was reflected in the difficult discussions on IMF quotas (country shares) and representation (chairs) on the fund's executive board, which remain ongoing.[1]

A year or so before the outbreak of the financial crisis, an existential debate was under way about the future role of the IMF. The new managing director, Dominique Strauss-Kahn, came into office with a mandate (principally by the G7) to bring about major changes in the organization. Significant cutbacks in IMF staff were implemented (although a number of the staff had to be brought back to assist when the financial crisis broke out). Questions were raised on what the role of the IMF should be going forward. Interestingly, at the time the G7 countries did not see the IMF as being especially relevant to them as far as their economies were concerned (interesting, in retrospect, given the origins of the global financial crisis), although they saw utility in the role that the fund might play vis-à-vis the emerging markets. The emerging markets, on the other hand, saw the IMF as lacking evenhandedness and questioned its policy advice. The role and mission of the IMF were not clear—and definitely not agreed on by the key players, whose contrasting views were clearly brought out in an evaluation by the IMF's Independent Evaluation Office (IEO) entitled "IMF Interactions with Member Countries." Those views are especially relevant today in that the emerging markets and the G7 countries—the two groups that had the least amount of time for the IMF—are now working together in the G20. The question now is "What's going to happen next?"

When the crisis broke out in 2008, the G20 became the principal coordinating body and in many ways provided the intellectual leadership while the IMF largely implemented what it was asked to do. Since the crisis, however, we have seen that the IMF has been nimble in trying to take a number of initiatives to reposition itself. We have also seen, through the so-called mutual assessment process (MAP) in the G20 to promote macro cooperation, that tensions regarding the role and evenhandedness of the IMF resulted in its role being limited to that of technical adviser. There is simply a lot of resistance to having the IMF play a leadership role. That leads to still another question: "What is the role of this institution?" It may be fine for the G20 if they want to use the MAP that way, but where does that leave the IMF and where does that leave the countries outside the G20?

Clarity and agreement on the role of and representation in the IMF lie at the heart of governance reform. In 2008, two important reports examined the

---

1. The IMF's executive board is composed of twenty-four directors and the managing director, who serves as its chair. Five of the directors (from the United States, Japan, Germany, France, and Great Britain) are appointed, and the rest are elected by member countries or by groups of countries. See www.imf.org/external/np/sec/memdir/eds.htm.

governance challenge—one by the Independent Evaluation Office and another by the Committee on IMF Governance Reform, chaired by Trevor Manuel, minister of finance of the Republic of South Africa. Both reports looked at a variety of governance issues and both strongly stated that there were important governance challenges that needed to be addressed—regarding in particular the effectiveness, efficiency, and legitimacy of the IMF.

With regard to legitimacy, the issues that have dominated the debate have been on quotas (country shares) and seats (country chairs), which were mentioned earlier. Two and a half years ago there was agreement to bring about a 2.5 percent shift in quotas, and now there is agreement in principle that there should be a further 5 percent shift in quotas. What is interesting is that the 2.5 percent shift agreed to over two years ago still has not been implemented because legislation must be passed by individual countries to effect that change, and that has not yet happened. The 5 percent still has not been agreed to in terms of a specific formula. Even assuming that it is and that the shift actually gets implemented (two big ifs), the question is whether it will really change anything; I would suggest not.[2]

With respect to seats on the executive board, this is by now a well-known story in which a third of the seats are currently held or controlled by Europeans (although interestingly, the European Central Bank, which one assumes should be represented in an international monetary organization, does not have representation). The Europeans do not represent a third of the 187 member countries, and clearly that is an issue that needs to be addressed. It is complicated, and it is political, but it is time for the situation to be changed. Currently there are twenty-four seats on the executive board. Through a quirk of history, agreement must be reached every two years to maintain the board at that number, and the United States holds a veto over the decision. The United States has now said that it will not agree to maintain the board at that number, thereby forcing a realignment of chairs. However, unless a political agreement is reached, it is two developing country chairs that will disappear, given the current rules, because they have the lowest voting shares among the groups that appoint or elect the twenty-four chairs. That obviously would be a step backward.[3] In short, this is a high-stakes political gamble that it is hoped will break a long-standing log jam

2. Since this article was written, the IMF has agreed to doubling of the quotas and a shift of 6 percent to emerging markets and other underrepresented countries. Commitments under the New Arrangements to Borrow will be rolled back. While that undoubtedly is progress, debate still ensues about the real impact on individual country quota shares.

3. Paulo Nogueira Batista, "Europe Must Make Way for a Modern IMF," *Financial Times*, September 23, 2010 (www.ft.com/cms/s/0/8b57a684-c744-11df-aeb1-00144feab49a.html).

and lead to an agreement on a smaller and more representative board. It is not yet clear whether that will be the result.[4]

On the issues of executive board representation and quotas (chairs and shares), it is abundantly clear to most observers that the current situation is inequitable and seriously undermines the legitimacy of and support for the IMF. It must be changed. However, absent a clear and widely shared view on the role and functioning of the IMF, achieving resolution of these long-debated issues is unlikely to change very much. Indeed, I would argue that it is the absence of agreement on the role of the fund that makes the current stalemate so tolerable—countries are unwilling to make the necessary political choices because it is unclear why they should do so.

The problem of "talk but no action" can be seen in other examples—for instance, in the new agreement on the New Arrangements to Borrow, a financial safety net for the IMF itself. That agreement was called for at the London G20 summit in April 2009 to increase the membership and the amount of funds that would be available to buttress IMF resources in times of crisis. The subsequent agreement was a step forward in terms of reforming the previous arrangements to borrow, but again, what is interesting is that the concerned countries—which are in large measure the G20 countries—have not taken the necessary steps to enact the national legislation that would allow the new agreement to be used. If a crisis broke out tomorrow, the New Arrangements to Borrow would not be available to the IMF to buttress its resources (and now it is to be scaled back because of the agreement to double quotas).

Reform seems to be something that one talks about when there is a crisis, but implementation seems a long ways off. What is to be done about that—particularly at upcoming G20 summits? First, the G20 needs to come out and state unequivocally that its member countries will implement what they have previously agreed to. The New Arrangements to Borrow needs to be put in place so that it can be used if needed. Members also need to implement what was agreed to earlier on quotas. In addition, countries also need to implement what they have agreed to already on allocations of special drawing rights.

Second, the G20 countries need to make the necessary decisions with respect to further quota reform and seats on the executive board. This is a sine qua non for addressing current perceptions about the unbalanced representation of

4. Again, since this article was originally written, it has been agreed that advanced Europe will give up two seats in 2012, that all chairs will be elected (rather than five being appointed by the largest members), and that the board will remain at twenty-four members. Details remain to be worked out over the next two years, and therefore the implications for the composition of the board remain uncertain. Even more important, it leaves European representation still at more than 25 percent and leaves the board at a size that many observers argue is simply too large to allow it to exercise effective oversight of the institution.

many emerging and other countries at the IMF. Technical obfuscation should no longer be allowed to block progress on this political imperative. However, it is a necessary but insufficient reform if the IMF is to be restored at the center of the international financial architecture.

Third, to address the more fundamental issue of governance, G20 countries need to start to address the issue of ministerial oversight of the institution, including whether to have a Ministerial Council and whether G20 finance ministers should constitute such a body, as well as the issue of the role of the executive board—how is it to be reformed to be much more effective in holding management and staff accountable rather than being marginalized, as is currently the case.

Fourth, there is the question of mandate: What is to be the role of the IMF? What role do countries want it to play? The IEO evaluation referenced earlier, "IMF Interactions with Member Countries," clearly brings out that there is no current agreement among G20 countries on the role of the fund. Unless its role is defined, one simply cannot hold the institution and its management and staff accountable.

That is the agenda of the G20 going forward if it is to clarify the role of the IMF and its relationship to it. It can be done, but some tough decisions will be required. Can the G20 succeed where the G7 failed? That is the test, and the answer remains to be seen.

Postscript

As mentioned in the notes, some progress has been made on IMF issues. If measured against the lack of progress over the last years, that is indeed an accomplishment. If measured against the reforms necessary to achieve meaningful governance reform as set out in the two governance reports cited in this chapter, the reforms fall far short of what was argued to be necessary to achieve real change and may simply reduce the pressure to make more significant progress. And the central question of the role of the IMF remains—calls from the Seoul summit for the IMF to play a greater role in identifying cross-country spillovers simply repeat a call that many have made over the last fifteen years. That role is already within the IMF's formal mandate but remains a largely unfulfilled aspiration. And so, the question asked in the title remains. Will the G20 push for the further progress needed, or has the limited agreement reached in Seoul simply lessened the pressure for more fundamental reform?

20

How the G20 Can Break the Stalemate in the Reform of the Multilateral Development System: Proposals for Action

JOHANNES F. LINN

Prior to the creation of the G20 summit forum, the much-needed reform of the global governance system faced a stalemate.[1] All major global institutions—the United Nations and its manifold agencies, the international financial institutions, and the many other multilateral and regional institutions that had developed since World War II—confronted a crisis of legitimacy due to serious questions about their representativeness and effectiveness. But there were no drivers, internal or external, that could bring about real change in the governance of the major institutions.

The perception that only the leaders of key countries could break the stalemate was one of the arguments underpinning the call to set up the G20 summit. Now that the G20 summit has been established and the G20 leaders have given the summit clear preeminence in addressing global concerns, especially in the financial, economic, and development arenas, the question is whether future summits will live up to expectations.

This chapter considers the architecture, governance, role, and funding of multilateral organizations in the development area, focusing in particular on the World Bank as the oldest and most eminent of the multilateral development

---

1. For more documentation and background on the argument in this paragraph, see Bradford and Linn (2007).

institutions.[2] The chapter reviews selected key issues, including the multilateral development architecture, the resource needs of the poor countries, and the need for a greater voice for developing countries in the global economic institutions. For each of those issues the chapter makes recommendations for the G20 leaders to consider at future summits.

Reform of the Multilateral Development Architecture

According to estimates of the Development Assistance Committee (DAC) of the Organization for Economic Cooperation and Development (OECD), the number of multilateral agencies engaged in providing development support increased from thirty in 1950 to 196 in 1980 and to 263 in 2008 (OECD 2008). However, in terms of financial flows of official development assistance (ODA) as recorded by the DAC, multilateral development assistance has lost ground relative to bilateral aid flows over the last thirty years (OECD 2010). And among multilateral aid agencies, the traditional leaders—the World Bank's International Development Association (IDA) and the United Nations and its agencies—have a reduced share. At the time of its creation in 1960, IDA was the only multilateral soft-loan window. It was set up to bundle the resource flows to poor countries, reaping the benefits of scale, concentration, and burden sharing. Today IDA's share in multilateral concessional resource flows is below 25 percent and its share in total concessional official aid recorded by the OECD-DAC is only about 5 percent (OECD 2010).[3]

While there are clear benefits to having new donors on the scene—more money and more good ideas are foremost among them—there are also serious drawbacks when a large number of donors overwhelm the limited capacity of poor recipient countries to absorb aid. Lack of coordination, high transaction costs, and a jungle of different fiduciary requirements and safeguards (environmental, social, and legal) for the many donors contribute to a loss of effectiveness of aid flows.

---

2. For the purpose of this chapter, I include under the heading of "development" the provision of global public goods, such as mitigation of and adaptation to climate change, preparedness for and response to global epidemics, and safeguarding of a stable and open global trade and financial system.

3. This description underestimates the overall dimensions of the increasing fragmentation of the international development architecture, since it counts among the multilateral agencies only agencies that provide financial assistance (leaving out such agencies as the World Trade Organization) and does not reflect the additional substantial elements of fragmentation introduced by the proliferation of bilateral official and private donors. See Kharas (2007) for further information on the issue of fragmentation in the aid architecture.

This issue was recognized in the Paris Declaration on Aid Effectiveness and the subsequent Accra Agenda for Action, under which donor and recipient countries committed themselves to improve the effectiveness of aid through pursuit of five principles: ownership, alignment, harmonization, managing for results, and mutual accountability. However, implementation of this agenda, while carefully monitored by the OECD-DAC, has turned out to be difficult, especially with regard to effective in-country coordination. In the absence of clear and accepted leadership by either the government or a trusted donor, there remains the key issue of how to overcome the collective action problem that donors face on the ground.

In some countries, subsets of donors have tried to prepare joint country assistance strategies, generally with some involvement of the recipient government, but in the absence of a clear leadership from the government or any of the donors, those efforts have generally fallen short of their ambitious goals (Linn 2008). In the past, the World Bank—and to a lesser degree the United Nations Development Program (UNDP)—played the lead role in aid coordination in the absence of strong government capacity, but in recent years the two institutions have played that role less and less, reflecting their declining role as key players in the evolving aid architecture.

Of particular concern over the last decade has been the creation of many specialized multilateral funding windows. They have proven effective in pursuing a strong results orientation and in scaling up interventions in narrow areas of their mandates, especially in the health sector, and therefore they have proven attractive to donors.[4] But they also have added a new dimension to the fragmentation process. The global (or "vertical") funds, with their application of overwhelming financial resources and strong advocacy, have been accused of biasing recipient governments' priorities in the direction of the particular objectives of the funds.

The case of the Global Fund for AIDS, Tuberculosis, and Malaria is most frequently cited (Isenman and Shakow 2010). While specific illnesses are important current and potential future health threats, they are not generally the most important threat. Other causes of bad health and high mortality, such as poor hygiene, lack of clean water and sanitation, lack of maternal education, and weaknesses in the health system as a whole, may be more important systemic health problems than specific communicable diseases. Such systemic problems are generally not addressed by the vertical health funds. Scarce national resources, both financial and managerial, are at risk of being diverted away from the important systemic challenges as a result of the high-powered intervention of the vertical funds. Again, a key constraint in ensuring a balanced

---

4. See Kharas (2010) for an in-depth assessment of the reasons why donors have found these funds attractive.

approach toward global development challenges is the fact that the World Bank and UNDP, which have traditionally provided the resources for dealing with the "horizontal" or systemic issues, play a relatively much weaker role today than they did three or four decades ago.

With the current international focus on climate change, new vertical funding mechanisms are being set up, risking a repeat of the problems of vertical funds in the health sector (Isenman and Shakow 2010). Especially in the area of funding the costs of adaptation to climate change, separate funding mechanisms would duplicate the capacity of the multilateral development banks (MDBs) and in particular the World Bank, since interventions in support of adaptation are in many if not all regards identical to traditional development interventions, which historically have been the mandate of the MDBs.

The problem of fragmentation extends even into the traditional multilateral development institutions. For example, in the case of the World Bank, issues of internal fragmentation arise because of the establishment of a multitude of special-purpose trust funds inside the bank, financed by selected donors and often burdened with their own governance and administrative requirements. In 2008 those trust funds contributed US$2.4 billion to the bank's resources and numbered more than 1,000 (OECD 2010; World Bank 2008). For all multilateral agencies combined, 12 percent of all aid flows were so-called "non-core" or "multi-bi" funding mechanisms under which bilateral donors fund special programs carried out by specific multilateral institutions (OECD 2010).

A final aspect of the global development architecture that gives rise to concern is the fact that the number of development interventions funded by external official sources is on the rise, while their average size is on the decline. What is perhaps most surprising is the fact that the median project size now falls well below US$100,000. The rapidly rising number and declining size of projects is a reflection of the proliferation of new official donor agencies, multilateral as well as bilateral. But it also reflects the lack of effective control of the size and number of projects by many of the established agencies.

Multilateral donors follow the general trend, with a threefold increase in the project numbers (from about 6,000 to about 18,000 over ten years), while the average project size dropped from about US$5 million to the range of US$2 million to US$3 million. The median project size for multilateral donors dropped from about US$360,000 in 2000 to US$40,000 in 2008 (figure 20-1). It is notable, though, that projects of the multilateral development banks, in particular IDA, have by far the highest average and median size, even as the average size of the projects has also declined in recent years. The average and median size of an IDA project is about US$40 million and US$20 million respectively.[5]

---

5. Data compiled by Jonathan Adams, based on Findley and others (2010).

Figure 20-1. *Project Numbers, Average Size, and Median Size for All Multilateral Donors, 1999–2008*

2000 US$ millions   Number of projects

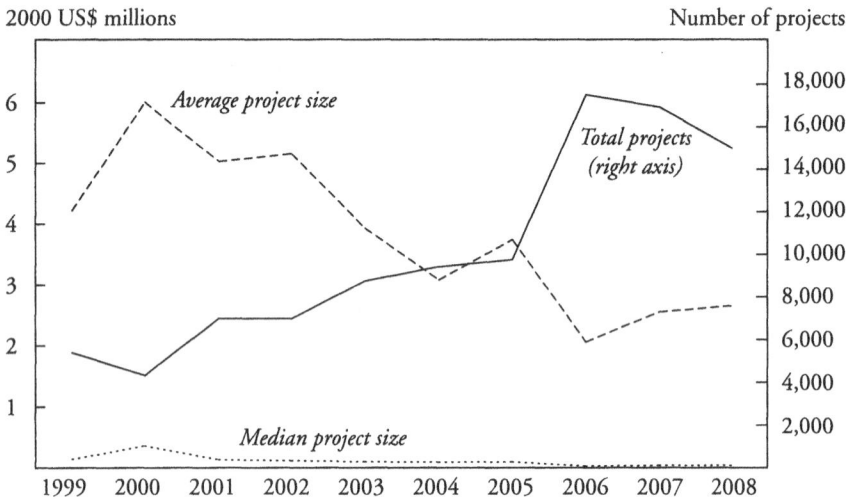

Source: Data compiled by Jonathan Adams, based on Findley and others (2010).

With a rising number of ever-smaller projects, the risk of aid fragmentation, lack of focus on scaling up successful development interventions, and rising transactions costs is reinforced. While bilateral donors contribute the bulk of small projects, the proliferation of multilateral organizations is also increasingly becoming part of the problem.

In his recent contribution to the debate about the future of the multilateral development institutions, Kharas observes that "multilateralism is being questioned because its initial raison d'être has disappeared" (Kharas 2010, p. 57) because of perceptions of institutional complexity, lack of transparency, higher absolute costs, remoteness, lack of accountability, and insufficient evidence of multilateral effectiveness. At the same time, a new rating of aid program effectiveness shows that the large multilateral development agencies are rated relatively highly.[6] In fact, IDA is the top performer among all large programs (comparable only to the much smaller aid program of Ireland) and far ahead of most bilateral programs.

Clearly the time has come for a serious assessment of the future of the multilateral development architecture—or rather "non-architecture," in view of the chaotic conditions of the current system.[7] Therefore I recommend that the G20

6. See Birdsall and Kharas (2010).
7. I am indebted to Pedro Malan for pointing out to me that the current multilateral institutional setup cannot be characterized as conveying a sense of "architecture."

set up a high-level commission to review the existing framework of multilateral development institutions and prepare recommendations for its reform. Such a commission can draw on the very useful work of the OECD-DAC[8] and, ceteris paribus, address the following set of questions:

—What should be the mandate for multilateral development agencies and the appropriate division of labor and resources between multilateral and bilateral aid agencies and among multilateral agencies?

—Should there be a moratorium on creating new multilateral agencies? Which agencies deserve support?[9]

—Are multilateral agencies the best channels for knowledge exchange?

—Can multilateral agencies be better leveraged to raise resources for development?

—What principles for governance of multilateral agencies will help ensure their legitimacy in terms of representativeness, effectiveness, and accountability?

—How can the processes and procedures of the multilateral agencies be streamlined and harmonized to minimize their administrative costs and the burdens placed on recipient countries?

Against the backdrop of this analysis of the multilateral development architecture, the G20 summit leaders should consider a number of actions:

—Establish a commission to review the multilateral development system and to assess ways to streamline the system. The commission would be expected to make recommendations to a future G20 summit.

—In the meantime, the World Bank should be asked to play the lead role in coordinating donor activities in countries where the government itself is unable or unwilling to play that role.

—Donors also should "think twice" before they set up new global (that is, "vertical") funds or endow new trust funds with narrow mandates in multilateral institutions, especially in the World Bank. Instead, they should extend their support for existing major multipurpose funds in the multilateral institutions while minimizing the practice of earmarking.

—Furthermore, rather than continue the trend to more and smaller projects, donors should be encouraged to increase the size of their projects and reduce their number, especially the many small projects that are proliferating among the bilateral donors.

8. The OECD-DAC has published two excellent reports on the multilateral aid system (OECD 2008, OECD 2010). They would provide an excellent factual underpinning for the work of this commission. The OECD-DAC is, however, not a good substitute for a high-level commission reporting to the G20, since it does not include important members of the G20, some of whom have large aid programs and have important stakes in the reform of the multilateral development system, especially Brazil, China, and India.

9. This and the next two questions draw on Kharas (2010).

—Finally, as a signal that they take seriously the need to harmonize donor requirements, G20 leaders should urge the multilateral aid organizations to apply a common set of fiduciary and safeguard standards. As a first step toward that goal, they should request that the multilateral development banks (including their soft-loan windows, such as IDA) give recipient countries a choice of which set of bank standards they wish to follow when receiving funding from any of the banks.

Resources for Poor Countries

Poor countries are not represented in the G20. It is therefore not surprising that they have not received much attention in the G20 summits so far. The global financial crisis, which originated in the industrial countries and required concerted action by the systemically important economies of the world, was another important factor in that lack of attention. However, as the crisis recedes, G20 leaders should focus on the specific needs of the poor developing countries.

One way to identify poor countries is by whether or not they have access to IDA, which currently includes seventy-nine countries with annual per capita incomes below US$1,135. With the support of the international community, these countries had made significant progress in recent decades. The share of extremely poor people (defined as having an income of below US$1.25 a day) in developing countries is expected to drop from 42 percent in 1990 to 15 percent in 2015, well below the Millennium Development Goal (MDG) target (IDA 2010a). China, South Korea, and Turkey, among others, have graduated from poor country status and are now contributors to IDA. Sub-Saharan Africa, long regarded as a stagnant continent, had been growing rapidly since the turn of the century until it was hit by the fallout from the global crisis.

Despite such progress, developing countries face many challenges in what might be called a "triple crisis." First, while the overall poverty reduction target of the MDGs will likely be met, a number of other global MDG targets will not be achieved (especially for child and maternal mortality), and many African countries in particular will fall well short of achieving many MDG targets.

Second, conflicts, natural disasters, and economic crises will continue to threaten the progress made. The global economic crisis of 2008–09 cut Sub-Saharan African economic growth from 6.7 percent in 2006–07 to 1.7 percent in 2009. According to World Bank estimates, almost 90 million people in low-income countries would be pushed into extreme poverty by the end of 2010 as a result of the crisis (IDA 2010b). The human impact of economic crises on key human development indicators is especially severe and takes years of economic growth to reverse.

Third, climate change will affect the poorest countries especially hard. They will be most severely affected by droughts, floods, and bad weather, and their capacity to cope with the impacts is very limited. The impact of climate change on IDA countries is expected to reach US$40 billion over the next forty years. Merely "climate proofing" IDA projects to ensure that they can withstand the heightened risks associated with climate change during their lifetime will cost in the order of US$800–$900 million a year (IDA 2010c).

So far the response of the international community to the global economic crisis and climate change has for the most part benefited the middle-income countries. For example, in response to the economic crisis, the World Bank, along with other MDBs, was able to triple its lending to these countries. The MDBs had a strong capital base going into the crisis or received substantial capital replenishments and thus were able to access international capital markets. In contrast, IDA and other multilateral soft-loan windows were constrained by their fixed resource base, provided by donors in multiyear replenishments. In the area of climate change too, funding has so far been directed mostly at middle-income countries. For example, of the total US$17 billion committed under World Bank–managed trust funds, only 17.5 percent have gone to IDA countries so far (IDA 2010b).

Therefore, in response to the triple crisis, the G20 leaders should commit to a significant increase in resources going to poor countries. The recent replenishments of the soft-loan windows of the Asian Development Bank, the African Development Bank, and the World Bank provided additional resources for the poor countries but reflected a relatively conservative approach by donors, relying more heavily on the internal resources of the institutions than on additional donor contributions.

Among the multilateral institutions, IDA in particular has a strong record of engagement and leadership in development. It works in a unique way at the country, regional, and global levels. It combines financing at a substantial scale with technical assistance and analytical support. And it meshes "vertical" (sub-sector-specific) interventions with "horizontal" (country- or sector-wide, systemic) support for an appropriate balance. As mentioned above, IDA can also provide leadership in donor coordination at the country level where needed. And IDA plans to respond to new challenges by devoting increased attention and resources to fragile and conflict-affected countries and by implementing an intensified response to the impact of climate change on poor developing countries (IDA 2010c).[10]

---

10. In addition, IDA plans to reinforce its focus on women, on its results agenda, and on more sharply focusing its assistance on countries with stronger policy and institutional performance.

Many donor countries currently face very difficult domestic economic, fiscal, and political challenges. Nonetheless, the right response for the G20 leaders is to commit to

—an increased focus in their future summit agenda on the needs and contributions of poor developing countries

—high-level replenishments for the soft-loan windows of the multilateral development banks over the next three to five years.

Greater Voice for Developing Countries

In recent years governance reform of the multilateral institutions has become a major issue. In the IMF and World Bank, from the time of their creation in 1944, the vote and voice of industrial countries predominated due to the economic weights that determined quotas, shares, votes, and chairs on the institutions' governing boards. Over the last five years, much debate has taken place inside and outside the two institutions on how to reflect the rapid rise of the emerging market economies in the formulas that determine member representation. Some limited progress has been made with respect to reform of IMF and World Bank governance to date.

At the Pittsburgh summit in September 2009, G20 leaders agreed that they would support a reform of the share distribution formula in the IMF and World Bank that would give the developing countries, in particular the emerging market economies, a larger role. However, the amounts to be redistributed were calibrated so as to ensure that the industrial countries would retain a majority of shares and votes. Moreover, the summit gave no guidance on the distribution of chairs on the executive boards of the IMF and the World Bank, which is even more heavily biased in the direction of industrial, and especially European, countries. In the case of the World Bank, the change was adopted in April 2010. In the case of the IMF, the change was adopted by its board of directors in November 2010.

For IDA, the critical governance forum is the group of IDA deputies, which meets every three years to decide on the replenishment of IDA's resources. Since IDA's creation, the replenishment meetings have in effect determined the strategic directions and policies that IDA applies in its operations, although the IDA executive board, which broadly mirrors the board of the World Bank, has to issue a pro forma endorsement of all decisions taken by the IDA deputies. The directions and policies adopted by IDA generally also have become the basis for all World Bank operations, including those of the International Bank for Reconstruction and Development (IBRD), the World Bank affiliate that lends to middle-income countries.

This practice has given the IDA deputies great de facto influence on the activities of the World Bank as a whole. Until the 1990s, only donor countries were invited to send IDA deputies to replenishment meetings. Since then, representatives from recipient countries are also invited to participate. However, they remain a small minority. As a result, donor countries retain effective control of the directions and policies of IDA and, to a lesser extent, of the World Bank.

Another important dimension of governance relates to the selection of the organizational leadership in multilateral agencies. By convention since the creation of the organizations, the head of the IMF has been a European and the head of the World Bank has been an American. This convention is obsolete today. It reflects past economic and geopolitical conditions rather than today's need for broader representation and greater inclusiveness of the emerging market economies and developing countries. G20 leaders confirmed at the Pittsburgh summit that future heads of the IMF and World Bank are to be selected on merit in an open and transparent process, but they did not specifically indicate that leaders would be selected without regard to their nationality. That leaves open the possibility that the old convention will be revived when the current heads need to be replaced.

Other multilateral development institutions have a more balanced representation of donor and recipient interests. In the regional development banks, regional representatives predominate and in some of them borrower countries have equal representation (for example, the Inter-American Development Bank). Some regional development banks also select heads from their borrowing member countries (African Development Bank and Inter-American Development Bank); others (Asian Development Bank and European Bank for Reconstruction and Development) have so far selected representatives from nonborrowing members (Japanese and Western European, respectively). The Global Environmental Fund has an elaborate system of double voting in which majorities of weighted donor votes and of unweighted member votes are needed for decisions to be adopted. Recently created vertical funds, such as the Global Fund for AIDS, Tuberculosis, and Malaria, have even more inclusive representation, with participation of civil society members on their executive boards. In terms of leadership, most of the funds appear to have no restriction on nationality.

G20 leaders have recognized that twenty-first-century global problems require legitimate global institutions and hence have taken on the task of reforming the governance structures, with some initial steps now being implemented by the IMF and World Bank. However, if they want to develop truly inclusive, credible, and effective global institutions, they will have to go further. For the IMF and World Bank, further reform of the distribution of quota, shares, votes, and chairs is needed to ensure that developing countries have at least an equal share in the decisionmaking forums of these critical multilateral organizations. More-over, a true commitment is needed by the traditional G8 powers not to cling to the past practice of leadership selection from a restricted set of nationalities in any of the major multilateral organizations.

That will not be easy politically for the G8 countries. The Europeans have to show the greatest degree of flexibility in giving up their traditional prerogatives in the international institutions, since they are the most overrepresented as a group. However, Japan and the United States also need to give up what in some political and bureaucratic quarters are cherished privileges.[11] Ultimately, how-ever, it will be in the European, Japanese, and U.S. interest to give up some con-ventional privileges, as that is necessary to ensure that the international institu-tions are effective in addressing global problems that have a direct bearing on the welfare of the populations of the G8 countries. Only if these institutions have the acceptance and support of the greatest possible number of members will they be able to function effectively. The initiative of the G20 leaders is needed pre-cisely because only they can be expected to overcome the domestic political and bureaucratic obstacles that will inevitably get in the way of significant reform.

Therefore, in regard to governance reform of the multilateral institutions, the G20 leaders should commit to

—push for further reform of the governance structures in the IMF and World Bank to ensure more effective representation of the emerging market economies and developing countries

—ensure that heads of multilateral agencies are selected on merit and without restrictions on their nationality.

Conclusion

The creation of the G20 summit was a major breakthrough in the stalemate that characterized global governance until 2008. It now offers an opportunity to promote much-needed reforms in the multilateral governance structures. It is encouraging that in the summits to date the G20 leaders have taken up some of the issues that need to be addressed. However, more is needed to ensure suf-ficient progress.

Among the recommendations in this chapter, three are of particular impor-tance and urgency:

11. A recent staff report of the Committee on Foreign Relations of the U.S. Senate strongly rejected possible moves to give up the U.S. privilege to name the World Bank president or to give up the U.S. veto over certain decisions of the World Bank board of governors (Committee on For-eign Relations 2010).

—Establish a commission to review the multilateral development system and to recommend ways to streamline the system.

—Commit to an increased focus on the needs and contributions of poor developing countries.

—Push for further reform of the governance structures in the IMF and World Bank to ensure more effective representation of the emerging market economies and developing countries, and select the heads of the organizations on the basis of merit and without restrictions on their nationality.

References

Birdsall, Nancy, and Homi Kharas. 2010. "Quality of Official Development Assistance Assessment." Washington: Center for Global Development and Brookings Institution.

Bradford, Colin I., Jr., and Johannes F. Linn. 2007. *Global Governance Reform: Breaking the Stalemate*. Washington: Brookings.

Committee on Foreign Relations. 2010. "The International Financial Institutions: A Call for Change." U. S. Senate (March 10).

Findley, Michael G., and others. 2010. "AidData: Tracking Development Finance." Paper presented at "Aid Transparency and Development Finance: Lessons and Insights from AidData," Oxford, United Kingdom, March 22–25, 2010.

IDA. 2010a. "The Demand for IDA16 Resources and the Strategy for their Effective Use." Washington: IDA Resource Mobilization Department (May).

———. 2010b. "Setting the Agenda for IDA 16." Washington: IDA Resource Mobilization Department (February).

———. 2010c. "Summary Note: Supporting Development Results." Washington: IDA Resource Mobilization Department (May).

Isenman, Paul, and Alexander Shakow. 2010. "Donor Schizophrenia and Aid Effectiveness: The Role of Global Funds." *Practice Paper* 2010, no. 5 (April). Brighton, U.K.: Institute of Development Studies.

Kharas, Homi. 2007. "Trends and Issues in Development Aid." Wolfensohn Center Working Paper 1. Brookings.

———. 2010. "Rethinking the Roles of Multilaterals in the Global Aid Architecture." In *Making Development Aid More Effective*. Global Economy and Development Program, Brookings (September) (www.brookings.edu/~/media/Files/rc/papers/2010/09_development_aid/09_development_aid.pdf).

Linn, Johannes F. 2008. "Aid Coordination on the Ground: Are Joint Country Assistance Strategies the Answer?" Wolfensohn Center Working Paper 10. Brookings.

OECD. 2008. *2008 DAC Report on Multilateral Aid*. Paris.

———. 2010. *2010 DAC Report on Multilateral Aid*. Paris.

World Bank. 2008. *2008 Partnership and Trust Fund Annual Report*. Washington: Global Partnership and Trust Fund Operations Department.

21

The United Nations and the G20: Synergy or Dissonance?

PAUL HEINBECKER

This chapter assumes that to achieve effective global governance, the world needs both the nascent G20 and the sexagenarian UN to succeed and that the success of each can be greater if the two cooperate. The chapter examines in summary form some of the main factors in play between the two.[1] It makes a plea for perspicacity and wisdom from G20 members vis-à-vis the UN, so that they do not inadvertently undermine the institution as the new group evolves, and for open-mindedness and good sense on the part of the non-G20 UN members, so that they do not discourage cooperation.

The world is changing dramatically, and largely for the better. People around the world are richer, better fed, better educated, and safer than they have ever been before. Since 1980, world income has doubled. Since 1990, almost half a billion people have climbed out of poverty, notwithstanding the stubborn, tragic exception of the billion poorest. Our world is more successful and more integrated, and it is a more complex governance challenge than ever before. Although the United States remains uniquely powerful and China and others are growing rapidly, no country is in a position to determine unilaterally the

1. Other works by Paul Heinbecker in the same field include "Canada's World Can Get a Lot Bigger: The Group of 20, Global Governance, and Security," School of Public Policy, University of Calgary, April 2011; "The Future of the G20 and Its Place in Global Governance," Centre for International Governance Innovation, April 2011; and "The 'New' Multilateralism of the 21st Century" (with Fen Hampson), in *Global Governance, a Review of Multilateralism and International Organizations*, forthcoming 2011.

course of world events in the twenty-first century. The single-superpower era is following its two-superpower predecessor into history. We are entering a time of either enhanced cooperative governance if we are wise or destructive international competition if we are foolish. In this changing context, the UN remains a necessary but not sufficient response to the world's issues. The G20 is a further necessary but insufficient response. Effective global governance depends considerably on the success of both institutions. Further, the world needs the two to cooperate in order to benefit from the synergies that cooperation can generate.

It is too early for certitude about the future of the G20, whose course is not yet established. Its agenda will likely go still deeper into economic and financial cooperation and reform of the international monetary system before it addresses other issues. Thanks in part to Korea's leadership, development has, however, become the first "new" issue on the G20 agenda, in the sense that development—albeit economic and financial (and social) in character—goes well beyond the immediate self-interests of the G20. Over time, but likely not very much time, the G20 will probably complement its financial and economic agenda with deliberations on other issues that require agreement among the most senior players in global governance, including possibly climate change; global governance reform, including UN and Security Council reform, as President Sarkozy has mused; and international security and arms control. The experience of the G8 has been that when leaders come together, they take advantage of each other's presence to discuss the pressing issues of the day, whatever they are. Most G20 leaders will not be content for long dealing exclusively with economic and financial issues. Nor will their finance ministers and treasury secretaries want them to do so. Nor will the world need them to.

For many years, the G8 served as the locus for high-level political discussions among its members, notably on terrorism, arms control and disarmament, regional crises, and so forth. Some see a continuing, albeit narrowed, role for the G8, focusing on development, democracy, and peace and security. According to Canada's prime minister, Stephen Harper, those are all matters that can best be addressed through close cooperation among friends and like-minded allies. President Sarkozy has said that he intends to focus the 2011 G8 Nice summit on Africa and security and leave it to the future to decide if the G8 should endure.

It does seem very likely that the G20 will ultimately absorb the G8. The time demands of summit diplomacy—exceeding a dozen gatherings a year and more for some leaders—as well as the wear and tear of travel across time zones and impatience with any redundancy of forums seems likely to result in consolidation of the groups. The more diverse membership of the G20 means fewer areas of common interest and possibly shallower consequent agreements. But there would be offsetting advantages in terms of the breadth of support for any agreement reached. The G20 is the best solution so far to the legitimacy/effectiveness conundrum.

The UN and the G20 in Perspective

Universal adherence to its charter by member states confers unique legitimacy on the United Nations. Further, in part because of the international legal system derived from the charter and the international law and treaties built on the charter, the UN has become the world's central operating system, a kind of motherboard of global governance. The UN performs its own core functions and at the same time also enables myriad subsystems to work better, both within the ambit of the UN organization—for example, UNICEF—and beyond. The UN makes it possible for other organizations to function more effectively, notably NATO, which needs the UN to certify the legitimacy of its operations in Afghanistan and elsewhere. The UN also makes it possible for initiatives as such as the Millennium Development Goals to be subcontracted out efficiently. The reverse is also true. The products of other entities, notably of the G8, can be imported into the UN for consideration by its larger membership. Most fundamental, the UN and its charter provide the rule book for the conduct of international relations, which all states, including G20 states, see it as in their interest to respect.

At the same time, the United Nations suffers from the scleroses and frailties of a sixty-five-year-old very human institution. A lot of water has gone under the UN bridge since 1945. It is plagued by divisions, often grounded in genuine differences in interests (or perceptions thereof), between rich countries and poor; between the Security Council and the General Assembly; between the five permanent members of the Security Council (P5) and the rest; between the nuclear powers and others; between the climate changers and the climate victims; between the Israelis and Arabs and Muslims more generally; between the Indians and Pakistanis; between North Korea and its neighbors (and the United States); and, during the Bush years especially, between a unilateralist, excessively exceptionalist Washington and a steadfast, multilateralist New York.

What is not always clear is whether the intractability of the problems that the UN faces causes the divisions among the members or whether the divisions among the UN's members make its problems intractable. In my judgment and experience, the latter is more often the case; the UN's own hoary groupings are probably a greater threat to the organization's viability in the twenty-first century than the G20 is. These many weaknesses hinder the UN's effectiveness and consequently diminish its efficacy, prompting some to look elsewhere for solutions to the day's problems.

Despite its problems, the UN retains its unique legitimacy, derived from its universal membership and the adherence of all 192 members to the UN Charter as the basis of international law. It is also more effective than its detractors think. Overlooked in the criticism of the UN is the fact that the organization has undergone extensive innovation and renovation and, in the process, substantial reinvention. From peacekeeping to peace enforcement and peacebuilding, to international criminal justice systems, to sustainable development, to refugee protection, to humanitarian coordination and food relief, to democracy and electoral support, to human rights conventions, to health protection, to landmine removal, and to managerial accountability and oversight, the organization has been changing and equipping itself to acquit its increasingly demanding responsibilities. As a consequence, the UN has broader political presence than any other organization and much substantive expertise in dealing with contemporary challenges, such as instability and fragile states.

The G20 enjoys its own legitimacy, derived principally from its effectiveness in addressing the crucial economic and financial crises of 2008. Its legitimacy also comes from the fact that its membership accounts for 85 percent of global gross national product, 80 percent of world trade, and 67 percent of the planet's total population. Those factors do not constitute universality, of course— the least developed countries are notably missing, as are some of the very constructive smaller powers—but nor are they trivial assets. When the G20 reaches agreement among its members, a large part of whatever problem it is addressing is on the way to resolution.

Consensus is difficult to generate at the UN, and it is not yet clear whether it will be easier to create at the G20. Present in both entities are the main protagonists and the main disputes, notably the intractability of trade and budget imbalances, climate change, and nuclear disarmament. Further, ways of thinking and acting established over generations cannot be modified quickly. For the heretofore hegemonic United States, partnership will need to mean not just hearing others before deciding and acting, but also developing shared assessments and acting cooperatively. For some others among the G20, notably China and India, national interests will have to be reconceived to include more directly the well-being of the international system itself. All twenty governments will have to reconcile self-interest with the common interest and to privilege co-operation over domination, multilateralism over unilateralism, the effective over the merely efficient, and the legal over the expedient. All of that is easier said than done, especially in the absence of common threats.

Restricted groups of governments, even the G20, can bind themselves if they wish, but they can only commend their decisions to others, not command compliance. Absent the UN and its universal membership and legal framework, smaller, exclusive groups, especially the G8 but also the G20, would be much more controversial and their legitimacy more contested. As a consequence, they would also be less effective.

How the G20 Could Help the UN

It is a truism that the UN works best when the major powers are not at loggerheads. The G20 countries are members of disparate UN political and geographic groups—notably the Non-Aligned Movement (NAM), the Group of 77 members of the "South," and the democratic countries of the "North"—that are often at ideological odds with each other and frequently at political cross-purposes too. To the extent that G20 membership induces a sense of solidarity among the twenty and diminishes identification with other groups, cooperation under UN auspices will be made easier, helping the UN to work more productively, generally, on day-to-day issues and on specific topics. Indeed, as we have seen in the case of the IMF, consensus among the G20 is a powerful stimulus to action and reform.

Permanent representatives at the UN are often constrained by the institution's divisions—notably between the Security Council, where the five veto powers dominate, and the Economic and Social Council and the General Assembly, in which the "South" prevails—and hobbled by instructions from their capitals. Leaders, however, are blessedly far removed from the hothouse of New York and the antique ideologies, accumulated grievances, and diplomatic delusions that impede progress there. The G20, operating at the head-of-government level, has the luxury of focusing on the substance (and domestic politics) of a given issue and ignoring institutional prerogatives and inertias, thereby catalyzing action that individual bodies of the UN find difficult or impossible to achieve on their own. The G20 can encourage and facilitate cooperation within the UN and between the UN and other bodies. Further, the very existence of the G20 and its evident capacity to act outside of UN parameters if the UN is dilatory or obstructive create an incentive in New York for action and cooperation among those who do not want the UN to be bypassed.

With one or two exceptions, the gap between the power of several of the candidates for permanent seats and the power of the lesser permanent members of the Security Council is becoming so wide that it risks destroying the legitimacy and effectiveness of the institution. For the aspirant countries, an unrepresentative and anachronistic council that does not reflect contemporary power realities is an illegitimate one. Worse, it is an ineffective one.

Not everyone equates enlargement with reform. Some opponents of an increase of permanent seats think that the council has a performance and accountability deficit—Darfur, Rwanda, Srebrenica, and so forth. They contend that more members do not necessarily increase the council's effectiveness and that permanent seats are incompatible with accountability. Further, there is also the issue of principle. Opponents of adding permanent seats prefer democratic practices to anachronistic privileges. Some are also opposed partly as a matter of self-interest, presuming that their own countries would not get a permanent seat and, in some cases, what would be worse—that a regional rival would.

For a generation, progress on this key question has foundered on the rocks of competing interests. Reconciling the positions of those who want permanent seats for themselves and those who prefer other solutions to UN governance challenges has thus far proved impossible. But, as all the protagonists are members of the G20 and all enjoy more or less permanent seats in the G20, which is in some respects the economic equivalent of the Security Council, it should be possible for professional politicians, leaders for whom compromise and the politics of the art of the possible are everyday realities, to find practical political accommodations. It happens that there will be a potentially useful overlap between the G20 and the Security Council in the next period. Ten G20 members (six G8 members) will be on the council, as will five of the leading six aspirants for permanent council membership.

The leaders' G20 was created to deal with the last economic crisis. The next economic crisis might well be driven by an inadequate response to climate change. Stopping and reversing climate change, the mother of all tragedies of the commons, was never going to be easy. There are precious few examples of humanity managing to come together in its own enlightened self-interest to change its collective course on a major governance issue. But there are some such examples: notably, World War III has been avoided (so far), the proliferation of nuclear weapons has (largely) been averted, and the ozone layer has been (mostly) preserved.

Negotiations among all 192 members of the United Nations, while an essential component of any ultimate climate change agreement, has nevertheless proven too unwieldy, too susceptible to conflicting interests and contradictory ideologies, and too vulnerable to the actions of a handful of spoilers to be able to reconcile competing and diverging climate change interests within a responsible timeframe. For climate change as for most overarching global issues, the crucial negotiations have usually taken place in back rooms of large gatherings, among groups of twenty or so of the most engaged countries. In Copenhagen, even that process was bypassed as five countries—the United States, China, Brazil, India, and South Africa, some of the worst polluters—cut a deal among themselves that they then offered to others on a take-it-or-leave-it basis. The Copenhagen solution, however, was inadequate substantively and unfair procedurally. While it had some merit—more than seventy countries, including thirty-five developing countries, signed on to the deal and pledged to take "nationally appropriate actions"—it lacked targets and timetables, and it back-end loaded its promises of financial transfers. Further, G20 members from the European Union, Japan, South Korea, Mexico, Saudi Arabia, Mexico, Australia, Turkey, Indonesia, and Russia were all sidelined —as was Canada, which is a significant generator of greenhouse gases (GHG) in its own right and the leading foreign supplier of oil, gas, electricity, and uranium to the United States, now the world's second-leading GHG emitter, having recently been surpassed by China. The G20 would have constituted a much more representative group for negotiating agreement. Further, a deal acceptable to the G20, with its complex membership, would likely have attracted less opposition.

Copenhagen will not save us from climate change, nor, in the absence of progress in the U.S. Congress, has Cancun. It is possible that the follow-up gathering in South Africa in 2011 will not do so, either. Partly in frustration with the difficulty of devising a fair global treaty expeditiously, coalitions of the willing are turning to "bottom-up" actions on a national and regional basis, although that course risks making the world a crazy quilt of incompatible regulations and trade protectionism masquerading as climate sensitivity.

Whether the solution is to be an overarching mega-deal or a series of internationally sanctioned issue-specific deals, the world has to be brought to "yes" on the necessity to act. What is needed is a group big enough to include all the nations whose cooperation is indispensable but still small enough to facilitate agreement—that is, to be effective on substance and efficient in negotiation. There are two alternatives that, happily, can add up to one solution: the Major Economies/Emitters Forum (MEF) and the G20. The MEF has the requisite vocation, reducing emissions, and the G20 has the requisite focus, economics and finance. The G20 is by its own declaration the world's "premier economic forum," and climate change mitigation and adaptation raise primordial economic issues, including the probability that not acting is going to be more costly for all than acting would be, as British economist Nicholas Stern has persuasively argued. For both substantive and procedural reasons, it would make sense for the MEF to morph into the G20 (all the MEF countries are already in the G20) and for climate change, starting perhaps with its economic and development dimensions, to be made a standing item on the G20 agenda.

The UN Security Council is equipped by chapter VII of the UN Charter with the power to "legislate" in member countries, a power that the G8 and G20 do not (and should not) have. The decisions of the council taken under chapter VII are binding on member countries whether they are council members at the time or not. The post-9/11 decision to deny terrorists access to the world's financial system is an example. The council's writ covers peace and security, fairly broadly defined. Major international political and security issues continue to be brought to the UN for deliberation and decision. The response to 9/11, the Iraq war, the Israeli-Lebanese war, and the Iranian nuclear program are high-profile examples.

The UN Security Council normally operates at the permanent representative level, and the G20 functions as a body of heads of state and government. Vastly more effort and money are allocated to the latter in capitals than to the former, a fairly accurate barometer of the importance to political leaders of the two bodies. At the same time, each has its own capacities. There is a strong argument in favor of the G20 members investing major effort in the work of the council, including in the creation of UN military missions. There has been a perceptible reluctance on the part of some G20 countries to participate in UN-led operations, out of concern for the effectiveness of such missions. The G20 could contribute to upgrading the UN's capacity to act effectively. The G20 could also inject high-level political energy periodically into council deliberations, as President Obama did in 2009 in chairing a Security Council session devoted to arms control and disarmament.

How the UN Could Help the G20

The UN can extend the G20's effectiveness. G20 decisions enjoy greater legitimacy if they are endorsed by the UN than if they are not, making the UN a kind of political "force multiplier." Further, global problems require global solutions, and, as Bruce Jones of the Brookings Institution has pointed out, "However much influence the G20 have, the problems they confront are the kind where the weakest link can break the chain."[2] Unless smaller states see that their views are reflected in decisionmaking or at least that their interests have been duly and fairly considered, they are unlikely to "buy into" the deal in question. Unresponsiveness can have repercussions in, for example, the attitude of the G172 toward illegal migration, the drug trade, and international terrorism and piracy. It can also affect their willingness to cooperate to prevent evasion of climate change regulations by unscrupulous industries and the spread of pandemics of infectious disease and their willingness to collaborate on financial regulation, notably regarding tax and banking reforms.

Much of the membership of the UN sees the G20 in positive, albeit apprehensive, terms. The G20's efficacy is generally acknowledged at the UN. Many UN members recognize that the G20 came into existence when and how it did because a myriad of political and structural problems prevented existing institutions, principally the G8 and IMF, but also the UN proper, from addressing the global financial crisis effectively. They realize that similar impediments are obstructing progress on other global issues more directly under the UN's purview. Further, they are well aware that smaller, powerful groups are capable of bypassing the UN when disagreements there prevent effective action. At the same time, the G172—that is, the 172 countries that are not in the G20—have legitimate concerns about the latter's possible evolution. To quote Vanu Gopala Menon, Singapore's permanent representative to the UN, speaking on behalf of the Global Governance Group, an informal group of moderate countries that have joined forces to deliberate on the need to strengthen the UN role in global economic governance:

> We firmly believe that the G-20 process should enhance and not undermine the UN. All countries, big and small, will be affected by how the

---

2. Bruce Jones, "Making Multilateralism Work," Policy and Analysis Brief for the Stanley Foundation, April 2010 (www.stanleyfoundation.org/publications/pab/Jones_PAB_410.pdf).

G-20 deals with the issues it takes under its charge. Given the complexities and interdependencies of the global economy, it is important for the G-20 to be consultative, inclusive and transparent in its deliberations for its outcome to be effectively implemented on a global scale.[3]

The most fundamental problem is that the lack of seats at the G20 table for the G172 greatly reduces the latter's ability to protect their peoples' interests, or at least to air those interests in the hope that doing so will, ipso facto, afford some protection. The more the G172 members are excluded, the less confidence their populations will have in the ultimate fairness and efficacy of the multilateral system and the less interest they will have in responding to the G20's wishes. There are two further problems. Despite the presence at the G20 table of some developing countries, no place is reserved for the poorest and no one is carrying their proxy. Equally problematic, the capable smaller countries, such as Norway, Switzerland, Chile, Singapore, and New Zealand, are absent as well, effectively depriving G20 deliberations of those countries' generally constructive and frequently innovative diplomacy.

The G20 therefore needs to take seriously the need for outreach and, to an extent consistent with efficacy, inclusion. There are several steps that the G20 can take, none of which will be really satisfactory to those who are absent but all of which are likely to be better than nothing. First and most fundamental is that the chair of the G20 in a given year should make it a solemn responsibility to consult others besides his or her G20 counterparts on the G20 agenda and seek substantive rather than pro forma input. The chair or the appropriate high-level representative could do so by attending major meetings of, for example, the African Union, ASEAN, the Shanghai Cooperation Organization, the Gulf Cooperation Council, the Organization for Economic Cooperation and Development, the Organization of American States, and so forth. Unless a leader is prepared to commit to such an effort and to commit the country's diplomacy to genuine consultation, he or she should not seek to host the event. Second, the G20 should to the extent feasible adopt a constituency approach, as is done in the IMF (for example, Canada's executive director represents a constituency including Ireland and the Caribbean). Third, in order to ensure a voice for the G172 at the G20 table, especially for the poorest, the UN secretary-general should attend the G20 as a matter of right (as should the heads of the IMF and, when development is on the agenda, the head of the World Bank). The secretary-general should be represented at the G20 preparatory meetings by his

3. Statement by Ambassador Vanu Gopala Menon, Permanent Representative of Singapore to the United Nations, "Strengthening the Role of the UN in Global Economic Governance," June 2, 2010 (www.un.org/esa/ffd/events/2010GAWGFC/7/Stmt_Singapore.pdf).

own sherpa. As is the case with the EU, the African Union head should attend as a matter of convention. Further, the UN (and the Bretton Woods organizations) should be encouraged to contribute their perspectives and ideas at G20 ministerial meetings.

At the same time, to obtain the maximum benefit from the meetings of the G20, the number of people at the table needs to be tightly restricted. It is imperative that the table be small enough that those sitting around it be able to look each other in the eye and interact directly when necessary. They need proximity and intimacy to really understand each other's perspectives, especially their disparate political interests and limitations, and to engage each other. Distance across large tables destroys spontaneity and favors formality and disengagement. As a consequence, the table should be small and only government leaders should have dedicated seats at it. One or two additional rotating seats, as in the UN Security Council, could be allocated to nongovernment leaders to use when invited by the host chair to speak.

The annual G20 meeting could be held at UN headquarters or elsewhere in New York or that vicinity. Having the G20 and the UN meet side by side would help to make the work of each more coherent. As all of the leaders come to New York for the General Debate in September anyway, parallel G20 sessions would spare leaders the wear and tear of an extra trip. Further, as major security infrastructure is already in place, meeting in New York would greatly reduce the expenses of a summit (the Toronto G20 summit is said to have cost Canadian taxpayers more than $1.1 billion). The leaders could stay an extra day or two in New York at the trivial, incremental cost of a few extra nights in a hotel. The chairmanship could continue to rotate as it now does.

The inescapable conclusion is that the UN and the G20 need each other. The UN embodies universality and the G20 efficacy. If the United Nations and the G20 behave constructively and sensibly, they can produce synergies. The G20 can strengthen the UN by reducing the gaps among the major powers on contentious issues, making decisionmaking in the world body easier and more effective, and the UN can return the favor by extending the G20's efficacy vis-à-vis the G172, a group that the G20 cannot command but whose cooperation it needs. The UN, for its part, needs to be sensibly responsive and strategically savvy, resisting the blandishments of its ideological "spoilers." And the G20 needs to take the initiative to develop an effective modus operandi with nonmembers to resolve genuine issues of inclusion and exclusion and to find a way to give voice in its deliberations to the less powerful poorer countries and to the small but competent richer ones. More generally, the G20, which can undoubtedly harm as well as help the world body, should take care to reinforce rather than diminish the UN and its charter and the body of treaty law derived from it. Otherwise, to paraphrase Joni Mitchell, you won't know what you had 'til it's gone.

VI

New Dynamics of Summitry and Institutional Innovations for the G20

22

The Cultural Foundations for the New Dynamics of Summitry

COLIN I. BRADFORD

The central quest of this volume is to assess the degree to which the newly created sequence of G20 summits will make the transition from crisis committee to global steering committee. This is potentially a transformative moment in summitry. The G20 could not only replace the G8 as "the premier forum for international economic cooperation" but also assume more global responsibility on a broad range of issues and, further, generate a new kind of global leadership. For the G20 to become an enduring global steering committee, it will have to succeed in its role as crisis committee to have credibility, develop the capacity to move beyond economics to other types of issues, and create new modalities of global leadership derived from the cultural diversity of its members and the world. If these three goals were achieved in the next few years, that would indeed constitute "transformative" change, not only in summitry but also in the broader international system.

Beyond the transition from G8 to G20 as a summit group, the transformation of global leadership that would be required can best be understood as a new sequence in a larger narrative between G20 leaders and their publics, as suggested by Martin Albrow (Albrow 2010). When G20 summits are thought about as "narratives," it is evident that summit communications, the media, and new channels for information and news become central to the effectiveness of the summits. Summits need to provide a sense of strategic leadership in "the global age," when most local and national challenges have distinctly global dimensions; communications are central to providing that sense, linking leaders and publics on crucial global issues.

The notion of summits as narratives—and specifically as narratives between leaders and their publics—provides us with a larger prism through which to view the importance of the transformations taking place in the G20 today, as it evolves from crisis committee to global steering committee.

The current crisis is indeed a triple crisis. First, it is a crisis of *confidence* in markets; second, a crisis of *trust* in leadership; and third, a crisis of *faith* in institutions charged with preventing crises. The new form of global leadership and global responsibility created by G20 summitry will be crucial to the resolution of every one of the three dimensions of the current crisis. The actions of the G20 must be effective in addressing the economic crisis of confidence; the political dynamics of the G20 between leaders and their publics must be credible in order to restore trust in leadership; and the governance reform efforts of the G20 must be forceful enough to ensure the international institutional capacity to address global challenges and generate renewed faith in global institutions.

The Grand Narrative of Our Times: Cultural Diversity in the Global Age

The ascendance of G20 summits is emblematic of a wholly new moment in international life for still another reason. G20 summits are not just meetings of leaders of nations; the G20 represents a meeting of historically diverse cultures. The G20 represents a global encounter of cultures, a powerful new interface of cultural differences. This is the "grand narrative," which involves all of us as individuals—including our identities, our communities, and our cultures, all of which are now interpenetrated by "others" of different cultures, traditions, and sensibilities.

Whereas the G8 was and is a symbol of a dichotomous encounter between "the West and the Rest," between those who are "in" and those who are "out," the G20 embodies within itself a more complex nexus of diverse cultures. The G20 has six Asian countries, whereas the G8 had one; the G20 has three Islamic countries, whereas the G8 Plus 5 had none; the G20 has ten emerging market economies from the non-Western developing world, whereas the G8 had none. There are significant nations within the G20 that were "out" in the era of the G8.

In the minds of many, the G20's larger size and especially its broad cultural diversity are a problem that will make consensus building and decisionmaking more difficult. Some in the West, especially, still cling to the notion that "like-mindedness" is a sin qua non for finding common ground and forming alliances. By its very composition, the G20 challenges the notion that cultural similarity is a major asset in the politics of leadership; rather, it is the cultural diversity of the G20 that is an asset. Once fully grasped, it can be exploited as a foundation for the new dynamics of summitry and, as such, a powerful transformative force of G20 summitry. That is not only because of the cultural diversity within the G20 itself, but because in the global age, cultural diversity is a foundational element in our individual lives and in our national cultures and societies.

Globalization as we now experience it includes far more than the growing importance of global trade in goods and services. Global cultural diversity is a force that penetrates far more deeply into our personal lives—our mindset, worldview, literature, art, architecture, music, and sense of individuality and identity. Society, culture, and our public and private lives are in a continuous process of "encounter" with "the other" in broader and deeper ways and on a greater scale than ever before.

What is important about the transition from G8 to G20 is that it embodies, reflects, and participates in this more profound social phenomenon, which strengthens the rootedness and connectedness of our time and our lives. The cultural diversity of the countries in the G20, in stark contrast to that of the G8 countries, embraces the cultural encounters occurring daily across the world in the lives of all of us and in our societies. This is the "grand narrative" of G20 summitry, which extends beyond leaders to everyone everywhere. This is what makes the success of the G20 as a global steering mechanism built on cultural difference such a critical test not only of the G20 but of our times.

Will leaders of civil society, business, finance, the arts, education, and the new and the old media as well as the leaders of nations be able to create principles, norms, rules, institutions, and social and economic organizations based on global cultural diversity? The global crisis will be prolonged if new processes and governance mechanisms are not developed that will facilitate the emergence of this new world in which cultural diversity is foundational not only for summits but in our daily lives. The answer is not yet clear. But these are the central challenges posed by cultural diversity, and meeting them is the key to unlocking its great potential.

Cultural Diversity as a Foundation for Economic Diversity

Cultural diversity is foundational to the agenda and the work of G20 summits, not just to its processes of interaction. Cultural diversity generates institutional diversity, which leads to different national economic models of interaction between the private and public sectors. Those in turn lead to systemic differences in financial regulation, business practices, leadership styles, and management techniques. The current economic crisis reopens the centuries-long debate about economic systems, models, and ideologies in which the relative roles of the market and the state are again up for grabs. The crisis has raised serious questions about the universalist pretensions of the Anglo-Saxon model of hands-off capitalism, deregulated financial systems, and fully liberalized markets and the notion that "governments that govern best are those that govern least."

Korea itself represents a sterling example of economic diversity in its highly dynamic growth trajectory over the last forty years (Lim 2011). Beginning in the 1980s, Korea's experience and that of other "newly industrializing countries" were hotly debated in international economics. The conventional wisdom of mainstream (Anglo-Saxon) economics maintained that the economic dynamism of East Asia was attributable to free trade, free enterprise, and free markets. It is widely understood now that Korea's economic dynamism was due to a powerful combination of market forces and strategic government interventions that generated externalities, synergies, and high-yield "outlier" outcomes in economic performance.

The international economic debate has now moved from trade-offs between market and state-led approaches to acceptance of diverse economic models and experience. It turned out there was no single "East Asian Miracle" in the 1980s; that Japan, Korea, and China, not to mention Hong Kong, Thailand, and Malaysia, have different and unique economic histories and experiences. Asia provides diverse models of a mixed economy, not a single vision of economic success based exclusively on market fundamentalism. The G20 embodies a still greater breadth of national economic experiences that can be relevant to reforms and policy direction for G20 member countries and other countries as well.

Cultural diversity is not an irrelevant backdrop to the economic policy debate and separate from it. To the contrary, cultural diversity that embraces differences in balance between, for example, individualism and communitarianism, formal and informal modes of expression, hierarchical and egalitarian structures, abstract and representational forms, and critical and conformist tendencies has a direct and important impact on institutional forms, such as organizational, behavioral, and leadership styles and patterns. These variants in institutional forms, derived from cultural differences, have a direct and important impact on differences between countries in terms of their economic systems and experiences; that in turn has effects on divergent economic patterns and performance.

The differences among G20 countries, all of which have experienced sustained periods of economic success, mean that the breadth of economic experience represented by the countries at the G20 table is much greater than that in the G8 group. These differences provide a source of innovation and insight not present in the G8. They can contribute to the core G20 agenda on such issues as financial regulatory reform, strengthening institutional capacity, and enhancing the effectiveness of economic policies in addressing diverse demands and trade-offs.

Instead of cultural diversity being a problem for the G20, cultural diversity and its institutional and systemic manifestations are an asset. Nations and governments are looking for new approaches and innovations that can combine public responsibility and market economy dynamics. G20 peer review, exchange of views on best practices, and collaboration on oversight and supervision can generate changes in how nations pursue the combined goals of greater financial stability, economic growth, and sustainable balance in the future, all central goals of the G20. *Cultural diversity is a foundational element of G20 summitry.*

Cultural Encounters with "Difference" as a Defining Dynamic

Globalization has generated fears of homogenization of cultures. Dissenters and critics have not worried only about the perceived disequalizing effects of globalization but also about the power of modern materialism and consumerism, which they believe will inevitably lead to the erosion of cultural distinctiveness. Worries abound that the modernization that all countries seek will be translated into westernization under the influence of the global market economy. That concern is without doubt one of the reasons why the G8 was an insufficient and inappropriate group to deal with the global economic crisis: it embodied the confrontation between "the West and the Rest" rather than a means of resolving it.

Insights can be drawn from the millennia-long experience of cultural encounters as metaphors for and foreshadowing of the evolution of globalization and the global economy in the twenty-first century. Again, Korea represents a useful example. The only books in English on contemporary Korean art are written by Youngna Kim (Kim 1998 and 2005), a professor of art history at Seoul National University, and Jaeryung Roe (Roe 2001), former curator at the Museum of Contemporary Korean Art. These two authors elucidate the evolution of the interaction between Korean artists in the twentieth century and the outside world, beginning with Japan in the late nineteenth and early twentieth centuries and with Western art in the last half of the twentieth century. They clarify the tension between traditional Korean art, which developed largely without reference to the world outside of Asia, and its encounter with the modern art of the Western world.

Both authors highlight two dynamics of interaction between traditional and modern aesthetics and influence. One is the degree to which Korean art was stimulated and enhanced by interaction with Western influences and expressions rather than inhibited or overwhelmed by them. New levels of Korean artistic expression were generated by the struggle to come to terms with Western modernism. The second is the degree to which the new creativity stimulated by the interaction with the West not only retained a distinctly Korean character but actually deepened Korean culture rather than weakening it.

Korean artists and critics were engaged in a debate about the tensions between modernity and tradition that heightened public interest and engagement in Korea's search for an authentically Korean form of modernism that expressed

Korean identity in contemporary, modern, and even postmodern ways. The evolution of distinctly Korean cultural forms of expression reflected intellectual and
social tensions associated with the rapid economic and social modernization of
Korea in the late twentieth century and beyond (Kim 1998, 2005; Roe 2001).
The struggle and debate in the artistic community in Korea were part of a much
broader public debate in Korean society, not isolated from it.

Korea's rapid economic modernization occasioned and accelerated its cultural development of a distinctly Korean form of artistic modernism. Korea's
artistic evolution informed and contributed to strengthening Korean identity,
authenticity, and uniqueness, which helped shape Korea's approach to its own
economic modernization. Neither Korea's economic development nor its contemporary artistic culture emulated Western models of modernization and modernism, as might have been expected.

These trends in the history of contemporary Korean art are mirrored in the
experience of other non-Western countries experiencing rapid economic transformation. There is ample evidence from recent scholarship on the history of
modern art in G20 countries that the patterns of artistic development in G20
countries are similar to those of Korea. Those trends and patterns define the
dynamics of "the grand narrative" of cultural diversity that constitutes a major
force in the evolution of G20 summitry.

The cultural diversity of large, successful G20 countries demonstrates that
their cultural vitality is greater than the forces of cultural globalization and
potential homogenization, that their cultural growth is greater than the tendencies toward emulation, that authentic internal cultural deepening is more powerful than "flattening" (Friedman 2005), that the cultural hybrids characteristic of
the global age are greater than the forces toward homogenization, and that cultural "convergence" (Paz 1987), in which societies engage in selective borrowing,
combining internal and external elements, carries more weight than "the clash of
civilizations" (Huntington 1996).

Conclusion: Cultural Diversity as a Foundation for the New Dynamics of Summitry

The cultural diversity of the "global age" (Albrow 1997) is one of its defining
characteristics. The pervasiveness, power, and impact of cultural diversity are
underestimated in the world of diplomacy, politics, and economics. Its potential
as a transforming force of societies, economies, and governance is indeed great.
It is a major asset of the G20 in its effort to define new modalities of global leadership and responsibility. Achieving the transition in the evolution of the G20
from crisis committee to global steering committee and the transformation of
G20 summitry into new modalities and stronger narratives between leaders and

society will require seizing this moment and grasping the centrality of "the grand narrative" of global cultural diversity as the foundation for the new dynamics of G20 summitry.

Grasping the centrality of global cultural diversity for G20 summitry could strengthen the content of G20 peer review and the exchange of best practices in economic policy and institutional reform, enrich the public discourse on global leadership, provide vital elements for the development of new styles of global leadership, and give rise to a new notion of consensus based on the incorporation of varied perspectives into a composite vision of strategic leadership rather than simply a compromise between trade-offs. It also could provide insights into how leaders from vastly different cultures reach decisions given widely different cultural approaches to public decisionmaking. A broader representation of the cultural diversity in the contemporary world as manifested in the G20 could also facilitate more complex and varied diplomatic alignments, depending on the issue, leading to shifting coalitions of consensus to prevail over traditional alliances (see chapter 23 in this volume).

Because of the lack of attention to cultural diversity in G20 summitry so far, G20 summits have barely begun to capture and realize the new dynamics of summitry as forces for transformation. Korean cultural and economic development in recent decades illustrates the case for keeping a focus on both culture and economics rather than isolating one from the other.

Seizing this moment and grasping the centrality of "the grand narrative" of cultural diversity for our times as the foundation for a new dynamics of summitry is the key to making G20 summitry a transformative force in global leadership.

References

Albrow, Martin. 1997. *The Global Age: State and Society beyond Modernity.* Stanford University Press.

———. 2010. "Summits as Narratives between Leaders and Their Publics." In *Toward the Consolidation of the G20: From Crisis Committee to Global Steering Committee,* edited by Colin I. Bradford and Wonhyuk Lim. Seoul and Washington: Korea Development Institute and the Brookings Institution, 2010.

Friedman, Thomas L. 2005. *The World Is Flat: A Brief History of the Twenty-First Century.* New York: Farrar, Straus, and Giroux.

Huntington, Samuel P. *The Clash of Civilizations and the Remaking of World Order.* New York: Touchstone, 1996.

Kim, Youngna. 1998. *20th Century Korean Art.* London: Laurence King Publishing, in association with the Korea Literature Translation Institute.

———. 2005. *Tradition, Modernity, and Identity: Modern and Contemporary Art in Korea.* Elizabeth, N.J., and Seoul: Hollym International Corporation and the Korea Foundation.

Lim, Wonhyuk. 2011. "Joint Discovery and Upgrading of Comparative Advantage: Lessons from Korea's Development Experience." In *Postcrisis Growth and Development: A Development Agenda for the G-20*, edited by Shahrokh Fardoust, Yongbeom Kim, and Claudia Sepulveda, pp.173–226. Washington: World Bank, 2011.

Roe, Jae-Ryung. 2001. *Contemporary Korean Art*. St. Leonards, Australia: Craftsman House.

Paz, Octavio. 1987. *Convergences: Essays on Art and Literature*. New York: Harcourt Brace Javanovich.

23

The G20: Shifting Coalitions of Consensus Rather than Blocs

STEWART PATRICK

The emergence of the Group of Twenty (G20) marked a watershed moment in global governance. Since the end of the cold war, global forums had consistently failed to reflect shifts in global power. But the G20 now allows major established and emerging players to meet exclusively in a setting of formal equality—a setting that is not offered by the two-tiered Security Council or the international financial institutions, which have weighted voting systems.

The emergence of the G20 acknowledges that global governance cannot be accomplished by the West alone, and it provides a flexible framework in which established and emerging powers can hammer out agreements on pressing global issues. While the G20 has focused on economic issues, it will almost inevitably—like the Group of Eight (G8) before it—be drawn into a broader agenda including development, climate, energy, and eventually peace and security issues.

As the G20 matures and expands its agenda, it has the potential to shake up the geopolitical order, introducing greater flexibility into global diplomacy and transcending the stultifying bloc politics that have too often hamstrung cooperation in formal, treaty-based institutions (including the United Nations). The very size and diversity of the G20—while not without drawbacks—may inject

This chapter draws on the author's forthcoming report for the Century Foundation, *The G20 and the United States: Opportunities for More Effective Multilateralism* (2010). He expresses his gratitude to Preeti Bhattacharji of CFR for her superb editorial assistance in completing this chapter.

new dynamism into global governance by facilitating the formation of shifting coalitions of interest. If it does, the G20 will present particular strategic advantages for the United States, which will likely remain the indispensable partner for most winning coalitions within the new steering group.

Balancing Like-Mindedness, Effectiveness, and Representation

When it comes to constructing a global steering group, there are inevitable trade-offs to be made involving three essential values: like-mindedness, effectiveness, and representation. Let me touch on each of these, because they are worth bearing in mind when one considers possible negotiating dynamics within the G20—as well as outside of it.

One possible organizing construct is *like-mindedness,* in terms of political values. If the United States were looking merely for this quality, it might have stuck with the G7 (the G8 being partially hamstrung by Russia's inclusion) rather than elevate the more ideologically diverse G20. What the financial crisis revealed, however, is that a coalition of Western market democracies can no longer manage global issues alone. Moreover, evidence suggests that democratic and authoritarian governments are quite capable of finding common ground on some global governance challenges as long as they do not address norms of *domestic* governance. (The Obama administration continues to see some value in a like-minded body, however, and still leans on the G8 for some politically sensitive issues like Iran.)

A second construct is *effectiveness.* Truly implemented, this would envision a larger steering group than the G7 but one limited to the smallest number of states that really matter. On that basis, one might have stopped at a "G13," by formalizing the G8+"Outreach 5" dialogue that emerged through the Heiligendamm–L'Aquila process. Such a scenario would have brought Brazil and other big countries in, while keeping Argentina and other lesser players out.

The third construct—and one to which the G20 has moved (arguably too far)—is *representation,* which places a premium on an entity that looks like the world and presumably enjoys stronger (though hardly perfect) legitimacy as a result. The inclusion of Muslim countries (Indonesia, Saudi Arabia, and Turkey) is a positive development in this regard, even though the underrepresentation of Africa—South Africa is its sole representative—remains a problem. The G20's size comes at some cost to effectiveness, as discussions typically require a time-consuming "tour de table"—a challenge that has only increased with the presence of gatecrashers like Spain and the Netherlands. Such a large steering group risks reproducing the unfortunate dynamics of organizations that have a large membership, including the pursuit of lowest-common-denominator policies.

To maximize the like-mindedness, effectiveness, and representativeness of global forums, the United States will invariably make use of multiple frameworks of consultation. In a world of "multi-multilateralism," countries will inevitably forum shop, adopting the institutional arrangement or coalition that fits their needs and creating issue- or context-specific coalitions of limited membership. Such a pattern has already emerged in the realm of climate change (with the creation of the Major Economies Forum) and in the sphere of nuclear nonproliferation (where like-minded states have created the Proliferation Security Initiative and met at the Nuclear Security Summit).

At the same time, the transaction costs of establishing a new "Gx" group for each new problem as well as "summit fatigue" among the world's leaders may well drive leaders toward some institutional consolidation. Given the structural limitations of "variable geometry" outside the G20 context, we are likely to see the emergence of complicated coalition dynamics within the G20 itself. States will shift alignments across issue areas, and they may form separate coalitions based on *weight, like-mindedness,* and *representation.*

Divergences among the G20 were masked during the first year of the financial crisis, as countries focused on the short-term, urgent goal of preventing a global financial meltdown. As the world has begun, unevenly, to come out of the crisis, the underlying diversity of opinions, interests, and perspectives in the G20 has started to reemerge—including, as the Toronto summit amply demonstrated, among the venerable members of the G8. In the near term, the credibility of the G20 will depend on its ability to grapple with important legacy tasks, particularly implementation of the Pittsburgh G20 Framework for Strong, Sustainable, and Balanced Growth, as well as implementation of coordinated financial regulations. Beyond this immediate agenda, the G20 has the potential to make the transition to a standing global steering group, with some profound implications for global governance.

The G20's Potential to Shake Up Global Diplomacy

To date, analysts have focused overwhelmingly on the role of the G20 as a global crisis committee; they have devoted less attention to its potential to transform global diplomacy. The G20 could reshape diplomatic coalitions in at least four important ways.

First, it promises to inject fresh air into stale negotiations over global governance that frequently split along North-South lines, thus avoiding the destructive bloc dynamics that exist in the United Nations and other large membership forums. As President Obama bemoaned at the 2009 opening of the UN General Assembly, multilateral cooperation is often stymied by rigid ideological divisions reflecting outdated cold war and postcolonial experiences.[1] For example, the tendency of disaffected fringe countries in the Group of Seventy-Seven (G77) to invoke developing country solidarity against the "rich and powerful" countries and derail consensus on realistic goals displays not only ignorance of potential consequences but also an unwillingness to accept that the solutions to global challenges lie in multilateral agreements and partnerships that cross traditional lines.

The advent of the G20 may begin to alter those dynamics. Several prominent members of the G77—including Brazil, China, India, and Indonesia—are now at the table, bargaining directly with powerful states from the wealthy world. Such rising players may find themselves whipsawed between their new status in the inner sanctum and their continued links to the developing world. India, in particular, is a critical country here. Perhaps even more than China, it faces a tug between its traditional orientation and more recent political, economic, and geostrategic needs.

This presents both a challenge and an opportunity. Badly managed, such diversity of opinion could lead to antipathy, cacophony, or (at best) lowest-common-denominator multilateralism. Adroitly handled, it could create opportunities for forging agreements between Western and non-Western countries. With space to engage in a flexible manner, developing states may undertake a more detailed approach to policy than was previously possible. And ideally, the new alignments and strange bedfellows that will emerge within the G20 will be exported back to the United Nations, the international financial institutions, and other standing organizations.

The greatest threat to this more flexible diplomatic dynamic would be the development of standing bloc caucuses within the G20—something that fortunately has not occurred to date. Given the comfort that the United States has gained within the like-minded G7, some have suggested that Washington should promote a formal caucus of Western countries within the G20. Although superficially appealing, that approach could well backfire, as others—perhaps G77 members, the BRICs (Brazil, Russia, India, and China), or the BASICs (Brazil, South Africa, India, and China)—respond in kind.[2] The United States should accordingly avoid actions likely to lead others to import toxic bloc dynamics into the G20.

1. "The traditional division between nations of the South and the North make no sense in an interconnected world; nor do alignments rooted in the cleavages of a long-gone Cold War. The time has come to realize that the old habits, the old arguments, are irrelevant to the challenges faced by our people." President Barack Obama, Remarks by the President to the United Nations General Assembly, September 23, 2009 (www.whitehouse.gov/the_press_office/Remarks-by-the-President-to-the-United-Nations-General-Assembly).

2. Already, a number of voices, including scholars at Australia's Lowy Institute, have called for the creation of an Asian caucus within the G20. See Grenville and Thirlwell (2010).

A second major advantage of the G20 lies in its ability to offer a potential framework on which to build multilateral consensus on—and persuade rising powers to accept—the responsibilities inherent in power. As members of the G20 club, rising states—as well as established ones—will be expected to assume a greater share of obligations for the provision of global public goods, and they may also feel some pressure to comport with established international norms.

Forging consensus about global obligations and burden sharing will be vital but tricky. Unlike the relatively homogenous G7, the G20 includes countries of different political and economic orientations. None of the world's major emerging powers is revolutionary or bent on overthrowing the established (and historically liberal) order. But most are at least moderately revisionist, intent on becoming rule makers, not simply rule takers.

Generally speaking, all emerging players want to increase their weight *in* global governance but they do not necessarily want *more* global governance.[3] The reform agenda of the International Monetary Fund (IMF) is a case in point. Many Western governments in the G20 seek to give the IMF a more overt surveillance and early-warning role to identify systemic risks to the global financial order, including the capacity to monitor member states' fiscal and macroeconomic policies. But most major emerging-market governments—including China, India, and Saudi Arabia—oppose such a step. They seek bigger voting shares in the IMF, not an IMF that infringes on their sovereignty.

The ongoing challenge will be to persuade emerging powers, now that they are at the table, to help pick up the check. Convincing China, India, and Brazil to behave as global stakeholders rather than just self-interested participants is crucial. As these countries increasingly find themselves on the international stage, much of their focus continues to be drawn to significant domestic challenges, and they worry that spending resources to tackle broader global problems poses a risk to national development. The G20 offers a valuable forum for established and emerging powers to debate—and ideally forge agreement on—the substance of the global agenda, and it provides a mechanism to enlist the tangible contributions of rising powers to maintaining global order, in areas ranging from currency imbalances to climate change, peace operations, development cooperation, and nuclear nonproliferation.

Third, the G20 has the potential to drive reform within the United Nations. The world is being transformed, but many parts of the UN remain in a state of torpor. The G20 promises to give the United Nations a bit of healthy competition in shaping the global agenda as well as in providing a forum in which the world's most powerful actors can reach preliminary agreement on constructive approaches to common global problems. The G20 will not replace the

---

3. I am indebted to David Gordon for this insight.

world body and its specialized agencies, which retain unmatched legitimacy and impressive technical expertise and capacity to implement programs. But the G20 has the potential to become an important complement to the UN by serving as a "pre-negotiation forum" on important global matters and catalyzing much-needed reform of UN management, budget, personnel, and bloc dynamics.[4]

In the short term, the G20 may act as a pressure valve on the question of UN Security Council (UNSC) reform, reducing agitation among leading aspirant states (particularly from the developing world) to alter its composition. Over the longer term, however, the creation of the G20 is likely to redouble pressure to reform the increasingly anachronistic UNSC by highlighting the disparity between that latter body and global power trends. To the degree that the G20 begins to address issues of peace and security, it may serve as a testing ground for gauging the willingness of aspirant states to contribute to global order consistent with the provisions of the UN Charter.

Fourth, the more fluid negotiating environment presented by the G20 could empower the United States to find a wider range of potential alignments with nontraditional partners. For all the domestic hand-wringing over alleged U.S. decline, the United States will remain the premier, often indispensable, partner for other G20 members seeking to push particular initiatives. And as the linch-pin in many winning coalitions, Washington will have the freedom to advance its interests with a flexible set of G20 coalitions and a policy of variable geometry.

For instance, on counterterrorism cooperation, one could imagine the United States having a natural convergence of interests not only with the Europeans but also with Russia, China, Saudi Arabia, Indonesia, India, and Turkey—all of which have been vulnerable to homegrown terrorism. The G20 might also cre-ate new possibilities for cooperation on global energy by providing a forum in which producer and consumer countries might reach common ground.[5]

Expanding the G20's Agenda

The G20 will have these impacts, of course, only if it expands its agenda over time. The G20 signaled a potential enlargement of its mandate as early as November 2008, when its communiqué from the Washington summit under-lined its members' commitment "to addressing other critical challenges such as energy security and climate change, food security, the rule of law, the fight against terrorism, poverty, and disease."[6]

---

4. Jones, Pascual, and Stedman (2009).
5. This paragraph builds on insights from Bruce Jones.
6. Washington Declaration, G20 Summit on Financial Markets and the World Economy, Washington, D.C., November 15, 2008 (www.pittsburghsummit.gov/resources/125136.htm).

To date, G20 members have resisted significant mission creep, insisting that the body retain a focus on recovery from the economic crisis and promote strong, sustainable, and balanced growth through international economic cooperation. But as the global economy recovers, G20 leaders will likely broaden their horizons, making use of the G20 to consider a wider array of global economic, social, environmental, political, and security challenges.

Already, the G20 has moved beyond the immediate financial crisis to address several larger issues in the economic sphere, touching on topics like energy, anticorruption, labor, and development. In Pittsburgh, for example, leaders launched an initiative to phase out fossil fuel subsidies, asking their relevant ministers to return with a preliminary report as to how that might be accomplished. G20 meetings remain dominated by finance ministers and central bank governors, but G20 labor ministers also met in Washington in 2010.

The Korean government allotted a portion of the Seoul agenda to two new items. The first is the creation of a global financial safety net to enhance the IMF's capacity to preempt crises and help vulnerable countries, reducing their need to accumulate excessive foreign reserves. The second is a foray into development, focusing on its importance for global economic growth—a departure from the G8's focus on the foreign assistance components of development.

Going forward, leaders will need to avoid overloading the G20 agenda. Ideally, the G20 agenda should be limited to pressing issues that require the attention of leaders from the most powerful countries in the world, developed and developing. Otherwise, the G20, like the G7/G8, could become a "Christmas tree," festooned with a dozen separate ministerial processes. Rather than weighing down the G20 with every global matter, leaders should regard it as only one (if often the most important) of a number of overlapping networks of varying membership and competency. On the other hand, it may sometimes make sense for logistical reasons to schedule ad hoc meetings on specific issues—along the lines of the April 2010 Nuclear Security Summit—adjacent to G20 summits, to take advantage of the presence of G20 leaders.

As the G20 expands its agenda to include a broader array of foreign policy issues, foreign ministers should naturally play a larger role. Currently, finance ministries—including the U.S. Treasury Department—provide the lion's share of support for the sherpa process and the summits themselves. As the G20's ambit expands, it should follow the trajectory of the G7/G8, which shifted increasingly to foreign ministries—including the U.S. Department of State. That would ensure that cross-cutting issues receive the full political and diplomatic consideration that they deserve.[7]

7. Choe (2010).

Conclusion

The new dynamics of coalitions within the G20 may well produce some strange bedfellows. The Toronto summit provided tantalizing indications of the G20's potential to shake up global diplomacy. China's preemptive decision to relax its currency policy, announced just days before, was clearly intended to placate not just the United States, but also important emerging powers—notably Brazil and India, whose economic fortunes have been damaged by the undervalued yuan.

Moving forward, the G20 will likely continue to shake up diplomatic coalitions in new and productive ways. By injecting fresh air into North-South negotiations, offering a venue for rising and established powers to forge consensus, and providing the United States with a more fluid negotiating environment, the G20 can inject new dynamism into global governance.

References

Choe, Wongi Choe. 2010. "The Role of Korea in G20 Process and the Seoul Summit." Paper prepared for the international conference "The G20 Summit: From Crisis to Cooperation," organized by the Korean Association of Negotiation Studies, Seoul, May 20.

Grenville, Stephen, and Mark Thirlwell. 2010. "An Asian Regional Caucus for the G20." *Tempo* [Jakarta], March 24 (www.lowyinstitute.com/Publication.asp?pid=1273).

Jones, Bruce, Carlos Pascual, and Steven John Stedman. 2009. *Power and Responsibility: Building International Order in an Era of Transnational Threats.* Brookings.

24

The G20 and Regional Dynamics

ANDREW COOPER

In many of the original conceptualizations of the G20, regional bodies were viewed as being complementary to the "hub" model for this mode of sum-mitry at the leaders' level. That positive image was strengthened by the pres-ence of key regional drivers within the G20. All members of NAFTA were included, each of the EU4 (the United Kingdom, Germany, France, and Italy), plus Japan and the BRICs (Brazil, Russia, India, and China). Additional space was made available for Turkey, Saudi Arabia, South Africa, Australia, Indonesia, South Korea, and Australia, making the forum global in its reach. This structure allowed for the presence of a number of regional and/or global middle powers.

Such a diverse membership also opened the way for connections of different forms with a wide number of regional organizations—the African Union (AU) and ASEAN as well as MERCOSUR, the Gulf Cooperation Council (GCC), and the Economic Cooperation Organization (ECO). To give just one exam-ple of how those connections were made to justify membership, Saudi Arabia defended its position in the G20 by referencing not its leadership position in the Middle East but its role in the GCC (Zawya 2009).

Since the advent of the G20, however, the regional dynamics attendant to this forum have become points of serious contestation rather than a source of strength. Regional summits have entered into those dynamics in a number of ways. Significantly, some have been used to champion alternative designs for the G20. Greater inclusion has been called for in terms of enhanced status for a regional organization. In the lead-up to the Toronto G20, for example, the Norwegian foreign minister, Jonas Gahr Støre, explicitly criticized the G20 for its inadequacies in terms of regional representation (Spiegel 2010).

Equally, though, regional summits or regional dynamics more generally have come to the fore as motors for new forms of cooperative engagement within the context of the G20. Not only are these innovations significant in themselves, they also allow for platforms for spillover activities in other regional machinery. From its inception as the finance ministers' G20, there was a strong degree of recognition of the regional dimension, punctuated by the decision in 2002 to rotate the role of chair along regional as much as North/South lines. G20 countries agreed that "there should be an equitable annual rotation among all regions and between countries at different levels of development" (G20 2007, p. 23; Mo and Kim 2009).

Building on that model, the G20 at the leaders' level has proved to be a catalyst for a number of new and significant regional consultation initiatives. Although implemented in an awkward and inconsistent fashion, these initiatives have become embedded as an increasingly salient component of the overall architectural structure of the G20, extending from the European Community to Asia and Africa. Framed either as an impediment to the institutional legitimacy of the G20 or a catalyst for new types of innovation, a messy design exists in which regional dynamics act as both critic and driver for the G20.

Regional Critiques as a Manifestation of Diverse Grievances

It must be acknowledged that the regional critiques have had only minimal impact on the workings of the G20. That is to say, specific proposals made at the regional level have not made any difference in the way that the G20 has proceeded in advancing its agenda. On the contrary, the crisis orientation of the G20 has accented the concert nature of the G20, which privileges a small group of pivotal countries.

The impact of the regional critiques has been felt not on an instrumental but on a legitimacy basis, with some erosion of the G20's credibility in presenting itself as the hub institution of global governance. Although the sources of grievance are quite distinct from a regional perspective, all share the sentiment that their interests need to be taken into much stronger account by the G20.

A number of cases can be used to illustrate this point. The first is the critique from the Caribbean region, through the fifteen-member CARICOM, that the G20 has unfairly targeted the economic practices of that region. The most obvious source of tension is in the area of offshore financial centers (OFCs) or tax havens. There are also concerns on issues such as airline taxes, which could be detrimental to the tourism industry (see Fletcher 2009).

The theme of exclusion dominates in the Caribbean critique. As Bruce Gold-ing, Jamaica's prime minister, put it on a trip to China: "We do not sit in the G20. Our voice, where we are allowed to sit, is weak and so the imbalances in the economic architecture need to be addressed" (Brown 2010). Yet the politi-cal/diplomatic response was not one of rejection. Rather than actively resisting the G20's mandate, Jamaica—the biggest country in CARICOM—sought entry (not distance) from the process. In so doing it teamed up not with countries such as Venezuela or Bolivia in the UN General Assembly (the G192) but with countries in the Global Governance Group (or 3G) coalition, led by Singapore.

A second similar source of criticism came from countries that can be consid-ered to be in the middle-power category but that have not been accorded mem-bership. The sense of grievance coming from Norway stands out here. Again, however, there was a disjunction between normative discourse and diplomatic/ political objectives. As noted above, the Norwegian foreign minister, Jonas Gahr Støre, offered a robust critique of the G20, labeling it as "a grouping without international legitimacy" or a "mandate" concerning "its functions" (Spiegel 2010). Yet the focus of his instrumental proposals was directed at broadening the G20, not at replacing it. His prime objective was that the members of the Nor-dic Council—Norway, Sweden, Denmark, Finland, and Iceland—should share a rotating seat together with the Baltic states. Extending that line of thought, it was also suggested that similar arrangements could be made for other underrep-resented groups, such as African and Arab countries (Norway 2009).

A third source of criticism came from countries that can be considered regional rivals of countries that had gained membership in the G20. For exam-ple, African rivals used regional gatherings to express their sense of grievance at being left out of the G20, based largely on the grounds that because South Africa was the only G20 member, Africa was underrepresented and marginal-ized. One country that used that approach was Nigeria. Having been left out at the first three summits, Nigeria reasserted its claims for membership at a meet-ing of African finance ministers (on the sidelines of the IMF annual meeting), with its own finance minister, Mansur Muhtar, arguing that "we have been clam-oring for a greater role. . . . For us the key concern is to see that the principle [of greater African representation] gets accepted" (Reuters 2009).

Still, as noted, while such illustrations are interesting, they have not been det-rimental to the central purpose or instrumental workings of the G20; in each case the grievances of the outsiders could be largely ignored. Nigeria, most nota-bly, kept up the pressure for its inclusion through the June 2010 G20 summit—aided by its more positive national image with the succession of Jonathan Good-luck to the presidency. Yet, notwithstanding some enhanced access (for example, to the G20 business forum), Nigeria was invited to take part in the G8 outreach activities (in the same mode as Jamaica), not to sit at the high table of the G20.

Other regional grievances, however, proved to be so formidable that diplomatic action was deemed necessary. In those situations it was not simply individual countries pressing their own candidacy. In contradistinction, criticism came
from important regional groups themselves, most notably the AU and ASEAN.
Their complaints could not as easily be ignored, given the degree of the asymmetry between their exclusion and the out-of-proportion inclusion of the EU in
the G20. ASEAN advocated for a formal seat at the table of the G20 instead of
just simple representation by its chair. For example, at Davos in January 2010,
the Vietnamese prime minister, Nguyen Tan Dung, pushed the notion that
there should be an "increase [in] the representation of G20 [and] I think that
it is important to institutionalize the participation of regional organizations like
ASEAN" (Dung 2010).

The AU complained vociferously from the outset about its status among the
excluded. At a crisis summit held in Tunis, hosted by the African Development
Bank, Jean Ping, head of the African Union's executive commission, stated that
"Africa . . . was not associated even slightly with the preparation when it's a
question of deciding the future of the world to which this continent belongs, in
fact and by right." Ping appealed to organizers of the G20 meeting to think of
Africa's right to be an active player in the process and "not to suffer, as always,
the consequences of other people's mistakes" (cited in Muiruri 2008). Countries
such as Uganda added their sense of grievance. Uganda's Central Bank governor,
Emmanuel Tumusiime Mutebile, argued that "Uganda is a rich country and well
governed for the last 15 years, so why should its voice not be heard? . . . The
G20 represents part of the old architecture, which I hope will end next weekend" (Pfeiffer 2008).

The official state-centric sense of grievance relating to the G20 was embel-
lished by the support that this attitude of resentment received from components
of global civil society, led by the Global Campaign against Poverty (GCAP). By
formally launching the "Africa AU at the Table" initiative at the Addis Ababa
summit of the AU Assembly in February 2010, GCAP added some momentum
for G20 reform (GCAP 2010). The major thrust of the argument was voiced by
Adelaide Sosseh, GCAP co-chair and member of the GCAP Africa governing
council: "Africa's lack of united representation on the global scene is sidelining
the continent. Successes are going unnoticed and even help given in some areas
is becoming redundant. Africa's inclusion as a recognized bloc in the G20 will
give her a unified negotiating point in the G20" (AU Monitor 2010).

In contrast, representatives from the G20 countries defended the nature of
the limited membership not on grounds of legitimacy but of instrumentality.
French cooperation minister Alain Joyandet, who attended the Tunis ADB meeting, contended that as a crisis committee, the G20 needed to be arranged among
major powers and that South Africa was called on to represent Africa's views.

Given the extent of the improvised structure of the G20, the rationale tilted to "limit the number of organizations present, undoubtedly for more effectiveness" (Pfeiffer 2008).

This type of logic came under increased stress, however, as the overrepresentation of the EU became more apparent. The expectation was that the EU would be able to rationalize its own participation in the G20. After all, with both the EU Commission and the EU presidency at the table, there appeared ample opportunity for coordination between the EU4 as insiders and the wider EU23 as outsiders. Yet, despite this impressive institutional presence, Europe has added to, not subtracted from, its representation at the country-specific or national level. The most obvious illustration is the engagement of Spain. Spain got into the first G20 summit in Washington on the coattails of French president Sarkozy, who, after some intense lobbying, gave up one of France's two seats (as one of the EU4 in the G20 and in France's capacity as the EU president) to Spanish prime minister José Luis Rodríguez Zapatero. Spain subsequently consolidated its position when it took up the EU presidency, using an EU summit to situate itself as a "permanent guest" in the G20 (ANSAmed 2010).

The porous architecture of the G20 may be seen as having two major consequences—one for the EU and one for the G20. Within the EU, Spain's entry—along with the presence of the Netherlands and countries holding the EU presidency (the Czech Republic and Sweden)—led to demands for even more additional members. The Eurozone has made one bid for an institutional membership (Strupczewski 2010). Poland has also claimed this status (Associated Press 2010).

The other consequence, as alluded to, is the far more detrimental one that the EU's overrepresentation reinforced the claims of critics that the G20 lacked the ingredients needed to make it a hub of economic global governance. To charges that the G20 lacked equality were added those of even European critics, such as the European Council on Foreign Relation's Jose-Ignacio Torreblanca, that too many voices did not multiply influence: "The fact that there are a lot of Europeans in a room doesn't mean that they are being listened to" (cited in Pop 2010).

Efforts to Ameliorate Regional Grievances

Notwithstanding the privileging of a small group of pivotal countries, the G20 has promoted some innovative efforts that helped ameliorate regional grievances concerning the summit process. One significant example of how innovation can be initiated has come with the rapid move by South Korea to embark on new forms of regional outreach—embracing ASEAN in particular. As his first destination, Changyong Rhee, the secretary-general of South Korea's Presidential Committee, visited the ASEAN secretariat and smoothed sensitivities through the declaration that "we are shaping the agenda as early as possible to include the views of ASEAN" (ASEAN 2010).

In terms of substance, the main attraction offered by the evolving G20 agenda has been South Korea's proposals regarding a global financial safety net and development issues. According to Junkyu Lee, senior adviser to the South Korean Ministry of Strategy and Finance, in talks with Vietnamese Ministry of Finance officials (representing Korea as host of the G20 and Vietnam as president of ASEAN in 2010, respectively), in the near term the G20 could set up a regional-scale cooperation regime or mutual agreement on financial safety assistance (Vietnam Business News 2010).

As witnessed by that type of interaction, ASEAN has proved receptive to greater inclusion in the G20 process. At the ASEAN leaders' summit in Hanoi, April 9, 2010, the leaders stated that "ASEAN strongly believes that it can contribute to the deliberations of the G20 through continued participation of the ASEAN Chair and the ASEAN Secretary General in the future G20 Summits" (quoted in Rana 2010, p. 12). Outreach efforts to regional organizations, such as ASEAN and others, offers the G20 an opportunity to enhance inclusion and address legitimacy concerns. ASEAN participation at the June 2010 Summit in Toronto (see Xinhua 2010) followed this model, through the participation of the ASEAN chair and secretary general.

Even more structurally advanced, South Africa has creatively and successfully implemented a stellar form of indirect representation through the regional Committee of Ten (C10) finance ministers and governors of central banks under the auspices of the African Development Bank, the Economic Commission for Africa, and the African Union Commission. This enterprise, it should be acknowledged, has been a risky endeavor. Not only did it expose South Africa's position as the one African member of the G20 to increased scrutiny, it stretched South Africa's resources. Yet, despite the risks, the initiative has worked well. The scope of the committee's membership is impressive, including as it does countries that sought membership (Egypt and Nigeria) in a reformed G8 themselves. Indeed, Egypt was embedded as the C10 vice chair in the ongoing process featuring another meeting in Washington, D.C., on October 5–6, 2010, in the run-up to the Seoul G20 summit (C10 2010; All Business 2010).

However important these efforts to ameliorate regional grievances, they do not address the fundamental legitimacy deficit of the G20: the overrepresentation of the EU. Innovative moves toward enhanced consultation with nonmembers therefore need to be complemented by pushback on EU participation. Such an ambitious approach can be implemented through a number of techniques. First, above all, rather than allowing further EU representation, a process of rollback and contraction should be implemented. That will help build legitimacy for the G20 outside of the EU. But just as important, it will encourage more innovative forms of coordination inside the EU.

To be sure, the political/diplomatic pressures to add, not subtract, will continue to be intense. A case in point is that of the Netherlands at the Toronto G20. Having initially signaled that the Dutch would not be invited, Canada relented (not out of just a sense of like-mindedness but good personal chemistry at the leadership level) and allowed the Netherlands in, with a cluster of other countries (Ethiopia, Malawi, and Vietnam) implicitly under the banner of regional representatives. Whatever the political/diplomatic advantage gained by this supplementary move, it was offset by the problematic logic of letting in another EU claimant. Instead of lending credence to the notion that the G20 represented a shift of global governance for a world that was realigning its power and normative foundations, it reinforced the image of the G20 as having an arbitrary "club" design (MacCharles 2010).

Still, the ability of a determined host to push back on additional European participation was demonstrated when South Korea said no to the Netherlands at the November 2010 Seoul summit. A key test of legitimacy will be whether France in 2011 and Mexico in 2012 will display the same sort of resolute behavior.

Second, the move by South Korea to embrace a form of host/regional institutional mode of consultation should be refined and institutionalized. This part of the approach to strengthen the legitimacy of the G20 could come through varied means; for example, in addition to the initiatives taken by the host country, moves could be made through a G20 secretariat (if one is established as proposed by President Sarkozy) or more loosely through a team of sherpas (either in a troika format or in a more ad hoc fashion). The focus would be on select groups of excluded countries, with a functional orientation. A prime target for consultation beyond regional organizations would be the 3G group, which, under the leadership of Singapore along with Switzerland and Qatar, has gained some momentum.

Third, some serious thought needs to be given to whether a formal caucus system within the G20 is a good idea or not. If the EU is pressed to coordinate internally, it will have the effect of becoming a de facto caucus. Moreover, the African C10 reveals the power of innovative activity in alleviating criticisms about exclusion of Africa. A proposal for an East Asian caucus has been put forward by the Lowy Institute in Australia; an A8, as suggested by the Brookings Institution, would serve as a similar model in the Americas.

Still, even if the full-blown caucus idea is rejected, there are other ways that regional consultation could be enhanced. Above all, ASEAN consultation through the G20 process could be enhanced through a meeting of an expanded ASEAN+3 prior to the G20 summits. One possible conduit for this type of consultation is the ASEAN+3 Economic Review and Policy Dialogue (ERPD), which brings together the finance ministers and deputies of thirteen countries (ASEAN plus China, Japan, and Korea) (Rana 2010).

Regional dynamics have proven up to now to be one of the most obvious defects in the G20 model. Instead of serving a complementary purpose, the asymmetrical gaps in representation have weakened the legitimacy and arguably the efficiency of the G20, especially in allowing multiple EU voices to be heard instead of a single voice.

While states will retain their primacy within the G20 context, it will be advantageous if the club orientation at the regional level could be stretched to embrace a more networked approach. For one thing, a regional dimension could be built into the G20 business forum, either directly or through connections with gatherings such as the APEC CEO summit (the two meetings fell back to back, with the Korea G20 business forum being held on November 10–11, 2010, and the APEC CEO summit taking place in Yokohama, Japan, November 12–13, 2010). As revealed at the South Korea summit, the G20 business forum contains the potential for becoming a major embedded constituency for the forum (Kim 2010). But as the G20 grows, the attractions of some mode of regional subforums or coordinated practices will become more apparent, as the anticipated scale of the forum highlights the organizational complexity of this form of activity (over 100 chief executives organized through twelve working groups were in attendance in South Korea).

The role of NGOs at the regional level is more sensitive, as witnessed by the exclusion of NGOs up to now from the South Africa–led C10. Yet, as demonstrated by the actions of GCAP on the AU representation issue, African civil society is mobilizing around the G20 on a regional basis. While it is AU and pivotal national governments, notably South Africa (which allows some considerable access to NGOs on specific economic issues), that will remain the core and rightful targets, some complementary activities will be worthwhile. One such endeavor has been the "20 African Outreach" meeting held in tandem with the August 2010 Korea Africa Economic Cooperation conference in order to gather African voices for the November G20 Summit (Na 2010).

In conclusion, it may be suggested that with some innovative reforms along these lines, the regional dynamics surrounding the G20 could move from being a weakness to a source of strength. As emphasized throughout this chapter, the "rejectionists" of the G20 have not been many in number, with most regional bodies wanting to find ways to work within the summit process. What is desired is some greater openness to participation in and beyond the state dimension. If formal G20 membership is closed, it should not preclude innovative mechanisms that would broaden the forum's input and legitimacy on a more improvised basis. As suggested, there are a number of viable alternative means of engagement through which that objective can be reached.

References

All Business. 2010. "African Development Bank Group–C-10 to Discuss Development Agenda for G20 Summit in Seoul," October 4 (www.allbusiness.com/economy-economic-indicators/economic-conditions-recovery/15156351-1.html).

ANSAmed. 2010. "Spain: Press Announces Permanent Seat at G20" (March 26).

ASEAN. 2010. "Views of ASEAN Sought for G20 Agenda." Press release. Jakarta (February 10).

Associated Press. 2010. "Poland, with World's 18th Largest Economy, Wants in G20." *ABC News*, February 3.

AU Monitor. 2010. "GCAP Applauds Initiative by the AU to Seek G20 Membership" (www.pambazuka.org/aumonitor/comments/2640/).

Brown, Calvin G. 2010."Jamaica Calls on China to Advocate for Developing Countries in the G20." *Caricom News*, February 7.

C10. 2010. "Communiqué of the Meeting of the Committee of African Ministers of Finance and Planning and Governors of Central Banks." Cape Town (February 21).

Dung, Nguyen Tan. 2010. "Generating Democratisation in Global Governance an Urgent Demand, Says PM." Speech to WEF, Look at Vietnam (January 28).

Fletcher, Pascal. 2009. "Caribbean Finance to Survive G20 Pressure—Caricom." Reuters (December 10).

GCAP. 2010. "Launch of 'Africa AU at the Table' Campaign." Press release. Addis Ababa (February 2).

G20. 2007. "The Group of Twenty: A History" (http://www.g20.org/Documents/history_report_dm1.pdf).

Kim, Tong-hyung. 2010. "Seoul Business Summit Starts to Take Shape." *Korea Herald*, August 22.

MacCharles, Tonda. 2010. "The Expanding G8 Adds up to a G20 in Huntsville, while Toronto's G20 Will Be a G33 or 34." *Toronto Star*, June 14.

Muiruri, Rebecca. 2008. "Africa Disappointed at Exclusion from G20." Kenya Broadcasting Corporation (November 12).

Mo, Jongryn, and Chiwook Kim. 2009. "Power and Responsibility: Can East Asian Leadership Rise to the Challenge?" Seoul: Hills Governance Center at Yonsei (September).

Na Haejung. 2010. "S. Korea to Host Ministerial Conference on Economic Cooperation with Africa." Xinhua New Agency (August 24).

Norway. 2009. "Norwegian Call for Nordic Membership in the G20." Press release. Oslo: Ministry of Foreign Affairs (www.regjeringen.no/en/dep/ud/selected-topics/Trade-policy/membership_g20.html?id=587984&epslanguage=en-GB).

Pfeiffer, Tom. 2008. "Africa Dismayed at Exclusion from Crisis Summit," November 12 (http://uk.reuters.com/article/2008/11/12/us-africa-g20-sb-idUKTRE4AB4JM20081112).

Pop, Valentina. 2010. "Van Rompuy and Barroso to Both Represent EU at G20." EUobersver.com (March 19).

Rana, Pradumna R. 2010. "Reform of the International Financial Architecture: How Can Asia Have a Greater Impact in the G20?" RISI Working Paper 201 (June 9).

Reuters. 2009. "African FinMins Call for G20 Voice, More Support" (October 5).

Spiegel. 2010. "Norway Takes Aim at G20" (June 22).

Strupczewski, Jan. 2010. "Juncker Wants Euro Seat at G20, Budget Cooperation." *The Guardian*, January 18.

Vietnam Business News. 2010. "ASEAN's Position towards the G20 Seoul Summit" (September 5) (http://vietnambusiness.asia/asean%E2%80%99s-position-towards-the-g20-seoul-summit/).

Xinhua. 2010. "ASEAN to Attend G20 Summit in Toronto." China.org.cn (June 22) (www.china.org.cn/world/2010-06/22/content_20322748.htm).

Zawya, Maria Abi-Habib. 2009. "AMF Chairman: Saudi Arabia Not Overrepresented in G20–AMF" (http://en.news.maktoob.com/20090000379378/Saudi_Arabia_not_over_represented_in_G20_AMF/Article.htm).

25

A G20 "Non-Secretariat": President Nicolas Sarkozy's Conversations with Philosopher Lao Tzu, Strategist Sun Tzu, and Clio, the Muse of History

BARRY CARIN

The G20 decided it would be the "main global forum" for economic and financial issues. But it must still give itself the means to work more effectively. Shouldn't we create a G20 Secretariat to continuously monitor the implementation of decisions and deal with issues in conjunction with all pertinent international organizations?[1]

Act I

A little known fact is that deep in the cavernous basement of the Louvre in Paris, there exists a time machine. It is a closely held secret; the machine is made available only to the president of France, restricted for use to help resolve only the most intractable problems. President Sarkozy, host of the 2011 G20, decided to use the time machine to go back to 495 BC to consult the wise Lao Tzu at the height of his powers. What follows is the transcript—any errors or omissions are the fault of the translator, working from Mandarin and French.

President Sarkozy: My dear sir, please excuse me for dropping in unannounced, but I desperately need some advice. I am hosting a meeting of the leaders of the world's most powerful countries in a year's time. The issues on the agenda

---

1 . President Nicolas Sarkozy (www.diplomatie.gouv.fr/en/ministry_158/events_5815/speech-by-the-president-of-the-republic_14177.html).

are extraordinarily complex—coordinating global fiscal policies, with each country facing difficult economic conditions, as well as financial regulation, safety nets, and development. There is constant pressure to expand the agenda to include multifaceted problems like climate change, trade, and nuclear proliferation. There are high expectations, intense media scrutiny, and resentment from excluded countries and international civil society—everyone clamors to provide input, if not be at the table. We leaders lack technical expertise and, despite our different cultural approaches to decisionmaking, are supposed to effectively deal with these issues, as well as the crisis of the day, in an informal two-day meeting, with little preparation time.

I think I need a new institution—it is impossible to reform the existing international organizations. To make progress and provide continuity, an institutional memory is required. The new institution must be nimble and flexible, controlled by our informal group of leaders, not run by some invisible elite. We need a mechanism to direct the extensive preparations for our two-day meeting, to manage the outreach and consultation efforts. We must have an apparatus to report on the various invitations and requests for reports that we extend to international organizations, our ministers, and working groups and to discretely monitor and report on the performance of our own commitments.

Lao-Tzu[2]: I understand. Governing a large country is like frying a small fish. You spoil it with too much poking. The solution to your problem is simple. You need a "non-secretariat."

President Sarkozy: A "non-secretariat"? Please do not speak in riddles. I need your best advice.

Lao-Tzu: Some say that my teaching is nonsense. Others call it lofty but impractical. But to those who have looked inside themselves, this nonsense makes perfect sense.

President Sarkozy: But with all due respect—a "non-secretariat"—that is a paradox.

Lao-Tzu: True words seem paradoxical. Nothing in the world is as soft and yielding as water. Yet for dissolving the hard and inflexible, nothing can surpass it. The soft overcomes the hard; the gentle overcomes the rigid.

President Sarkozy: OK. A "non-secretariat." What kind of institution is that?

Lao-Tzu: When you have names and forms, know that they are provisional. When you have institutions, know where their functions should end.

---

2. Lao-Tzu, *Tao Te Ching*, trans. by S. Mitchell (http://academic.brooklyn.cuny.edu/core9/phalsall/texts/taote-v3.html).

President Sarkozy: All right, I think I see. "Provisional" means no permanent staff to prevent the process being captured by an entrenched elitist bureaucracy. So the "non-secretariat" will be composed of seconded staff borrowed from interested countries for a limited period of time.

Lao-Tzu: When the Master governs, the people are hardly aware that he exists.

President Sarkozy: Are you serious? Can we make progress without a powerful central organization?

Lao-Tzu: We join spokes together in a wheel, but it is the center hole that makes the wagon move. We shape clay into a pot, but it is the emptiness inside that holds whatever we want. We hammer wood for a house, but it is the inner space that makes it livable. We work with being, but non-being is what we use.

President Sarkozy: I am not sure I understand. It seems that your advice is a contradiction in terms.

Lao-Tzu: The gentlest thing in the world overcomes the hardest thing in the world. That which has no substance enters where there is no space.

President Sarkozy: What about a communication plan?

Lao-Tzu: Those who know don't talk. Those who talk don't know. True words aren't eloquent; eloquent words aren't true. Wise men don't need to prove their point; men who need to prove their point aren't wise.

President Sarkozy: I am not sure I understand. Should I not publicize this brilliant non-secretariat initiative?

Lao-Tzu: Look, and it can't be seen. Listen, and it can't be heard. Reach, and it can't be grasped. Approach it and there is no beginning; follow it and there is no end.

President Sarkozy: But making progress on this global quandary will help my reelection efforts. Should I not take credit for the "non-secretariat"?

Lao-Tzu: The Master doesn't talk, he acts. When his work is done, the people say, "Amazing: we did it, all by ourselves!"

Act II

President Sarkozy returned to the Élysée in 2010 and had dinner with Carla. He was enthusiastic about his conversation with Lao-Tzu and recounted the Taoist idea of a "non-secretariat." Carla was skeptical. She advised him to get a second opinion, from the other end of the philosophical spectrum. President Sarkozy agreed and, after cognacs, returned to the basement of the Louvre. He dialed up the Kingdom of Wu in the fifth century BC and located Sun Tzu, author of *The Art of War.*

President Sarkozy: Excellency, please give me some advice on a matter of state, albeit a nonmilitary problem. I have to chair a meeting of nineteen other leaders of major countries—most speak neither French nor Mandarin. They are not experts, but they are expected to make progress on complex global deadlocks.

Sun Tzu: Excuse me, you think you have problems! I have just been commanded to train a harem of 180 concubines into soldiers.

President Sarkozy: What do you think of the concept of a "non-secretariat"—an informal support unit to prepare summits, composed of seconded agents of the other countries involved and led by a troika?

Sun Tzu: Be extremely subtle, even to the point of formlessness. Be extremely mysterious, even to the point of soundlessness. Thereby you can be the director of the opponent's fate.

President Sarkozy: One problem with this secondment idea is that I have no control of the caliber of people seconded by other countries.

Sun Tzu: The skilful employer of men will employ the wise man, the brave man, the covetous man, and the stupid man.

President Sarkozy: Will advice and preparation performed by the non-secretariat work?

Sun Tzu: The enlightened ruler is heedful, and the good general full of caution.

President Sarkozy: I worry that with a low-profile "non-secretariat" I won't get any credit.

Sun Tzu: The general who advances without coveting fame and retreats without fearing disgrace, whose only thought is to protect his country and do good service for his sovereign, is the jewel of the kingdom.

President Sarkozy summoned his G20 sherpa and his foreign policy adviser. He instructed them to listen carefully and laid out the blueprint for the G20 non-secretariat. They concurred but advised him to act now, before another G20 leader decides to propose a permanent G20 secretariat. They noted that some Canadians had already published an op ed suggesting that it would be worth it for Canada to sound out the other G20 countries and offer to place a permanent secretariat—and to pay for some of the costs—in an international city such as, say, Montreal. The Canadians' argument could be persuasive:

Canada could argue that it is not a major power such as the United States or China, and not a European country, there already being too many international institutions located there. Canada does know how to organize events, is relatively innocuous yet more or less efficient, and once had a reputation for being constructive, even innovative, in international affairs.[3]

President Sarkozy decided to act, preempting the Canadians. He placed phone calls to President Lee Myung-bak of the Republic of Korea and President Felipe Calderón of Mexico. He noted that the G20 needed a more integrated approach to its administrative, technical, and logistical functions. He suggested that the G20 summit be prepared and managed by the sherpas of the Korean-French-Mexican troika. He encouraged them to assign their G20 personal representatives to help co-lead the preparatory effort. The three sherpas forming the troika could remain in their host countries and manage the secretariat's work remotely. He also invited the Koreans and the Mexicans to second senior trusted officials to be resident in Paris to work as an integral part of the sherpa team preparing the 2011 G20 summit.

President Sarkozy had a plan to staff the "non-secretariat." His staff would invite G20 member countries and international organizations to second administrative and technical staff. Liaison contact points and implementation reporting requirements would be established in the key international institutions that were tasked with following up on G20 summits. The OECD secretariat, located in Paris, would be asked to provide analyses and to be especially responsive to requests from the "non-secretariat."

In the first year, the budget of the non-secretariat, except for salaries of seconded officials, would be funded by France. President Sarkozy suggested that in subsequent years the operating costs be funded in equal parts by the members of the serving troika. The fact that salaries of seconded officials would be borne by their own home organizations would finesse the fear of an independent bureaucratic organization. Leaders would feel comfortable that they indeed controlled the process, rather than an invisible illegitimate organization. Sarkozy, Lee, and Calderón agreed that the functions of this "non-secretariat" secretariat would be to provide support for

—preparation of the summits (agenda and technical background)

—follow-up of summits (monitoring implementation of commitments)

—managing relations with nonmember countries and organizations.

President Sarkozy, a voracious reader, had seen an article by Johannes Linn that suggested that given the sensitivity concerning expansion of the

3. Roy Culpeper and Joe Ingram, "Make Canada the G20's Permanent Home" (www.theglobe andmail.com/news/opinions/make-canada-the-g20s-permanent-home/article1664535/).

international bureaucracy and the aversion to a new formal structure, it might be better to refer to the proposed "non-secretariat" by an innocuous term. Sarkozy agreed and henceforth the "non-secretariat" would be referred to in public in all G20 countries as the G20 summit staff.[4]

Act III

A few days after President Sarkozy decided to establish the G20 non-secretariat, Clio, the muse of history, was in Paris doing some research. She was well aware of his commitment to reform international institutions. Dining with President Sarkozy, Clio asked for an update on current developments in international governance.

President Sarkozy (quoting Valerius Flaccus): *"To thee, O Muse, has been vouchsafed the power to know . . . the ways by which things come to be."*[5] Aren't you up to date on all these developments, such as the recent G20 leaders' meetings and the event in Seoul?

Clio responded that she needed a briefing to ensure that she inspired future historians appropriately.

Clio: I just re-read Barbara Tuchman's *The March of Folly,* which traces human foolishness across the millennia. Her thesis is that even when political leaders have the information that they need to make an intelligent decision and know what decision ought to be made, they consistently fail to make it. They act against both common sense and self-interest. Why would we expect different outcomes from the G20?

President Sarkozy: The challenge is to craft governance institutions to maximize rationality. The G8 summit has been replaced by the G20, with all the key players involved from the beginning. The G20 summit will be well-prepared by a unique non-secretariat, a governance innovation invented jointly with the Koreans and the Mexicans. Paul Martin, the former Canadian prime minister, is one of the parents of the ideas of both the G20 and this mechanism that will make it work. Working together in this Taoist-type entity, officials and experts are highlighting common-sense options that will lead to win-win-win legacy-enhancing outcomes. Intelligent decisions can be made and both enlightened self-interest and the global public good will be served.

Clio: Well, thank you, President Sarkozy. You have brilliant ideas. And may I say that yours is the most crisp analysis I have received in the last four centuries.

4. Johannes Linn, "Preliminary Suggestions for a G20 Summit Secretariat" (www.kdi.re.kr/upload/15230/2-3.pdf).
5. See *Argonautica Book 3,* trans. by J. H. Mozley (www.theoi.com/Text/ValeriusFlaccus3.html).

President Sarkozy: I guess you haven't checked in for a while. As Herodotus said, "Very few things happen at the right time, and the rest do not happen at all: the conscientious historian will correct these defects." Clio, I rely on you, so future historians will give me the credit that I deserve, because the non-secretariat will ensure the future success of the G20.

Commentary: Non-Secretariat versus Permanent Secretariat

We need a mechanism to ensure effective information collection, outreach, and policy implementation while avoiding bureaucratization. Some may infer that Sarkozy's call to create a G20 secretariat implies a conventional *permanent* secretariat rather than a Taoist non-secretariat. There are two major issues. First is the question of a troika and seconded staff versus a conventional organization with one secretary-general and permanent staff. Second is the question of location of a permanent organization.

The Staff

We must avoid bureaucratization and the loss of leaders' control and with it the loss of leaders' commitment. To address concerns about bureaucratization and agenda setting by unaccountable technocrats, the secretariat, even if permanent, should have staggered secondments from troika countries for three years (for example, Mexican officials would serve in 2011, 2012, and 2013) and sherpas from the troika countries should serve as co-secretaries-general (that is, from Korea, France, and Mexico in 2011) to ensure direct accountability to the host countries. There is merit to limiting terms to three years and refreshing the staff by turning over one-third each year. If sherpas are running the show, there is no danger of lifelong bureaucrats capturing the process. A troika-based non-secretariat, with seconded staff, is workable in practical terms. (Staff would not be restricted to troika countries—it would make sense to encourage the best available people for three-year terms.)

Location

One argument for a permanent location for the G20 non-secretariat is that an unenthusiastic host country could wreak havoc on the whole enterprise. It is bad enough that the technical staff would have to move every year, but logistical issues would be complicated by an uncooperative host. Furthermore, in a permanent structure, each G20 member country would probably eventually have a mission at the venue of the secretariat, in the manner of the OECD.

Another argument for a permanent location is the need to build effective mechanisms for peer learning and peer evaluation. As the G20 issue space expands from macro-financial policy to a growth-oriented development agenda, climate change, and so on, it will become increasingly important to have in place peer mechanisms within the G20 based on rigorous analytical standards (à la OECD). One can argue that only a permanent secretariat with a strong technical staff can do an adequate job in this regard. Supporters of the non-secretariat argue that the peer learning and peer evaluation functions do not require permanence—quality staff work and institutional memory can be provided by personnel on three-year terms.

A permanent secretariat would need a permanent location, but people will disagree on the criteria for the location of a permanent secretariat. There is an advantage to putting the secretariat in Beijing (signaling the recent changes in economic gravity), a good case for Korea and Australia, and a case for New York or Geneva, as being UN cities. Proponents for Canada will point out Canada's critical role in launching the G20 finance ministers group and advocating its elevation to the G20 summit, its good relations with all members of the G20, and the fact that it is home of the leading information center on the G8/G20 and of the Centre for International Governance Innovation (CIGI), the leading think tank specializing in global governance.

In contrast, a non-secretariat would be located in the host country for the G20 summit and move every year. There is little difficulty moving every year—all the documents are electronic. The officials loaned to the non-secretariat would be elite cosmopolitan experts and would willingly accept two international assignments of a year's length, split by a year at home. Koreans would go to France in 2011—French secondees would go to Mexico in 2012.

On balance, a "non-secretariat" is an idea whose time has come.

VII

The Leaders, Their Publics, and Communications

26

Public Attitudes in G20 Countries

BRUCE STOKES

The G20 met in Seoul in November 2010 at a time of widespread despair among the publics in G20 countries. In the wake of the global financial crisis, people are hurting, unhappy about the way that things are going in their societies, disconsolate about the state of the economy, and yet generally hopeful about the future. Most fault their government for the bad economic times and think that governments are doing a poor job of coping with current troubles. There is, however, widespread support, especially in the West, for more financial regulation. Faith in capitalism and globalization still remains strong. And the message that publics are sending to their leaders—with majority backing in the United States and plurality support in France, Germany, Britain, and Italy—is that they want them to make the management of international economic problems their top priority.

The G20 Mood

The recent deep economic downturn has taken a human toll in G20 countries. In all six of the G20 countries surveyed by the German Marshall Fund in June 2010, majorities say that they or their family have been greatly or somewhat

Survey data presented here are from the 2010 Pew Global Attitudes Survey (http://pewglobal.org/2010/06/17/obama-more-popular-abroad-than-at-home/) and the German Marshall Fund 2010 Transatlantic Trends Survey (ww.gmfus.org/trends/2010/).

Table 26-1. *Current versus Future Situation*

Percent

Country	Dissatisfaction with country direction	Current economic situation bad	Economic situation improving
United States	62	75	56
Britain	63	79	47
France	74	87	22
Germany	59	55	48
Russia	59	65	39
Turkey	60	65	25
China	9	7	87
India	54	43	64
Indonesia	56	50	56
Japan	76	88	14
South Korea	74	80	40
Argentina	74	72	29
Brazil	49	36	75
Mexico	79	75	47

Source: Pew Global Attitudes Project.

affected by the economic crisis. They include three in four (76 percent) Americans and Turks, who claim to be the most personally affected by the Great Recession. It is little wonder then that in nearly all G20 nations surveyed, people are unhappy with the direction of their country, disgruntled about the state of their nation's economy, and divided about the economic future. (See table 26-1.)

In the fourteen G20 nations that the Pew Global Attitudes project surveyed in April, three in five (61 percent) people were dissatisfied with the way things were going in their society. That discontent divides into three tranches of G20 members.

The first group comprises frustrated former powers, such as Japan and France, and emerging economies, such as Mexico and Argentina, where three-quarters or more of the population in each nation is unhappy. The lone exception is South Korea, where three in four Koreans are dissatisfied despite their economy's strong growth. But the Pew data suggest that the Koreans are hard to please; they have been unhappy for the last decade, through bad times and good.

The second tranche of G20countries, in which three in five people are discontented, largely comprises old line powers: Britain, Germany, Russia, and the United States. Turkey is the lone exception in this group, despite its relatively good economic performance through the crisis. But Turks' discontent may lie at the microeconomic, not the macroeconomic, level: 46 percent of Turks told the

German Marshall Fund pollsters that they personally had been *greatly* affected by the crisis, an intensity of unhappy sentiment that far exceeded what the German Marshall Fund found in the other five G20 countries that it surveyed.

The third group, in which only about half of the population told Pew that they were unhappy with the way things were going, comprises emerging market nations: Brazil, India, and Indonesia.

Among G20 populations, only the Chinese refused to be gloomy, doubtless a reflection of the buoyant Chinese economy. Nine in ten (91 percent) Chinese surveyed say that they are satisfied with conditions in their society.

The root of the general discontent is dissatisfaction with the state of the economy. Economists report that the world is recovering from the worst downturn since the Great Depression. But strong majorities in ten of fourteen G20 nations still give their country's current economic situation a thumbs down. That includes 88 percent of Japanese, 87 percent of the French, 80 percent of Koreans, 79 percent of the British, and 75 percent of both Mexicans and Americans.

In most nations, the portion of the public that thinks that their economy is doing well is only a fraction of what it was before the Great Recession hit. In 2007 in the United States, 50 percent of the public thought that the economy was doing well; in 2010, only 24 percent thought so. Similarly, the portion of the public saying that the economy is good in France (13 percent) and Japan (12 percent) is less than half the portion that felt that way just three years ago. And while 57 percent of Indians think that their economy is doing well today, that is down from 74 percent in 2007.

But G20 populations remain optimistic about the future. Pluralities in eight of the fourteen G20 countries that Pew surveyed think that their economy will improve in the next twelve months. The most optimistic are the Chinese (87 percent), with 22 percent saying that their economy will improve "a lot"; the Brazilians (75 percent), with 36 percent saying "a lot"; the Indians (64 percent), with 17 percent very optimistic; the Indonesians (56 percent), with 13 percent saying "a lot"; and the Americans (56 percent), with 13 percent very optimistic.

The most pessimistic, believing the economy will worsen over the next year, are the French (43 percent) and the Turks (40 percent).

Among those surveyed who think that their economy is currently doing poorly, people overwhelmingly blame their own government. Only in Germany does a plurality blame the banks and other financial institutions. And only in China does a significant minority (26 percent) blame the United States for the crisis. (See table 26-2.)

Whoever is accountable, half or more of the population in ten of the fourteen G20 countries that Pew surveyed thinks that their government is doing a poor job of dealing with the economy. That includes more than two-thirds of the people in Japan (84 percent), Korea (72 percent), and Argentina (68 percent).

Table 26-2. *Who's to Blame for Current Economic Problems?*
Percent

Country	Our government	Banks and financial institutions	United States	European Union	Ourselves
Britain	68	76	17	10	18
France	63	70	20	27	18
Germany	60	77	20	17	10
Russia	72	45	20	4	17
Turkey	79	18	24	12	26
China	51	35	42	19	11
India	89	14	9	3	63
Indonesia	95	26	7	1	45
Japan	86	26	17	2	47
South Korea	92	34	12	2	44
Argentina	87	21	9	1	39
Brazil	80	26	5	2	55
Mexico	88	29	25	2	32

Source: Pew Global Attitudes Project.

And close to one-third of the people in Japan and Turkey and one-quarter in the United States and Britain are even more judgmental, saying that their government has done a *very bad* job managing the economy. (See figure 26-1.)

Satisfaction with the government's handling of the economy tracks with a positive assessment of the current economy and high hopes for the future. The Chinese, Brazilians, and Indians are all among the most upbeat about economic conditions, the most optimistic about the next twelve months, and most likely to praise their public officials' handling of the economy. (See table 26-3.)

People in most G20 economies would like their governments to do more, at least when it comes to regulating the financial sector, a task that has been one of the principal objectives of the G20's work. That is particularly the case in Western Europe, where overwhelming majorities— 91 percent in Germany, 85 percent in Britain, and 78 percent in France—think that it would be a good idea for the government to more strictly regulate the way that large financial companies, such as banks, do business. A smaller portion of Americans (62 percent) agree. However, the Asians that Pew surveyed are not so sure that more regulation is in order. Barely half of South Koreans (52 percent) and only one-third of Japanese (34 percent) think that tighter financial regulation is a good idea. As the G20 wrestles with implementation of agreed-on financial reforms and new financial challenges, that divide may foreshadow problems.

Figure 26-1. *Rating of Own Government's Effort in Dealing with the Economy*

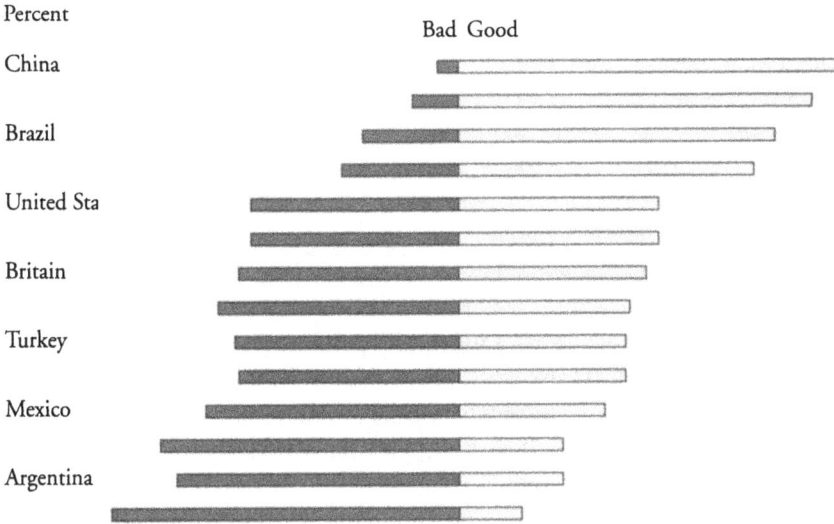

Source: Pew Global Attitudes Project.

Impact on the Free Market System

Contrary to widespread fears that the global recession would undermine public support for free markets and globalization, backing remains strong among most G20 publics. (See table 26-4.)

There is less than majority support for the proposition that people are better off in a free market economy, even though some people are rich and some are poor, *only in* Japan (43 percent), Argentina (40 percent), and Mexico (44 percent). Somewhat ironically, the most supportive of capitalism are the Chinese, 84 percent of whom back the free market system, up from 70 percent in 2002. It would appear that nothing breeds support for capitalism like economic success.

Since 2007, of the twelve G20 countries that Pew has surveyed for which there are comparable data, support for the free market is actually up in eight countries, down in three, and unchanged in one: United States. Free market support is down 8 percentage points in Britain and 6 points in Japan, but it is up 18 points in Indonesia, 11 points in France, 8 points in Germany, and 6 points in South Korea.

Similarly, contrary to warnings against protectionism in G20 statements and pundits' predictions of rising anti-globalism in the wake of the crisis, there is, as yet, little evidence of a protectionist backlash. Trade is given overwhelming support in all G20 countries, especially in China (93 percent), Germany (90

Table 26-3. *Support for Strict Financial Regulation*

Percent

Country	Good idea	Bad idea	Don't know
United States	62	32	6
Britain	85	10	5
France	78	21	0
Germany	91	8	1
Japan	34	50	16
South Korea	52	37	11

Source: Pew Global Attitudes Project.

percent), India (90 percent), and South Korea (88 percent). Notably, the weak-est support among the G20 countries surveyed is found in the United States. Only 66 percent of Americans think growing business ties between countries are good for the United States. Overall, support for trade has gone up in seven of thirteen countries with comparable data.

With trade held in such a favorable light by such a large portion of the global public, the intensity of such feelings may be a better indicator of sentiment. More than half of Turks and almost as many Indians (47 percent) say trade is *very* good for their country. But Americans (17 percent) and Japanese (16 percent) are far less passionate.

In one sign of the adverse impact of the global recession on China's exports and thus on people's jobs, only one in five (20 percent) Chinese now think trade is *very* good for China, down from 38 percent in 2007, before the downturn in world trade. Moreover, 27 percent of Americans say trade is bad for the United States.

Nevertheless, support for trade among Americans of all political persuasions has actually increased since 2008, contrary to predictions that the crisis would stoke protectionist fires. And, contradicting the widely held view that Republicans are free traders and Democrats are protectionists, 75 percent of self-identified Democrats say trade is good for the United States, up 4 percentage points from 2009, while only 61 percent of Republicans and 63 percent of independents, whose support remained unchanged, feel the same. This counterintuitive finding has also been identified by the German Marshall Fund and other independent pollsters.

The G20

The G20 was created to broaden responsibilities for the leadership of the global economy. But among G20 publics, economic leadership is still equated with a country's GDP and recent economic performance, not with some new multilateral governance structure. In eight of fourteen G20 countries surveyed by Pew,

Table 26-4. *Support for Free Markets and Trade*
Percent

Country	Are most better off in a free market economy?			Are trade and business ties good for country?		
	Percent agree			Percent good		
	2007	2009	2010	2007	2009	2010
United States	70	76	68	59	65	66
Britain	72	66	64	78	82	84
France	56	57	67	78	83	79
Germany	65	61	73	85	85	90
Russia	53	51	60	82	80	86
Turkey	60	60	64	73	64	83
China	75	79	84	91	93	93
India	76	81	79	89	96	90
Indonesia	45	49	63	71	79	82
Japan	49	41	43	72	73	72
South Korea	72	76	78	86	92	88
Argentina	43	36	40	68	65	72
Brazil	. . .	. . .	. . .	. . .	. . .	87
Mexico	. . .	52	44	77	79	71

Source: Pew Global Attitudes Project.

the United States is considered the world's leading economic power. Support for the United States is strongest in South Korea (77 percent).

People in five other countries see China as the leader. Support for China is greatest in Germany (51 percent) and Japan (50 percent), and Japanese backing for Beijing has grown 29 percentage points since 2009. Notably, Americans are more likely to pick China than their own country as the world's leading economic power. (See table 26-5.)

Looking ahead, publics believe that it is most likely that the United States will exercise strong leadership in world affairs in 2015. According to the German Marshall Fund survey, 70 percent of Americans strongly believe that Washington will play that role five years from now and 58 percent of the British strongly agree. But only 27 percent of the French are that certain. A much smaller portion (16 percent) of the six G20 publics that the German Marshall Fund surveyed see Russia as the likely world leader in 2015.

There is a wide variance in opinion about the future role of China. Seven in ten (71 percent) Americans say that Beijing is very likely to exercise strong leadership, but only 38 percent of Germans and 27 percent of the French strongly agree.

Table 26-5. *World's Leading Economic Power*

Percent

Country	Country named as the world's leading economic power				
	United States	China	Japan	EU	Other/ Don't know
United States	38	41	8	6	7
Britain	38	44	5	8	6
France	41	47	5	7	0
Germany	18	51	8	19	4
Russia	23	27	25	9	16
Turkey	69	12	4	5	10
China	45	36	2	6	11
India	60	11	7	10	12
Indonesia	49	20	18	7	6
Japan	40	50	2	4	3
South Korea	77	15	1	5	3
Argentina	43	24	12	10	10
Brazil	51	18	13	5	14
Mexico	53	22	9	8	9

Source: Pew Global Attitudes Project.

There are similarly mixed reviews of the leaders of the G20. U.S. president Barack Obama is clearly seen by the global public as the first among equals. His popularity is remarkably high. It did not suffer appreciably in his second year in office, and it far exceeds that of any of the other G20 leaders. He is widely trusted to do the right thing in world affairs. Nine in ten Germans say that they have at least some confidence in Obama, as do more than eight in ten respondents in France (87 percent) and Britain (84 percent). Ratings of Obama are also overwhelmingly positive in Japan (76 percent), South Korea (75 percent), India (73 percent), and Indonesia (67 percent), according to Pew. A smaller percentage of Americans (65 percent) share that view. (See figure 26-2.)

Meanwhile, a much narrower majority in China (52 percent) expresses at least some confidence in the American president. A majority of Brazilians (56 percent) say they have at least some confidence in Obama, a view shared by nearly half of Argentines (49 percent). Mexicans are evenly split; 43 percent express confidence in Obama and 43 percent do not.

Backing for Obama has declined in Turkey since he first took office, dropping 10 percentage points with respect to 2009 data. Support for the American leader has also fallen 12 points in Argentina, 9 points in Japan, and 9 points at home in the United States. The U.S. drop-off primarily reflects a loss of support

Figure 26-2. *Confidence in World Leaders*

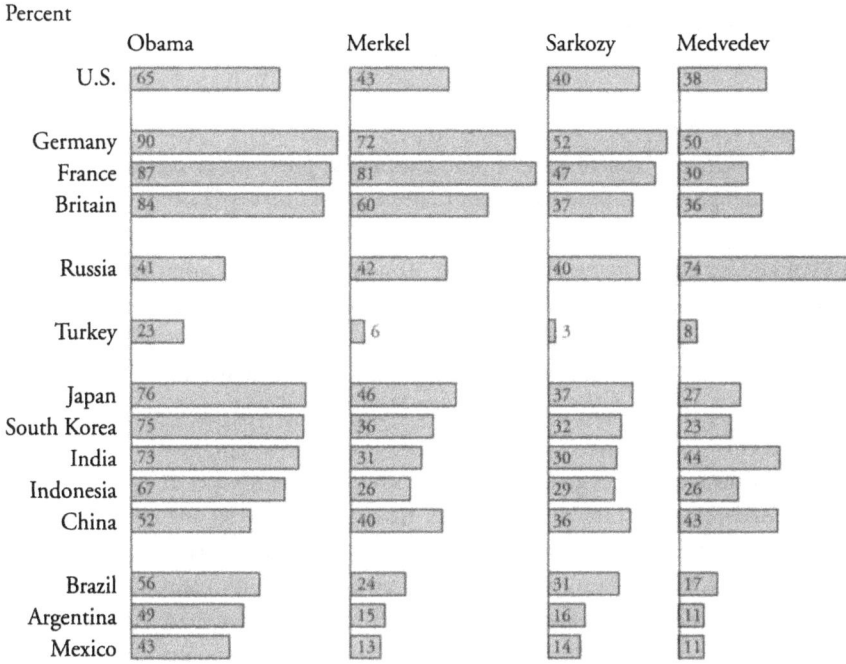

Percent

	Obama	Merkel	Sarkozy	Medvedev
U.S.	65	43	40	38
Germany	90	72	52	50
France	87	81	47	30
Britain	84	60	37	36
Russia	41	42	40	74
Turkey	23	6	3	8
Japan	76	46	37	27
South Korea	75	36	32	23
India	73	31	30	44
Indonesia	67	26	29	26
China	52	40	36	43
Brazil	56	24	31	17
Argentina	49	15	16	11
Mexico	43	13	14	11

Source: Pew Global Attitudes Project.

among Republicans, who were split in their views of the newly elected president in 2009—about half (49 percent) said they had at least some confidence in Obama to do the right thing in international affairs and 51 percent said that they had little or no confidence in him. Today, just 32 percent of Republicans have confidence in the president, while 68 percent say that they have little or no confidence in him. Democrats are as likely as they were in 2009 to say that they have at least some confidence in Obama, but considerably fewer now say that they have *a lot* of confidence in him (56 percent today versus 74 percent in 2009). The decline in overall and strong support for Obama has been less dramatic among independents.

In the Western European G20 countries that Pew surveyed, where overall support for Obama is unchanged, fewer give the American president the enthusiastic endorsement that they gave him when he first took office. In Germany, 46 percent say they have *a lot* of confidence in Obama to do the right thing in world affairs, while 56 percent expressed similar levels of support in 2009. In France, one-quarter (25 percent) now say that they have *a lot* of confidence in Obama, down from 34 percent who said the same in 2009. And in Britain, where 36 percent expressed similarly intense levels of confidence in the U.S. president in 2010, 43 percent did so in 2009.

With regard to the international economy, majorities in nine of fourteen G20 nations overwhelmingly approve of Obama's handling of the economic crisis. The least supportive are the Turks, only 17 percent of whom give Obama's record a thumbs up. Americans are divided: 46 percent approve; 46 percent disapprove.

The German Marshall Fund found similar support. Three-quarters (76 percent) of people in the four European G20 members surveyed think that Obama is doing a good job of handling the international economy. Only 52 percent of Americans agree, however, and only 30 percent of Turks approve. Moreover, approval of Obama's international economic policy is down 14 percentage points in France, 9 points in Germany, and 17 points in Turkey since 2009.

Leaders of other G20 countries are less well known than Obama. A majority of Argentines (62 percent) and Mexicans (53 percent) and a plurality of Indians (46 percent), Indonesians (39 percent), and Koreans (37 percent) say that they do not know enough about German chancellor Angela Merkel to voice an opinion. Moreover, one-third of Americans, Russians, Japanese, and Brazilians and one-quarter of Turks also say that they do not know her well enough.

Among G20 populations that do have an opinion, confidence in Merkel is most widespread in France, where she is even more popular than she is at home and more popular than French President Sarkozy. About eight in ten French respondents (81 percent) have confidence in the chancellor to do the right thing in international affairs. A large majority (72 percent) in Merkel's home country hold the same view. In Britain, 60 percent express confidence in Merkel, up from roughly half (51 percent) the previous year. The most negative view of the German leader's foreign policy skills is found in Turkey. A large majority in Turkey (69 percent) have little or no confidence in Merkel's international decisions, while only a few have confidence (6 percent).

French president Nicolas Sarkozy, the leader of the G20 in 2011, suffers from the same lack of widespread recognition among many G20 publics. Nearly half of Mexicans (49 percent), Argentines (48 percent), and Chinese (47 percent) told Pew pollsters that they have no opinion of him. The same was true for a large portion of Indonesians (36 percent), Russians (33 percent), Koreans (32 percent), Americans (28 percent), and Chinese (28 percent). Moreover, publics in European G20 member countries, who do know Sarkozy, express far less confidence in him than in Merkel. Germany is the only European nation surveyed in which a majority (52 percent), albeit a slim one, expresses confidence in Sarkozy to do the right thing in world affairs. In France, fewer people have confidence (47 percent) in their president than do not (53 percent). In 2009, positive views of Sarkozy (53 percent) outranked negative ones (47 percent). Favorable views of the French president are even less common in Britain (37 percent). Four in ten people in Russia and the United States have confidence in Sarkozy's global leadership. In Turkey, 71 percent currently have little or no confidence in Sarkozy's handling of foreign affairs, while only a few (3 percent) have a positive view.

Confidence in Russian President Dimitry Medvedev to do the right thing is limited, although the public's assessment is more positive than last year. Pluralities in India (44 percent), China (43 percent), and the United States (38 percent) express confidence in his ability to handle foreign policy. American opinions of Medvedev have grown more positive since 2009, when 30 percent expressed confidence in him. Many in Argentina (62 percent), Mexico (52 percent), India (39 percent), and Indonesia (35 percent) offer no opinion of the Russian leader.

Overwhelmingly, Medvedev remains popular at home, where a large majority of Russians (74 percent) have confidence in their president. Positive views of the Russian leader have also become more common in Europe. Germans give Medvedev his highest marks among the European G20 nations polled by Pew; one-half now express confidence in him, up 18 percentage points from 2009. Significant increases also took place in France (up 13 percentage points) and Britain (up 9 points) from 2009 to 2010. However, in Turkey, negative assessments of Medvedev continue to prevail; 69 percent say that they lack confidence in him, up slightly from 2009 (64 percent). Many Turks say that they are unfamiliar with the Russian leader.

The China Challenge

Public attitudes toward China, the second-largest economy among the G20 countries, highlight the difficulties that G20 governments may have in cooperating on key international economic issues. Majorities in Japan (69 percent), Germany (61 percent), France (59 percent), South Korea (56 percent), and India (52 percent) give China an unfavorable rating, according to Pew. One-third of Americans (36 percent) agree. Among G20 publics, only in Russia (60 percent), Indonesia (58 percent), and Brazil (52 percent) do people see China in a favorable light.

Concerns about China's economic might are high among many publics. People in France (67 percent) are the most likely of those in all the G20 countries that Pew surveyed to say that China's growing economy is a bad thing for their country. Majorities in Turkey (60 percent), Germany (58 percent), and India (56 percent) agree. Pluralities in South Korea (49 percent) and the United States (47 percent) share similar concerns. But pluralities in Russia (49 percent) and Mexico (41 percent) actually think China's growing economy is a good thing. And the portion of the public that is negative about China has gone down significantly in the last year in Mexico, Japan, and even the United States.

The Chinese receive mixed reviews for their global economic leadership. A plurality of the British (46 percent), Germans (42 percent), and Americans (40 percent) think that Beijing plays a positive role in managing the world economy, according to the German Marshall Fund. A plurality of the French (43 percent) and the Italians (43 percent) think that they play a negative role.

The G20 publics that the German Marshall Fund surveyed disagree on whether China and their country share sufficient values and interests to be able to cooperate on international problems. A majority of Americans (53 percent) think that they have common values with the Chinese, and 58 percent think that they have common interests. But a strong majority of the French (65 percent), Germans (78 percent), British (56 percent), and Italians (65 percent) say that the Chinese do not share their values. A majority of the French (57 percent) and Germans (60 percent) and a plurality of the British (48 percent) and Italians (46 percent) do not think that they and the Chinese have common interests.

Climate Change

Despite the toll exacted by the economic crisis, majorities in all fourteen G20 countries that Pew surveyed believe that protecting the environment should be given priority, even if it causes slower economic growth and some loss of jobs. The strongest support was in countries that have best weathered the economic downturn: India (86 percent), South Korea (82 percent), China (80 percent), and Brazil (80 percent). The least willingness to sacrifice growth and jobs for the good of the environment was found in Japan (57 percent) and France (54 percent).

The crisis has clearly taken its toll on public support for the environment. Willingness to sacrifice was down in seven of eleven G20 countries for which comparable data exist, with the biggest drop in Japan, down 10 percentage points.

In all but one of the fourteen G20 nations that Pew surveyed, at least three-quarters of the population perceives global climate change to be a serious or *very* serious problem. But publics differ in just how much they are worried. Brazilians show the greatest intensity of concern about global warming by far, with 85 percent reporting that climate change is *very* serious. Anxiety regarding climate change is also high in Turkey, where 74 percent of the population is *very* worried, as are large portions of the population in South Korea (68 percent) and Mexico (68 percent). Americans and Chinese, the world's two worst emitters of carbon dioxide, are relatively less troubled by global warming, with only 37 percent of Americans and 41 percent of Chinese saying that climate change is a *very* serious challenge.

In the United States the intensity of views about climate change clearly divides along partisan lines. Over one-half (56 percent) of people belonging to the Democratic Party say that global warming is a *very* serious problem, and nearly one-third of self-styled independents (32 percent) agree. But only 18 percent of Republicans are intensely concerned about climate change. Moreover, more than one in four Republicans (28 percent) think that climate change is *not* a problem at all, while only 3 percent of Democrats dismiss the threat posed by global warming.

In Western Europe, as in the United States, people who identify themselves as being on the political left are more likely than those on the right to be *very* concerned about climate change, with left-wing Germans the most concerned. The greatest ideological rift is in the United States, where a gap of 30 percentage points exists between conservatives and liberals. Conservative Europeans are far more concerned about climate change than are conservative Americans.

Of even greater salience for the G20 summit in Seoul, concern about climate change has been ebbing in many key G20 societies. The intensity of sentiment has declined, notably in several of the wealthier G20 countries. The portion of the public saying that climate change is a *very* serious problem is down 22 percentage points in France (from 68 percent to 46 percent), down 20 points in Japan (from 78 percent to 58 percent), and down 10 points in the United States (from 47 percent to 37 percent) from 2007 to 2010.

Despite the general consensus that the environment should be protected, even to the detriment of economic growth, G20 publics are divided about whether individuals should pay higher prices specifically to address climate change. In six of the fourteen G20 nations that Pew surveyed, majorities or pluralities think that consumers should not pay more to slow atmospheric warming. That included a majority of Indonesian (63 percent), French (61 percent), Mexican (60 percent), and American (58 percent) respondents. In contrast, even though the Chinese are less likely than most other publics to consider global warming a *very* serious problem, they are by far the most willing (91 percent) to see prices rise to cope with the challenge. Indians (73 percent) and South Koreans (71 percent) agree.

Beijing and Washington are given distinctly different report cards for their efforts in fighting climate change. Three in five (64 percent) of the European members of the G20 nations surveyed by the German Marshall Fund approve of President Obama's handling of the climate issue in the last year. The most satisfied were the Italians (71 percent). China's efforts, however, are harshly criticized: two-thirds (66 percent) of European and American members of the G20 think that Beijing plays a negative role in fighting climate change.

Development

Development in Africa, Asia, and Latin America and the responsibilities of the G20 members to aid in the recovery and growth of these economies were major subtexts of the Seoul summit. Pew asked people in nine of the G20 countries who they think is doing the most to help poor countries develop. The results were illuminating.

In five of the nine countries—Russia, Turkey, China, Argentina, and Brazil—people were most likely to name their own country as doing the most for the world's poor. Indonesians, Indians, Koreans, and Mexicans think that the United States is having the greatest positive impact on third world development, and America was the second-most-named country in Turkey, Argentina, and Brazil. Nevertheless, it is clear that there is no general consensus on who among the G20 is doing the most for the poor. Even though the United States is the top pick in four countries, only in South Korea did a majority of the public name America as the most helpful to poor nations.

China's contribution to third world development is judged more severely. The German Marshall Fund asked people whether they think that China plays a positive or negative role in fighting world poverty. In the European G20 nations and the United States, only 52 percent think that Beijing plays a positive role. The French are especially critical; three in five (61 percent) surveyed say the Chinese have a negative impact on the effort to ease the plight of the poor.

Conclusion

In all but a handful of G20 societies, the public mood is bleak, largely because of concern about the economy. That is true even in nations such as South Korea and Turkey, which have fared better than most during the Great Recession. Only in countries that have weathered the economic downturn significantly better than others, notably China, are people upbeat. Nevertheless, most people remain optimistic about the future and have not lost faith in either the free market system or in globalization.

But people blame their governments for mishandling the economy, and they want them to do more to improve economic conditions. Among G20 leaders who might provide direction for the world economy, President Obama is by far the most popular around the world, and the United States is expected to provide global leadership for some time to come. G20 publics are more divided about China's current and future role.

The message that publics are sending to the G20 leaders is clear: fix the economy. There is support, at least in the West, for stronger financial regulation. People will hold their leaders accountable for improving the economic outlook and preventing further financial setbacks. And they look to American, and to a certain extent Chinese, leadership to make that happen.

27

G20 Summitry: Domestic Leadership in a Polarized and Globalized World

THOMAS MANN

In the wake of the global financial crisis and Great Recession, the G20 emerged as an important institutional instrument for addressing critical global economic problems. The substantive challenges facing G20 leaders—not least among them fashioning policies that deliver on the promises of the Framework for Strong, Sustainable, and Balanced Growth—are daunting. A central component of the overall challenge, however, is managing the complex interplay between domestic politics and global diplomacy.

The domestic politics of global cooperation are inevitably difficult. Globalization produces gains and losses, winners and losers. National interests and preferences are shaped through political processes—dominated by myopic voters, aggrieved interests, and responsive politicians—that tend to favor short-term thinking. Yet consequential global agreements require longer-term perspectives that can frustrate the desires of those who focus only on the here and now. Under those circumstances, national interests can easily overwhelm global cooperation. States, of course, are not simply unitary actors; interests compete within nations as well as between them. Opportunities as well as constraints arise as political actors operate at the intersection of domestic politics and global diplomacy. Resourceful domestic leadership is essential if the G20 is to be effective.

Can G20 leaders work cooperatively on pressing global challenges, which often appear to require tough and unpopular domestic policies, and still represent and satisfy the interests of their national constituencies? Is it possible to reach constructive, consequential agreements at global summits that can be sold to domestic publics as likely to improve their lives and future prospects? What resources and strategies are available to leaders to increase the payoff from this two-level game? In short, what can the G20 do to ease the tension between essential global policies and the domestic political imperatives of its member countries?

An initial step in addressing these questions is to identify and seek to understand the political forces that shape the environment in which today's global summitry occurs. First, trust in national governments is at record lows. Publics are deeply skeptical of the capacity of government and the willingness of their elected leaders to deal responsibly with the pressing problems confronting their country. This is not primarily an embrace of a libertarian ideology by mass publics. Most of those who have lost faith and hope in government and its leaders have neither a well-defined ideology nor a deep-seated animus toward the idea of government providing essential services and protecting consumers from the excesses of market economies. People's distrust flows more from a distaste for intense conflict among elected officials; a belief that many politicians are entirely self-serving if not downright corrupt; the apparent influence of well-heeled interests; perceptions of bureaucratic incompetence; and a sense of diminishing economic and social opportunities for themselves and their progeny. The contemporary media surely contribute to public cynicism and distrust, all of which weakens the capacity of leaders to fashion and sustain policies responsive to the problems that they confront.

Second, in these difficult times publics often view the global community more as a threat than a solution to problems that cross national boundaries. Terrorists, drug traffickers, and crime syndicates from abroad threaten security at home. Immigrants, especially those without a legal basis for entry or permanent residence, are often seen as socially disruptive, culturally estranged, and economically burdensome. Trade agreements and mercantilist policies of other countries ship good jobs overseas and reduce wages at home. Summits are all too easily cast as cushy meetings of elites detached from the interests and aspirations of ordinary citizens and conspiring to protect wealthy individuals and powerful multinational corporations and organizations.

Third, increasing ideological polarization, hyperpartisanship, and the permanent campaign have vastly complicated the task of assembling stable governing coalitions on behalf of responsible policymaking. The hung parliament produced by the recent Australian election, only months after the U.K. general election led to the same outcome, means that for the first time in history not a single Westminster-style parliamentary government is led by a majority party. In the United States, governance has become little more than a permanent state of war between the competing parties. The ideological sorting of the parties over a number of decades has produced two armed camps, reinforced by party activists and ideological media outlets and generously funded by aligned interests, with starkly contrasting visions of the role of government. A set of institutional arrangements designed to check and balance, deliberate and debate, and negotiate and compromise are now routinely used to try to destroy the other party and its president. A procedural arms race in Congress has removed any semblance of regular legislative order. The routinization of the filibuster in the Senate has allowed a minority to run out the clock in order to kill or discredit legislation produced by the majoritarian House.

Low public trust in government and its leaders, fear of threatening global players, and partisan polarization complicate the inherently difficult task of advancing domestic interests by fostering global cooperation and coordination. Identifying policies that are substantively credible—that hold real promise of advancing the economic well-being of member countries and others represented at the G20 and that have a reasonable chance of being implemented—is, of course, an essential step. Virtuoso leadership and brilliant political strategies may be necessary, but they surely are not sufficient conditions for successful summitry. Without wise policies that enjoy some measure of success in their respective countries, G20 leaders and their successors will have little incentive to engage in the hard work required to produce enlightened global cooperation. There is no substitute for getting the policy right.

Two additional dimensions of leadership merit consideration. The first is the nature of the public discourse that surrounds summits and the decisions taken by them and how attention to language and messaging might build domestic political support. The second is the possibility of engaging other domestic institutional players—most important, parliaments—in the dynamics of summits to boost prospects for policy development and implementation.

Public interest in and knowledge of policy issues and governance is very limited. Most citizens are inadvertent rather than purposeful consumers of information about politics and policy. They use various simplifying or economizing devices to cut through arcane discussions of politics and policy: viewing public life through their own partisan lenses; treating elections as referendums on the performance of the economy (if times are bad, throw out the party in power); and reacting to powerful symbols or revealing language that indicate whose side a politician or party or political institution is on.

Deliberative democracy is much more a goal of political theorists than a description of political reality. Rather than thoughtful exchanges between citizens and leaders that produce learning, understanding, and responsiveness, political communications tend to be top-down, manipulative efforts to sell preexisting positions. Parties, politicians, and interest groups employ well-paid language mavens to construct the most appealing narratives and phrases to advance their own proposals or to disable those of their adversaries. The recent battle over health reform in the United States is a classic example. Most members of the public had little knowledge of the contents of the legislation as it worked its way through Congress, but Republican messaging about a "government take-over," "a bureaucrat between you and your doctor," and "death panels" easily trumped "bending the cost curve" and other language used by President Obama to sell his reform proposals. Without a compelling narrative, he lost the political war in spite of almost miraculously winning the legislative battle.

Can more and better messaging by individual G20 leaders and the collective entity strengthen the position of those leaders with their domestic publics and help nurture a responsible and effective global institution? It might, and it is surely worth making additional efforts along these lines. The widespread public skepticism of global governance combined with the inevitable opposition of interests within member countries to difficult G20 agreements puts the burden on the summiteers to think carefully about how best to package and market those agreements to their domestic publics. The difficulty lies in constructing narratives that are both true (that is, honest descriptions of the problems confronted, the solutions agreed to at the summit, and the steps that must be taken to implement them) and simple, understandable, and appealing to domestic audiences. Successful leadership is so daunting because it requires responsibility and responsiveness.

Domestic public opinion is shaped more by fundamental forces and objective reality than tactical brilliance or seductive rhetoric. If the latter are to be successful, they must be consistent with the former. At the very least, greater investment by G20 leaders and summit organizers in the stories that they must tell after the meetings to be successful back home might positively shape the substance of agreements and the process by which they come to agreement.

The second dimension of global leadership that merits consideration is the early and continuous engagement of key institutional players in member countries. These certainly include critical ministries, major interest groups and NGOs, and parliaments. Legislative bodies play a special role in reconciling law-making with representation of constituents, which makes them key sources of political intelligence and essential partners in implementing summit agreements. In the United States, statutory requirements or accepted informal practices often lead to early engagement of members of Congress in international negotiations. In the trade arena, "fast-track" or "trade promotion authority" involves a bargain between the executive and legislative branches: in return for numerous opportunities to monitor and influence an agreement negotiated by the president, Congress agrees to a timely, up-or-down vote, not subject to amendment or filibuster. Similarly, arms control treaty negotiations have traditionally provided an opportunity for bipartisan groups of senators to play an important role before the terms of an agreement are settled.

To be sure, summits are different. They are relatively short-term events in which country leaders play a paramount role. Leaders must be careful not to devalue their singular executive positions. Nonetheless, the elaborate and lengthy sherpa-led process of preparing for summits provides opportunities for informing and consulting with key legislators, a practice that some G20 members might pursue more systematically.

These efforts may be constructive, but they are often circumscribed by the structure of partisan politics in each country. In the United States, the Republican opposition in Congress has as its primary objective the political miniaturization and electoral defeat of President Obama. The market for consultation and good-faith bargaining and negotiation has crashed. The permanent campaign in the United States extends to global summitry. This is a reality that must be recognized and managed in the best way possible.

28

The G20 Takes Center Stage as a Twenty-First-Century Leadership Forum

WENDY R. SHERMAN

Like many of us, I wear a variety of hats: in my case, that of a former government official; of a businesswoman who consults around the world and works in investment in emerging markets; of incoming chair of the board of Oxfam America, an NGO that pursues a rights-based approach to eliminating poverty; and of mother, wife, and citizen of my country. I also recognize that those of us involved in this volume are a unique group with respect to our level of intellectual interest in the G20. I think that it is safe to assume that most people are not aware of the G20, or do not have any idea what the G20 does, or simply do not care.

All of us who spend time as diplomats, policymakers, and thinkers might keep in mind something that I learned early on during my years as a social worker: the importance of understanding where in life the client is and what he or she wants out of life. To answer the question of what the G20 sound bite might be, we need to understand what domestic constituencies care about—having a job now, not later; being able to send their children to school; being healthy; having their livelihood intact; and being able to aspire to a better life than they have now.

If the G20, representing all of the major countries and 90 percent of the world's GDP, can come together and help make that happen, then citizens of the world will be supportive of the G20. People want answers, outcomes, and evidence that their lives will improve. If the G20 can deliver those things, then it will be a sustainable forum.

Although the ultimate bottom line is meeting people's day-to-day needs, the G20 still has value in its current state. As Marshall McLuhan famously said, "The medium is the message." The mere existence of the G20—and what that says about the world in the twenty-first century—sends an incredibly powerful message to the public. It demonstrates change—from the time when developed economies led the world to an era in which emerging countries, often those with great poverty but also with the fastest growth trajectories, jointly lead the economic future of the world.

These changes will not be the result of one leader alone. They will be the result of a group of leaders who control the world's power and influence working together—and together they may have the ability to effect change in people's day-to-day lives. The evolution of the G20 should not, in my view, reflect the institutions of the twentieth century, with bureaucracies and tightly scripted agendas. It should reflect the reality of today's world, including the 24/7 multimedia context in which we live and the struggle by states for sovereignty in an increasingly interconnected world.

The balance to be struck is *not* one between global governance and the nation-state, between international and domestic agendas and the media. It is between the need to create balanced global growth and the need of every individual to hold onto his or her way of life in the midst of modernity and urbanization and challenges and opportunities that know no borders.

The PEW Global Attitudes project, an annual survey based on interviews with thousands of people in dozens of countries, has long noted that while people like what globalization brings them in terms of medicine, technology, and food, at the same time they remain anxious about the pace of change and potential loss of cultural identity. That tension was evident throughout the evolution of the G20, and it remains today.

The Historical Perspective

In 1975 a group of developed industrialized nations began a group to focus principally on economic issues. At Rambouillet, where the first summit meeting was held, the group was the G6; when the United States added Canada in 1976 to offset the preponderance of Europeans, the G7 came into being. The developed economies faced a stock market freefall and global recession in 1973–74. 1973 had been an especially tumultuous year. There was an oil crisis as a result of an OPEC-mandated oil embargo on top of the erosion of the real price of oil due to U.S. inflation. At the same time, South Vietnam weighed heavily as the United States withdrew combat troops in 1973, overwhelmed by the costs of war. The message of Rambouillet was clear. As British prime minister Harold Wilson put it, "The coming together of the six heads of government this weekend was a recognition of our shared responsibility for the recovery of the world economy."[1]

It was not until 1997, more than twenty years later, that the G7 became the G8, with the addition of Russia to the fold. The 1998 Birmingham G8 summit focused on the aftermath of the Asian financial crisis along with debt relief, commitment to the European Union and Eurozone, energy, combating crime and drugs, and welcoming the Kyoto Protocol.

On May 16, 1998, Dan Balz of the *Washington Post* wrote these prescient words:

In the wake of the Cold War, the world is changing around the G-8. . . . The proliferation of subjects that G8 leaders now deal with also affects who should be involved. No longer is this gathering designed largely for discussion of macroeconomic policy issues. Political issues are regularly on the agenda. . . . The organization will continue to feel the strain of the new world order. Since its inception, the G8 has been forced to evolve and enlarge. More changes are likely.[2]

Although technically the G20 was created in 1999, it took a worldwide economic crisis some twelve years after Balz's article was published for the G20 to overtake the G8 as the center of decisionmaking.

The point of this brief history is that concerted international action and institutional transformations—whether small or large—take place during times of historic change and often in response to crisis. No sustainable changes occur quickly or without controversy and some growing pains. That was true of the founding of the United Nations, which followed the failed League of Nations. That was true of the ratification of a constitution for the European Union. It was true also of the evolution of ASEAN, which is still evolving. The list could go on and on.

Institution building—particularly international institution building—is a messy affair in which compromise is fundamental. As with national legislative bodies, it is characterized by incremental change; only on rare occasions is there a revolutionary dash to historic change. By that yardstick, the G20 has already created historic change by its very existence. In less than two years, the G20 is seen as the premier forum for economic issues broadly defined, having acted collectively to save the world from falling into an economic abyss.

Did its members do everything that was needed to ensure strong, sustainable, and balanced global growth? Decidedly not. But they took the formidable step

1. Original telegram statement by Harold Wilson, available at www.margaretthatcher.org/document/110954.

2. Dan Balz, "A Volatile World Tests G8 Leaders; Crises in India, Indonesia Challenge Summit Striving to Retain Its Relevance," *Washington Post*, May 16, 1998 (www.highbeam.com/doc/1P2-657506.html).

of putting in place mechanisms to strengthen progress toward those objectives. How were the outcomes of the initial meetings viewed by the world? *The Economist*, following the Washington summit in November 2008, had this editorial comment: "Judged by the hubristic promises that preceded it, the G20 meeting was bound to disappoint."[3]

After elaborating on the limitations of what was accomplished, it went on to ask: "So was it all a waste of time? There are some reasons to think not. For one, this was the first time that leaders of this group of rich and emerging economies—which between them represent almost 90 percent of global GDP—had gathered for an economic summit." That was a pretty fair and accurate summary of the first meeting. But it is important to note that the media were laser-focused on the mere fact that the meeting took place—the headline was that one of the world's premier decisionmaking bodies had shifted from a group of eight to a group of twenty.

Most citizens of the world, with all due respect to the media and to national leaders, probably did not pay much attention to the fact that this first-ever G20 summit or the follow-up meetings even took place. If they heard anything, it was probably their national media telling them that their leader was part of an important decisionmaking body that was protecting their interests. Most of the world's citizens were rightly focused on whether *their personal situation* was going to improve or whether the financial crisis would continue.

It is this tension between personal security and the intrusion of global forces, events, and shocks that challenges the ability of summits to deliver their message and engage publics in a positive narrative. Backlash, suspicion, and skepticism abound due to the disparity between the desire of ordinary citizens for greater control over their personal lives and the impact of global forces on them. To average citizens, summits seem to provide more evidence of the problem than the solution.

Subsequent G20 meetings have seen mixed media attention. Some believe that the media have been overly critical in highlighting tensions, conflicts, and incomplete actions. None of that especially bothers me. That is the role of the media—to report. They look for stories. They push and prod and shine a spotlight. Even the smaller G8 could not control the message in a sustainable fashion. International political events, protests in the street, unfulfilled commitments to Africa, and sovereign electoral politics often overtook the meeting. And the G8, for the most part, did not operate in a 24/7 multimedia world of Twitter, blogs, and events going viral. I have seen this interaction between the media and the policy world from a myriad of professional positions, discussed below.

3. "The G20 Summit in Washington, D.C.: Not a Bad Weekend's Work," *The Economist*, November 16, 2008 (www.economist.com/node/12623258).

Governance and the Media from Various Vantage Points

As counselor and assistant secretary for legislative affairs for the U.S. State Department, I experienced the media as both an occasional nemesis and a critical channel for communication. During the Clinton administration, my daily reality could involve calling a senator to share some fast-breaking decision by the president, only to find that CNN had already reported the news. We would spend hours fashioning our message for a multilateral meeting, only to be overtaken by events happening somewhere else in the world. And—although the president of the United States had an unparalleled bully pulpit, even in the 1990s, and as skilled as President Clinton was and is—message delivery was less sharp at virtually every multilateral meeting by virtue of the multilateral nature of the beast. Every president has a strong urge to go it alone, if only to control what is said and what is done. But the world no longer accommodates a solo act for very long—if it ever did. While leadership requires a strong point of view, knowing where you want to go, and using carrots and sticks to your advantage to achieve as much as possible in a complex situation, it also requires successful communication with others.

In the 1990s, the world did not yet have blogs or Twitter, Blackberries, or iPhones. In fact, State Department officials had only classified computers, making e-mail communication with the outside world virtually impossible. Now government officials are on Blackberries, on the World Wide Web, and in real-time video conferences. The luxury of travel time has virtually disappeared, and the age of sending a cable and getting a response hours later is long gone. The world now expects a virtually instantaneous response to virtually any comment, inquiry, complaint, or event.

Today, as a businesswoman and investor, I watch with interest what happens during the G20. I care what is decided and, equally as important, what is not decided. I'm glad that more countries are engaged because I believe that over time it will force leaders to confront dislocations and imbalances in the markets and, it is hoped, to create mechanisms to manage economic mismatches and more. When the media report that countries are watching out only for their own interests rather than the world's economic needs, it is frustrating, but usually it is not the whole truth. Markets have generally priced-in anticipated summit outcomes, and most want to know what direction we are heading in; they want to be reassured that we are not heading off a cliff.

Now, as the new chair of the board of a rights-based NGO, I applaud Korea for focusing on development and models for growth. But I want to know that citizens' voices are heard, not only through their elected officials but through civil society forums and through the voices of the poor themselves. I want to make sure that the dynamism of the G20 extends to all segments of society, and not just through the trickle-down effect.

How to Create and Deliver a Narrative

So where does this lead with respect to creating and delivering a narrative? There are several critical elements: organizational elements and evolution; the message; and expectations, both ours and those of others.

Organizational Elements and Evolution

Let me begin with organizational elements, which can often be a metaphor for progress or an anachronism. The G20 should reflect this century, and it should be an agile organization. We can best ensure collective action if we leave space for dynamic sovereign leadership. The Seoul G20 summit was a case in point. As the first non-G8 country to host a G20 summit, Korea provided dynamic leadership, including extensive outreach prior to the meeting; a robust but manageable agenda; and, most important, a point of view. If the G20 were a bureaucracy, this kind of sovereign dynamism would be lost. Everyone has been aware of the exceptional effort made by Korea as chair of the G20 to push forward the economic and institutional agenda of the G20.

I know that there are debates about representation—whether the G20 should be the G24 or G30. The Koreans are role modeling how to take a fresh approach by exercising regional leadership in their regions by undertaking the first-ever consultation visit to ASEAN. Indeed, the G20 will have a short shelf life unless leaders engage a wider audience, because the world is not static. Tomorrow's emerging nations may want to begin having a say today. But just as the G7 gave way to the G8 and then to the G20, whatever morphing needs to take place will happen when and if events demand an adjustment.

The Message

In sum, the message for the G20 is that it is a dynamic conversation between major emerging and developed economies that represent 90 percent of the world's GDP. The G20 underscores the diversity and dynamism of each sovereign leader and his or her citizens, and it is committed to engaging all the citizens of the world, recognizing the ever-changing—and faster-changing—times.

The G20 must also connect with a broad range of stakeholders, including business, civil society, the media, and opinion leaders. Korea wisely held a robust business leaders' forum in tandem with the Seoul summit. In addition, every nation in the G20 should, as many have suggested, meet with all elements of its population before and after each summit; the way that will be done will be different in each country. In twenty-first-century think, those countries that ignore civil society—especially those, like the poor, who often do not have a voice—do so at their own peril. That also applies to opinion leaders, including the media.

Expectations

Next are expectations—our own and those of others. Here are some of my personal expectations: I want to resolve global economic imbalances, ensure growth around the world, end unemployment and underemployment, eliminate poverty, provide quality educational opportunities and health care for our children, and make sure that we address climate change so that there is, quite literally, a world in which to do all of these things. I want my leaders and the worlds' leaders to work toward those ends. I believe that the G20 is a crucial—perhaps *the* crucial—forum in which to work toward those goals. But there are obstacles, and it will take time, creativity, and pushing and pulling to get there. There are also political events, crises, conflicts, tragedy, natural catastrophes, and other, unpredictable factors that often intervene and make achieving those ends harder. Nevertheless, they occasionally have the opposite effect—of focusing our attention and sovereign political will to make more progress.

So, let's keep our collective expectations in check. Let's be ambitious but not arrogant regarding what can be done. Let's acknowledge the fundamental change that has taken place in the move from the G8 to the G20, without hyperinflating what it will mean in the short run. Let's understand the power of those leaders, all in one room, while recognizing that, for the most part, they barely know each other. Let's acknowledge ever-changing leadership and national electoral politics and accept that it takes time to build trust, or at least a basis for common understanding if not collective action.

The Seoul G20 Summit: Balancing Strategic and Adaptive Leadership

Korea made significant contributions to G20 summitry by laying out an ambitious and compelling agenda for the November 2010 summit, both by building on the past and seeking the future in addressing models of development. In an important departure from past summits, the Seoul summit addressed development not only in terms of aid but also, more sustainably, in terms of blueprints for growth, using its own and others' success to do so.

But summits will always have to cope with any number of world events. An earthquake, a conflict, or a regional economic crisis somewhere in the world could always recast even the most carefully prepared summit agenda. The strength and sustainability of the G20 will reside, then, in its agility and ability to remain focused on its core economic mission while addressing, as appropriate, events that color the prospects for economic success. As with all other things in an Internet world, in capital markets reacting to world events, there is no decoupling of those events from the G20's leaders.

Finally, we come back to the G20's message. Demonstrated, effective, and strong global leadership is critical to the success of G20 summits at a time when people want more security and control over their lives and the times generate economic and social discontinuities, dislocations, and disturbances. The politics of leading through cooperation combined with responsiveness to public anxieties is tricky, made all the harder by the need for clear messages and strategic direction.

I do not want the G20 summit to become a twentieth-century institution. It is a crucial twenty-first-century leadership forum that provides guidance in the economic sphere and takes action when it must. If it remains agile, dynamic, and accountable to all of the world's stakeholders, including the media, the G20 summit will be a conversation worth having and, at the very least, a fail-safe mechanism against economic disaster. That would be no small achievement.

29

Successful Communications Strategies for G20 Summits

ALAN BEATTIE

In November 2011 the G20 will celebrate its third anniversary as a group that meets regularly at the head-of-government level. Having started this phase of its life in the middle of a global financial crisis, it is evolving. The G20 is now less an emergency task force and more a steering group and discussion forum for the policy framework governing the international economy, trade and financial regulation, and more general questions of international relations.

The biggest mistake that its communications strategy could make, in my view, is to operate as though the world were still deep in crisis and an impression of international unity urgently needed to restore confidence. The G20 is moving into a phase in which it hosts and informs in-depth, medium-term policy discussions. To enhance its credibility, its communications need to reflect the increasing detail and the lengthening time horizon of those discussions.

There are some intrinsic difficulties in trying to create an effective communications strategy for the G20. Most obviously, the G20 is not actually an organization. It has neither a permanent staff nor a large and dedicated research function. For stand-alone organizations with a single mission, a single area of expertise, and a substantial group of staff, it is relatively simple to work out what the body should be saying and to say it. Once the organization becomes more diffuse, turning into a forum in which member countries have discussions, it becomes harder, not least because differences of opinion are an intrinsic part of such group. Presenting a unified message risks either misrepresenting the views of some participants or being forced to sink to a lowest common denominator of such blandness ("The G20 calls for a stable financial system and balanced global recovery") that its communications become essentially as meaningless as the saying "Have a nice day."

Comparisons with existing international institutions are instructive. The International Monetary Fund, World Bank, and Organization for Economic Cooperation and Development have large full-time staffs and generate a lot of research. That does not mean that the research ends up being the policy of the organization, since policy is under the control of the shareholder governments, but we can at least talk meaningfully of the institution itself having a position. In the recent debate over financial taxes to be applied internationally, for example, the IMF produced a paper—commissioned by the G20, by the way—that laid out a range of options and gave its own clear view on which was preferable. That did not mean that the IMF staff's preferred solution would necessarily be adopted, but the fund has sufficient expertise and resources to make such a statement without risking its impartiality too much.

Toward the somewhat more diffuse end of the organizational spectrum is the World Trade Organization. The WTO does maintain a small secretariat and a research operation, and it does undertake assessments of its member countries' trade regimes and other general issues of interest. But when it comes to the real function of the organization—helping in the actual negotiation of trade deals— the WTO's role is that of facilitator and provider of technical assistance; it is not an executive body. Only under exceptional circumstances has the WTO or its predecessor, the General Agreement on Tariffs and Trade, ever come up with a strong view itself, communicated it to the outside world, and sought to corral the membership into agreeing with it. Most of the WTO's communications with the media involve giving as neutral and dispassionate a view as possible of the current state of negotiations, as indeed they should— most usefully in the form of background briefings—and of organizing member governments to talk to the media during ministerial meetings.

If the WTO suddenly decided to take a strong view on what the outcome of negotiations should be, it would very rapidly lose the support of its member states and endanger not just its credibility as a communicator but its effectiveness as an organization. On the other hand, if it spent its entire time issuing enthusiastic bromides for trade, arguing that everything in the world trade system was just fine and that the Doha round was on the brink of completion, it would rapidly lose credibility with journalists, particularly the specialists among them. (The specialist/generalist distinction among journalists is an important one to which I shall return.)

The G20 is even further down the spectrum of diffuseness than the WTO. It is a convenor of other countries' conversations rather than an organization in itself. Some of the communication function is in the hands of whichever happens to be the host country, but the member governments will obviously have their own messages to convey. It has no substantial permanent secretariat and no permanent research unit. It confines its work to organizing meetings and seeking to clarify the terms of conversation. It is also still quite new and thus concerned with establishing itself as the main discussion forum for international economic issues as much as pushing the debate in any particular direction.

In these circumstances, I think the G20 and its host country should avoid overselling the degree of unity and progress that the group as a whole is making. In considering the experiences of other organizations, I see that there are essentially three ways that the organizers of any given G20 can try to communicate in the run-up to and during its summits.

—Create a one-off hit of publicity oriented around a particular achievement on which the entire G20 can unite, expressed in a simple and media-friendly way.

—Push a particular point of view hard (for example, a particular plan for what should be done with financial regulation) and claim consensus.

—Treat each G20 summit as the latest stage of a conversation in progress across a variety of topics, and try to give an accurate sense of where each of those conversations has got to.

Many journalists, particularly nonspecialists and journalists who cover politics broadly rather than specific subjects, would, I suspect, prefer the first of these. It is much easier for a reporter to tell her or his news desk in a single sentence that a G20 summit has achieved one particular goal than it is to have to explain what incremental changes have been made in discussions on macroeconomic assessments, fiscal policy, financial regulation, the Basel accords and capital requirements, bank taxes, governance of the International Monetary Fund, and a raft of other equally arcane topics.

It was to fulfill this kind of demand, I strongly suspect, that the London summit of April 2009 focused on the supposed $1 trillion-plus package of support for the global financial system. I say "supposed" because in my view and that of my colleagues on the *Financial Times* that number involved exceedingly creative accounting—heroically assuming, for example, that a few billion dollars of support for trade finance would support $250 billion in trade over several years and then counting the $250 billion number as part of the trillion-dollar package. In terms of creating positive publicity for the hosts, the tactic seemed to work well. Although the Labour government was facing hostile domestic media at that time, it got relatively good coverage from the U.K. papers for the summit. Even papers that were more sceptical of the underlying solidity of the number did at least report it.

But whether putting so much effort into creating a favorable short-term media narrative is in the long-term interests of the organization or indeed the cause of global economic stability is much more doubtful. The outcome of an event similar to the London G20, which took place four years previously, should give cause for concern. The announcement at the London summit was in some way reminiscent of a similar stage-managed announcement at the G8 heads-of-government summit in Gleneagles, Scotland, in 2005, back when the G8 rather than the G20 was the main forum for international cooperation. That meeting was designated by the host as the summit for Africa, and eye-catching targets for rises in overall aid and assistance to Africa, usefully expressed in media-friendly round numbers of $25 billion and $50 billion, were set. As with the London summit in 2009, the coverage was largely favorable, particularly from the kind of political journalist who regarded such summits as events in the career of Tony Blair rather than significant landmarks in the history of Africa.

The downside of that media-oriented, announcement-focused approach became clear only over the succeeding years. The progressive breaching of the Gleneagles promises by the G8 countries seems to have induced considerable cynicism in the public about aid in general and G8 pledges in particular. Even the nongovernmental organizations that cheer-led the announcements now accept that by overhyping announcements in order to make a short-term impression, they may have ended up doing more damage than good to the image of development aid.

And as the years went on, the number of journalists actually covering the detail of the G8 aid pledges and indeed the overall issue dropped. Once most of the generalists had gone and the specialists were left, it became progressively harder to try to manipulate newspapers like the *Financial Times* into believing that things were going better than they were. And though specialist journalists write for a smaller audience, their coverage, I suggest, has a way of spreading out slowly into the wider media.

Thus a communications strategy that looks successful in the short term may be damaging to the institution itself and to the wider issue in the long term. The G8 has fallen out of favor and ceded way to the G20 partly because of the obvious need to include more rising giants from the developing world in discussions of the global economy. But many participants and experts that I have spoken to suggest that the pattern of overpromising, and then failing to deliver, progressively emptied G8 summits of real meaning. Just before the Toronto G8/G20 summit in 2010 I spoke with Nancy Birdsall, who heads the Center for Global Development, a think tank in Washington, and her verdict was blunt: "All the G8 really does in development is aid, and it doesn't do that very well."

If the G20 and its summit hosts follow a policy of manufacturing announcements, the same could easily happen to its summits. A series of announcements that the G20 governments have saved the global economy and financial system will look increasingly hollow if the world slips back toward recession or if there is renewed distress in the financial system. Protestations of unity will start to look increasingly incredible in the light of obvious disagreements over issues like Basel III.

Indeed, if the G20 gives the impression of agreeing all the time, there is not much point in the G20. The G7, perhaps, could get away a bit more with projecting an image of perpetual unity, since its members do all have some attributes in common, being rich democracies. But if an organization representing half of the world's population and a rich variety of countries agrees on everything all the time, it is going to risk appearing so bland as to be pointless or being accused (probably correctly) of hiding disagreements.

The second way that the G20 could communicate is for the host country to push its own strong opinion regarding the subjects under discussion. That seems to me, if anything, fraught with even more danger than the process of manufacturing announcements. Having reasonable discussions and disagreements on the substantive issues is one thing. Risking opening up divisions within the G20 about bad faith and misuse of the process seems to me even worse.

The more sensible and responsible approach is the third of the options above: communicate in a lower-key, more detailed, and more nuanced way. Give more background briefings on exactly what is being discussed and what is at stake, and make fewer bland statements of international unity. Provide more access to officials who can explain exactly what the discussions are about, and place less emphasis on promoting bland communiqués and a series of content-free press conferences with heads of government. That will, of course, require cooperation from the member governments—it is not something that the host can achieve on its own.

It will produce fewer quick results in terms of media coverage, certainly, but it should have less of a downside in the future. Nor does it preclude the host making its own case or having something in particular to propose at a summit, so long as it does not insist that all other G20 members agree with its proposal. And as the corps of journalists covering the summits is winnowed down to include primarily the specialists, as it most likely will, it will be easier to have serious conversations and acknowledge differences without the media trying to look for and exaggerate splits in opinion all the time.

If you want people, and particularly the specialist media, to write that the G20 is a unique success in global governance and has saved the world, you have to convince them of it and work from the details up, not from the statement of intent down. You cannot just assert it and expect them to write it, summit after summit. Maybe in the midst of a full-blown financial crisis there is a premium on conveying unity at some cost to the truth. That is no longer the case when the world's leading economies are working on long-term reform, when it is more important to get it right than to give the impression of concord at all times.

Along with the financial crisis seems to have come a marked fall in trust in political leaders and many institutions. Continuously making statements that appear to be at odds with the facts will not help restore it. At the moment, the G20's biggest risk with respect to the media is not that it will not get as much coverage as it wants. It is that its summits create unrealistic expectations, which are widely broadcast by the media at the time but are later disappointed. Historically, it is the disappointment of expectations that makes institutions most vulnerable to a rapid loss of popularity. That is the outcome that the G20 communications strategy should seek to avoid.

30

A Healthy Fear Factor:
The Media as Action-Forcer at Summits

PAUL BLUSTEIN

If you wish the G20 well—and who doesn't?—then you should hope that the media will be hard-nosed and probing, if not downright cynical, in their coverage of G20 summits. Indeed, one of the biggest favors that the media could bestow on the G20 would be to produce a few scathing headlines at each summit lamenting that the gathering is plagued by disarray, or proclaiming that the summiteers are producing little more than photo-ops, or pointing out that important issues are going unaddressed.

Calling on the media to make such assertions may seem counterintuitive, to say the least. Politicians and bureaucrats, who devote enormous time and energy to presenting summits as triumphs of statecraft, do not appreciate seeing their efforts depicted as futile. And the G20, still in the fledgling stage of development in its new role as global economy steering committee, surely cannot withstand a constant diet of bashings in the media, lest its member governments themselves lose faith in its potential.

But the key fact to bear in mind about summits is that they are action-forcing events, and it is the media that force the action. The knowledge that cameras will be rolling and laptop keys will be tapping as leaders emerge from the meeting room creates an incentive for policymakers to reach substantive agreement and take concrete measures, both at the summit and during the preceding period. One might even say that it is fear that drives the process—fear on the part of politicians that they will be publicly derided for traveling great distances at public expense merely to engage in a gabfest, and fear on the part of senior officials that such criticism will incite their bosses' wrath.

The media will therefore play a valuable—and, I would argue, welcome—function by maintaining a healthy and profound skepticism toward summits. By "valuable" I am referring not just to the value to society of critical media capable of ferreting out truth, but the value to the G20 itself. The G20 needs to produce results, both for the world's sake and for its own viability. The threat of blistering media coverage is essential to attaining that end.

Perhaps this perspective makes me sound like a sadistic schoolmaster who feels obliged to rationalize the beatings that he inflicts on students as good for building their character. But it is just common sense to recognize that criticism, meted out with something approaching fairness, serves as a powerful spur to performance. Weighty forces are working against the G20's success at reaching collective decisions in the global interest, as chapter 27 of this volume, by Thomas Mann, elucidates. So media that err on the side of excessive negativity may be no bad thing. Yes, the G20 has made tremendous strides, but it needs to do much more. And it will do much more only if its failings and shortcomings are brought glaringly to light—which is precisely the media's role.

Interestingly, worries about media reaction played some part in the process that led to the G20's elevation to the leader-summit level in the autumn of 2008. Proposals for a global leaders' meeting came initially from French president Nicolas Sarkozy and British prime minister Gordon Brown. According to interviews that I conducted with former officials of the Bush administration, the United States at first rejected those proposals, despite the arguments by some in the White House that the public wanted to see leaders getting together. President Bush was especially cool toward the idea. One of the main reasons for Washington's negative stance was concern that the summit would be depicted as having no substance to it. Bush felt that while European leaders seemed inclined to hold summits all the time, the world would naturally expect some major "deliverables" from a meeting attended by the president of the United States. The president began to come around only when he saw the prospect that the meeting could achieve one goal in particular—that is, to help prevent the global economy from moving in a protectionist direction, by agreeing on pledges to keep markets open. It is clear in retrospect that Bush's instincts were sound; indeed, I would venture to say that had the initial G20 summit been held in haste with little regard for those sorts of concerns, the group might well have been hooted off the world stage—and deservedly so.

So it is fortunate that the media have a penchant for adopting a somewhat caustic view of summits, and in this context it is important to understand the reasons for journalists' attitudes. Negative press is often thought to be the result

of pressure from media bosses, based on the theory that bad news attracts readers and viewers (and thus, ultimately, advertising dollars) while good news does
not. Based on my long experience as a newspaper reporter, I don't think that this
explanation is quite as persuasive as is commonly assumed, at least not when
it comes to the G20. Although bad news surely trumps good news as a reader
attractant and ad-generator in stories about subjects such as celebrity divorce,
crime, and financial market trends, I doubt that it matters much in the case of
more arcane topics like economic summits.

The most plausible reason for the media's behavior at summits is that reporters, like the politicians that they cover, are fearful—that is, afraid of being seen
by their peers and colleagues as gullible suckers for official spin. I vividly recall
the feeling of sitting in a huge summit press room, eyeing my colleagues from
other papers as they typed out their stories, wondering how my account of events
would stack up the next day when readers—most important, my editors—compared my coverage with theirs. Reporters are naturally anxious to avoid the possibility that their stories strike colleagues and superiors as "puffy" and naively
tilted toward the line being dispensed by officials. To be sure, reporters are sensitive to concerns about fairness too, and they do not want their editors or sources
to perceive them as so relentlessly antigovernment as to lack objectivity. But if
journalists have a collective bias, it puts them closer to the cynical end of the
spectrum than the credulous end.

Two important kinds of fear, then—one on the part of policymakers, the
other on the part of journalists—are at work at summits, and I believe that they
enhance rather than diminish the G20's chances for going down in history as
a group that steered the global economy for a sustained period rather than as a
mere crisis-management body.

Could the media go overboard in the negative direction and, by failing to give
due attention to significant accomplishments, inflict serious damage on the G20?
After all, why would world leaders make strenuous efforts to cooperate if they
never got any credit for doing so? Such a development cannot be dismissed as
inconceivable, but a quick review of some of the articles that blazed across front
pages on the occasion of G20 summits reveals its unlikelihood. "Nations Craft
Hard-Fought Pledge to Repair World Financial System; Plans Aims to Tighten
Regulation, Increase Lending, Aid Poor Nations," was the headline of an article
about the G20's London summit that ran in the *Washington Post* (Shear and
Faiola 2009). Six months later, a *New York Times* story on the Pittsburgh summit, headlined "Leaders of G20 Vow to Reshape Global Economy," began with
the following: "One year after a financial crisis that began in the United States
tipped the world into a severe recession, leaders from both rich countries and
fast-growing powerhouses like China agreed on Friday to a far-reaching effort to
revamp the economic system" (Andrews 2009).

Not that those headlines are typical of all G20 coverage. At the time of the London summit, considerable media attention was devoted to the dispute between the United States and Britain on one hand and the continental Europeans on the other over how to count and compare stimulus packages (Erlanger and Castle 2009; Giles, Parker, and Tett 2009). The *Financial Times* published a trenchant analysis of the "numerical inflation" involved in the London summiteers' claims to have increased IMF resources to the $1 trillion level (Giles 2009), and another *FT* article following the London summit (Beattie 2009) acerbically concluded:

> Groupings that produce grandiloquent promises of international action are only worthwhile when they materially affect the domestic policy debates in their member countries. . . . In that regard, there is scant evidence yet that the G20 can perform any better than its widely discredited older cousin [the G8].

In advance of the Toronto summit, a number of stories again focused on conflicts between leading member countries (Davis and Walker 2010; Schneider and Wilson 2010); those culminated in a memorably mordant assessment by *FT* columnist Clive Crook, who wrote: "Simple ineptitude seems to be a bigger problem [for the G20] than disinclination to cooperate" (Crook 2010).

Such coverage has dismayed some observers (Bradford 2009 and 2010; Bradford and Linn 2010). Bradford is understandably concerned that the public will not properly appreciate the subtle but important advances that the group is making if too much media attention is showered on squabbles that may ultimately be of little consequence. To my journalist colleagues, I commend his analyses, which present a number of highly illuminating insights into the nature of the G20 process and the goals that the G20 is attempting to achieve. As Bradford astutely notes, "The purpose of the G20 is not to standardize everything, to homogenize differences, and to achieve uniformity; it is to achieve equivalence, consistency, and coherence in the otherwise disparate actions of the major players in the world today." I do not share the depth of his concern about the articles in question; I thought their authors acquitted themselves well and in some cases brilliantly. But it is not the purpose of this chapter to delve into their merits and demerits. Rather, I wish to highlight the paradox that the "bad press" that the G20 receives at the hands of writers like Crook can have a beneficial impact overall.

For the G20, one problem related to media coverage that may be seriously troublesome is the pressure on summits to address non-economic and nonfinancial issues that are unrelated to the central G20 agenda. Again, a fear factor is at work here; national leaders and their staffs are afraid that they will be ridiculed in the media if they fail to address topics such as a deadly natural disaster, or a terrorist attack, or a military conflict that erupted just as the summit was getting under way. Unfortunate as it may be that the G20 must divert its attention from the crucial economic and financial problems that are its raison d'être, leaders will understandably wish to avoid appearing insensitive, feckless, or obtuse about other issues.

At a Brookings conference in 2010, I proposed a way to mitigate this problem (Blustein 2010). I noted that when summits end and delegations are rushing to catch their planes home, reporters typically have very little time to digest the flood of information that starts to come at them from all directions, in communiqués, final news conferences, briefings, and so forth. I proposed that summits therefore should be organized so that the first portion would be devoted to economic and financial coordination issues and the second portion would be devoted to other issues. As soon as leaders are finished with the first section, briefings and press conferences should be held on those matters only, thereby giving the media a good chance to get a handle on that material while the leaders are moving on to their discussion of non-economic issues. Adopting this proposal would not completely eliminate the problem of non-economic issues drowning out economic ones. But it might help, and it would at least ensure that journalists get the time necessary to make sense of complex economic topics.

I conclude with a challenge to the G20 to take even greater advantage of the media as summit action-forcer. The G20 is striving to achieve a coordinated rebalancing of the global economy using "mutual assessments" of member country economies, and I cannot help but think that the process would benefit from novel forms of media involvement. Imagine, for example, a requirement that at each summit, member countries whose policies were deemed by the IMF to be inconsistent with the rebalancing goal would have to hold a special news conference on the subject. Perhaps that idea is politically unrealistic, and I'm not sure that it would have a significant impact even if it were implemented. But I hope that it might inspire more creative thinking along the same lines.

In the meantime, as the G20 matures from fledgling to the full flower of youth, hopefully it will receive continued sustenance from the nattering nabobs of negativism.

References

Andrews, Edmund L. 2009. "Leaders of G20 Vow to Reshape Global Economy." *New York Times*, September 26.

Beattie, Alan. 2009. "G20 Aid Pledges Must Be More Than Just Hot Air." *Financial Times*, April 5

Blustein, Paul. 2010. "Meat at the G20 for the Baying Hounds of the Press." In *Toward the Consolidation of the G20: From Crisis Committee to Global Steering Committee,* edited by Colin I. Bradford and Wonhyuk Lim, pp. 447–49. Seoul and Washington: Korea Development Institute and the Brookings Institution.

Bradford, Colin I. 2009. "The G20 Stimulus Split: A False Debate." April 1 (www. brookings.edu/opinions/2009/0401_g20_bradford.aspx).

———. 2010. "Doom and Gloom before the G20 Summit Still Again!" Unpublished paper (June).

Bradford, Colin I., and Johannes F. Linn. 2010. "The April 2009 London G20 Summit in Retrospect." April 5 (www.brookings.edu/opinions/2010/0405_g20_summit_linn.aspx).

Crook, Clive. 2010. "Fiscal Disarray Is the Least of the G20's Sins." *Financial Times*, June 27.

Davis, Bob, and Marcus Walker. 2010. "Spending Fight Looms at Coming G20 Talks." *Wall Street Journal*, June 22.

Erlanger, Steven, and Stephen Castle. 2009. "European Leader Assails American Stimulus Plan." *New York Times*, March 26.

Giles, Chris. 2009. "Large Numbers Hide Big G20 Divisions." *Financial Times*, April 2.

Giles, Chris, George Parker, and Gillian Tett. 2009. "Paris and Berlin Take G20 Stand." *Financial Times*, April 2.

Schneider, Howard, and Scott Wilson. 2010. "Disagreements Loom Over G20 Summit." *Washington Post*, June 18.

Shear, Michael D., and Anthony Faiola. 2009. "Nations Craft Hard-Fought Pledge to Repair World Financial System." *Washington Post*, April 3.

CONCLUSION

Priority Innovations and Challenges for the G20

COLIN I. BRADFORD AND WONHYUK LIM

A theme of this volume is that the G20 at the leaders' level was brought into being to address the current crisis, which is in fact a three-dimensional crisis: an economic crisis that has created a *crisis in confidence* in markets that has affected nearly everyone on the globe; a *crisis in public trust* in political leaders, manifested in opinion polls in many countries; and a *crisis in faith* in the capacity of the system of international institutions to avoid crises and better represent public concerns for financial stability, growth, and development.

To address the three dimensions of the crisis, Korea's Presidential Committee for the G20 Summit asked the Brookings Institution in Washington and the Korea Development Institute (KDI) in Seoul to look at them in connection with the underlying tension inherent in modern summitry between the legitimacy of summits with respect to their representativeness and their legitimacy with respect to their effectiveness. Brookings and KDI, along with the Canadian Centre for International Governance Innovation (CIGI) in Waterloo, organized an off-the-record exploratory conference at Brookings on April 21–22, 2010, to generate new ideas for "institutional, policy, and political innovations for G20 Summits." The G20 Seoul International Symposium, a large public conference sponsored by KDI, Brookings, and *Dong-A Ilbo,* was held at the G20 summit site in Seoul on September 27–29, 2010. The two conferences provide the basis of this book.

What follows here are those innovations for the G20 that seem to hold the greatest potential for generating the highest yield in terms of making the G20 simultaneously both more representative and more effective and that can help G20 leaders address all three aspects of the current crisis. Innovations such as these could help the G20 to become an enduring forum for global leadership and to shift from being a crisis committee to being a global steering committee for the world economy.

Political Innovations

Strategic Preparation for Domestic and Global Leadership

It is likely to strengthen the national standing of G20 leaders in public opinion in their countries and the visibility of global leadership if governments prepare national strategies for each G20 summit in which national economic interests, active domestic political leadership, geopolitical positioning, and the nature of the public interest in summit outcomes are identified. The question is whether G20 countries already are doing this as part of their summit preparation process or whether more deliberate and more explicit efforts need to be made to strengthen the relationship between national leaders and their publics and the connection between concerted actions of the G20 and high-priority public concerns in G20 countries and in global public opinion.

Communications Strategies for G20 Countries

Given the importance of communications for leadership, it would be worthwhile for G20 leaders to have a deliberate communications strategy prior to G20 summits that sends a message linking their involvement in issues at the summits with high-priority public concerns at home in order to strengthen the relationship between them and their publics (see chapters 27 and 28).

National Press at Global Summits

It has been observed that if journalists from national media outlets are not present at G20 summits, the resulting dependence on international wire services and media eliminates the visibility of the national leader in domestic public perception. This problem can be summarized in the phrase "no story teller, no story." The presence of national journalists is essential to connecting global summitry to domestic politics.[1]

Public Engagement in Other Countries

Critical questions arise on how to engage the publics of non-G20 countries. There is a real danger that if other countries are not present, they will not be

---

1. See Colin Bradford, "National Perspectives on Global Leadership" (www.cigionline.org/project/national-perspectives-global-leadership).

interested. That affects the ability of the G20 to achieve legitimacy in the eyes of the countries not included in the G20.

PARLIAMENTARY SUPPORT

Parliaments ultimately decide national outcomes on major issues addressed by G20 summits, especially those that require legislation. And yet it seems that the involvement of parliaments and parliamentarians in the preparations for and follow-up after G20 summits may be less than fully realized, with potentially high costs for the effectiveness of the G20. How could each G20 country develop a specific form of focused communication with key parliamentarians?

PRESS CONFERENCE ON CORE ECONOMIC ISSUES FIRST

Paul Blustein has pointed out that the issuance of G20 declarations at the closure of G20 summits gives national media representatives no time to write stories before departing the summit site themselves.[2] He suggests that the summits complete the core economic agenda first, issue the declaration on it immediately, and move on to other issues, giving journalists time to write lengthier and more thoughtful stories on the priority economic issues after interaction with experts, while the rest of the summit agenda is being dealt with (see chapter 30).

CIVIL SOCIETY ENGAGEMENT

Since G20 summits deal with issues of major public concern, a deliberate effort to involve leaders from civil society, business, academia, think tanks, and the media in the run-up to and the follow-up after G20 summits would make them more effective, since communications and civic engagement are keys to successful summitry.[3]

Policy Innovations

THE G20 AND DEVELOPMENT

The Korean government had already secured agreement in Toronto to create a G20 working group on development of developing countries. This group will emphasize the roles of economic growth, infrastructure, human capital investment, and knowledge sharing in the G20's approach to development. This policy innovation in the G20 agenda is itself a form of greater inclusion and increases

2. Paul Blustein, "Meat at the G20 for the Baying Hounds of the Press," in *Toward the Consolidation of the G20: From Crisis Committee to Global Steering Committee,* edited by Colin I. Bradford and Wonhyuk Lim (Seoul and Washington: Korea Development Institute and the Brookings Institution, 2010), pp. 447–49.

3. Martin Albrow, "Summits as Narratives between Leaders and Their Publics," in *Toward the Consolidation of the G20,* edited by Bradford and Lim.

the G20's representativeness and thereby its legitimacy. Further thought is being given to how developing countries can participate in the G20 development discussion; the goal is to fully engage them without enlarging the G20 table and also to avoid creating a second-class category of participants within the group (see part IV).

THE G20 FRAMEWORK, INNOVATION, AND INCLUSION

The G20 Framework for Strong, Sustainable, and Balanced Growth (FSSBG) is a major policy and institutional innovation for G20 summits. It creates a medium-term framework within which to assess, review, and adjust G20 macroeconomic policies to achieve "collective consistency" among them. The "framework" and the "mutual assessment process" that goes with it create the potential for putting the world economy on a path toward mutually consistent policies for growth, stability, balance, and development. This is a global approach; it will involve developing countries and countries not in the G20 in a strategic approach to restoring balance and steadiness to the global economy. Much will depend on the capacity of G20 member countries to negotiate firmly and fairly with each other to accommodate the requirements for both distinctiveness and consistency. G20 peer review is the centerpiece of this new process; the success of the framework depends upon the willingness of systemically important countries to be influenced by the need to have complementary and consistent policies for achieving overall global balance (see part III).

Institutional Innovations

THE G20 AND REGIONAL SUMMITS

Regional summits in Africa, Asia, and Latin America could generate views on substantive issues that could be systematically fed into the preparations for G20 summits. The G24, the Commonwealth of Nations, and other forums at the leaders' level could also funnel ideas, viewpoints, and perspectives into the G20 process. Indeed, time could be reserved at G20 summit discussions of priority issues for consideration of views from countries outside the G20 as a way of enhancing the inclusiveness and global representativeness of the G20 (see chapter 24). In addition, using its four or five rotating invitations, the summit host country can invite as special guests the chair countries of regional organizations from underrepresented regions.

SYSTEMATIC CONSULTATION AND OUTREACH EFFORTS

Regular interaction between the G20 chair and non-G20 countries provides a good way of strengthening external support for the G20's activities and initiatives. Consultation and outreach efforts, led by the chair, should be an ongoing requirement. The chair, in turn, should inform other G20 members of its consultation and outreach results on a regular basis to receive feedback and craft effective responses to the concerns expressed by nonmembers.[4]

A G20 Non-Secretariat

One way of enhancing the G20's effectiveness without encumbering it with bureaucracy would be to second a few senior staff from the three G20 troika governments to the G20 host capital each year to focus specifically on eliciting, processing, and preparing the input from countries outside the G20 for use in the G20 preparatory process (see chapter 25). A two-tiered secretariat at a permanent location may be considered, including troika-based officials with staggered three-year secondments from troika countries who set the direction based on instructions from their capitals; and merit-based technical staff who provide analytical and administrative support, in cooperation with specialized international organizations. The sherpa (or deputy) of the G20 chair should serve as the secretary-general of the secretariat to ensure accountability and prevent bureaucratization.[5]

Greater Staff Support for the Financial Stability Board and the IMF

G20 governments should consider the need to allocate additional financial resources to the Financial Stability Board and to the IMF to buttress their analytical capacities in systemic financial issues and open economy macroeconomics in order to generate stronger policy results and strengthen the peer review processes in both institutions (see part II).

The G20 and the International Institutions

The G20 is an informal leaders-level strategic guidance mechanism; the international institutions are formal, treaty-based universal membership organizations. More thought needs to be given to how to create complementarities and enhance the functional relationships between the G20 and the IMF, World Bank, United Nations, and other international institutions to ensure that the international system as a whole operates more effectively and is also more representative. G20 leadership on international institutional and governance reform is one aspect; greater functional coherence between the policies and programs of international institutions could also be achieved by more interactive relationships between the G20 and the international institutions (see part V).

---

4. See Wonhyuk Lim and Françoise Nicolas, "From the Korean to the French Presidency: Ensuring Continuity." KDI-IFRI Joint Paper (Seoul and Paris).
    5. Ibid.

The New Dynamics of Summitry

CULTURAL DIFFERENCE AS AN ASSET

Whereas the G8 is largely made up of Western industrial democracies from Europe and North America, along with Japan, the G20 is a more diverse group, in geographical, economic, and cultural terms. The G20 has six Asian countries rather than one, as in the G8; three Islamic countries rather than none, as in the G8 or in the G8+5; and ten emerging market countries from different regions of the world. Cultural differences lead to institutional differences, which lead to systemic differences among major economies. In a globalized world economy, where there is a search for innovative ways to combine public institutions and private markets to advance the public interest in economic outcomes, these cultural, institutional, and systemic differences can be assets in the peer review process, in learning, and in adjusting policies in the G20 (see chapter 22).

SHIFTING COALITIONS OF CONSENSUS

Given the diversity of the G20 members and the complexity of the global challenges facing them, it would be in the interest of all G20 member countries to develop policy positions derived from their different substantive analyses of the issues involved, which would result in different country alignments and coalitions depending on the issues. A priori alliances, ideological position taking, and bloc politics need to be trumped by greater pragmatism, differing leadership configurations on different issues, and shifting coalitions of consensus in G20 summitry for the G20 to generate effective, inclusive, and innovative outcomes (see chapter 23).

The Collision of Domestic Politics and Global Rebalancing

The three sets of innovations and the new dynamics of summitry could provide a positive agenda for the G20 that would strengthen it as an effective global leadership forum. If the urgency of the current crisis and the momentum toward summit innovations continue and capture the new dynamics of summitry, then that forward movement may facilitate the transition of the G20 from "global responder," in the words of Paul Martin, to global steering committee. The G20 leaders might be able to meet the triple crisis—of confidence in markets, trust in leaders, and faith in institutions. G20 leaders must address simultaneously the dimensions of strategic, political, integrative, institutional, pragmatic, and inclusive leadership.

On the other hand, the increasing polarization in domestic and global politics and the growing disconnect between leaders and their publics pose major challenges to global leadership and concerted, cooperative actions fostered by the G20. In addition, the inability of major countries to agree on a way to manage current global imbalances and distortions, as in the annual meetings of the World Bank and IMF in October 2010 and in the Seoul G20 summit itself, poses a fundamental challenge to G20 members and global institutions.

These two challenges—the growing intensity of political polarization and of anxiety among ordinary citizens and the unwillingness of governments of major economies to agree on a set of long-term, consistent, and mutually reinforcing polices that provide a feasible path to global recovery—threaten the credibility of the G20 and its sustainability as well as its potential as an enduring global leadership forum into the future.

The G20 Seoul International Symposium anticipated these threats. Global rebalancing was seen to be a daunting political challenge for the sovereignty of nations, an institutional problem for the effectiveness of multilateral surveillance, and a difficult economic policy issue (see part III.) And an entire segment of the conference was devoted to public attitudes in G20 countries (see chapter 26), domestic leadership in a polarized and globalized world (chapter 27), and leadership, publics, and communications (chapter 28), with prominent journalists contributing to the discussion (see part VII.)

Indeed, it was well understood that these two challenges interact and collide with each other. The global rebalancing by the G20, whereby nations must shape their domestic policies to align with globally consistent goals beyond their internal ramifications, generates resistance by leaders because of the polarization of domestic politics, which itself is being intensified by the effects of globalization. Global economic rebalancing would be challenging enough without the domestic political repercussions, and managing domestic political polarization would be daunting enough if it were separate from the economic policy challenges.

This collision of domestic politics and global rebalancing adds still another layer of difficulty for countries that host the G20 summits in the future. Paths forward out of the "currency wars" must be found that are compatible with the growing intensity of domestic political reactions to the economic crisis that the G20 is trying to manage. There are no easy solutions; but there are some perspectives and propositions that grew out of the G20 Seoul International Symposium on these matters that are worth setting out here.

Ten Propositions for Avoiding Collision

First, the global imbalances are much broader than fiscal deficits in the United States and exchange rate undervaluation in China and much broader than the external deficit and surplus countries within the G20. Global imbalances are global in scope and require approaches, strategies, and policies that are global in reach. More instruments, institutions, and countries must be involved.

Second, global imbalances require time for policies to adjust and for their impact to be felt in the real economy. They cannot be fixed by actions taken by G20 countries at a single G20 summit alone; a series of summits is required, over time. The G20 countries and others need to maintain a continuous focus on global imbalances and the effects of policies on them over a number of years into the future.

Third, G20 fiscal and monetary policy actions do not have to be identical, but they must, as a whole, be coherent and complementary. The myth that policy coordination means that everyone does the same thing at the same time is getting in the way of everyone doing the right thing in the context of the global economy over the medium term.

Fourth, international institutions, especially the IMF, must play an independent and vigorous role in providing the rigorous analysis and synthesis of country economic policies that is vital to the G20 global rebalancing exercise. Kemal Derviş, former finance minister of Turkey, made clear that the policy harmonization role of the IMF is as important for the future as its lending and financing role has been in the past.

Fifth, the policy purview of the exercise must extend beyond exchange rate and macroeconomic policies to structural reforms, as outlined in chapter 11 by Pier Carlo Padoan, deputy secretary general and chief economist of the OECD.

Sixth, the new G20 peer review of country policies, based on G20 country economic submissions and IMF analyses, is crucial to the process of reconciliation and rebalancing. Pedro Malan, former finance minister of Brazil, points out in chapter 13 that new arrangements like this depend on the governments behind them and are only as effective as the governments want them to be. Therefore, a great responsibility for the effectiveness of the G20 peer review of macropolicy management now rests on the governments of the G20 countries themselves.

Seventh, in addressing the collision of rebalancing policies and domestic politics, Thomas Mann points out that there is no substitute for getting the policies right. As important as communications and clear "messaging" is to global leadership and successful summitry, policy should drive the message, not the reverse. Mann agrees that it is worth investing in messaging but cautions strongly against manipulating the message for public effect without credible policy actions on which to base public statements (see chapter 27).

Eighth, Wendy Sherman argues that G20 summits should focus on concrete, credible outcomes that affect the jobs, personal security, and livelihoods of people in their day-to-day lives as a way of addressing the underlying public anxieties of today (chapter 28). Simple, direct communications need to link G20 policy actions, which are often complex, to daily practical concerns of people.

Ninth, Alan Beattie from the *Financial Times* made the point that summiteers should not overstretch G20 narratives to describe more positive efforts and more optimistic results than can be substantiated in fact (chapter 29). Paul Blustein, a former reporter for the *Washington Post,* argued that bad press is good for the G20 in that criticism helps strengthen the G20 process and keep officials on their toes (chapter 30).

Tenth, several commentators observed that engaging broader publics and more intense consultation with institutional actors, especially G20 parliaments, will be vital for the long-term sustainability of G20 summits.

These ten points, articulated in the G20 Seoul International Symposium at the end of September 2010, seem even more poignant and relevant to G20 efforts after the Seoul G20 summit. The "global clash over the economy,"[6] unresolved in the eyes of most observers by the Seoul summit, adds pressure on G20 leaders to address collectively the tough challenges facing them in order to identify a credible path forward for global economic adjustment and to create an integrated package of actions on global recovery, financial regulatory reform, international institutional changes, and innovations for the G20 in future summits.

The package needs to be rich and complex enough to convince markets, consumers, investors, and financial actors that G20 leaders have a vision for the future of the global economy that can integrate instruments to promote financial stability, economic growth, and institutional reform together over time. Those instruments need to be strongly utilized and clearly articulated so that they will provide the framework and foundation for a "strong, sustainable, and balanced" world economy in the years ahead.

Amid serious concern that the currency war issue could derail a cooperative summit, the significant success achieved by the finance ministers' meeting in Gyeongju, South Korea, on October 22–23, 2010, showed that commitment to cooperation has been strong among the G20 despite the sometimes divergent evaluations of the difficult issues. In the Seoul summit, too, more progress was made than met the eye. But the collision of domestic politics and the requirements of global rebalancing generated policy conflicts before, during, and after Seoul.

That means that G20 leaders still have a way to go to demonstrate to their publics, to markets, and to global public opinion that their concerted actions can restore confidence in markets, trust in leaders, and faith in institutions.

6."Global Clash over the Economy," *Financial Times,* October 12, 2010.

Contributors

ALAN BEATTIE is the international economy editor of the *Financial Times*.

THOMAS BERNES is the executive director and vice president for programs of the Centre for International Governance Innovation, Waterloo, Canada.

SERGIO BITAR served as minister of public works of Chile from 2008 to 2010, president of the Partido por la Democracia (PPD) from 2006 to 2008, minister of education from 2003 to 2006, and senator from 1994 to 2002.

PAUL BLUSTEIN is an economic journalist and author, a former reporter for the *Washington Post*, a nonresident senior fellow at the Brookings Institution, and a senior visiting fellow at the Centre for International Governance Innovation.

COLIN BRADFORD is a nonresident senior fellow of the Brookings Institution and of the Centre for International Governance Innovation.

BARRY CARIN is a senior fellow at the Centre for International Governance Innovation and associate director of the Centre for Global Studies at the University of Victoria, British Columbia, Canada, where he is also adjunct professor of public administration.

ANDREW F. Cooper is a distinguished fellow at the Centre for International Governance Innovation and a professor of political science at the University of Waterloo.

KEMAL DERVIŞ is vice president of the Global Economy and Development program at the Brookings Institution and former minister of economic affairs and the treasury, Turkey.

PAUL HEINBECKER is the inaugural director of the Laurier University Centre for Global Relations, Waterloo, Canada; a distinguished fellow at the Centre for International Governance Innovation; and former Canadian permanent representative to the United Nations.

OH-SEOK HYUN is the president of the Korea Development Institute.

JOMO KWAME SUNDARAM is assistant secretary-general for economic development in the Department of Economic and Social Affairs, United Nations.

HOMI KHARAS is a senior fellow and deputy director of the Global Economy and Development program at the Brookings Institution.

HYEON WOOK KIM is director of the Macroeconomics Department at the Korea Development Institute.

SUNGMIN KIM is director general of the G20 Affairs Office at the Bank of Korea.

JOHN KIRTON is a professor of political science and co-director of the G20 Research Group and director of the G8 Research Group at the Munk School of Global Affairs at the University of Toronto.

WONHYUK LIM is director of policy research at the Center for International Development of the Korea Development Institute.

JOHANNES LINN is a resident senior scholar at the Emerging Markets Forum, Washington, D.C., and a nonresident senior fellow at the Brookings Institution.

PEDRO MALAN is chairman of the International Advisory Board of Itau Unibanco; he was Brazil's minister of finance for eight years (1995–2002) and president of the Brazilian Central Bank from September 1993 to December 1994.

THOMAS MANN is the W. Averell Harriman chair and senior fellow in the Governance Studies program at the Brookings Institution.

PAUL MARTIN was prime minister of Canada from 2003 to 2006, minister of finance from 1993 to 2002, and the inaugural chair of the Finance Ministers' G20 in 1999.

SIMON MAXWELL is senior research associate of the Overseas Development Institute in London and executive chair of the Climate and Development Knowledge Network.

JACQUES MISTRAL is a professor of economics and head of economic research at the Institut Français des Relations Internationales (IFRI) and a former economic adviser to the prime minister, Paris.

VICTOR MURINDE is director of the Corporate Finance Research Group at Birmingham Business School, University of Birmingham, United Kingdom.

PIER CARLO PADOAN is deputy secretary-general and chief economist of the Organization for Economic Cooperation and Development, Paris.

YUNG CHUL PARK is distinguished professor of international studies at Korea University.

STEWART PATRICK is a senior fellow and director of the International Institutions and Global Governance program at the Council on Foreign Relations, Washington, D.C.

IL SAKONG is the chair of the Presidential Committee for the G20 Summit, which comprises ministers and senior secretaries to the president of the Republic of Korea.

WENDY R. SHERMAN is vice chair of the Albright Stonebridge Group and a member of the Investment Committee of Albright Capital Management.

GORDON SMITH is executive director of the Centre for Global Studies, a distinguished fellow at the Centre for International Governance Innovation, and adjunct professor of political science and public administration at the University of Victoria.

BRUCE STOKES is senior transatlantic fellow for economics at the German Marshall Fund, international economics columnist for the *National Journal,* and one of the authors of the annual Pew Global Attitudes Survey.

NGAIRE WOODS is professor of global economic governance, academic director of the Oxford Blavatnik School of Government, and director of the Global Economic Governance Programme.

LAN XUE is a professor and the dean of the School of Public Policy and Management at Tsinghua University, Beijing.

YANBING ZHANG is a lecturer at the School of Public Policy and Management at Tsinghua University, Beijing.

Index

Access to information, 33
Accountability, 34. *See also* Transparency
Accounting standards, 77–78, 97–100
Accra Agenda for Action on Aid Effectiveness, 166, 226
Adaptive leadership, 310–11
Advanced internal ratings–based approach (AIRBA), 109
Advanced measurement approach (AMA), 110
AERC (African Economic Research Consortium), 116
AfDB. *See* African Development Bank
Afghanistan: and G8, 52; Soviet invasion of, 21, 25
Africa: bank regulation in, 101–21; and development agenda, 168; G8 partnership with, 53; IDA access in, 230; and knowledge sharing, 212. *See also* Middle East and North Africa; *specific countries*
Africa Clearinghouse, 52
African Development Bank (AfDB), 108, 116, 231, 233, 270
African Economic Research Consortium (AERC), 116
African Union: and Committee of 10, 270; and development agenda, 189; and G20

legitimacy, 42, 115, 244, 268; and regional dynamics, 265
AfT. *See* Aid for trade
Agenda setting: climate change, 22, 29, 31; development, 13, 32, 38, 167–70, 179, 188–89, 263, 326–27; financial regulatory reform, 22, 45, 65–69, 100; for G8, 257; for G20, 38, 56–57, 262–63; infrastructure development, 170–71; institutional reform, 38; stimulus spending, 2, 9, 18; trade, 30
Agricultural development, 173
Ahmadinejad, Mahmoud, 17
Aid donors. *See* Official development assistance (ODA)
Aid for trade (AfT), 178, 193, 198
AidWatch, 182–83
AIG (American Insurance Group), 77
AIRBA (advanced internal ratings–based approach), 109
Airports, 204
Albrow, Martin, 249
Algeria, G20 participation of, 42
Al Jazeera on G20 inclusiveness, 39
AMA (advanced measurement approach), 110
American Insurance Group (AIG), 77
Anti–money laundering (AML), 82

ABOUT BROOKINGS

The Brookings Institution is a private nonprofit organization devoted to research, education, and publication on important issues of domestic and foreign policy. Its principal purpose is to bring the highest-quality independent research and analysis to bear on current and emerging policy problems. Interpretations and conclusions in Brookings publications should be understood to be solely those of the authors.

ABOUT KDI

Established in March 1971 by the Korean government, the Korea Development Institute (KDI) is Korea's oldest and best-known research institute in the fields of economic and social sciences. Its primary mission is to contribute to Korea's development by setting long-term national agendas and providing policy recommendations based on rigorous analysis. KDI has also sought to share Korea's development knowledge with other countries that are facing the challenge of initiating and sustaining development.

www.ingramcontent.com/pod-product-compliance
Lightning Source LLC
Chambersburg PA
CBHW030637270326

41929CB00007B/104